# THE POCKET GUIDE TO WINE
## (REVISED EDITION)

A freelance wine journalist based in New York, Barbara Ensrud writes the weekly syndicated wine column for the *New York Daily News*. She established the monthly wine column in *Vogue* Magazine and now contributes regularly to such publications as *House & Garden, Cuisine, Harper's Bazaar, GQ* and *The Wine Spectator*. She has also contributed to several best-selling wine books, including *The Joys of Wine*, Time-Life's *Wines & Spirits*, and *The New York Times Book of Wine*. A member of the New York Wine Writers Circle, the International Wine & Food Society and Les Dames d'Escoffier, Ms. Ensrud has traveled extensively in vineyard regions of the world and frequently lectures on wine.

# The Pocket Guide to
# WINE

## (REVISED EDITION)

Barbara Ensrud

## NEW ORCHARD EDITIONS

New Orchard Editions Ltd
Robert Rogers House
New Orchard
Poole, Dorset BH15 1LU

ISBN 1-85079-021-3

Printed in Great Britain by
Pitman Press Ltd., Bath

# CONTENTS

# INTRODUCTION

For some years now I have heard friends and others plead for a practical, down-to-earth wine book that didn't tell them more than they wanted to know or had time to absorb. When I was approached to do this little book, it seemed the perfect answer to such a need. Mostly it is for those who already enjoy wine, who do not profess to know a great deal but want ready access to the kind of serviceable information that will aid them in choosing the right wine for the moment. It makes no pretense of being complete or encyclopedic— that job has been superbly done by several others on large scale and small. This is a more selective guide, geared to the wine labels we are most likely to encounter in trying to select wine.

As a sort of "field guide" to the principal wines from some 20 countries, this book can be used on several different levels. Beginners, for example, can dip into its various sections and explore the wines described with some guidance to the level of quality they are getting for their money. Even the most knowledgeable consumer will find it a useful reference on occasion—in a wine shop, confronted with the myriad of wine labels from all over the world, or perhaps abroad, winding along the slopes of Burgundy, through the hills of northern Italy, or the valleys of California or the Rhineland.

The guide includes thumbnail sketches of more than 1,500 wines—including quality ratings for the majority of them. While it does not include, by any means, all the wines made in each country, it does cover a broad range of those most commonly seen in wine shops and restaurants of the world's leading wine markets, with enough indication of style, quality, and value to enable you to choose intelligently.

Another reason for doing yet another wine book is the effort to keep pace with the exciting changes that are going on in the world of wine. The tremendous surge of interest in wine moved from a brisk trot in the late sixties to a lively canter by the close of the seventies, and shows no signs of breaking stride, especially in places like California, Italy, Australia, and even France. Winelovers of the eighties can look ahead to greater variety than ever before. Increased demand for wines at every level of quality and price has ushered in an abundance of wines new to many markets. As prices for the best and rarest escalate, wines from other and newer regions come into their own. One has only to take a look at chapters such as Australia, the United States, Italy, and France to get some idea of what I mean.

Wine, in all its facets, from vineyard to barrel to bottle and glass, fascinates me endlessly. One of the things I love most about wine is the interesting variety of people involved with growing, making, and selling it. Nature, of course, assures that each vintage will be different, and the greatness of any wine must begin in the grape, but

1

it is the human element at each step along the way that determines the ultimate outcome, whether modest or grand. The simple but sound wine for everyday use is as important as the great wine saved for rare moments. Indeed, how could we so thoroughly appreciate the latter without some casual experience of the former?

Wine is a very sociable substance. It requires cooperative efforts among those who make it available—the growers, the winemakers, the tradesmen—and promotes conviviality among those who share it when it is poured. And wine, most definitely, is a thing to be shared. In the company of others, be they friends or strangers, wine is a common language, and the easy flow and exchange of opinion provides one of the best and most pleasurable ways to learn; hence, the proliferation of wine clubs and tasting groups. Many a friendship is born through a kindred love of the grape.

The forbidding "mystique" that surrounded wine until recently has begun to subside as more and more people enjoy wine for themselves. But there is still, and always will be, a certain mystery as to how the juice of crushed grapes becomes in some instances a sublime and exalted beverage—whose experience, though it has incited poets to rhyme, is quite beyond anything the mere printed word can evoke. It is something you must taste and experience for yourself to understand why that is so. It is my hope that this little book will prove not only a useful companion at moments of need but a stimulus to delve more deeply into a subject—and substance—that offers some of life's most rewarding experiences.

# HOW TO USE THIS BOOK

To make this book as simple and quick to use as possible, it has been geared primarily to interpreting the information given on the labels themselves. Each of the major wine-producing countries has been given a separate chapter, the main part of which is composed of a Wine Guide—an alphabetical listing of wines, grape varieties in instances where useful, and some specific wine-growing regions. The important wine-growing regions are listed (keyed to maps for the largest producers) at the start of each chapter and, where necessary, a Glossary of Wine Terms is given.

Wines from the leading producers, such as California, France, Italy, and Germany, are rated. I have not rated wines I have not personally tasted, except in a few instances when the evaluation has been based on discussions with members of the trade whose opinions I respect. Nor have I rated wines that are only just beginning to appear on the world's markets or those from regions that are still in the process of establishing an identity, such as the wines from New York State, for example. To some extent, this is true for California, but a great deal more has been achieved there; present ratings could change in the next few years and future editions will be revised accordingly.

# HOW TO READ AN ENTRY

For easier reading, as few symbols and abbreviations as possible are used. Sweet and sparkling wines (and a few fortified wines) are identified as such within their entries. In all other instances, the wine may be assumed to be dry table wine (the fortified wines of Spain and Portugal have a chapter of their own).

Each Wine Guide entry is listed under the principal name that appears on the label (whether place name, grape variety, or producer) and gives all or most of the following information:

1. **Wine Colors.** At the left of each entry, the color or colors of the wine.

   - (R) red wine
   - (W) white wine
   - (RO) rosé wine
   - (3) red, white, and rosé wines

   **Note:** If the principal wine is red, however, and only a little white or rosé is produced under the same name or vice versa, that information is indicated within the text entry rather than in the symbol at the left.

2. **Wine Regions.** The region of origin or where the wine comes from. Most regions are given in abbreviated form; the full terms are given under Principal Wine Region listings.

3. **Vintage Years.** Good to excellent vintage years (where useful).

   **Note:** Only those years that were good to excellent, and still drinkable, are cited; few are noted beyond the early 1960s; vintages for port include the 1950s.

4. **Wine Ratings.** Ratings of one to four stars in ascending order of quality.

   - ★      acceptable, everyday quality
   - ★ ★      good, above average
   - ★ ★ ★      very good, notable, distinctive
   - ★ ★ ★ ★      very finest, outstanding, expensive

   **Note:** A " + " sign indicates a wine that is a little above its rating but not quite up to the next level. A range of quality among the various wines produced in a given region is indicated thusly: ★ /★ ★ ★ ★ (acceptable to outstanding), ★ ★ /★ ★ ★ (above average to very good).

5. **Cross References** to glossary entries in each chapter are in SMALL CAPS.

# THE WINES OF FRANCE

**F**rance is the world's premier wine-producing nation. Not in terms of quantity, where she is now surpassed by Italy, but rather for the quality and variety of her best wines. Bordeaux, Burgundy (the red and white wines of both), Champagne—these are the famous wine-producing areas against whose products most of the world's wines are judged. They, as well as the best from other regions—the Rhône, the Loire, and Alsace—are the prototypes for most of the wines we consume, no matter where they are made. Yet they are a mere 10 percent of France's total production of 25 million gallons, the average annual yield from her 3 million acres of vineyards. Eighty percent are sold in bulk or as *vin ordinaire*, which is the lowest level of French wines.

French wines are the most strictly regulated in the world. All the best and most famous wines are covered by *Appellation Contrôlée* laws. These laws do not rate the wines qualitatively, as in Germany; primarily, they are the government's guarantee that the wine in the bottle corresponds precisely to what the label says it is. They guarantee denomination of origin, determine grape variety, yield per acre, and alcoholic strength and regulate vinification techniques and vineyard practices. The laws cover appellations as broad as the whole of Bordeaux or as minute as a 2-acre vineyard in Burgundy, with a staggering range of regions and vineyards in between. Eighty-five percent of French wines imported to this country are Appellation Contrôlée wines.

Below this level there are three others:

*Vins Délimités de Qualité Supérieur* (VDQS), a secondary level that includes many creditable wines of sound regional character, mostly for everyday us.

*Vins de Pays*, wines that may come from 44 specified regions. Much experimentation is going on at this level, introducing grape varieties to regions where they were not grown before. Some authorities feel this will eventually result in a good quantity of fresh, young table wines suitable for immediate consumption. As yet, very little is available outside France.

*Vins de Marque*, proprietary brands or trademarks, usually blends of different grape varieties and from various regions. Some are better than others, depending on the firm that makes them, but they are usually a better grade than vin ordinaire.

THE WINE REGIONS OF
# FRANCE

## PRINCIPAL WINE REGIONS

**Alsace** (Als.) Province in northeastern France with vineyards on lower slopes of the Vosges Mountains west of the Rhine producing mostly dry, rather full-bodied white wines named for their grape varieties—Riesling, Gewürztraminer, Sylvaner, Pinot Gris, Pinot Blanc.

**Bordeaux** (Bord.) City and region in southwestern France straddling the estuary of the Gironde and extending along the slopes and plains of the Dordogne and Garonne river valleys. Subdivided into several delimited areas, the best of which are the Médoc, Haut-Médoc (which includes the communes of Saint-Estèphe, Pauillac, Saint-Julien, and Margaux), Graves, Saint-Émilion, and Pomerol. Principal grape varieties are Cabernet Sauvignon, Merlot, and Cabernet Franc. Red wines noted for intense fruit, harsh with tannins in youth but classically structured and capable of maturing into elegant, long-lived wines. Average to good dry whites from Graves and adjacent areas, exquisite sweet whites from Sauternes and Barsac. See map on page 10.

**Burgundy** (Burg.) France's other world-famous wine region, renowned for its full-bodied, intensely fragrant reds and whites along the Côte d'Or (see maps on pages 15 and 16) and the light fruity reds of Beaujolais. Also Chablis to the north between Paris and Dijon.

**Champagne** (Cham.) France's northernmost wine region, about 90 miles east of Paris. Producer of the world's first and best sparkling wines at principal cities of Reims and Épernay. Chardonnay and Pinot Noir grapes do well in the chalky limestone soil and cool climate.

**Côtes de Provence** (Prov.) Hilly region between Marseilles and Nice producing red, white, and rosé. Popular locally and on the Riviera, the wines are light, fresh, and pleasant but not distinguished. Some better known names are Bandol, Cassis, and Bellet.

**Jura** (Ju.) Very small region near Swiss border with vineyards along the foothills of the Jura Mountains. Average reds, whites, a good rosé called Arbois, some sparkling wine, and unique whites known as *vins jaunes.*

**Languedoc** (Lang.) One of France's oldest wine regions, producing mostly VIN ORDINAIRE but also several recently upgraded appellations such as Côtes de Rousillon, Corbières, and Fitou.

**Loire Valley** (L.V.) Vineyards follow the long, sinuous course of the Loire for most of its 600 miles until it empties into the Atlantic at Nantes. Mostly whites of fresh, flowery character are produced along its banks; the names Muscadet, Sancerre, Vouvray, and Pouilly-Fumé are well known. See map on page 26.

**Rhône Valley** (R.V.) Region in southeastern France below Burgundy known mostly for ripe, stalwart reds such as Hermitage and Châteauneuf-du-Pape and a few similarly full-bodied whites. See map on page 21.

# WINE GUIDE

ⓡ **d'Agassac Ch.** Bord. 81 80 79 78 76 75 73 71 ★ ★
Property at Ludon near Margaux owned by same owners of the fifth-growth Calon-Ségur, with well-made wines, getting better.

**Aligoté.** Grape variety used for the lesser white wines of Burgundy; yields large quantities of dry, drinkable wines; best when young. Usually seen as Bourgogne Aligoté.

ⓡⓦ **Aloxe-Corton.** Burg. 81 80 79 78 76 73 72 71 69 ★ ★/★ ★ ★ ★
Northernmost town on Côte de Beaune with fine, long-lived reds, elegant full-bodied whites, including top white Corton-Charlemagne. Reds: Corton, also Bressandes, Clos du Roi, Rénardes.

**Alsace.** See Principal Wine Regions or grape names, such as Riesling, Gewürztraminer.

ⓡ **l'Angelus, Ch.** Bord. 81 80 79 78 76 75 71 ★ ★
Classed growth of Saint-Émilion, generally softer wines that mature early and agreeably.

ⓡ **d'Angludet, Ch.** Bord. 81 80 79 78 77 76 75 71 70 ★ ★ +
Good CRU EXCEPTIONNEL property near Margaux, often ranks with higher classed growths. Good value.

**Anjou.** Province along the Loire producing light fruity wines, mostly from Chenin Blanc, some rosé, around towns of Angers and Saumur. Both sweet and dry. See Coteaux du Lyon, de la Loire, Saumur.

**Appellation Contrôlée.** See Introduction.

ⓢ **Arbois.** Ju. ★/★ ★ ★
Light, fruity wines of varying quality though generally agreeable from town near Swiss border. Best known for *vin jaune,* unusual dry, sherry-like white.

ⓦ **d'Arche, Ch.** Bord. 80 79 78 73 71 70 ★ ★ +
Good-sized estate in Sauternes producing sweet wines, often good value. Second wine under Ch. d'Arche-Lafaurie label.

(R) **Ausone Ch.** Bord. 81 80 79 78 77 76 75 71 70 66 ★ ★ ★ ★
A top-ranked growth of Saint-Émilion; slipped in stature for a time, but seems again to be moving toward excellent wines, especially since 1975.

(RW) **Auxey-Duresses.** Burg. 81 80 79 78 76 74 73 71 ★ ★ +
Village on the Côte de Beaune producing quality reds and whites of second degree and generally lighter, less distinguished but quite pleasant. Good value.

(R) **Balestard-la-Tonnelle, Ch.** Bord. 81 80 79 78 76 75 71 70 ★ ★ +
Very old, good estate among classed growths of Saint-Émilion, situated near the town gate of Saint-Émilion.

(3) **Bandol.** Prov. ★ ★
Village on western edge of Côtes de Provence producing light wines from lesser grape varieties; red rather better than white or rosé. Best when young, and slightly cooled.

**Banyuls.** Coastal village in the foothills of the Pyrénées above Spain's Costa Brava, producing France's portlike fortified wine, Banyuls.

(RW) **Baret, Ch.** Bord. 81 80 79 78 77 76 75 71 70 ★ ★
Good reds, better whites from small estate in Graves near city of Bordeaux. Good value.

(W) **Barsac.** Bord. 81 79 78 76 75 73 71 70 67 ★ ★ / ★ ★ ★
Town and region near Sauternes producing similarly luscious sweet wines. Best vineyards: Climens, Coutet, also Doisy-Daëne.

**Barton-Guestier.** B&G. Large, well-known shipping firm of Bordeaux, average to good wines.

(R) **Batailley, Ch.** Bord. 81 80 79 78 77 76 75 73 71 70 66 64 61 ★ ★ ★
Excellent fifth growth of Pauillac (adjacent to Haut-Batailley), some 20,000 cases deep, firm long-lived wines.

(W) **Bâtard-Montrachet.** Burg. 81 80 79 78 77 76 73 71 ★ ★ ★
One of the finest whites of the Côte de Beaune, ranks with Chevalier and just under Le Montrachet itself. Expensive.

(R) **Beaujolais.** Burg. 81 79 78 76 ★ / ★ ★ ★
France's most delightful light red—full flavored, berryish fruit, lively charm. Best value: Beaujolais-Villages. Best when young and slightly cooled. See also CRUS such as Brouilly, Fleurie, Morgon.

(R) **Beaujolais nouveau, primeur.** The earliest Beaujolais available, bottled within a few days of fermentation and shipped as of November 15 (PRIMEUR) or December 15 (NOUVEAU). Fragile, drink by spring following harvest.

(R) **Beaujolais Supérieur.** A grade higher than simple Beaujolais but not in the class of Villages or the CRUS.

(3) **Beaumes-de-Venise. R.V.** ★ / ★ ★ ★
Mainly, a sweet muscat dessert wine from the southern Rhône; beguilingly delicious aromas and flavors; also agreeable dry reds, some rosé.

(R) **Beaumont, Ch.** Bord. 81 80 79 78 77 76 75 71 70 ★ ★
Generally good and consistent CRU BOURGEOIS, between Saint-Julien and Margaux communes. Good value.

(RW) **Beaune.** Burg. 81 80 79 78 76 73 72 71 69 ★ ★ / ★ ★ ★
Major wine center of the Côte d'Or, as well as appellation for some very fine PREMIER CRU wines from several top-rated vineyards: Clos des Mouches, Gréves, Féves, Marconnets, Cras, among others.

(R) **Beauregard, Ch.** Bord. 81 80 79 78 77 76 75 71 70 ★ ★
One of the better properties of Pomerol (and not to be confused with lesser estates of same name in other parts of Bordeaux); round, graceful wines. Good value.

(R) **Beauséjour, Ch.** Bord. 81 80 79 78 77 76 75 71 70 ★ ★ +
Several châteaux of this name in Bordeaux but not of this Saint-Émilion class. Property now divided, other half known as Beauséjour-Duffau-Lagarosse; both very good. Good value.

(R) **Beau-Site, Ch.** Bord. 81 80 79 78 76 75 ★ ★
CRU BOURGEOIS vineyard in Saint-Estèphe making agreeable wines in better vintages.

(R) **Belair, Ch.** Bord. 81 80 79 78 76 75 70 ★ ★

Classed growth of Saint-Émilion set on steep, chalky hill; and under same ownership as Ausone. Good value.

(R) **de Bel-Air, Ch.** Bord. 81 80 79 78 76 75 ★ ★

Reputable estate in Lalande-Pomerol, a district adjacent to Pomerol; similar but lighter wines.

(R) **Bel-Air Marquis d'Aligre, Ch.** Bord. 81 80 79 78 76 75 71 70 ★ ★

Small but distinguished CRU EXCEPTIONNEL at Soussans (Margaux).

(R) **Belgrave, Ch.** Bord. 81 80 79 78 76 75 ★ ★

Minor classified growth near Saint-Julien; variable but better of late, with firm, fullish wines.

(3) **Bellet.** Prov. ★ ★

Small production near Nice, popular on the Riviera and quite pleasant, especially the rosé.

(R) **Bellevue, Ch.** Bord 81 80 79 76 75 71 ★ ★ +

Best of numerous properties of the name, round and agreeable wines from this GRAND CRU CLASSÉ of Saint-Émilion.

(R) **Bel-Orme-Tronquoy-Lalande, Ch.** Bord 81 80 79 78 76 75 ★ ★

Agreeable CRU BOURGEOIS above Saint-Estèphe but lacks the latter's sturdy density.

# GLOSSARY OF WINE TERMS

**Appellation Contrôlée.** *Highest level of French wine laws guaranteeing origin and authenticity of label information. These words appear on labels of all France's best wines.*

**Blanc de Blancs.** *White wine from all white grapes.*

**Blanc de Noir(s).** *White wine made from black-skinned grapes.*

**Botrytis cinerea.** *Mold that grows on grapeskins, desirable for varieties like Sémillon and Sauvignon Blanc where it concentrates sugars and results in the luscious sweet wines of Sauternes.*

**Brut.** *Dry.*

**Caves.** *Cellar. (Mise en bouteilles dans no caves means "bottled in our cellars" and is no guarantee of anything else.)*

**Chai.** *Storage shed for maturing wine.*

**Chambre.** *Room temperature; in old days rooms were much cooler than the 68° to 78°F (20° to 22°C) they are today.*

**Château.** *Term used in Bordeaux for the manor house of a property. Some are grand, but others are little more than modest country homes.*

**Château-bottled.** *Term indicating wines grown, produced and bottled on the property. Formerly a strong indication of quality; somewhat less so today. See MISE EN BOUTEILLES AU CHÂTEAU.*

**Claret.** *English term for red Bordeaux.*

**Clos.** *Enclosed vineyard, or property.*

**Classé.** *Classified.*

**Commune.** *Vineyard area surrounding a town. A commune is specifically delimited.*

**Côte.** *Hillside.*

**Cru.** *"Growth," used to designate a specific property or vineyard.*

**Cru Bourgeois.** *A large classification of Médocs not included in the 1855 classification.*

**Cru Classés.** *The classified growths of the Médoc, Saint-Émilion, Graves, and Sauternes. Pomerol has no official classification.*

**Cru Exceptionnel.** *A grade higher than CRU BOURGEOIS.*

(RW) **Bergerac.** Bord. 81 80 79 78 76 75 ★/★★
Town on the Dordogne river east of Bordeaux; some drinkable reds and an interesting sweet white, Monbazillac.

(R) **Beychevelle, Ch.** Bord. 81 80 79 78 76 75 71 70 66 64 61 ★★★
Superior classed growth of Saint-Julien, known for its splendid texture, elegance, and breed.

**Beyer, Leon.** Respected producer in Alsace, good Riesling, Gewürztraminer, Sylvaner.

(RW) **Blagny.** Burg. 81 80 79 78 76 73 ★★ +
Village on the Côte de Beaune near Meursault and Puligny; whites similar in style to Meursault. Good value.

(W) **Blanquette de Limoux.** Lang. ★
Sparkling wine produced near the city of Carcassone in southern France. Dry version fresh and agreeable.

(RW) **Blaye.** Bord. 81 80 79 78 77 76 75 ★/★★
Good-sized region opposite the Médoc producing average reds and whites, the best entitled to name Premières Côte de Blaye.

**Blanc-Fumé.** Local name for the Sauvignon Blanc along the Loire at Pouilly-sur-Loire.

---

Cuvée. *In Champagne, a blend.* Téte de cuvée *signifies top blend, or best wines of a harvest.*

Demi-sec. *Half-dry (quite sweet for Champagne).*

Domaine. *An estate, or single holding; equivalent to château in Burgundy and the Rhône.*

Doux. *Sweet.*

Grand Cru. *Great growth, the rank awarded by French wine authorities to the best vineyards of Burgundy and Chablis, also Saint-Émilion in Bordeaux.*

Premier Cru. *First growth in Bordeaux, but actually the second (and quite good) level of wines in Burgundy and Chablis.*

Méthode champenoise. *Original Champagne method of putting the sparkle in wines by refermenting in the original bottle and other specialized techniques.*

Mise en bouteilles au château. *Château-bottled, that is, wine bottled on the property where grown; once a definite sign of quality but now commonly used and not necessarily a mark of distinction.*

Mise en bouteilles á la proprieté, Mise au domaine. *Estate-bottled, same as above but used in Burgundy, the Rhône, and elsewhere outside Bordeaux.*

Monopole. *Vineyard with single owner.*

Mousseux. *Sparkling, term used for all French sparkling wines outside the district of Champagne.*

Négociant. *Merchant who buys directly from growers, often bottling the wine at his own firm.*

Pétillant. *Lightly sparkling.*

Récolte. *Harvest.*

Sec. *Dry.*

Sur lie. *Wine left on its lees, or yeast sediments, after fermentation, until bottling. In some cases such as Muscadet, this gives it an appealing freshness. Recent laws have altered the term somewhat to mean the wine must be bottled before June after the harvest.*

Vin ordinaire. *Table wine of ordinary, everyday level.*

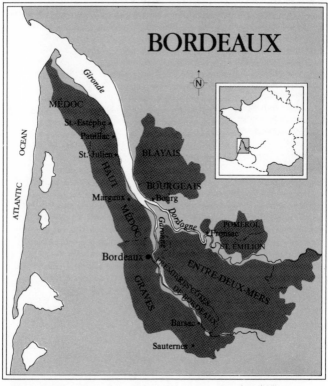

**BORDEAUX.** Bordeaux produces nearly a hundred million gallons of wine a year. Some of France's finest wines come from its best districts—the Médoc, Graves, Pomeral, and Saint-Émilion for elegant, long-lived reds; Sauternes and Barsac for sweet whites and Graves for dry, full-bodied whites. Attractive wines are also produced in such other regions as Haut-Médoc, Entre-Deux-Mers, Bourg, Blaye, and Canon Fronsac, and they are often very good value.

(W) **Bollinger.** One of the leading Champagne houses, producing full-bodied classic-style champagnes. Top of the line: Tradition R.D. This Champagne spends several years on yeast before disgorgement.

**Bommes.** Village in Sauternes with several top vineyards: Rayne-Vigneau, Sigalas-Rabaud, La Tour Blanche, Lafaurie-Peyraguey.

(R) **Bonnes-Mare.** Burg. 81 79 78 77 76 73 72 71 69 66 ★ ★ ★ ★
GRAND CRU vineyard between Chambolle-Musigny and Morey-Saint-Denis; powerful as Chambertin but rather more refined, one of the top dozen reds of the Côte-d'Or.

**Bordeaux, Bordeaux Supérieur.** Broadest and lowest appellations for Bordeaux. Supérieur is slightly higher in alcohol. Usually blended wines that cannot use a more specific place-name.

**Bouchard Aîné.** Long-established shipping firm based in Beaune, owners of several average-to-good properties along the Côte de Beaune.

**Bouchard Pére et Fils.** Very old, distinguished Burgundy shippers, with considerable (and venerable) vineyards on the Côtes de Beaune.

(R) **Bourg, Côtes de.** Bord. 81 80 79 78 76 75 ★/★ ★
Good to average reds, some whites from region on the Gironde opposite the lower Médoc. Occasionally full-bodied and good value in strong vintages.

(RW) **Bourgogne.** Burg. 81 80 79 78 76 72 71 ★ ★
Basic appellation for wines of Burgundy, some pleasant, round, and fruity but lacking the distinction of more specific appellations of the region that include village or vineyard names. See also Aligoté.

(R) **Bourgogne Passe-tout-grain.** Burg. ★
Lesser red Burgundy blended from half Gamay and half Pinot Noir. Somewhere between Burgundy and Beaujolais but lacking the personality of either, though sometimes agreeable. Drink young.

(R) **Bourgueil.** L.V. 81 79 78 76 ★ ★ +
A light, good Cabernet from the Touraine.

(RW) **Bouscaut, Ch.** Bord. 81 80 79 78 77 76 75 71 70 ★ ★
Good quality reds and dry white Graves at property south of Bordeaux, formerly owned by Americans, now sold back to French.

**Bouzy.** Important village in Champagne with the best of Pinot Noir vineyards; also a still red, Bouzy Rouge, delightful but limited production, occasionally available in Paris, rarely exported.

(R) **Boyd-Cantenac.** Bord. 81 80 79 78 77 76 75 73 71 70 66 ★ ★ ★
Classed growth of Margaux; under consultant Emile Peynaud, wines have improved considerably in the last decade.

(R) **Branaire-Ducru, Ch.** Bord. 81 80 79 78 76 75 73 71 70 66 61 ★ ★ ★
Fourth-growth Saint-Julien, with typical round elegant fruit and Saint-Julien finesse.

(R) **Brane-Cantenac, Ch.** Bord. 81 80 79 78 77 76 75 74 71 70 66 61 ★ ★ ★
Reliably good second growth of Margaux, fragrant, supple, sound wines, often good value; large estate of 180 acres. Good value.

(R) **Brouilly.** Burg. 81 79 78 ★ ★ ★
One of the nine GRANDS CRUS of Beaujolais, characterized by round, full lively fruit, though not long-lived. Best: Château de la Chaize, Château Thivin from adjacent Côte de Brouilly.

(RO) **Cabernet d'Anjou.** L.V. ★ ★
Light, fruity, off-dry rosé made around Saumur from Cabernet Franc. Usually better, drier than Rosé d'Anjou. Drink young.

**Cabernet Sauvignon.** Principal red wine grape of Bordeaux, mostly Médoc.

(R) **Cahors.** South West France 81 80 79 75 70 ★ ★
Once a hard, dark wine mostly from Malbec grape but vinified in lighter style today with addition of Merlot and other grapes. Still capable of aging well into interesting but not extraordinary wine.

(W) **Caillou, Ch.** Bord. 81 79 76 75 73 71 70 67 ★ ★ ★
Excellent sweet wines from this old property in Barsac. Good value.

(R) **Calon-Ségur, Ch.** Bord. 81 80 79 78 77 76 75 71 70 67 66 61 ★ ★ ★
One of the best classified growths of Saint-Estèphe, with typical heartiness and body; among the longest-lived of Saint-Estèphe, and of good value.

(R) **de Camensac, Ch.** Bord. 81 80 79 78 76 75 71 70 ★ ★ +
Minor Haut-Médoc classified growth, lackluster for years but expanded vineyards and modern techniques have resulted in much improvement in recent years; big, good depth, powerful aromas. Good value.

(R) **Canon, Ch.** Bord. 81 80 79 78 77 76 75 71 70 66 ★ ★ ★
Fine, generous full-bodied wines from this classed growth of Saint-Émilion.

(R) **Canon-La Gaffelière, Ch.** Bord. 81 80 79 78 76 75 ★ ★
Second-level growth on western slopes, generally typical Saint-Émilion; earthy, full-bodied, quick-maturing. Good value.

(R) **Cantemerle, Ch.** Bord. 81 80 79 78 76 75 71 70 ★ ★ ★
Fifth growth of the 1855 Haut-Médoc classification but better than its level. Well-balanced, supple wines of great finesse. Good value.

(R) **Cantenac-Brown, Ch.** Bord. 81 80 79 78 77 76 75 73 71 70 66 62 61 ★ ★ ★
Third-growth Margaux (Cantenac) showing breed and elegance typical of the commune but generally fuller-bodied than other Margaux.

11

(R) **Capbern, Ch.** Bord. 81 80 79 78 76 75 ★ ★
Full-bodied Saint-Estèphe, same owners as Calon-Ségur.

(RW) **Carbonnieux, Ch.** Bord. 81 80 79 78 77 76 75 74 71 70 ★ ★ ★
Vigorous reds, fine dry whites from old property in Léognan, Graves.

(R) **Cardonne, La.** Bord. 81 80 79 78 75 ★ ★
Recently purchased by the Lafite branch of Rothschilds, this CRU BOUR-
GEOIS in the northern Médoc has produced variable quality wines so far,
but a good firm 1975.

**Carraudes de Lafite.** Second label of Chateau Lafite, from younger
vines; less depth and class but still very good; not produced since 1967,
when new plantings reached maturity. See Moulin de Carruades.

(3) **Cassis.** Prov. ★ ★
Village on the Riviera producing light, agreeable reds, rosés, and dry
whites (best) for drinking young. Cassis is also the name of a black
currant liqueur made in Dijon.

(W) **Cerons.** Bord. 81 80 79 ★/★ ★
Medium sweet or off-dry whites from this region between Graves and
Sauternes. Not widely known but can be quite pleasant.

(R) **Certan-de-May.** Bord. 81 80 79 78 77 76 75 71 70 ★ ★ ★
One of the smallest vineyards in Pomerol producing big, long-lived
wines, often firmer than most Pomerols.

(W) **Chablis.** Burg. 81 79 78 76 75 71 70 ★ ★ ★
Famous white Burgundy quite different from southern Burgundy
whites, though also made entirely from Chardonnay. Flinty, dry, full-
bodied whites, somewhat austere but with classic elegance in good
years; thin and acidic in poor years. Classic with shellfish, especially
oysters.

(W) **Chablis Grand Cru.** The finest Chablis, consisting of seven vineyards—
Vaudésir, Les Clos, Grenouilles, Blanchots, Preuses, Bougros, Valmur.
Elegant richness in great years like 1978, 1976, 1975.

(W) **Chablis Premier Cru.** The second level of vineyards ranking just below
GRAND CRU, often quite superb. Best vineyards: Les Fôrets, Four-châume,
Montée de Tonnere, Monts-du-Milieu, Vaulorent.

(R) **Chambertin.** Burg. 81 80 79 78 77 76 73 72 71 70 69 66 61 ★ ★ ★ ★
The most famous red Burgundy, and deservedly for its sturdy vigor and
splendid proportions, heady perfumed aroma, and durability.

(R) **Chambertin-Clos de Bèze.** Burg. 81 80 79 78 77 76 73 72 71 70 69 66
★ ★ ★ ★
Estate adjoining Chambertin, the wines virtually indistinguishable in
some years, of at least equal greatness.

(R) **Chambolle-Musigny.** Burg. 81 79 78 77 76 73 71 69 ★ ★/★ ★ ★ ★
A top commune on the Côte de Nuits. Village wines of supple elegance.
GRAND CRU: Le Musigny; PREMIERS CRUS: Amoureuses, Les Charmes.

(W) **Champagne.** World's best sparkling wine from delimited region east of
Paris, made solely by special method known as MÉTHODE CHAMPENOISE.

(R) **Champigny.** L.V. 81 80 79 78 ★ ★ +
Very pleasant fruity, light red from the Loire Valley around Saumur,
somewhat Beaujolais-like in style. Also labeled Saumur-Champigny.

(R) **Chapelle-Chambertin.** Burg. 81 80 79 78 76 73 72 71 70 69 66 ★ ★ ★
Ranked a GRAND CRU but rather less grand than Chambertin, though still
impressive.

**Chardonnay** (sometimes Pinot Chardonnay). Noble white grape used
exclusively for white Burgundy, Chablis, Mâcon, BLANC DE BLANCS Champagne.

(R) **Charmes-Chambertin.** Burg. 81 80 79 78 76 73 72 71 69 66 ★ ★ ★
Lighter than most of the Chambertins but shows similar finesse.

(RW) **Chasagne-Montrachet.** Burg. 81 80 79 78 76 73 72 71 69
Important commune on the Côte de Beaune with several superb white
wine vineyards, including Montrachet, Bâtard-Montrachet, Criots-
Bâtard-Montrachet, Ruchottes, followed by (and including good reds)
Boudriotte, Caillerets, Morgeot.

®® **Chasse-Spleen, Ch.** Bord. 81 80 79 78 77 76 75 71 70 ★ ★ +
Estate at Moulis, Haut-Médoc, ranked as CRU EXCEPTIONNEL. Round, full wines of depth and breed. Good value.

Ⓦ **Château-Chalon.** Ju. ★ ★ ★
Unusual dry white wine with character of a dry sherry due to formation of flor yeast on the surface of fermenting wine. Limited production but worth trying.

®® **Château de la Chaize.** Burg. 81 79 ★ ★ ★
Best-known estate of Beaujolais, in Brouilly, full, fruity charm.

Ⓦ **Château Grillet.** R.V. 81 80 79 78 76 72 71 70 ★ ★ ★
One of France's smallest appellations covering a single vineyard (3.5 acres) on the northern Rhône; rich golden dry wines, spicy aromas.

®® **Châteauneuf-du-Pape.** R.V. 81 80 78 76 72 71 70 69 67 ★ ★ */★ ★ ★
Popular and widely known sturdy red from southern Rhône Valley made mostly from Syrah and Grenache. Widely variable quality, at best has soft, round richness that is most appealing.

®® **Chénas.** Burg. 81 79 78 76 ★ ★ ★
One of the nine GRAND CRUS of Beaujolais, fuller-bodied, sturdier than most.

**Chenin Blanc.** Fruity white grape planted mostly along the Loire.

®® **Cheval-Blanc, Ch.** Bord. 81 80 79 78 76 75 73 71 66 64 62 61 ★ ★ ★ ★
Top-ranked growth of Saint-Émilion, superbly rich, round wines of great depth and long life, though generally drinkable sooner than comparable Médocs.

Ⓦ **Chevalier-Montrachet.** Burg. 81 80 78 76 74 73 71 70 ★ ★ ★ +
The "rightful son" of Montrachet (see Bâtard-Montrachet), almost as rich and beautiful, though less powerful; only 17 acres and expensive.

®® **Chinon.** L.V. 81 80 79 78 76 75 ★ ★ +
A red from the Touraine made from Cabernet Franc; usually light and fruity but ages well in good vintages.

®® **Chiroubles.** Burg. 81 79 ★ ★ ★
One of the loveliest, fruitiest of the nine Beaujolais CRUS; early maturing, soft, and fragrant.

**Cissac.** Commune in the Haut-Médoc near Pauillac with several good CRUS BOURGEOIS growths, including Ch. Cissac.

®® **Citran, Ch.** Bord. 81 80 79 78 76 75 73 71 ★ ★
Sound, solid wines from one of the best CRUS BOURGEOIS in the Haut-Médoc. Good value.

**Clairet.** Light red wine, though not quite rosé.

Ⓦ **Clairette de Die.** R.V. ★ ★
Sparkling wine popular in southern France, made from Clairette and Muscat grapes; sweet, with Muscat aromas.

®® **Clarke, Ch.** Bord. 81 80 79 78 ★ ★
Large CRU BOURGEOIS property at Listrac, recently purchased and re-planted by a branch of the Rothschilds.

®® **Clerc-Milon, Ch.** Bord. 81 80 79 78 77 76 75 71 70 ★ ★ ★
Fifth-growth Pauillac of Haut-Médoc now owned by Baron Philippe de Rothschild; well-made wines with typical Pauillac depth and character.

Ⓦ **Climens.** Bord. 81 79 78 76 75 73 71 70 67 ★ ★ ★
Superb sweet whites from commune of Barsac, possibly its best.

®® **Clinet, Ch.** Bord. 81 80 79 78 76 75 71 70 ★ ★ +
Small but quite good Pomerol, classic light Bordeaux. Good value.

®® **Clos de la Roche.** Burg. 81 79 78 77 76 72 71 70 69 ★ ★ ★ +
GRAND CRU at Morey-Saint-Denis on the Côte de Nuits with almost the grandeur of Chambertin, but a shade less majestic. Good value.

®® **Clos des Lambrays.** Burg. 81 79 78 77 76 72 71 70 69 ★ ★ ★
Excellent PREMIER CRU vineyard on the Côte de Nuits at Morey-Saint-Denis; powerful and long-lived.

®ⓦ **Clos des Mouches.** Burg. 81 80 79 78 76 74 72 71 70 69 ★ ★ ★
Full-bodied red and distinguished white from PREMIER CRU vineyard near Beaune. One of the Beaune's best vineyards.

®  **Clos de Vougeot.** Burg. 81 80 79 78 77 76 74 73 72 71 70 69 66 ★ ★ ★ /
★ ★ ★ ★

Magisterial chateau on the Côte de Nuits, 124-acre vineyard with numerous owners, and thus wines of variable quality; at its best generously full-
flavored, with intense, lingering bouquet. A small quantity of white,
Clos Blanc de Vougeot, also quite fine.

®  **Clos l'Église.** Bord. 81 80 79 78 76 75 71 70 ★ ★ ★
Polished, graceful Pomerol, one of its best vineyards. Good value.

®  **Clos Fourtet.** Bord. 81 80 79 78 77 76 75 71 70 ★ ★ ★
A great growth of Saint-Émilion, producing lighter wines of late but still
elegant.

®  **Clos des Jacobins.** Bord. 81 80 79 78 76 75 71 70 ★ ★
Classed growth of Saint-Émilion, same owners as Talbot, Gruaud-Larose
in Médoc. Modest, pleasant wine.

®  **Clos du Roi.** Burg. 81 80 79 78 76 73 72 71 69 ★ ★ ★
Two excellent PREMIER CRU vineyards on the Côte de Beaune, one at
Beaune, the other at Corton-Clos du Roi richer and more distinctive.

®  **Clos René.** Bord. 81 80 79 78 76 75 71 70 66 61 ★ ★ ★
Good Pomerol classed growth of second level, mature wines often lush
and highly perfumed after 8 to 12 years.

®  **Clos St. Denis.** Burg. 81 80 79 78 77 76 73 72 71 70 69 ★ ★ ★
Excellent GRAND CRU of Chambertin-like constitution; complex, long-
lived. Good value.

®  **Clos St. Jacques.** Burg. 81 80 79 78 77 76 73 72 71 70 69 66 ★ ★ ★
PREMIER CRU at Gevrey-Chambertin, probably tops on the Côte d'Or in
that class. Rich, full, substantial, very near to Chambertin itself.

®  **Clos St. Jean.** Burg. 81 79 78 77 76 73 72 71 69 ★ ★ ★
Best PREMIER CRU vineyard for red wine from Chassagne-Montrachet on
the Côte de Beaune; sound value.

Ⓦ  **Condrieu.** R.V. ★ ★ +
Interesting Rhône Valley white, mostly dry but some semisweet, unusual fragrance; most consumed locally and worth looking for.

®  **La Conseillante, Ch.** Bord. 81 80 79 78 76 75 71 70 66 ★ ★ ★
Among the top properties of Pomerol, often rich, plush-textured wines,
but may need a decade at least to show it.

®  **Corbières.** Lang. 81 80 79 78 76 ★ ★
A light to medium-bodied red of VDQS level; Corbières du Rousillon
also good, a bit coarser. Some lesser white and rosé also made.

®  **Cornas.** R.V. 81 80 79 78 76 75 72 71 70 69 67 ★ ★ +
Robust, attractive red from the northern Rhône that ages quite well in
strong vintages.

**Corsica.** Island in the Mediterranean belonging to France, lately expanded production of robust, mostly average-quality wine. Best are
A.C. Patrimonio and Ajaccio, *vins de pays* L'Ile de Beauté.

®  **Corton.** Burg. 81 80 79 78 77 76 73 71 70 69 66 ★ ★ ★ ★
Top red of the Côte de Beaune at Aloxe-Corton and a GRAND CRU that can
stand with the best reds of the Côte de Nuits. Staunch, rich, and long-
lived.

Ⓦ  **Corton-Charlemagne.** Burg. 81 80 79 78 76 73 69 ★ ★ ★ ★
Superb white Corton from celebrated vineyard named for Charlemagne
who once owned vineyards in the region in the eighth century (though
maybe not these). Steely elegance, rich fruit, long-lived.

®  **Cos d'Estournel, Ch.** Bord. 81 80 79 78 77 76 75 71 70 67 66 64 61
★ ★ ★
Outstanding second growth in Saint-Estèphe now owned by Prats
family; rich, sturdy wines that mature with considerable finesse of flavor
and bouquet. Good value.

®  **Cos Labory, Ch.** Bord. 81 80 79 78 76 75 71 ★ ★
Good, robust Saint-Estèphe with reputable though not especially distinguished wines.

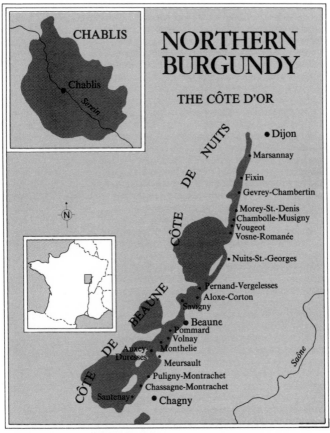

**NORTHERN BURGUNDY.** Burgundy's wine regions are among the oldest in France but produce only a third as much wine as Bordeaux. The Côte d'Or of northern Burgundy is subdivided into the Côte de Nuits—known for its famous red wines from the communes of Fixin to Nuits-St. Georges—and the Côte de Beaune—known for both reds and whites from Beaune, center of Burgundy's wine trade—to Santenay. Chablis lies north and west of the Côte d'Or.

ⓦ **Coteaux Champenois.** Cham. ★ ★ ★
   The still dry white wine of Champagne, made from Chardonnay. Often quite good but expensive; best within two or three years.

ⓦ **Coteaux de la Loire.** 81 80 79 78 76 75 ★ ★ ★
   Fragrant, full-flavored whites made from Chenin Blanc in Anjou. Best appellation: Savennières. Good value.

ⓦ **Coteaux du Layon.** L.V. 81 80 79 ★ ★ +
   Sweet whites with appealing fruit and fragrance from Chenin Blanc grape; among the best are Bonnezeaux, Quarts de Chaume. Also some rosé. Angers is center of the region.

③ **Coteaux du Loir.** L.V. ★ ★
   The Loir is a tributary of the Loire near Tours; a lesser region for mild reds, whites, rosés, best of which is Jasnières.

15

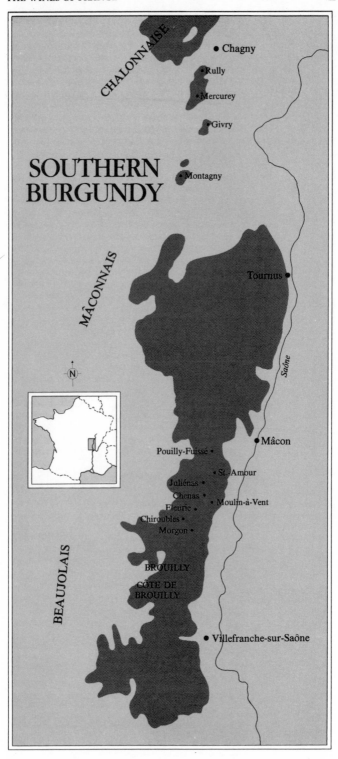

**SOUTHERN BURGUNDY.** The wines of southern Burgundy are not as illustrious as those of the north, but the dry white wines of Mâcon and the fruity reds of Beaujolais offer excellent value and delightful drinking. Along the Côte Chalonnaise, Givry and Mercurey are best known for fullish reds and Montagny and Rully mainly for dry whites that are increasingly better known.

(R) **Coteaux du Tricastin.** R.V. 81 80 79 78
Area around Valence in the northern Rhône, recently elevated to APPELLATION CONTRÔLÉE. Lighter than Côtes du Rhône. Good value.

**Côte de Beaune.** Northern half of Burgundy (see map, page 15), known for softer reds (exept Corton) and exquisite whites such as Meursault, Corton-Charlemagne, and Montrachet. Also an appellation for lesser reds and whites from vineyards around Beaune; Côte de Beaune-Villages is of similar rank and, unless a town name is attached, covers the general region.

(R) **Côte de Brouilly.** Burg. 81 79 78 ★ ★ ★
Excellent CRU-ranked Beaujolais, from the upper slopes of the Mont du Brouilly, generally more substantial fruit than Brouilly with a bit more finesse. Look for Chateau Thivin.

**Côte de Nuits.** The northern half of Burgundy's Côte d'Or, taking its name from the commune of Nuits-Saint-Georges. As a regional appellation, covers blended wines that are little seen outside France or Burgundy itself.

**Côte d'Or.** Literally, "golden slope," the name for the strip of vineyards between Dijon and Santenay that produces Burgundy's finest wines (see map, page 15).

(R) **Côte Rotie.** R.V. 81 80 79 78 76 71 70 69 67 66 ★ ★ ★
One of the northern Rhône's best wines, tough and tannic in youth but becomes mellow, rich, and smooth-textured with age. Good value.

(R) **Côtes Canon-Fronsac.** Bord. 81 80 79 78 76 75 ★ ★
Small area west of Pomerol and Saint-Émilion; robust little wines best after four years or so of aging, generally age better than Côtes de Fronsac; both, however, good value.

(3) **Côtes de Provence.** ★ / ★ ★
Elevated in 1977 from VDQS to APPELLATION CONTRÔLÉE. Light, unassuming reds, whites, rosés, best consumed young and along the Riviera or hilly country back of it where they are made. Better value there.

(3) **Côtes du Rhône.** R.V. 81 80 79 78 76 ★ / ★ ★
Light, agreeable wines, mostly red and rosé from the southern Rhône Valley. Côtes du Rhône-Villages more substantial.

(3) **Côtes du Ventoux.** R.V. 81 80 79 78 76 ★ +
Light wines from a portion of the southern Rhône, similar to Côtes du Rhône; recently elevated from VDQS to APPELLATION CONTRÔLÉE.

(3) **Côtes du Rousillon.** Lang. 81 80 79 78 76 ★ ★
Red, white, and rosé from the foothills of the Pyrénées near Perpignan; the medium-character, full-bodied reds are good everyday wines.

(W) **Couhins.** Bord. 81 80 79 ★ ★
Well-made dry white from Graves; insignificant amount of red also. Good value.

(R) **La Couronne.** Bord. 81 80 79 78 77 76 75 71 70 ★ ★
Fine CRU EXCEPTIONNEL at Pauillac made by owners of Ducru-Beaucaillou and Haut-Batailley; good depth, well-balanced. Good value.

(RW) **La Cour Pavillon.** Bord. 81 80 79 78 76 ★ ★
Red and white proprietary brands marketed by Gilbey, reds from northern Médoc more consistently attractive.

(W) **Coutet, Ch.** Bord. 81 79 78 76 75 73 71 70 67 62 ★ ★ ★ +
Top vineyard at Barsac producing luscious golden sweet wines remarkable for breed and bouquet. Good value.

(R) **Fitou.** Lang. 81 80 79 78 76 ★ ★
Hearty red of some depth with good aging potential. Good value.

(R) **Fixin.** Burg. 81 79 78 76 71 70 69 ★ ★/★ ★ ★
Lesser commune at northern end of Côte de Nuits. Not as generously endowed as bigger reds to the south but well structured and among the best values in quality. Best vineyards; Clos de la Perrière, Clos du Chapitre, Hervelets. Good value.

(R) **Fleurie.** Burg. 81 79 78 ★ ★ ★
Beaujolais CRU, generously fruity and joyous wine, noted for flowery bouquet.

(R) **Les Forts de Latour.** Bord. 81 79 78 76 75 70 66 ★ ★ ★
Second wine of Château Latour; very high-class Pauillac, with strength, depth, and distinctive aroma; ready sooner than Latour.

(R) **Fourcas-Hosten, Ch.** Bord. 81 80 79 78 76 75 71 ★ ★ +
Superior CRU BOURGEOIS at Listrac in central Médoc. Good value.

(R) **la Gaffelière, Ch.** Bord. 81 80 79 78 77 76 75 71 70 ★ ★ ★
Formerly known as La Gaffelière-Naudes; very strong comeback in recent years, situated near slopes of Château Ausone, Saint-Émilion.
**Gamay.** Grape variety best known for the fruity wines of Beaujolais.

(R) **le Gay, Ch.** Bord. 81 80 79 78 76 75 74 71 70 ★ ★ +
One of the better second-level Pomerols, warm, full-bodied, generally early maturing.

(R) **Gazin, Ch.** Bord. 81 80 79 78 76 75 71 70 66 ★ ★ +
One of Pomerol's largest estates; good, robust wines though not quite top level.

(R) **Gevrey-Chambertin.** Burg. 81 79 78 76 73 72 71 70 69 66 ★ ★/★ ★ ★
Important commune of the Côte d'Or, site of Chambertin vineyards. Wines with the village name can be quite good; PREMIERS CRUS even better from vineyards like Clos Saint-Jacques, Varoilles, Aux Combottes.

(W) **Gewürztraminer.** Als. 81 80 79 78 77 76 71 ★ ★ ★
Dry, full-bodied whites with enticing spice aromas, rather austere fruit. Often age well; reserve wines intense and rich.

(R) **Gigondas.** R.V. 81 80 79 78 76 71 70 67 ★ ★ +
Variable quality reds from the southern Rhône that can be sturdy, full-bodied, warmly attractive—good value when they are.

(RW) **Givry.** Burg. 81 80 79 78 76 72 71 ★ ★ +
Light reds and whites of the Côte Chalonnaise; sound, if not impressive Burgundian character. Good value in good vintages.

(R) **Giscours, Ch.** Bord. 81 80 79 78 77 76 75 71 70 67 66 61 ★ ★ ★
Large, well-run estate at Labarde, Margaux, owned by Tari family; highly perfumed, consistently fine wines, very long-lived.

(R) **Gloria, Ch.** Bord. 81 80 79 78 77 76 75 71 70 67 66 61 ★ ★ +
A CRU BOURGEOIS but portions of vineyards were part of other famous Saint-Julien vineyards, so wines show typical fullness and a certain dash. Good value.

(R) **Grancey, Ch.** Burg. 81 79 78 76 73 72 71 69 66 ★ ★ ★
Estate-grown Corton of well-known shipper Louis Latour; big and long-lived.

(R) **Grand-Barrail-Lamarzelle-Figeac.** Bord. 81 80 78 76 75 71 70 ★ ★ +
Good, typical full-bodied Saint-Émilion; good value.

(R) **Grand-Puy-Ducasse.** Bord. 81 80 79 78 76 75 71 70 66 ★ ★ +
Fifth-growth Pauillac, vigorous and sound but lighter than most of that commune; drinkable sooner. Good value.

(R) **Grand-Puy-Lacoste.** Bord. 81 80 79 78 76 75 73 71 70 66 61 ★ ★ ★
Fifth-growth Pauillac but more classically structured than Ducasse, with more breed and considerable depth; highly regarded (and pricey).

(R) **Grands Échezeaux.** Burg. 81 79 78 77 76 73 72 71 70 69 66 ★ ★ ★ ★
Among the greatest of red Burgundies, luxuriant fruit, magnificent bouquet, great finesse.

(RW) **Graves.** Bord. 81 80 79 78 77 76 75 71 70 ★ ★ / ★ ★ ★
District of Bordeaux producing top wines such as Château Haut-Brion and other fine reds; fewer but also excellent dry whites and an abundance of fair to good whites, both sweet and dry.

(W) **Graves Supérieur.** Bord. 81 80 79 78 ★ / ★ ★
Now, by law, the sweet whites of Graves; some improvement in recent years but still rather clumsy and too often oversulfured.

**Graves de Vayre.** Part of Entre-Deux-Mers producing mediocre reds but acceptable whites, especially if young and fresh.

(R) **Griotte-Chambertin.** Burg. 81 79 78 76 73 72 71 70 69 ★ ★ ★ +
Worthy younger brother of the great Chambertin, which it adjoins.

(W) **Gros Plant du Pays Nantais.** L.V. ★ ★
Fresh, dry pleasant white of the Loire near the Atlantic; good, inexpensive choice for seafood but not as full as Muscadet. Drink young. Good value.

(R) **Gruaud-Larose, Ch.** Bord. 81 80 79 78 76 75 71 70 66 62 61 ★ ★ ★ +
Second-growth Saint-Julien and one of the best; abundant fruit, noble structure and breed.

(RW) **Guiraud, Ch.** Bord. 81 79 76 75 71 70 67 ★ ★ ★
A Sauternes ranked just after Yquem; less concentrated and luscious but quite as elegant. Small quantities of dry white and red also produced. Good value.

(R) **Haut-Bages-Libéral, Ch.** Bord. 81 80 79 78 76 75 ★ ★
A fifth growth but not up to the best of that level. Pauillac estate recently purchased by Cruse family and appears to be improving; recent wines fairly robust, smooth.

(R) **Haut-Bailly, Ch.** Bord. 81 80 79 78 76 75 73 71 70 ★ ★ ★
Sturdy, full-flavored Graves; needs time in bottle but exhibits great finesse when mature. Good value.

(R) **Haut-Batailley, Ch.** Bord. 81 80 79 78 77 76 75 73 71 70 66 ★ ★ ★
Formerly part of Batailley, Pauillac; though smaller it is equally as good with sturdy character and depth.

(R) **Haut-Brion, Ch.** Bord. 81 80 79 78 77 76 75 74 73 71 70 67 66 64 62 61 ★ ★ ★ ★
A Graves ranked with Lafite, Latour, Margaux in 1855, the only wine outside the Médoc so honored. Supremely fine still, if not always on a par with the others. Velvet-textured, very long-lived, often good in off-vintages.

**Haut-Médoc.** The best portion of the Médoc embracing its most famous châteaux; also a regional appellation for above-average wines, superior to those labeled simply "Médoc."

(RW) **Hautes-Côtes de Beaune.** Burg. 81 79 78 76 ★ ★
Vineyards on slopes behind the Côte de Beaune, lighter reds and whites but can be good value.

(W) **Heidsieck, Charles.** One of the top houses of Champagne. Classic, full-bodied style. Luxury CUVÉE: Royal.

(W) **Heidsieck, Dry Monopole.** Champagne firm at Rheims. Luxury CUVÉE: Diamant Bleu.

(W) **Henriot.** Small but top Champagne house producing rich, very full-bodied wines. Luxury CUVÉE: Rèserve de Baron Philippe de Rothschild.

(R) **Hermitage.** R.V. 81 80 79 78 76 74 72 71 70 69 66 ★ ★ ★ +
Big generous reds of the northern Rhône that become round and velvety after several years' aging; great ones very long-lived. Good value.

**Hospices de Beaune.** Famous charity hospital in Beaune, scene of annual auction of Burgundy wines each autumn, and owner of portions of several outstanding vineyards on the Côte de Beaune. Wines named for owners include Docteur Peste, Charlotte Dumay, Nicolas Rolin.

**Hugel.** A leading firm in Alsace, one of the largest, producing Riesling, Gewürztraminer, Sylvaner.

**Jadot, Louis.** Well-respected shipper in Burgundy with several fine vineyards at Corton, Pommard, for example.

19

Ⓡ **d'Issan, Ch.** Bord. 81 80 79 78 76 75 73 71 70 ★ ★ ★
Historic château at Cantanac, Margaux, recently upgraded wines with the suppleness of Margaux but more robust.

Ⓡ **Juliénas.** Burg. 81 79 78 76 ★ ★ ★
One of the sturdier Beaujolais CRUS: not as immediately engaging but balanced and longer-lived.

Ⓡ **Kirwan, Ch.** Bord. 81 80 79 78 76 75 71 70 ★ ★
Good-sized third growth at Cantenac, Margaux, rather lackluster to date but steadily improving.

**Klug.** A major producer in Alsace; good Riesling, Gewürztraminer, good value.

Ⓦ **Krug.** One of the smaller Champagne houses; classic, full-bodied wines often considered the connoisseur's Champagne. Luxury CUVÉE: Grande Réserve Blanc de Blancs.

Ⓡ **Lafite-Rothschild, Ch.** Bord. 81 80 79 78 77 76 75 71 70 67 66 62 61 ★ ★ ★ ★
Among the world's greatest wines, from Pauillac. The classic claret of elegance and breed, stylish, subtle but astonishing power in great vintages, of this century and the last.

Ⓡ **Lafleur-Pétrus, Ch.** Bord. 81 80 79 78 76 75 71 70 66 ★ ★ ★
Charming, flavorful wines from one of the smaller Pomerol estates.

Ⓡ **Lafon-Rochet, Ch.** Bord. 81 80 79 78 77 75 73 71 70 66 61 ★ ★ +
Fourth-growth Saint-Estèphe now owned by the Tesseron family, who have restored the château and vineyards. Dark, sturdy, typically Saint-Estèphe. Good value.

Ⓡ **La Lagune, Ch.** Bord. 81 80 79 78 76 75 73 71 70 66 ★ ★ ★
A third growth of the 1855 classification at Ludon (below Margaux). Vineyard replantings and modernization have put this wine in the front ranks; meatier fruit than most Médocs; good balance.

Ⓡ **Lanessan, Ch.** Bord. 81 80 79 78 76 75 71 70 ★ ★
One of the more reputable CRU BOURGEOIS of the Haut-Médoc, firm, full-bodied wines known for long-lived delicacy. Good value.

Ⓡ **Langoa-Barton, Ch.** Bord. 81 80 79 78 76 75 73 71 70 67 66 ★ ★ ★
Third-growth Saint-Julien and sister château to Léoville-Barton; somewhat lighter than the Léoville but quite good.

Ⓦ **Lanson Père et Fils.** A Champagne firm in Rheims. Best value: the nonvintage, which is light, dry, and fruity.

Ⓡ **Lascombes, Ch.** Bord. 81 80 79 78 76 75 72 71 70 66 64 62 61 ★ ★ ★
Second-growth Margaux property restored to excellence largely by former owner Alexis Lichine; fine bouquet and rich, smooth texture. Now belongs to Bass-Charrington shipping firm.

Ⓡ **La Tache.** Burg. 81 80 79 78 77 76 74 73 72 71 70 66 62 ★ ★ ★ ★
To some, the noblest of all Burgundies, certainly one of the world's most outstanding (and expensive) wines; deep color, extravagant perfume, lavishly rich yet tremendous noblesse; great vintages live for decades.

Ⓡ **Latour, Ch.** Bord. 81 80 79 78 76 75 74 73 71 70 69 67 66 64 62 61 ★ ★ ★ ★
First-growth Pauillac, the most forceful and intense of all, remarkably consistent quality; dark, tannic, and harsh when young but matures into a wine of great nobility and breed with strength for very long life; often superb in off-vintages and excellent value.

**Latour, Louis.** Large, well-known, and highly respected Burgundy shipper, owner of several vineyards such as parts of Corton-Charlemagne.

Ⓡ **Latour-Pomerol, Ch.** Bord. 81 80 79 78 77 76 75 74 73 71 70 ★ ★ ★
Small Pomerol estate but ample, fruity, beautiful wines made by a member of the Moueix family of Chateau Pétrus.

Ⓡ **Latricières-Chambertin.** Burg. 81 80 79 78 77 76 74 72 71 70 69 66 ★ ★ ★
A GRAND CRU vineyard approaching the strength and nobility of Chambertin but less weighty.

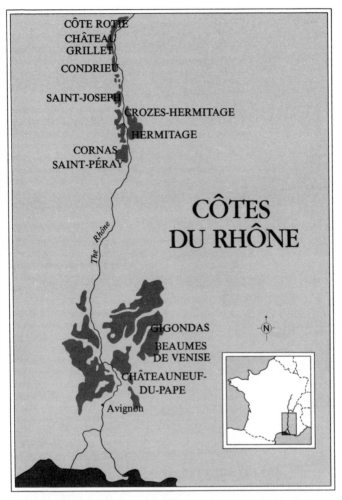

CÔTE ROTIE
CHÂTEAU GRILLET
CONDRIEU
SAINT-JOSEPH
CROZES-HERMITAGE
HERMITAGE
CORNAS
SAINT-PÉRAY

CÔTES DU RHÔNE

The Rhône

GIGONDAS
BEAUMES DE VENISE
CHÂTEAUNEUF-DU-PAPE
Avignon

N

**THE RHÔNE.** Rhône Valley wines, predominantly red, range from the very fine, full-bodied reds such as Côte Rotie, Hermitage, or Châteauneuf-du-Pape to light regionals labeled simply Côtes du Rhône or Coteaux du Tricastin. Unusual and distinctive whites are made in the region also, such as Condrieu, Château Grillet, Hermitage, and Beaumes-de-Venise, but in far smaller quantities.

Ⓦ **Laurent-Pérrier.** One of the top shippers in Champagne; luxury CUVÉE, La Grand Siècle, has excellent fruit and finesse.

Ⓡ **Léoville-Barton, Ch.** Bord. 81 80 79 78 77 76 75 73 71 70 67 66 64 62 61 ★★★
Excellent second-growth Saint-Julien, full body, fruit, not quite as fine as Léoville-Las-Cases, though occasionally richer.

Ⓡ **Léoville-Las-Cases, Ch.** Bord. 81 80 79 78 77 76 75 74 73 71 70 67 66 64 61 ★★★ +
Second growth of Saint-Julien and the most outstanding; full, rich fruit, wonderfully perfumed, with great breed, finesse, and long-lasting delicacy at maturity.

(R) **Léoville-Poyferré, Ch.** Bord. 81 80 79 78 76 75 73 71 70 67 66 61
★ ★ ★
Excellent second-growth Saint-Julien, usually better than Léoville-Barton with whom it jockeys for position just under Las-Cases; has style and verve.

(R) **Loudenne, Ch.** Bord. 81 80 79 78 76 75 74 73 71 70 ★ ★ +
Imposing château and well-run CRU BOURGEOIS, of the northern Médoc, owned by Gilbey. Small quantity of dry white Bordeaux Supérieur also produced. Good value.

(R) **Lynch-Bages, Ch.** Bord. 81 80 79 78 76 75 71 70 66 61 ★ ★ ★
Popular fifth-growth Pauillac without the classic breed of the best Pauillac, but robust, rich, and roundly attractive at earlier age.

(R) **Lynch-Moussas, Ch.** Bord. 81 80 79 78 76 75
Hardly notable fifth-growth Pauillac now under ownership of the family that has Batailley nearby; improvements and expansions underway.

(W) **Macon.** Burg. 81 79 78 ★ ★/★ ★ ★
Good, dry, full-bodied whites (and small amount of less notable reds) from southern Burgundy seen under appellations Macon-Villages, Macon-Viré, Saint-Veran, and Pouilly-Fuissé. First three appellations very good value. Good value.

(R) **Magdelaine, Ch.** Bord. 81 80 79 78 76 75 71 70 ★ ★ ★
A great growth of Saint-Émilion near Ausone; full, early maturing, superb.

(RW) **Malartic-Lagravière, Ch.** Bord. 81 80 79 78 77 76 75 71 70 ★ ★ +
Good, sound reds and dry, full-bodied whites from classified estate at Léognan, Graves. Good value.

(R) **Malescot-St. Exupéry, Ch.** Bord. 81 80 79 78 77 76 75 73 71 70 67 66
61 ★ ★ ★
One of the most charming Margaux, with lovely form and structure, beautiful fruit. Good value in its class.

(W) **de Malle, Ch.** Bord. 81 79 78 76 75 73 71 70 67 ★ ★ ★
Rich, well-balanced Sauternes from classified growth of the second level. Good value.

(R) **Margaux,** Bord. 81 80 79 78 76 75 71 70 ★ ★/★ ★ ★ ★
Notable commune of the Haut-Médoc, home of Chateau Margaux and several other fine properties. Known for its finely textured, perfumed wines with more delicacy than other Médocs. Appellation also includes communes of Cantenac Soussans and Labarde.

(R) **Margaux, Ch.** Bord. 81 80 79 78 77 76 75 71 70 67 66 61 ★ ★ ★ ★
One of the top four first growths of the Médoc, highly esteemed for its delicacy, breed and bouquet, exquisite texture; new owners and consultant Emile Peynaud have restored to top form since 1977.

(R) **Marquis-de-Terme, Ch.** Bord. 81 80 79 78 76 75 71 70 ★ ★ +
Fourth growth of Margaux, rarely great but consistently good, full, soft.

(RO) **Marsannay.** Burg. 81 80 79 78 76 ★ ★ +
Very good rosé from Pinot Noir grape from village in northern Burgundy; dry, full, and fruity. Smaller amount of light red also made. Good value.

**Maufoux, Prosper.** Shipping firm in Burgundy at Santenay offering good Beaujolais, dependable Burgundies mostly from Côte de Beaune.

(R) **Mazis-Chambertin.** Burg. 81 79 78 76 72 71 70 69 66 ★ ★ ★
A GRAND CRU member of the illustrious enclave of Chambertins.

(R) **Mazoyères-Chambertin.** Burg. 81 79 78 77 76 73 72 71 ★ ★ ★
Mostly sold under Charmes-Chambertin label, almost identical.

**Mèdoc.** Bordeaux appellation for reds outside the better district of Haut-Médoc; generally good value, never great.

(W) **Mercier.** One of the principal houses of Champagne, now owned by Moët et Chandon.

(R) **Mercurey.** Burg. 81 79 78 76 72 71 70 69 ★ ★
Good, occasionally distinctive Burgundies from south of the Côte d'Or; fairly good value in good vintages.

(RW) **Meursault.** Burg. 81 80 79 78 76 73 71 70 69 ★ ★ ★ +
Several superb vineyards produce this dry, full, intriguingly flavored white from the Côte de Beaune. Rich fruit, lingering aftertaste. Best PREMIERS CRUS: Perrières, Charmes, Genevrières. Also smaller quantities of good, sturdy reds, which may be labeled Volnay.

(R) **Meyney, Ch.** Bord. 81 80 79 78 76 75 71 ★ ★
Very good CRU BOURGEOIS at Saint-Estèphe near the Gironde; owned by Cordier, proprietors of Gruaud-Larose and Talbot. Good value.

(R) **Minervois.** Lang. 81 80 79 78 77 ★ ★
Appealing full-bodied reds of VDQS level produced în the hills of the Languedoc; some fresh rosé also made.

(RW) **La Mission Haut-Brion, Ch.** Bord. 81 80 79 78 77 76 75 73 71 70 66 61 ★ ★ ★ ★
Outstanding Graves, considered on a par with the great Haut-Brion across the road. Rich, broad, round flavors, distinctive bouquet. Small quantity of fine dry white sold as Laville-Haut-Brion.

(W) **Moët et Chandon.** One of the largest and oldest Champagne houses, a part of Moët-Hennessey. Luxury CUVÉE: Dom Pérignon, of worldwide fame.

(W) **Monbazillac.** Bord. 81 80 79 78 76 75 71 ★ ★ +
Sweet, golden dessert wine from Bergerac.

(R) **Monbousquet, Ch.** Bord. 81 80 79 78 76 75 ★ ★
Well-run estate owned by the Querre family of Saint-Émilion; light, attractive wines that mature early.

(R) **Monthélie.** Burg 81 80 79 78 76 72 71 ★ ★ +/★ ★ ★
Tender, fragrant red Burgundies near Volnay on the Côte de Beaune. Good value.

(W) **Montrachet.** Burg. 81 80 79 78 77 76 75 74 73 71 69 66 ★ ★ ★ ★
The legendary white of the Côte d'Or—dry, finely balanced, luxuriant fruit; lusciously scented; long, seductive finish. Best is the tiny portion of the vineyard owned by Domaine de la Romanée-Conti.

(R) **Montrose, Ch.** Bord. 81 80 79 77 76 75 71 70 67 66 64 61 ★ ★ ★
Highly respected second growth of Saint Estèphe; formidable, dark, intense wines that mature with great distinction.

(R) **Morey-Saint-Denis.** Burg. 81 79 78 77 76 72 71 70 69 66 ★ ★ ★
Notable commune on the Côte de Nuits with several GRANDS CRUS vineyards; and very fine PREMIERS CRUS, often very good value.

(R) **Morgon.** Burg. 81 79 78 76 ★ ★ ★
One of the fullest, sturdiest of the Beaujolais CRUS; needs a good year or two to show its best; also keeps well.

(R) **Moulin à Vent.** Burg. 81 80 79 78 76 74 73 ★ ★ ★
Biggest, most potent of the nine CRUS of Beaujolais; achieves with age the silkiness of a light Burgundy in superior vintages.

**Moulin des Carruades.** Second wine at Château Lafite. Soft, fruity, pleasant in superior large vintages but lacks the quality of Latour's other label, Les Forts de Latour.

(RW) **Mouton-Cadet.** A Bordeaux Supérieur produced by Baron Philippe de Rothschild. Agreeable red of variable quality; fresh dry white is better.

(R) **Mouton-Baronne-Philippe, Ch.** Bord. 81 80 79 78 76 75 74 70 66 61 ★ ★ ★
Large Pauillac estate owned by Baron Philippe de Rothschild; bold character and bouquet of typical Pauillac, but not as deep.

(R) **Mouton-Rothschild, Ch.** Bord. 81 80 79 78 77 76 75 73 71 70 67 66 62 61 ★ ★ ★ ★
Won official (and long deserved) rank among the first-growth Pauillacs in 1973; dark, intense, concentrated wines dominated by forceful, penetrating fruit of Cabernet Sauvignon: hard-edged in youth, slow to mature but ultimately rich, with persistent aromas of blackberries and hints of cedar.

(W) **Mumm, G. H. & Cie.** One of the leading houses in Champagne selling Cordon Rouge. Luxury CUVÉE: René Lalou.

(W) **Muscadet.** L.V. 81 80 79 78 ★ ★ ★

Fine, full-bodied dry white of the western Loire near Nantes, often labeled SUR LIE. Good acidity makes it superb with shellfish. Sèvre-et-Maine is the inner best district of Muscadet. Good value.

**Muscat.** Fruity, distinctively-scented grape that produces mostly sweet wines: Muscat Beaumes-de-Venise, Muscat di Frontignan from Languedoc, others.

(R) **Musigny.** Burg. 81 79 78 77 76 73 72 71 69 66 ★ ★ ★

GRAND CRU at Chambolle-Musigny, incomparably fragrant and refined though not as powerful as the biggest GRAND CRUS: has the nobility of Chambertin but more grace. A small quantity of excellent dry white produced also.

(W) **Nairac, Ch.** Bord. 81 79 78 75 73 71 ★ ★ +

Recently restored Sauternes estate; owned by a young American; balanced, well-made wines, steadily improving. Good value.

(R) **Nenin, Ch.** Bord. 81 80 79 78 77 76 75 71 70 66 ★ ★ ★

One of the larger estates in Pomerol; soft, fruity, engaging wines.

**Nicolas.** Paris's largest wine merchants, who buy wines from many parts of France to ship under their label; several retail stores around France.

(R) **Nuits-St.-Georges.** Burg. 81 79 78 77 76 73 72 71 70 69 ★ ★/★ ★ ★

Firm, earthy, full-bodied reds of the southernmost part of the Côte de Nuits just above Beaune. Best vineyards: Les Saint-Georges, Vaucrains, Les Pruliers, Les Cailles, Les Porrets.

(RW) **Olivier, Ch.** Bord. 81 80 79 78 76 75 71 70 ★ ★ +

Classified property of Graves producing dry whites and reds of sound, rugged character.

---

# PETITS CHATEAUX

Too numerous to mention individually are many of the better CRUS BOURGEOISES of the Médoc and unclassified chateaux from other Bordeaux regions, often referred to as *petits chateaux*. Generally, they mature earlier and are at their best within 5 years of the vintage. Here are some I particularly recommend, all producing red wines.

d'Agassac, Haut-Médoc
La Bégorce-Zédé, Margaux
Bellegrave, Pauillac
Bellerose, Pauillac
Capbern, Saint-Estèphe
La Cardonne, Médoc
Chasse-Spleen, Moulis
Cissac, Haut-Médoc
Coufran, Saint-Estèphe
La Couronne, Pauillac
Le Crock, Saint-Estèphe
Croque-Michotte, Saint-Émilion
Dutruch Grand Poujeaux, Moulis
L'Enclos, Pomerol
Fourcas-Hosten, Listrac (Margaux)

Le Gay, Pomerol
Du Glana, Haut-Médoc
Greysac, Haut-Médoc
Houissant, Saint-Estèphe
Lafleur, Pomerol
Lagrange, Pomerol
Lanessan, Haut-Médoc
Larose Trintaudon, Haut-Médoc
Laroze, Saint-Émillion
Maucaillou, Moulis
Patache d'Aux, Haut-Médoc
Potensac, Médoc
Reysson, Haut-Médoc
Ripeau, Saint-Émilion
La Tour de By, Médoc
La Tour-des-Mons, Margaux
Tronquoy-Lalande, Saint-Estèphe

(R) **Les Ormes-de-Pez.** Bord. 81 80 79 78 77 76 75 73 71 70 ★ ★ +
Mellow and full-bodied Saint-Estèphe CRU BOURGEOIS wine; reliable and consistent. Same owners as Calon-Ségur. Good value.

(R) **Palmer, Ch.** Bord. 81 80 79 78 77 76 75 73 71 70 66 61 ★ ★ ★ +
Third-growth Margaux very near in distinction to the first growths; big, classic, stylish wines of power and elegance.

(R) **Pape-Clement, Ch.** Bord. 81 80 79 78 77 76 75 74 72 71 70 66 ★ ★ ★
Fine, sturdy Graves from ancient vineyards at Pessac named for thirteenth-century pope. Frequently good value.

(R) **Pauillac.** Bord. 81 80 79 78 76 75 71 70 ★ ★/★ ★ ★ ★
Famed district and commune of the Haut-Médoc containing three first growths—Lafite, Latour, Mouton—and several other distinguished properties. Strongly individualistic wines but typically have great strength and authority, classic structure; are slow to mature but have great staying power. Regional Pauillacs also good value.

(R) **Pavie, Ch.** Bord. 81 80 79 78 76 75 71 70 66 ★ ★ ★
Round, generous and appealing Saint-Émilion from one of the largest of the classed-growth vineyards.

(RW) **Pernand-Vergelesses.** 81 80 79 78 77 76 72 71 69 ★ ★ ★
Very fine reds and whites from vineyards at Corton and sold mostly under that appellation or Corton-Charlemagne. Its own best: Ile de Vergelesses. Good value.

(W) **Pérrier-Jouet.** One of the top Champagne houses at Épernay. Deluxe CUVÉE: Fleur de Champagne, fruity, elegant, well balanced.

(R) **Pétrus, Ch.** Bord. 81 80 79 78 77 76 75 71 70 66 64 62 61 ★ ★ ★ ★
The outstanding Pomerol, ranks with the first growths of the Médoc, Cheval-Blanc and Haut-Brion as the top Bordeaux. Gravelly clay soil gives eloquent expression to Merlot here in full wines of extraordinary finesse and bouquet.

(R) **de Pez, Ch.** Bord. 81 80 79 78 77 76 75 71 70 ★ ★ ★
A CRU BOURGEOIS of Saint-Estèphe but deserves higher rank for consistently round, soft pleasing wines; excellent value.

(R) **Phélan-Segur, Ch.** Bord. 81 80 79 78 77 76 73 71 70
Very good CRU BOURGEOIS of Saint-Estèphe; sound, reliable, aromatic wines.

(R) **Pichon-Longueville-Baron, Ch.** Bord. 81 80 79 78 77 76 75 71 70 66 61 ★ ★ ★
Elegant, long-lived, aristocratic Pauillac wine but lighter than Pauillacs toward the north.

(R) **Pichon-Longueville-Lalande, Ch.** Bord. 79 78 77 76 75 74 71 70 66 61 ★ ★ ★
Across the road from Pichon-Baron, Pauillac wines of similar style but the Baron is weightier, the Lalande delicate, more supple fruit and, of late, more impressive. Second wine: Rèserve de la Comtesse.

**Pineau des Charentes.** Sweet aperitif from the Cognac region, made from juice of crushed grapes and cognac.

**Pinot Blanc, Pinot Noir.** White and red wine grapes of the Pinot family. Pinot Noir is the red grape for Burgundy and its white juice is used in Champagne. Pinot Blanc is grown mainly in Alsace and parts of Burgundy.

(W) **Piper-Heidsieck.** Long-established Champagne producer in Reims. Deluxe CUVÉE: Florens Louis Blanc de Blancs.

(R) **la Pointe, Ch.** Bord. 81 80 79 78 76 75 71 70 ★ ★ +
Popular Pomerol for good, fleshy wines that ripen quickly.

(W) **Pol Roger.** One of the top Champagne houses at Épernay. Deluxe CUVÉE: Reserve Special.

(R) **Pomerol.** Bord. 81 80 79 78 77 76 75 ★ ★ ★
Small but very important region of Bordeaux with several excellent properties noted for fine red wines, mainly from the Merlot grape and some Cabernet. Château Pétrus is leading vineyard. Small quantities with regional label, Pomerol, usually quite good.

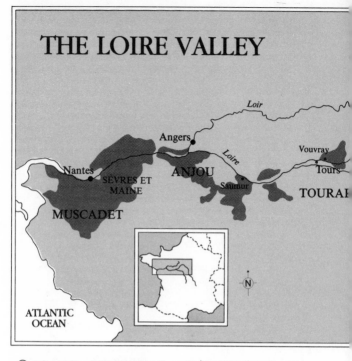

THE LOIRE VALLEY

Loir

Angers

Loire

Vouvray

Nantes

SÈVRES ET
MAINE

ANJOU

Saumur

Tours

MUSCADET

TOURAI

ATLANTIC
OCEAN

Ⓦ **Criots-Bâtard-Montrachet.** Burg. 81 80 79 78 76 73 71 ★ ★ ★
Superb dry white, almost indistinguishable from neighboring Bâtard-
Montrachet, generous fruit, body, and bouquet.

Ⓡⓦ **Crozes-Hermitage.** R.V. 81 80 79 78 76 74 72 70 ★ ★/★ ★ ★
Sturdy Rhône reds of lesser distinction than Hermitage but often as
attractively full-flavored. Whites okay but less interesting. Good value.

Ⓦ **Deutz & Geldermann.** Cham. ★ ★ ★
One of the top, though lesser known Champagne houses; classic full-
bodied style. Deluxe cuvée: William Deutz.

Ⓦ **Doisy-Daëne.** Bord. 81 79 78 76 75 71 70 ★ ★ ★
Full, opulent, sweet white wines near Sauternes; consistently first rate,
well-balanced wines. Also a good dry white. Both good value.

Ⓦ **Doisy-Védrines.** Bord. 81 79 78 75 71 70 ★ ★ ★
Older Barsac name, originally included Doisy-Daëne; also rich and full.

Ⓦ **Dom Pérignon.** Cham. 79 76 75 71 70 69 ★ ★ ★ ★
The deluxe cuvée of Moët et Chandon in Champagne; excellent classic,
full-bodied, elegant wine.

Ⓡⓦ **Domaine de Chevalier.** Bord. 81 80 79 78 77 76 75 72 71 70 66
★ ★ ★ +
Superb, firm, full-bodied red, richly textured with age and equal to
second-growth Médocs. The dry white is one of the best white Graves
but very little is made.

**Domaine Dujac.** One of the best young growers of the Côte de Nuits
with several excellent vineyards in Chambolle-Musigny, Morey-Saint-
Denis, and Gevrey.

**Dopff & Irion.** One of the leading producers in Alsace with good
Riesling, Gewürztraminer.

Ⓡ **Ducru-Beaucaillou, Ch.** Bord. 81 80 79 78 77 76 75 73 72 71 70 66 64
61 ★ ★ ★
One of the top two or three châteaux of Saint-Julien; beguiling fruit,
elegance, and bouquet, yet very long-lived. Good value.

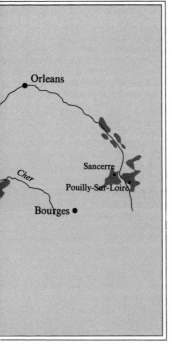

**LOIRE VALLEY.** Large quantities of white, rosé, and red wines are produced along the winding course of France's longest river, the Loire. The most famous wines are white: Pouilly-Fumé, Sancerre, Vouvray, and Muscadet. Good light reds such as Chinon, Bourgeuil, and Champigny, based on Cabernet varieties, are also made but in much smaller quantities. Chenin Blanc and Sauvignon Blanc grapes predominate for white wines.

Ⓡ **Duhart-Milon-Rothschild, Ch.** Bord. 81 80 79 78 76 75 71 70 66 ★ ★ +

Fourth growth of Pauillac now owned by the Rothschilds of Lafite, which it is near. Firm, powerful wines though not yet in the class with other Pauillacs.

Ⓡ **Durfort-Vivens, Ch.** Bord. 81 80 79 78 76 75 70 66 ★ ★ ★

Second-growth property of Margaux that languished for a while but is coming on strong again with fine, elegant wines of breed and alluring bouquet.

Ⓡ **Échézaux.** Burg. 81 79 78 76 72 71 70 69 ★ ★ ★

GRAND CRU at Flagey-Echézeaux on the Côte de Nuits; opulent fruit and bouquet but rather less density than the bigger Burgundies.

Ⓦ **Entre-deux-Mers.** Bord. 81 80 79 78 ★ ★

Dry white of average to good quality from a large area between the Dordogne and Garonne rivers, best when young and fresh.

Ⓡ **L'Évangile, Ch.** Bord. 81 80 79 78 76 75 74 71 70 ★ ★ ★

Full-bodied Pomerol of good repute; youthful hardness becomes delicate and very pretty with age.

Ⓦ **de Fargues, Ch.** Bord. 81 79 78 76 75 ★ ★ +

Notable, well-balanced Sauternes, not the richness and depth of top growths but quite good. Same owners as Chateau Yquem.

Ⓡⓦ **Fieuzal, Ch.** Bord. 81 80 79 78 76 75 71 70 ★ ★ +

Sound, generous red from Graves, increasingly attractive in last decade. Dry white also good, but both made in relatively small quantities.

Ⓡ **Figeac, Ch.** Bord 81 80 79 78 77 76 75 73 71 70 66 64 62 61 ★ ★ ★ +

Exceedingly fine classified growth of Saint-Émilion and one of the most popular for its lusty warmth in youth; can be quite long-lived with full-bodied roundness throughout.

Ⓦ **Filhot.** Bord. 81 79 78 76 75 72 71 70 67 ★ ★ ★

Lovely sweet wines from this second-growth Sauternes, occasionally somewhat drier but noted for classic balance, breed.

(R) **Pommard.** Burg. 81 79 78 76 73 72 71 69 ★ ★ ★
One of the largest communes on the southern half of the Côte d'Or, known for firm, very pleasant reds; some, unfortunately, overpriced. Top vineyards: Rugiens, Les Épenots, Les Arvelets.

(W) **Pommery et Greno.** Large Champagne shipping firm at Reims; classic, full-bodied style Champagne.

(R) **Pontet-Canet, Ch.** Bord. 81 80 79 78 77 76 75 71 70 67 66 61 ★ ★ ★
The top fifth-growth Pauillac and largest of the classified growths, nearly 200 acres, under forward-looking new owners, the Tesseron family, who are improving quality that had begun to slip. Good value.

(W) **Pouilly-Fuissé.** Burg. 81 80 79 78 77 ★ ★/★ ★ ★
Dry, full-bodied white, the best of the Maconnais but overpriced, lately pressed by more reasonable Macon-Villages, Saint-Véran. Similar wines of nearby Pouilly-Vinzelles and Pouilly-Loché are also worthwhile.

(W) **Pouilly-Fumé** L.V. 81 80 79 78 ★ ★/★ ★ ★
Fresh, fragrant, fruity dry whites from the Sauvignon Blanc grape, with a distinctly flinty aroma and flavor. (Pouilly-sur-Loire is a different wine of same area made from the lesser Chasselas grape.)

(3) **Premières Côtes de Bordeaux.** District opposite Graves producing average reds, sweet or dry whites and rosés, occasionally good value.

(R) **Prieuré-Lichine, Ch.** Bord. 81 80 79 78 76 75 71 70 66 ★ ★ ★
Lovely Margaux estate at Cantenac restored by present owner Alexis Lichine; soft, delicate, early-maturing wines with perfumed bouquet. Good value.

**Puisseguin-St.-Émilion.** A neighbor of Saint-Émilion producing robust, full-bodied wines, good but not distinguished.

(W) **Puligny-Montrachet.** Burg. 81 80 79 78 76 74 73 ★ ★ ★
With nearby Chassagne-Montrachet this village produces some of the great dry white wines of the world. Various Montrachet vineyards straddle the two districts; other top vineyards include Le Cailleret, Les Combettes, Pucelles, Clavoillon.

(W) **Quarts de Chaume.** L.V. 81 79 78 76 75 ★ ★ ★
Famous sweet golden wine of lush richness, more concentrated with age, made around Angers on the Coteaux du Layon (Anjou).

(W) **Quincy.** L.V. 81 80 79 78 ★ ★
Crisp, dry white similar to Sancerre but not as distinctive.

(R) **Rausan-Ségla, Ch.** Bord. 81 80 79 78 76 75 71 70 ★ ★ +
Second-growth Margaux but recent vintages patchy; can be full, typical Margaux with appealing bouquet.

(R) **Raussan-Gassies, Ch.** Bord. 81 80 79 78 76 75 71 70 ★ ★
Second-growth Margaux that once included Rausan-Ségla; poor quality in some years has hurt reputation but now under new ownership.

(W) **Rayne-Vigneau, Ch.** Saut. 81 79 76 75 73 71 70 67 ★ ★ ★
One of the best-known Sauternes, rich and full with great depth and power, though occasionally overblown and lacks balance.

(R) **Richebourg.** Burg. 81 80 79 78 77 76 75 73 72 71 70 69 66 ★ ★ ★ ★
One of the great GRANDS CRUS of Burgundy at Vosne-Romanée; gloriously rich fruit, plush textures, intense bouquet. Part of the vineyard belongs to the Domaine de la Romanée-Conti; other owners are Louis Gros, Charles Noellat.

(W) **Rieussec, Ch.** Bord. 81 79 76 75 71 70 67 ★ ★ ★ +
One of the top first growths of Sauternes, just under Yquem; concentrated, elegant golden sweet wines.

(W) **Roederer, Louis.** One of the leading Champagne shippers in Reims. Luxury CUVÉE: Cristal.

(R) **La Romanée.** Burg. 81 79 78 77 76 73 72 71 70 66 ★ ★ ★ ★
Tiniest of the GRANDS CRUS, barely 2 acres near Romanée-Conti; wines of great breed, luxuriant fruit, and fragrance.

(R) **La Romanée-Conti.** Burg. 81 80 79 78 77 76 73 72 71 70 69 66 ★ ★ ★ ★
4.5-acre plot at Vosne-Romanée yielding the most expensive wine in the world, questionably the best but undeniably great and rare.

SOCIÉTÉ CIVILE DU DOMAINE DE LA ROMANÉE-CONTI
PROPRIETAIRE A VOSNE-ROMANÉE (COTE-D'OR)

# ÉCHÉZEAUX

APPELLATION ÉCHÉZEAUX CONTROLÉE

*11.234 Bouteilles Récoltées*

N°   04216      L'ASSOCIÉ-GÉRANT

ANNÉE 1971      *H. de Villaine*

*Mise en bouteille au domaine*

**ÉCHÉZEAUX.** One of Burgundy's greatest wines, Échézeaux is a *Grand Cru* vineyard with an *Appellation Contrôlée* of its own, therefore it can stand alone on the label without the commune name or the words *Grand Cru*. The phrase *mise en bouteille au domaine* means the wine was bottled on the estate where the grapes were grown, the equivalent of chateau-bottled in Bordeaux. These terms do not necessarily carry the guarantee of superior quality they once did. The producer's reputation and track record over recent vintages is an important consideration. The Domaine de Romanée-Conti produces other of the world's greatest wines, including La Tache, Romanée-Conti, and Richebourg.

(R) **Romanée St. Vivant.** Burg. 81 79 78 77 76 73 72 71 70 69 66 ★ ★ ★ ★
Another of the noble GRANDS CRUS at Vosne-Romanée, similar to Romanée-Conti but softer, more grace than virility.

(RO) **Rosé d'Anjou.** L.V. ★
Mostly sweetish rosé made in Anjou, occasionally acceptable but Cabernet d'Anjou is better value. Drink young, well-chilled.

(R) **Ruchottes-Chambertin.** Burg. 81 80 79 78 77 76 73 72 71 70 69 66 ★ ★ ★
Laudable, durable member of the extended family of Chambertins.

(W) **Ruinart Père et Fils.** One of the oldest Champagne houses in Reims, which is now owned by Moët et Chandon. Delux CUVÉE: Dom Ruinart BLANC DE BLANCS.

(RW) **Rully.** Burg. 81 80 79 78 76 ★ ★
Good, dry reds and whites of the Côte Chalonnaise; also known for its sparkling Burgundy.

(R) **Saint-Amour.** Burg. 81 79 ★ ★ ★
Soft, fruity Beaujolais CRU and the northernmost commune; very tender and appealing wines.

(R) **Saint-Émilion.** Bord. 81 80 79 78 76 75 73 71 70 66 ★ ★ / ★ ★ ★ ★
Important village and district of Bordeaux producing full, rich wines from slopes overlooking the Dordogne River. Top vineyards: Cheval-Blanc, Ausone, Figeac. Several surrounding communes may also affix Saint-Émilion to their names; wines often quite good.

(R) **Saint-Estèphe.** Bord. 81 80 79 78 77 76 75 73 71 70 ★ ★ / ★ ★ ★ +
Northernmost of the five top communes of the Haut-Médoc with several excellent vineyards including Cos d'Estournel, Montrose. Dark, slow-maturing wines with a certain earthy richness of flavor and bouquet.

BURGUNDY
RED WINE
PRODUCT
OF FRANCE

U.S. REPRESENTATIVES
FREDERICK
WILDMAN
AND SONS
NEW YORK CITY

CONTENTS
750 ML
ALCOHOL
13°/. BY VOLUME

## *Fleurie*

### APPELLATION CONTROLÉE

◦

## *Louis Latour*

MIS EN BOUTEILLE PAR LOUIS LATOUR

### NÉGOCIANT A BEAUNE (COTE-D'OR)

**BEAUJOLAIS.** Fleurie is one of the nine *Grands Crus* of Beaujolais in southern Burgundy, all of which are more precisely regulated and produce wines with more definitive character than Beaujolais-Villages or simple Beaujolais. While there are some estate-produced wines, most Beaujolais is bought from local cooperatives or small growers by large shipping firms such as that of Louis Latour, headquartered in Beaune.

(R) **Saint-Julien.** Bord 81 80 79 78 77 76 75 71 70 ★ ★ ★
Commune in the heart of the Médoc noted for fine, classically balanced claret; no first growths but several superb vineyards, including the three Léovilles, Ducru-Beaucaillou, Beychevelle, Gruaud-Larose. Wines with the village name only are among the best regionals in Bordeaux.

(R) **Saint-Pierre-Bontemps-et-Sevaistre.** Bord. 81 80 79 78 77 76 75 71 70 ★ ★ +
Light but sound, well-balanced claret, a fourth-growth St. Julien.

(W) **Saint-Véran.** Burg. 81 80 79 78 ★ ★ ★
Dry, stylish, full-bodied white from Macon, good alternative to nearby Pouilly-Fuissé, though not quite as full. Good value.

(W) **Sancerre.** L.V. 81 80 79 78 ★ ★ ★
Excellent dry white from picturesque hill town on the upper Loire; crisp, racy fruit, stylishly rendered from Sauvignon Blanc. Region also produces a quite nice rosé from Pinot Noir.

(R) **Santenay.** Burg. 81 80 79 78 77 76 72 71 69 ★ ★ ★
One of the lighter Burgundies at the southern end of the Côte de Beaune. Some dry whites but the soft, full reds are better. Best vineyards: Les Gravières, Clos de Tavannes. Good value.

(3) **Saumur.** L.V. 81 80 79 78 77 ★ ★ +
Town on the Loire in Anjou and surrounding district produces pleasant fruity whites from Chenin Blanc, dry or lightly sweet, good sparkling wines, above average Cabernet Franc rosé, and a quite nice red, Champigny, also from Cabernet Franc. All good value.

(W) **Sauternes.** Bord. 81 79 78 76 75 73 71 70 67 ★ ★/★ ★ ★ ★
Region south of the town of Bordeaux (includes Barsac) producing luscious, sweet golden wines, some of the world's finest and perhaps *the* finest—Chateau d'Yquem. Also Climens, Suduiraut, Coutet, La Tour Blanche.

(W) **Savennières.** L.V. 81 80 79 78 76 75 73 ★ ★ ★
   Chenin Blanc from Anjou with considerable depth, body, and richness;
   ages well. Best vineyards: La Roche-aux-Moines, Coulée de Serrant.

(R) **Savigny-les-Beaune.** Burg. 81 79 78 77 76 72 71 ★ ★ ★
   Burgundian town near Beaune producing notable reds with attractively
   supple fruit; a very small quantity of dry white also made. Top vineyards; Vergelesses, Lavières, Jarrons, Marconnets. Good value.

(RW) **Savoie.** Ju. ★ ★
   Crisp whites, adequate reds similar to those of nearby Switzerland; best
   known are sparkling Crépy and Seyssel.

(W) **Sigalas-Rabaud, Ch.** Bord. 81 79 78 76 75 71 70 67 ★ ★ +
   One of the better classed growths of Sauternes, smaller than adjacent
   Rabaud-Promis, but often more balance and finesse. Good value.

(RW) **Smith-Haut-Lafitte, Ch.** Bord. 81 80 79 78 77 76 75 71 70 ★ ★ ★
   Good, sturdy, slow-maturing reds from Graves, bracing dry whites from
   Sauvignon blanc, often good value.

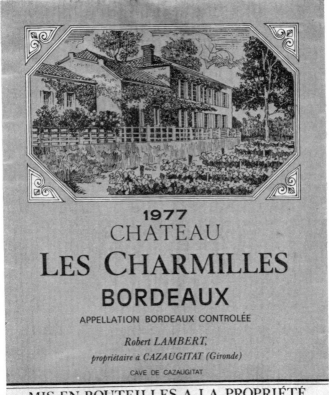

1977
CHATEAU
LES CHARMILLES
BORDEAUX
APPELLATION BORDEAUX CONTROLÉE

*Robert LAMBERT,*
*propriétaire à CAZAUGITAT (Gironde)*

CAVE DE CAZAUGITAT

MIS EN BOUTEILLES A LA PROPRIÉTÉ

**CHÂTEAU LES CHARMILLES.** The word "château" on a label does not always
signify a better wine. The real clue to this wine is in the words that appear beneath the
château name, *Appellation* Bordeaux *Contrôlée*, which signify that the wine may legally
have come from anywhere in the Bordeaux region. While the wine may indeed have
been bottled at the château named (implied by the words *mis en bouteilles á la
propriété*), the generalized appellation comes from a region with no appellation of its own.
Simple Bordeaux appellations such as this can, however, provide pleasant drinking in
good vintages if the price is right.

# French Vintage Chart

Vintage charts should be consulted only as a general guide to the quality of the wines in a given vintage. In every vintage, great or poor, there are exceptions that stand apart from the rest. This chart is, however, more reflective of the better wines of each region than lesser ones. The ratings note the original quality of the vintage—drinkability of the wines today is indicated according to the color code.

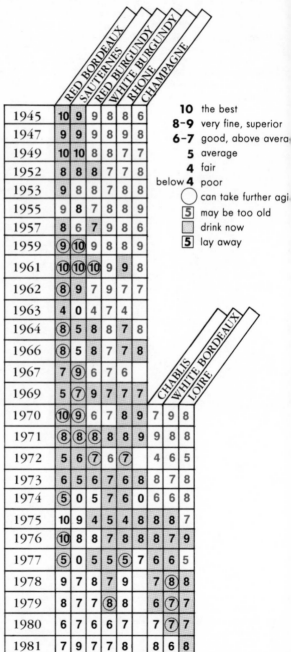

| | Red Bordeaux | Sauternes | Red Burgundy | White Burgundy | Rhône | Champagne | Chablis | White Bordeaux | Loire |
|---|---|---|---|---|---|---|---|---|---|
| 1945 | 10 | 9 | 9 | 8 | 8 | 6 | | | |
| 1947 | 9 | 9 | 9 | 8 | 9 | 8 | | | |
| 1949 | 10 | 10 | 8 | 8 | 7 | 7 | | | |
| 1952 | 8 | 8 | 8 | 7 | 7 | 8 | | | |
| 1953 | 9 | 8 | 8 | 7 | 8 | 8 | | | |
| 1955 | 9 | 8 | 7 | 8 | 8 | 9 | | | |
| 1957 | 8 | 6 | 7 | 8 | 6 | 6 | | | |
| 1959 | 9 | 10 | 9 | 8 | 8 | 9 | | | |
| 1961 | 10 | 10 | 10 | 9 | 9 | 8 | | | |
| 1962 | 8 | 9 | 7 | 9 | 7 | 7 | | | |
| 1963 | 4 | 0 | 4 | 7 | 4 | | | | |
| 1964 | 8 | 5 | 8 | 8 | 7 | 8 | | | |
| 1966 | 8 | 5 | 8 | 7 | 7 | 8 | | | |
| 1967 | 7 | 9 | 6 | 7 | 6 | | | | |
| 1969 | 5 | 7 | 9 | 7 | 7 | 7 | | | |
| 1970 | 10 | 9 | 6 | 7 | 8 | 9 | 7 | 9 | 8 |
| 1971 | 8 | 8 | 8 | 8 | 8 | 9 | 9 | 8 | 8 |
| 1972 | 5 | 6 | 7 | 6 | 7 | | 4 | 6 | 5 |
| 1973 | 6 | 5 | 6 | 7 | 6 | 8 | 8 | 7 | 8 |
| 1974 | 5 | 0 | 5 | 7 | 6 | 0 | 6 | 6 | 8 |
| 1975 | 10 | 9 | 4 | 5 | 4 | 8 | 8 | 8 | 7 |
| 1976 | 10 | 8 | 8 | 7 | 8 | 8 | 8 | 7 | 9 |
| 1977 | 5 | 0 | 5 | 5 | 5 | 7 | 6 | 6 | 5 |
| 1978 | 9 | 7 | 8 | 7 | 9 | | 7 | 8 | 8 |
| 1979 | 8 | 7 | 7 | 8 | 8 | | 6 | 7 | 7 |
| 1980 | 6 | 7 | 6 | 6 | 7 | | 7 | 7 | 7 |
| 1981 | 7 | 9 | 7 | 7 | 8 | | 8 | 6 | 8 |

Legend:

- **10** the best
- **8-9** very fine, superior
- **6-7** good, above avera[ge]
- **5** average
- **4** fair
- below **4** poor
- ◯ can take further agi[ng]
- ⑤ may be too old
- ▨ drink now
- ⑤ lay away

(W) **Suduiraut, Ch.** Bord. 81 79 78 76 75 71 70 66 ★ ★ ★ +
Outstanding first growth of Sauternes with rich, creamy texture, splendid balance.

(W) **Taittinger.** Major Champagne shipper at Reims. Deluxe CUVÉE: Comte de Champagnes Blanc de Blancs and Rosé (best of the pink).

(R) **Talbot, Ch.** Bord. 81 80 79 78 77 76 75 74 71 70 66 61 ★ ★ +
Generally good, richly flavored fourth growth at Saint-Julien.

(RO) **Tavel.** R.V. ★ ★ ★
France's best and most famous rosé; attractive coral bronze color, dry and full-bodied. Drink young.

 **Touraine.** Large region along the Loire, produces copious amounts of sweet and dry white wines, best known being Vouvray; also good reds Chinon and Bourgeuil.

(R) **du Tertre, Ch.** Bord. 81 80 79 78 77 76 75 71 70 ★ ★ +
Little-known fifth growth with attractive Margaux-style wines.

(W) **La Tour-Blanche, Ch.** Bord. 81 80 79 76 75 71 70 67 ★ ★ ★
First-growth Sauternes that once rivaled Yquem; wines much lighter today and not as concentrated. Estate is government-owned and has a viticultural school.

(R) **La Tour Haut-Brion.** Bord. 81 80 79 78 77 76 75 71 70 ★ ★ +
Small, excellent Graves property near the city of Bordeaux popular for stylish, full-bodied reds.

(R) **Troplong-Mondot, Ch.** Bord. 81 80 79 78 77 76 75 70 ★ ★ +
Among the first growths of Saint-Émilion; round, full-bodied reds, often good value.

(R) **Trotanoy, Ch.** Bord. 81 80 79 78 77 76 75 71 70 66 61 ★ ★ ★
Rich, flavorsome wines from one of the best Pomerol estates, retain remarkable power in great vintages like 1961.

(R) **Trottevielle, Ch.** Bord. 81 80 79 78 77 76 75 71 70 66 ★ ★ ★
Eminent first growth of Saint-Émilion; finely tuned wines with abundant fruit and body but well-balanced.

(W) **Veuve Clicquot.** One of the top Champagne houses named for the widow Clicquot; rich, full-bodied wines. Special CUVÉE: La Grande Dame.

(R) **Vieux-Chateau-Certan.** Bord. 81 80 79 78 77 76 75 71 70 66 61 ★ ★ ★ +
The leading Pomerol after Petrus; concentrated fruit, good depth and body, ages with great distinction.

(W) **Vin Jaune.** Ju. ★ ★
Unusual heavy-ish yellow wines produced at Arbois, a character similar to dry Sherry but lighter and not fortified.

(R) **Volnay.** Burg. 81 80 79 78 77 76 72 71 69 ★ ★ ★
Delicate, fragrant silky-textured reds of the Côte de Beaune; among the lightest of Burgundies but one of the most engaging. Best vineyards: Caillerets, Clos des Chênes, Clos des Ducs, Champans, Fremiets. Whites from here are labeled Meursault. Volnay-Santenots is red Meursault. Good value.

(R) **Vosne-Romanée.** Burg. 81 80 79 78 77 76 72 71 70 66 ★ ★ ★/★ ★ ★ ★
Home of the incomparable GRAND CRUS Romanée-Conti, La Tache-Richebourg, La Romanée, etc., and fine PREMIERS CRUS La Grande Rue, Malconsorts, Les Suchots, Les Beaux-Monts. Simple Vosne-Romanée also quite special.

(W) **Vouvray.** L.V. 81 80 79 78 76 ★ ★ ★/★ ★ ★
Full range of whites: dry, semisweet, very sweet, and sparkling. All fruity, fragrant, often delightful; the sweet wines luscious and can age impressively. Excellent value.

(W) **d'Yquem, Ch.** Bord. 81 79 78 76 75 71 70 69 68 67 66 62 59 ★ ★ ★ ★
The most celebrated sweet wine in the world from Sauternes; lush, concentrated sweetness with great depth and finesse, glorious aromas of honeyed fruit; ages exceedingly well, often several decades. A full-bodied semi-dry white known as Ygrec is occasionally made.

# THE WINES OF
# ITALY

I taly makes more wine than any country in the world. She also exports more and consumes more at home per capita than any other nation, some 30 gallons per person per year.

Vines grow in astonishing variety from one end of the country to the other—from the Tyrol in the extreme northeast to the orange groves of Sicily. Italy's winemaking traditions are centuries old, with wines that evolved largely as accompaniments to local cuisine. Generally, therefore, one will find the better wines in regions where the cuisine is distinctive and varied, such as Tuscany and Piedmont or the Veneto. The grilled meats and game birds so popular in Tuscany, for example, are handsomely set off by fine reds like Chianti Riserva, Vino Nobile, or Brunello di Montalcino. In the northeast around Venice seafood delicacies from the Adriatic are accompanied by fresh dry whites such as Pinot Bianco, Pinot Grigio, and others that are among Italy's best dry white wines.

The Italians' offhand attitude toward wine as a natural adjunct to meals and a part of everyday life has led to a profusion of rather ordinary wines without a great deal to recommend them. Though Italy has always produced excellent wines like Barolo, Barbaresco, Brunello, Chianti Riserva, and others, standards of quality were, for the most part, entirely up to the individual grower. The casual approach to winegrowing and winemaking techniques was prevalent.

All of this began to change in the early 1960s when the government stepped in to set controls for the best wines of each region. In 1963 legislation enacted the *Denominazione di Origine Controllata* (DOC) laws, outlining specific place-names and defining viticultural districts. Grape varieties and minimum alcohol levels were also prescribed. The effect of the DOC laws was a general upgrading of wines at every level, including the best. Improvement continues as more wines are admitted to DOC status.

Recently, a further classification has been instituted for the very finest wines, *Denominazione di Origine Controllata e Guarantita* (DOCG), denomination of origin controlled and guaranteed. To date, Barolo, Barbaresco, Brunello di Montalcino, and Vino Nobile di Montepulciano are so designated. Applications from Chianti and Albana di Romagna have been accepted for consideration.

# GLOSSARY OF WINE TERMS

**Abboccato.** *Semisweet.*

**Amabile.** *"Amiably" sweet—a little sweeter than* ABBOCCATO.

**Amaro.** *Bitter.*

**Bianco.** *White.*

**Cantina.** *Winery; cantina sociale are local grower cooperatives.*

**Classico.** *Term for superior zone within a* DOC. *Usually the best wine of the region.*

**Colli.** *Literally, "hills."*

**DOC.** *Denominazione di Origine Controllata, wine of controlled name and origin.*

**DOCG.** *Denominazione di Origine Controllata e Garantita, wine of controlled name and origin guaranteed.*

**Dolce.** *Sweet.*

**Frizzante.** *Lightly fizzy.*

**Liquoroso.** *Very sweet and alcoholic dessert wine, sometimes fortified with brandy.*

**Passito.** *Sweet wine from extra-ripe grapes dried before pressing.*

**Riserva, riserva speciale.** *Reserve wines, aged for a time specified by* DOC *laws, usually in barrel but also in bottle. Minimum, a year or more.*

**Rosato.** *Rosé.*

**Rosso.** *Red.*

**Secco.** *Dry.*

**Spumante.** *Sparkling.*

**Stravecchio.** *Very old.*

**Superiore.** *Indicates slightly higher alcohol content.*

**Tenuta.** *Wine estate.*

**Vendemmia.** *Grape harvest, or vintage.*

# PRINCIPAL WINE REGIONS

**Abruzzi** (Abr.)   Mountainous region on the Adriatic, Montepulciano-d'Abruzzi.

**Alto Adige** (A.A.)   Northern portion of Trentino-Alto-Adige. Fertile hills and valleys produce very good varietal wines such as Merlot, Cabernet Franc, Pinot Bianco, Pinot Nero (Noir), and Gewürztraminer. Also Caldaro, Santa Maddalena, Terlano.

**Apulia** (Apu.)   The southeastern heel of Italy's "boot," producing huge quantities of bulk wine, as well as San Severo and Castel del Monte.

**Basilicata** (Bas.)   In the south, known mainly for Aglianico del Vulture.

**Calabria** (Cal.)   Forms the "toe" of Italy's boot shape; noted for Ciró.

**Campania** (Camp.)   South of Naples; volcanic soil on slopes of Mt. Vesuvius produces Lacryma Christi and Vesuvio. Inland there are Taurasi, Fiano di Avellino and Greco di Tufo.

**Emilia-Romagna** (E.R.)   Central Italy, gastronomic capital is Bologna. Best known for Lambrusco.

**Friuli-Venezia-Giulia** (F.V.G.)   Hilly, cool climate of the northeast bordering on Yugoslavia; produces several good varietals; Pinot Grigio, Sauvignon, Tocai, Pinot Bianco, Collio Goriziano (around city of Gorizia).

**Latium** (Lat.)   Also known as Lazio. Region around Rome, best known are wines from hills south of the city known as Castelli Romani, which include Frascati, Marino, Colli Albani.

**Liguria** (Lig.)   Mountainous Mediterranean coast, capital Genoa. Steep hillside vineyards on rocky coast here produce Cinqueterre, Rossese di Dolceacqua.

**Lombardy** (Lomb.) Central northern region embracing the Valtellina, known for Grumello, Inferno, Sassella; in the south, Oltrepo' Pavese around the River Po.

**Marches** (Mar.) Mountainous region on Adriatic, producing Verdicchio, Rosso Conero. Principal wine center is Ancona.

**Piedmont** (Pied.) Northwestern region bordering France and the Alps. Several of Italy's most famous wines produced: Barolo, Barbaresco, Barbera, Gattinara, Asti Spumante. Turin is the capital: Asti and Alba are principal wine centers.

**Sardinia** (Sard.) Large island off west coast of Italy. Monica di Cagliari and Alghero.

**Sicily** (Sic.) Volcanic island off the southern tip of Italy, largest of Mediterranean. Etna, Corvo, Marsala.

**Trentino** (Tren.) Southern portion of region bordering Austria, always linked with Alto-Adige. Principal city is Trento, principal wines same as Alto-Adige, also Teroldego, good SPUMANTE. Large Chardonnay plantings.

**Tuscany** (Tus.) Italy's leading wine region along with Piedmont, producing Chianti Riserva, Classico (between Florence and Siena), Brunello di Montalcino, and Vino Nobile di Montepulciano.

**Umbria** (Umb.) Hilly region in central Italy; best-known wines are Orvieto, Rubesco Torgiano.

**Veneto** (Ven.) Large northern region embracing Verona (Soave, Valpolicella, Amarone), Venice (Colli Euganei), Treviso, and Conegliano (Proseco, Venegazzú, Raboso). Tre Venezie refers to areas north and west of Venice: Friuli, Trentino and Veneto.

# WINE GUIDE

Ⓡ **Aglianico del Vulture.** Bas. DOC 81 80 78 75 73 71 70 ★ ★
Made from Aglianico grape and one of southern Italy's better reds. Sturdy, full-bodied; becomes RISERVA after 5 years.

Ⓦ **Albana di Romagna.** E.R. DOC 81 80 79 ★/★ ★ +
Versatile white wines produced in southeastern Emilia-Romagna. Most dry, some AMABILE, some sparkling.

Ⓦ **Albano.** Lat. 81 80 79 78 ★ ★
One of the dry white village wines from the hills south of Rome; most consumed locally and best when quite young.

Ⓡ **Aleatico.** Red Muscat grape; also the full-bodied sweet wine made from it mostly in Apulia (DOC), Latium, and the island of Elba.

Ⓦ **Alghero.** Sard. 81 80 ★ ★
Fresh, fruity, fragrant dry white from the region around the town of Alghero on Sardinia's northwestern coast.

Ⓡ **Amarone (Recioto Amarone della Valpolicella).** Ven. DOC 81 80 78 77 69 67 ★ ★ ★
A full-bodied (14–15% alcohol) long-lived type of Valpolicella made from very ripe grapes that are dried after harvest to concentrate sugars. Intense flavors, slightly bitter aftertaste, expensive.

Ⓦ **Asti Spumante.** Pied. DOC 81 80 79 78 ★ ★ ★
Sparkling white wine from the Muscat grape made around Asti; fruity and fragrant, lightly to quite sweet. Good value.

THE WINE REGIONS
OF
**ITALY**

Ⓡ **Barbacarlo.** Lomb. DOC 81 80 79 78 ★ +
Light red with hint of almond taste, often FRIZZANTE when young,
softens with a year or two bottle age.

Ⓡ **Barbaresco.** Pied. DOCG 81 80 79 78 74 71 67 64 62 61 ★ ★ ★ ★
One of Italy's best reds from Nebbiolo grape in hills of the Piedmont.
Robust, tannic when young, but capable of aging with grace and
distinction. Matures sooner than Barolo, to which it is a sort of "younger
brother."

**Barbera.** Grape variety grown in Piedmont producing sturdy, full-
bodied reds, very fruity; best when young but some age well, up to 10
years or more.

Ⓡ **Barbera d'Alba.** Pied. DOC 81 80 79 78 74 71 ★ ★ ★
Robust, earthy fruit, somewhat more tannin than Barbera d'Asti; usually
best at 2 to 4 years but some age well a decade or more.

Ⓡ **Barbera d'Asti.** Pied. DOC 81 80 79 78 74 64 61 ★ ★ ★
Somewhat lighter but more refined Barbera than above. Needs minimum 3–4 years aging, best at 5 to 8. Good value.

37

(R) **Barbera del Monferrato.** Pied. DOC 81 80 79 78 74 71 64 ★ ★
Widely produced in central Piedmont, varies from light to heavy and full-bodied. Mostly dry, occasionally semisweet and FRIZZANTE.

(R) **Bardolino.** Ven. DOC 81 80 79 ★ ★
Light red produced near Lake Garda, best when young (and slightly cooled).

(R) **Barolo.** Pied. DOCG 81 80 79 78 74 71 70 67 65 64 61 ★ ★ ★ ★
One of Italy's best reds, certainly best of the Piedmont; dark, robust, powerful, distinctively scented, slow to mature but long-lived. Some spend 5 to 8 years in cask, but recent trend is to bottling earlier. Made from Nebbiolo; minimum 4 years for RISERVA, 5 for RISERVA SPECIALE.

(W) **Bianco di Custoza.** Ven. DOC 81 80 ★ ★ +
Fragrant, dry white made near Verona; as good as, sometimes better than, Soave.

**Bonarda.** Red wine grape widely grown in Piedmont and Lombardy. Also a light fruity DOC red, Bonarda dell'Oltrepo' near Pavia.

(R) **Brachetto d'Acqui.** Pied. DOC 81 80 ★
Cherry red dessert wine, slightly sparkling, with fruity muscat aromas. Best when young and slightly cooled.

(R) **Bramaterra.** Pied. DOC 81 80 79 78 76 ★ ★/★ ★ ★
Rich, ruby-colored red from Nebbiolo grape grown in small area north of Gattinara; spends 3 years in oak.

(R) **Bricco Manzoni.** Pied. 81 80 79 78 ★ ★ ★
Proprietary name for sturdy, lively red made from mix of Nebbiolo and Barbera grapes; chewy fruit, some finesse.

**Brolio.** Oldest and most famous Chianti Classico estate founded by the Ricasoli family.

(R) **Brunello di Montalcino.** Tus. DOCG 81 80 79 77 75 70 67 66 64 61 55 45 ★ ★ ★ ★
Dark, powerful, slow-maturing wine from 100% Sangiovese Grosso. Aged 4 years minimum in wood, 5 for RISERVA. Italy's most expensive wine and one of her most impressive.

(R) **Buttafuoco.** Lomb. DOC 81 80 79 78 74 71 ★ ★
Staunch and fruity red of the Oltrepo' Pavese region in southern Lombardy; name means "spitfire." Best within about 5 years of vintage.

**Cabernet.** The Bordeaux varieties of Cabernet Franc and Cabernet Sauvignon are widely grown in the northeast districts of Trentino-Alto-Adige, Friuli, TreVenezia; some also in Tuscany (see Sassicaia) and Umbria show great future promise.

(RRO) **Caldaro (Lago di Caldaro).** Tren.-A.A. DOC 81 80 79 78 77 ★/★ ★
Fruity, mellow red from near Bolzano, known locally as Kaltersee and sometimes served chilled.

(R) **Cannonau.** Sard. DOC 81 80 79 78 77 72 69 64 ★ ★
Very full-bodied (13–15% alcohol) Sardinian red, both dry and sweet versions; ages well.

(W) **Capri.** Average dry white from island of Capri.

(R) **Carema.** Pied. DOC 81 80 79 78 74 71 70 ★ ★
Smooth, medium-bodied, long-lived red from the Nebbiolo grape, produced north of Turin. Good value.

(R) **Carmignano.** Tus. DOC 81 80 79 78 77 75 ★ ★ ★
Warm, fragrant red made from Sangiovese, Cabernet Sauvignon, and other grapes. Similar to Chianti.

(W) **Cartizze.** Ven. DOC ★ ★/★ ★ ★
SPUMANTE, dry or AMABILE, produced from Prosecco and Pinot Bianco. Lively, good acidity but limited production.

(RW) **Castel Chiuro.** Good red and white wines of the Valtellina, proprietary labels of a single producer.

(3) **Castel del Monte.** Apu. ★ ★
Region in Apulia producing agreeable DOC reds, whites, rosés. Good value.

(W) **Castelli Romani.** Hilly region south of Rome producing several dry whites. See Frascati, Colli Albani, Marino.

**Chardonnay.** Increasingly important white grape used for SPUMANTE and dry, fruity, light-bodied white table wine. Best from Trentino, Veneto, Friuli but also Apulia, Umbria.

(R) **Chianti.** Tus. DOC 81 80 79 78 71 70 ★ ★
Light, quite pleasant reds from hills surrounding Florence. Includes subdistricts of Rufina, Montalbano, Aretini, Colli Fiorentini, Pisane, Senesi. RISERVA (aged 3 years) often quite good.

(R) **Chianti Classico.** Tus. DOC 81 80 79 78 77 75 71 70 ★ ★ ★
Superior central district of Chianti between Florence and Siena. Medium to full-bodied red from dozens of fine estates; better vintages capable of aging well, often becoming refined and elegant. RISERVA aged minimum 3 years.

(RO) **Chiaretto Bardolino.** Ven. DOC 81 80 79 ★ ★
One of Italy's best DOC rosés produced around Lake Garda. Best when young.

(W) **Cinqueterre.** Lig. DOC ★ ★
Fragrant whites from the Ligurian coast and La Spezia. Best consumed locally when young and fresh. Rare sweet PASSITO is Sciacchetrà.

(RW) **Cirò.** Cal. DOC 81 80 79 78 77 74 73 69 ★ ★
Sturdy, full-bodied reds, whites, some rosé; known in the time of the ancient Greeks and consumed at the Olympic games.

(W) **Colli Albani.** Lat. DOC ★ ★
Gentle dry whites of the Alban hills south of Rome, mostly from Trebbiano grapes, some Malvasia that is slightly sweet. Best when young.

(RW) **Colli Euganei.** Ven. DOC ★
Rather light reds and whites produced near Padua, the everyday wines of Venice. Best when young.

(RW) **Collio Goriziano.** F.V.G. DOC 81 80 79 78 77 ★ ★ +
Eleven wines, mostly white varietals, produced around Gorizia and named for grape varieties (near Yugoslavia); among the best whites are Tocai, Pinot Grigio, Sauvignon, Pinot Bianco. Light reds are Merlot, Cabernet Franc.

(RW) **Colli Orientali del Friuli.** F.V.G. DOC 81 80 79 ★ ★
Principal growing region within Friuli-Venezia-Giulia, producing several quite agreeable reds and good whites, such as Pinot Bianco, Pinot Grigio.

(W) **Cortese di Gavi.** Pied. DOC 81 80 79 ★ ★ ★
Mostly fresh, light wine from Cortese grape from southern Piedmont, best from town of Gavi. Full, crisp fruit, excellent with seafood.

(RW) **Corvo.** Sic. DOC 81 80 79 78 77 74 71 ★ ★
Warm, medium-bodied red, flavorful white wines produced near Palermo. Both among southern Italy's best wines, widely exported.

(R) **Dolcetto.** Pied. DOC 81 80 79 78 74 ★ ★
Robust, quick-maturing fruity reds from Dolcetto grape, best of which is Dolcetto d'Alba, dark, dry, faintly bitter.

(R) **Donnaz.** Pied. DOC 81 80 79 78 ★ ★
One of the lightest reds made from Nebbiolo grape in the Val d'Aosta. Agreeable locally, sometimes ages well but not much exported.

(W) **Erbaluce di Caluso.** Pied. DOC 81 80 70 ★/★ ★ +
Dry or sweet whites from hills near Ivrea; sweet versions from dried grapes (PASSITO) are full-bodied; LIQUOROSO (16% alcohol) quite potent and long-lived.

(W) **Est! Est! Est!** Lat. DOC ★
Rather ordinary whites, both dry and semisweet, from hilltop town of Montefiascone.

(3) **Etna.** Sic. DOC 81 80 79 78 77 75 70 68 ★ ★
Full, flavorful reds, rosés and whites from the volcanic slopes of Mt. Etna. Reds often age extremely well. Good value.

(R) **Falerno.** Camp. 81 80 79 78 77 76 ★ ★
Sturdy, full-bodied reds from Aglianico grape; descended from ancient

Falernum, a heavy sweet red praised by Romans such as Horace, Ovid, Pliny for longevity. Modern Falerno also made in Latium.

ⓡ **Fara.** Pied. DOC 81 80 79 78 74 71 70 67 ★ ★
Smooth, fragrant red from Nebbiolo grape, produced near Novara.

ⓡ **Faro.** Sic. DOC 81 80 79 78 ★ ★ +
Sound, medium full red of some complexity, unusual for southern Italy but very small production.

ⓡⓦ **Favonio.** Apu. 81 80 79 78 ★ ★ ★
Estate-bottled wines from French varieties like Chardonnay, Cabernet Franc, Pinot Nero under pioneering efforts of Attilio Simonini in vineyards near Foggia.

ⓦ **Fiano di Avellino.** Camp. DOC 81 80 79 ★ ★ ★
Fine, dry white made from ancient Fiano grape; elegant, balanced, with hint of hazlenuts in aroma. Ages well.

ⓡⓦ **Fiorano.** Lat. 81 80 79 78 ★ ★ ★
Reds from Cabernet, whites from Sémillon and Malvasia; very limited production, prized by cognoscenti.

ⓡⓦ **Franciacorta.** Lom. 81 80 79 78 ★ ★ +
Sturdy reds from Cabernet, Merlot, Barbera, Nebbiolo, best within 3 to 5 years; fresh dry white is from Pinot Bianco, sometimes SPUMANTE.

ⓦ **Frascati.** Lat. DOC ★ ★
Best of the whites from the Colli Albani south of Rome. Soft, fragrant, fruity, very dry. Best when young.

ⓡⓦ **Frecciarossa.** Lomb. 81 80 79 77 76 74 73 ★ ★
Good reds and whites from Oltrepo' Pavese in southern Lombardy. Whites better known, but red is mellow, balanced.

ⓡ **Freisa d'Asti.** Pied. DOC 81 80 79 78 74 73 70 ★ ★ ★
Two styles of red—one dry, fruity, slighty acidic in youth but ages into roundness; the other, sweet, slightly fizzy; most consumed locally.

ⓦ **Galestro.** Tus. 81 80 ★ ★ ★
New, fresh white, mostly from Trebbiano Toscano, some Pinot Bianco; crisp and dry, best when young, promises to be one of Italy's best whites.

ⓦ **Gambellara.** Ven. DOC 81 80 79 ★ ★ +
Dry white similar to Soave, sometimes better. Sweet version is Recioto Bianco; Vin Santo also produced.

ⓡ **Gattinara.** Pied. DOC 81 80 79 78 76 74 70 69 68 64 ★ ★ ★
Excellent red from Nebbiolo grape, lighter but more refined than Barolo when young and capable of aging up to 10 years or more. Good value.
**Gavi.** See Cortese di Gavi.

ⓡ **Ghemme.** Pied. DOC 81 80 79 78 74 ★ ★ ★
Another Nebbiolo wine produced near Gattinara. Not quite so fine as Gattinara but sound and appealing. Good value.

**Grappa.** Grape brandy distilled from mass of pulp left after grapes are pressed. Colorless, potent, often fierce spirit. Better ones have fine aromas and complex flavors.

ⓡⓦ **Grave del Friuli.** F.V.G. DOC 81 80 79 78 ★ ★/★ ★ ★
Red and white varietals from Cabernet, Merlot, Pinot Bianco, Pinot Grigio, Tocai, Riesling, and others. Good value.

ⓦ **Greco di Tufo.** Camp. DOC 81 80 79 78 ★ ★ ★
Flavorful, full-bodied dry white from ancient grape said to have originated in Greece, hence the name. Ages well.

ⓡ **Grignolino.** Pied. DOC 81 80 79 78 74 71 ★ ★
Light, almost rosé red, very fruity bouquet, produced in Monferrato area of the Piedmont near Asti.

ⓡ **Grumello.** Lomb. DOC 81 80 79 78 75 71 70 69 ★ ★
From the Nebbiolo grape; one of the best and firmest reds of the Valtellina.

ⓡ **Inferno.** Lomb. DOC 81 80 79 78 75 71 70 69 64 ★ ★ ★
Similar to Grumello but ages better, developing perfumed bouquet. Best at about five years.

*Vigneto* **Bricco Asili** Barbaresco

# Barbaresco
## 1974

VINO A DENOMINAZIONE D'ORIGINE CONTROLLATA

*prodotto ed imbottigliato da*
*Ceretto in Bricco Asili*
*Barbaresco zona d'origine*
*Produzione 7030 b. glie e 950 magnum*
*Bottiglia*

**CERETTO**
**BRICCO ASILI**
**BARBARESCO - ITALIA**

| CONT. NETTO LT. 0,720 | R.I. 4322 - CN | ALCOOL GR. 13,90 |

**BARBARESCO.** Most Italian wines are named for the region of origin. Barbaresco is one of the leading red wine districts of the Piedmont in northern Italy. The fact that it is a government-regulated DOC wine is shown by the words *Denominazione d'Origine Controllata* under the vintage date. "Bricco Asili" is the name of a hilltop in the Barbaresco region that yields superior grapes. Ceretto is one of the most reputable producers of Barolo and Barbaresco. 7,030 bottles and 950 magnums of this wine were produced.

(RW) **Ischia.** Camp. DOC 81 80 79 ★ ★
   Crisp, dry whites from the island off Naples. Some reds produced.
(W) **Lacryma Christi del Vesuvio.** Camp. 81 80 79 ★ ★
   The famous white wine of Naples grown on the slopes of Mt. Vesuvius; name means "tears of Christ." Pleasant but not distinguished. A full-bodied red (Rosso) also produced.
(RO) **Lacrimosa d'Irpinia.** Camp. 81 80 ★ ★ ★
   Lively, robust, bronze-colored rosé made from Aglianico grape. Quite appealing but not inexpensive.
   **Lago di Caldaro.** See Caldaro.
(R) **Lagrein.** Tren; A.A. DOC 81 80 79 78 77 75 ★ ★ +
   Robust, often meaty red of Bolzano; heartier than Caldaro, not quite as distinguished as Santa Maddalena. Also a dry, full-bodied rosé.

Ⓡ **Lambrusco.** E.R. DOC ★ ★
Widely popular light reds in a variety of styles, often FRIZZANTE, slightly sweet, and almost rosé. Best when very young and chilled.

**Langhe.** Hills in central Piedmont south of Alba where best Barolo and Barbaresco are produced.

Ⓡ **Lessona.** Pied. DOC 81 80 79 78 74 71 ★ ★ ★
Classically structured, often fruity red of northern Piedmont above Gattinara. Ages well like most Spanna (or Nebbiolo) wines but generally lighter in body.

Ⓦ **Lugana.** Lomb. DOC 81 80 79 78 76 75 ★ ★ ★
Fragrant, flavorful white (Trebbiano grape) from southern tip of Lake Garda. Fresh, dry, and appealing. Drink young. Good value.

**Malvasia.** White grape producing several sweet wines, the most famous being Malvasia delle Lipari of Sicily and Cagliari of Sardinia.

Ⓦ **Mamertino.** Sic. ★ ★
A sweet white wine from very ripe grapes, prized in ancient Rome where it graced banquet tables of Julius Caesar. Limited production today near Messina.

Ⓦ **Marino.** Lat. DOC ★ ★
Fragrant, pale gold white from south of Rome, similar to Frascati, but fuller flavor and body. Best when young.

**Marsala.** Sic. DOC ★ ★ ★
Dark, sweet, and/or dry fortified dessert wine from Sicily. Good by itself and much used in cooking desserts like zabaglione. Good value.

**Merlot.** The red wine grape of Bordeaux, grown mostly in northeastern Italy, producing good, lively reds.

Ⓡ **Monica de Cagliari.** Sard. DOC 81 80 79 77 73 72 70 ★ ★
Sweet, spicy red from Monica grape, native to Sardinia; a dry red is also made, both up to 13.5% alcohol. Monica di Sardegna is a lighter red with its own DOC.

Ⓡ **Montepulciano d'Abruzzo.** Abr. DOC 81 80 79 77 75 74 73 68 ★ ★ ★
Good red from mountainous coast of Abruzzo. Ages well, developing attractive bouquet. Not to be confused with Vino Nobile of Tuscany, made from different grape. Rosé called Cerasuolo.

**Moscato.** Fragrant, fruity grape grown widely throughout Italy. Most famous wine is Asti Spumante.

**Nebbiolo.** One of Italy's best red wine grapes, used for Barolo, Barbaresco, and Gattinara, as well as wines of the Valtellina.

Ⓡ **Nebbiolo d'Alba.** Pied. DOC 81 80 79 78 71 ★ ★
Attractive red, sometimes declassified Barolo that doesn't meet producer's standards.

Ⓡⓦ **Oltrepo' Pavese.** Lomb. DOC 81 80 79 78 ★ ★
Hilly region near Pavia that produces several good reds and whites from such grapes as Barbera, Bonarda, Moscato, Riesling, to which the suffix dell'Oltrepo' is added in the wine names—Barbera dell'Oltrepo', for example. Good value.

Ⓦ **Orvieto.** Umb. DOC ★ ★
Fruity, full-bodied whites from region around the hilltop town of Orvieto, near Perugia, mostly dry but some gently sweet, mainly from the Trebbiano grape. Drink young.

**Passito.** Concentrated sweet wines made from sun-dried or partially raisined grapes. Among the best are Tuscany's Vin Santo and Caluso Passito of the Piedmont.

Ⓡ **Piave Rosso.** Ven. DOC 78 77 74 ★
Light to medium-bodied reds made mostly from Merlot and Cabernet.

Ⓦ **Picolit.** F.V.G. DOC ★ ★ ★ ★
Rare and expensive golden dessert wine, sweet or off-dry; made from very ripe, late-harvested grapes in Colli Orientali. Once renowned and favored by popes; most vines now destroyed by disease. Unusual aromas and flavors, probably best sipped alone. Italians call it *vino da meditazione*, a wine for contemplation.

THE WINES OF ITALY

(w) **Pinot Bianco.** Fresh, fragrant, fruity white wines, several of DOC status
produced mostly in northeastern districts of Trentino and Friuli. Good
value.

(w) **Pinot Grigio.** Firm, dry, fruity white wines from grape of that name,
several DOC in regions like Friuli, Trentino, Tre Venezie. Excellent value.
Best when young.

(R) **Pinot Nero** F.V.G. Tren.-A.A. DOC 81 80 79 78 76 75 ★ ★
Light reds of the northeast made from Pinot Noir grape.

(R) **Primitivo.** Apu. 81 80 79 75 74 71 ★/★ ★
Potent, heavy, portlike red made from highly sugared or raisined grapes,
tentatively linked to California's Zinfandel. DOC is Primitivo di Mandu-
ria. Often sweet and 14% to 18% alcohol, but not fortified.

(w) **Prosecco di Conegliano.** Ven. DOC 81 80 ★ ★ ★
Crisp, dry white produced northwest of Venice from the Prosecco
grape, often sparkling and uniquely perfumed, occasionally AMABILE.

(R) **Raboso.** Ven. 81 80 79 78 76 75 ★ ★
Pleasant robust red made near Treviso and river Piave.

(3) **Ravello.** Red, white, and rosé wines from town of that name along the
Amalfi coast; the best are fresh and pleasant.

**Recioto.** Implies extra ripe; term used mostly for full-bodied reds from
the Veneto around Verona; wine made from upper portions of grape
bunches that get more sun and higher sugars, often sweet. May also be
dry and potent, as in Recioto Amarone della Valpolicella.

(R) **Recioto della Valpolicella.** Ven. DOC ★ ★
Sweet red, occasionally sparkling, or FRIZZANTE, popular in Verona.

(w) **Recioto di Soave.** Ven. DOC ★ ★
Still and semisparkling white made from extra-ripe grapes; more full-
bodied and strong-flavored than regular Soave. Drink young.

(R) **Refosco.** F.V.G. DOC 81 80 79 78 76 ★ ★
Robust, forceful red from native Refosco grape; some complexity, demands heartiest dishes.

(3) **Regaleali.** Sic. 81 80 79 78 77 ★
Agreeable red and rosé, less distinguished white from Sicily; often
overpriced.

**Riesling.** White grape variety used in northern Italy to make mostly DOC
wines in Oltrepo', Friuli and Trentino-Alto-Adige.

**Riserva.** See Glossary of Wine Terms.

(RO) **Riviera del Garda Chiaretto.** Lomb. DOC ★ ★
Well-known rosé made near Lake Garda. Strong-flavored, dry, vividly
colored. Drink young.

(R) **Riviera del Garda Rosso.** Lomb. DOC 79 78 77 76 71 ★
Very full-bodied red version of above, coarser and more robust than
other well-known red of the region nearby, Bardolino.

(R) **Rossese di Dolceacqua.** Lig. DOC 81 80 79 78 75 71 70 ★ ★
Warm, full-bodied ruby red wine, faintly bitter in aftertaste; popular
along Italian rivera. SUPERIORE bigger, longer-lived.

(R) **Rosso Conero.** Mar. DOC 81 80 79 78 77 75 74 ★ ★
Robust, fruity red based on Montepulciano grape, produced around
Ancona on Adriatic coast. Good value.

(R) **Rosso dell Colline Lucchesi.** Tus. DOC 81 80 79 78 77 75 ★ ★
Medium-bodied red that is produced around Lucca, similar in style to
Chianti.

(R) **Rosso Piceno.** Mar. DOC 81 80 79 78 75 ★ ★/★ ★ ★
Round, balanced red from Sangiovese blended with Montepulciano
grapes; best have good aging potential.

(R) **Rubesco Torgiano.** Umb. DOC 81 80 79 78 77 75 74 71 ★ ★ ★
Excellent red produced near Perugia. Robust, full-flavored, and capable
of aging extremely well. Excellent value.

**Rufina.** One of the subregions of Chianti.

(R) **Salice Salentino.** Apu. DOC 81 80 79 78 75 ★ ★ ★
Dark, sturdy reds from southern Apulia; better vintages age well, becoming rich, velvety, and smooth.

43

**Castello di Uzzano**

CHIANTI CLASSICO

DENOMINAZIONE DI ORIGINE CONTROLLATA

**1975**

RISERVA

*Conti Castelbarco Albani*
*Masetti*
GREVE in Chianti - Italia

MESSO IN BOTTIGLIA AL CASTELLO

PRODUCE OF ITALY

680/FI

750 ml.          ®          Alcohol 12,5% vol.

IMPORTED BY **ALMADÉN** SAN JOSE **IMPORTS** CALIFORNIA   Sole Agents for the United States of America

**CASTELLO DI UZZANO.** There are numerous fine estates in the Chianti Classico region of Tuscany, a specifically defined area between Florence and Siena with its own DOC separate from other Chianti regions such as Rufina of Fiorentina. As a *Riserva*, the wine by law must be aged a minimum of 3 years before release. "Greve" is one of the principal wine towns of the Classico region and "Castello di Uzzano" one of its best estates. *Messo in bottiglia al castello* means estate-bottled.

**Sangiovese.** Principal red wine grape used for Chianti and other reds of Tuscany. Sangiovese Grosso is used for big reds like Brunello, Vino Nobile di Montepulciano.

℗ **Sangiovese di Romagna.** E.R. DOC 81 80 79 78 75 71 ★ +
   Widely produced everyday red north of Bologna; in good vintages improves with age.

℗ **Sangue di Giuda.** Lomb. DOC 81 80 79 77 ★ ★
   Lively red from southern Lombardy (Oltrepo' Pavese). Name means "blood of Judas."

③ **San Severo.** Apu. DOC 81 80 79 78 77 ★ ★
   Dry, sturdy white and red wines, some rosé, produced near town of Foggia; quality has improved in recent years, especially for red.

℗ **Santa Maddalena.** Tren. DOC 81 80 79 78 76 75 74 ★ ★
   One of the best reds of northeastern Italy near Bolzano, made from Schiava, full-bodied, flavorful, generally well-balanced. Good value.

(R) **Sassella.** Lomb. DOC 81 80 79 78 75 71 ★ ★

Good, medium-bodied red from the Valtellina made from Nebbiolo. Ages well in good vintages. Good value.

(R) **Sassicaia.** Tus. 81 80 79 78 77 75 ★ ★ ★ ★

Relatively new and superior red made from 100% Cabernet Sauvignon produced on coastal heights near Livorno. Big and tannic in youth, ages well; very small production. Interesting, expensive wine.

**Sauvignon Blanc.** White grape variety used in northeast, principally Friuli, to produce dry, fragrant, fruity white labeled Sauvignon. Very good value.

(R) **Savuto.** Cal. DOC ★ ★

Big, sturdy red of southern Italy.

**Schiava.** Red wine grape used in northern Italy for superior reds such as Santa Maddalena and Lago di Caldaro.

(R) **Sfursat.** Lomb. DOC 81 80 79 75 71 ★ ★

Full-bodied concentrated red of Valtellina made of partially dried grapes. Ages well but limited production. Also known as Sforzato.

(R) **Sizzano.** Pied. DOC 81 80 79 78 74 71 ★ ★

Agreeable red made from Nebbiolo grape, produced around Novara.

(W) **Soave.** Ven. DOC ★ ★ +

Italy's best-known white wine produced near Verona in ancient walled town of Soave. Fresh, light, fruity, very pleasant wine, though popularity and expanded production have resulted in some unevenness. Best when young; often good value.

(R) **Spanna.** Pied. 81 80 79 78 76 74 71 68 64 61 ★ ★ +

Sturdy, full-bodied red made from Nebbiolo. *Spanna* is local name for Nebbiolo grape from lower slopes around Gattinara region. Capable of long aging, often requires it. Good value.

(R) **Taurasi.** Camp. DOC 81 80 78 77 75 71 68 58 ★ ★ ★

Full-bodied, complex red; tannic and harsh in youth but ages impressively into harmonious wine of some finesse. Expensive.

(W) **Terlano.** Tren. DOC ★ ★

Several dry agreeable whites produced around Bolzano. Drink young.

(R) **Teroldego Rotaliano.** Tren. DOC 81 80 79 78 76 71 ★ ★

Leading red wine of Trentino. Berryish fruit, well-balanced wine of medium body. Good value locally.

(R) **Tignanello.** Tus. 81 80 78 77 75 71 ★ ★ ★ ★

Proprietary label from Antinori estate in Chianti region of Tuscany. Fine, well-structured wine made from Sangiovese and Cabernet Sauvignon. Made in Bordeaux style, becomes elegant with age, though quite good at 5 to 7 years.

(W) **Tocai.** Tren.; F.V.G.; Ven. DOC 81 80 79 ★ ★ ★

One of the better whites of the northeast. Aromatic, with a dry, crisp, slight almond aroma. Good value.

(W) **Torre di Giano.** Umb. DOC ★ ★ ★

Fragrant, full-bodied, flavorful white from the Lungarotti estate near Torgiano. Drink young. Good value. Also lesser wines labeled simply Torgiano.

(3) **Torre Quarto.** Apu. 81 80 79 78 77 ★ ★ ★

Estate-bottled red made near Foggia from mostly Malbec grapes; ripe, smooth, and robust with an elegance untypical of the south. Good rosé and white wines also made.

(W) **Traminer.** Tren.; F.V.G. DOC ★ ★

Delicate fragrant white of the Italian Tyrol, mostly northeast. Traminer Aromatico is name for Gewürztraminer, spicy dry white. Drink young. Good value.

**Trebbiano.** Leading white grape of Italy, mainly Tuscany, Latium and Umbria, producing several DOC whites such as Frascati and Orvieto. Generally fruity, flavorful though some lesser local versions quite ordinary. Known in France as Ugni Blanc.

(W) **Trebbiano di Aprilia.** Lat. DOC 81 80 ★

Fruity, but not very interesting white wine; best when young.

# Italian Vintage Chart

Vintage charts serve primarily as general guides to the quality of wines in each vintage; in both good and bad years there are exceptions to the general rating. Some regional wines, such as Barolo or Chianti, have numerous producers, and one can expect to find on occasion considerable variation of style among them.

This vintage chart covers only red wines. For white wines, generally the younger and fresher they are, the better. There are three Italian whites, however, that improve with a few years of bottle age: Fiano di Avellino, Greco di Tufo, and Vernaccia di San Gimignano.

| | AMARONE | BARBARESCO | BARBERA | BARDOLINO | BAROLO | BRUNELLO DI MONTALCINO | CABERNET TRENTINO | CAREMA | CHIANTI | CHIANTI CLASSICO (RISERVA) | CIRO ROSSO | CORVO ROSSO | GATTINARA | GHEMME |
|---|---|---|---|---|---|---|---|---|---|---|---|---|---|---|
| 1961 | 8 | 9 | 8 | 6 | (10) | 6 | 6 | | 5 | 6 | 7 | | 8 | 6 |
| 1962 | 8 | 8 | 8 | 9 | 8 | | 4 | | 7 | 9 | 5 | | 5 | 8 |
| 1963 | 7 | 2 | 4 | 6 | 4 | | 6 | | 4 | 4 | 7 | | 2 | 4 |
| 1964 | 10 | 10 | 9 | 8 | 10 | (10) | 10 | | 6 | 9 | 5 | | 10 | 9 |
| 1965 | 6 | 6 | 6 | 6 | 7 | 6 | 2 | | 5 | 5 | 5 | | 5 | 6 |
| 1966 | 8 | 2 | 2 | 6 | 5 | (7) | 6 | | 5 | 5 | | | 5 | 5 |
| 1967 | 8 | (8) | 7 | 7 | 8 | (8) | 6 | | 5 | 8 | 5 | | 5 | 5 |
| 1968 | (8) | 6 | 6 | 7 | 7 | (6) | 4 | | 7 | 8 | 10 | | 8 | 7 |
| 1969 | 9 | 7 | 7 | 9 | 7 | (7) | 10 | | 7 | 8 | 2 | | 8 | 7 |
| 1970 | (7) | (8) | 8 | 7 | (7) | (10) | (10) | 8 | (7) | (9) | 5 | | 8 | 8 |
| 1971 | (8) | (10) | (10) | 8 | 10 | (9) | 7 | 8 | (7) | (9) | 5 | 8 | 5 | 5 |
| 1972 | (7) | 2 | 2 | 5 | 4 | 5 | 4 | 5 | 5 | 5 | 5 | 8 | 3 | 4 |
| 1973 | 8 | 6 | 5 | 7 | 5 | 6 | 4 | 5 | 5 | 5 | (7) | 8 | 5 | 5 |
| 1974 | (9) | (9) | (8) | 7 | (8) | 6 | 4 | 8 | 7 | (7) | (7) | (8) | (9) | (8) |
| 1975 | | (5) | (5) | 8 | (6) | 9 | (6) | (5) | (8) | (9) | (5) | (7) | (6) | (5) |
| 1976 | 6 | (5) | (5) | 8 | (6) | 5 | (6) | 5 | 5 | 5 | 2 | (5) | (8) | (7) |
| 1977 | 8 | 5 | 2 | 8 | 6 | 7 | (6) | 2 | (8) | (8) | (7) | (6) | 5 | (5) |
| 1978 | 8 | 9 | 7 | 6 | 7 | 8 | 8 | 7 | 7 | 7 | 6 | 6 | 7 | 6 |
| 1979 | | 8 | 8 | 8 | 9 | 7 | 7 | 8 | 9 | 8 | 8 | 7 | 8 | 8 |
| 1980 | 7 | 7 | 7 | 7 | 7 | 8 | 8 | 7 | 8 | 8 | 8 | 8 | 7 | 7 |

**10** the best
**8-9** very fine, superior
**6-7** good, above average
**5** average
**4** fair
below **4** poor

○ can take further aging
5 may be too old
drink now
5 lay away

| GRIGNOLINO | GRUMELLO | INFERNO | LAMBRUSCO DI SORBARA | MERLOT TRENTINO | MONTEPULCIANO D'ABRUZZO | NEBBIOLO D'ABRUZZO | SASSELLA | SFURSAT | TAURASI | TORGIANO | VALPOLICELLA | VINO NOBILE DI MONTEPULCIANO | |
|---|---|---|---|---|---|---|---|---|---|---|---|---|---|
| 8 | 8 | 8 | 10 | 8 | 6 | 10 | 8 | 8 | 10 |  | 7 | 6 | 1961 |
| 5 | 5 | 5 | 4 | 6 | 6 | 8 | 5 | 5 | 4 | 0 | 8 | 8 | 1962 |
| 4 | 5 | 5 | 6 | 4 | 7 | 4 | 5 | 5 | 4 |  | 7 | 4 | 1963 |
| 5 | 10 | 10 | 4 | 8 | 4 | 8 | 10 | 10 | 8 |  | 9 | 8 | 1964 |
| 5 | 4 | 4 | 5 | 4 | 7 | 6 | 4 | 4 | 6 |  | 6 | 4 | 1965 |
| 5 | 5 | 5 | 4 | 6 | 6 | 4 | 5 | 5 | 8 |  | 7 | 6 | 1966 |
| 5 | 5 | 5 | 5 | 6 | 6 | 8 | 5 | 6 | 8 |  | 8 | 10 | 1967 |
| 5 | 5 | 5 | 6 | 5 | 9 | 5 | 5 | 5 | 10 |  | 7 | 8 | 1968 |
| 5 | 7 | 7 | 6 | 9 | 4 | 5 | 7 | 8 | 6 |  | 8 | 8 | 1969 |
| 5 | 8 | 8 | 7 | 6 | 5 | 5 | 8 | 8 | 8 |  | 7 | 10 | 1970 |
| 7 | 8 | 8 | 8 | 8 | 5 | 10 | 8 | 8 | 8 | 9 | 8 | 5 | 1971 |
| 2 | 6 | 6 | 5 | 4 | 5 | 2 | 6 | 5 | 6 | 8 | 8 | 5 | 1972 |
| 5 | 6 | 6 | 6 | 4 | 7 | 5 | 6 | 6 | 8 | 8 | 7 | 8 | 1973 |
| 8 | 6 | 6 | 6 | 6 | 7 | 5 | 6 | 7 | 6 | 7 | 7 | 6 | 1974 |
| 2 | 6 | 6 | 7 | 5 | 8 | 5 | 6 | 6 | 8 | 7 | 8 | 10 | 1975 |
| 5 | 5 | 5 | 6 | 6 | 5 | 5 | 6 | 4 | 6 | 5 | 6 | 4 | 1976 |
| 4 | 5 | 5 | 6 | 5 | 8 | 5 | 5 | 5 | 10 | 6 | 8 | 8 | 1977 |
| 6 | 5 | 5 | 6 | 7 | 6 | 6 | 5 | 5 | 8 | 7 | 7 | 8 | 1978 |
| 7 | 8 | 8 | 8 | 8 | 7 | 8 | 8 | 8 | 9 | 9 | 8 | 9 | 1979 |
| 6 | 7 | 7 | 8 | 8 | 8 | 7 | 7 | 7 | 8 | 8 | 7 | 7 | 1980 |

47

**Trentino-Alto-Adige.** Extreme northeastern province of Italy. Mountainous cool climate producing several DOC wines mostly named for grape varieties.

(RW) **Valdadige.** Broad DOC category of reds and whites, mostly named for grape variety and made around Trento.

(R) **Valgella.** Lomb. DOC 81 80 79 78 71 70 69 ★ ★
Sturdy red wine of the Valtellina, slow to mature. After 4 years aging becomes RISERVA. Good value.

(R) **Valpantena.** Ven. DOC 81 80 78 77 ★ ★
Light red produced east of Verona, similar to Valpolicella but of lesser quality.

(R) **Valpolicella.** Ven. DOC 81 80 79 78 77 74 ★ ★ ★
One of Italy's best light reds produced northwest of Verona. Smooth, round, fruity wines generally best within five years of vintage, though some last longer. Often best when slightly cooled.

**Valtellina.** Principal wine-producing region of Lombardy, a mountainous region east of Lake Como known for sturdy, generous reds such as Grumello, Sassella, Inferno, and Valgella.

(RW) **Velletri.** Lat. DOC 81 80 79 78 ★ ★
Agreeable whites and rather better reds from town of Velletri in the hills south of Rome.

(R) **Venegazzú.** Ven. 81 80 79 78 77 74 ★ ★ ★
Very fine red wine from little town of that name above Treviso. Made from Cabernet Sauvignon, Malbec, and Merlot, very full-bodied (over 13% alcohol) and aged in small oak. At 4 years becomes Riserva di Casa, developing fine bouquet, complexity, and finesse. Expensive. Some white wine produced under the name as well.

**Verdiso.** A white grape producing light fresh whites around the town of Conegliano in Friuli and the sparkling wines of Prosecco.

(W) **Verduzzo.** F.V.G.; Ven. DOC ★ ★
Dry, fragrant whites from grape of that name produced near Piave above Venice. Some sweet sparkling wines also produced.

(W) **Vermentino.** Lig. ★ ★
Popular dry white wine along Italian Riviera, very good with seafood. Drink young. Good value.

(W) **Vermentino di Gallura.** Sard. DOC ★ ★
Full-bodied dry white wine produced in northern Sardinia from Vermentino grape.

**Vernaccia.** Old and honored white grape variety producing dry and sweet pale golden wines.

(W) **Vernaccia di San Gimignano.** Tus. DOCG 81 80 79 78 ★ ★ ★
Best-known whites made from Vernaccia grape. Mostly dry and somewhat austere in youth, softens with a couple of years in bottle. Some sweet wines also made. Other Vernaccias are Vernaccia di Oristano of Sardinia.

(R) **Vino Nobile di Montepulciano.** Tus. DOCG 81 80 79 78 77 75 70 68 67 ★ ★ ★ ★
Excellent noble red wine from Montepulciano near Siena. Made mostly from Sangiovese grosso. Deeply colored, rich flavors and aromas, ages extremely well. Good value.

**Vin santo.** Rich, usually sweet, white wines made from dried grapes. Not well known outside Italy, but many of the leading estates produce their own. Tuscany's are the most famous. A DOC in Trentino.

(W) **Zagarolo.** Lat. DOC ★ ★
Agreeable whites from hill town of Zagarolo south of Rome. Similar to Frascati, but smaller production and less well known.

# THE WINES OF GERMANY

**G**ermany's two million acres of vineyards produce some of the world's most delightful wine. Along her famous wine rivers (where Rhine wines come in brown bottles and Mosel wines in green bottles), the views are spectacularly scenic, with steep vine-covered hills rising dramatically from the river banks, and villages of quaint and picturesque charm clustered below. The overall quality of German wines—mostly white, though a little red is produced—is very high. Wines at the middle level, Qualitätswein, are light, fragrant, fruity, and very easy to drink. The best, and Germany's best represents extraordinary distinction at highest levels, are her naturally sweet wines made from the Riesling grape, considered by some the supreme white wines of the world.

Although German nomenclature seems forbiddingly complicated, especially when it appears in forceful gothic, it is worth trying to understand the terminology, for the sublime experience that certain wines afford. The label information for Germany is the most precise in the wine world, and very often what is *not* on the label tells you as much as what is there.

The key words indicate ripeness of the grapes at harvest or pinpoint geographic origin. The geographic breakdown is this: There are 11 regions designated for quality wines (the 9 most important are discussed in Principal Wine Regions). Within each region there are subdistricts known as *Bereichs*. Bereich Bernkastel, for instance, covers most of the Mittel-Mosel. Within each Bereich, several of the better vineyards may constitute a further subgroup known as *Grosslage,* such as Bernkasteler Badstube. These wines are of higher grade than Bereich wines. Better wines still come from the most precise geographic site of all, the individual vineyard, or *Einzellage,* as in Bernkasteler Doktor. The suffix "er" is usually added to wines using a village name. Thus, a wine from the town of Winkel becomes Winkeler, one from Graach, Graacher. This works similarly for certain outstanding vineyards where the vineyard name appears by itself (Steinberger, Scharzhofberger). The inclusion of a vineyard name following a village name is a good indication of superior quality.

The other quality indicators are based on ripeness of the grapes, or "must-weight," at harvest. The simplest quality category is *Tafelwein,* ordinary table wine that conforms to minimum quality standards. It is inexpensive, undistinguished, though often agreeable. The next step up is *Qualitätswein bestimmte Anbaugebiete* (QbA)—wine of specified region. Tafelwein and QbAs may legally add sugar before fermentation to make up for insufficient ripeness—a usual occurrence since Germany's vineyards are the northernmost

# GLOSSARY OF WINE TERMS

**Anbaugebiete** (Gebiet) *Wine region. There are 11 designated by German law, 9 of which are shown on the map on page 52; the two lesser ones are Hessiche Bergstrasse and Württemberg.*

**Edelfäule.** *Noble rot, the beneficial mold Botrytis cinerea that penetrates grape skins, releasing moisture but concentrating sugars and flavors.*

**Eiswein.** *Literally, "ice wine." Rare, sweet wine made in the unusual instance when a drop in temperature freezes grapes that are still on the vine. The grapes are pressed while still frozen. Usually of the Auslese level of sweetness, and expensive. Can occur as late as January or February after harvest.*

**Erzeugerabfüllung.** *Estate-bottled, wine from a single vineyard.*

**Halb-Trocken.** *Half-dry.*

**Keller.** *Cellar.*

**Perlwein.** *Semisparkling.*

**QbA.** Qualitätswein bestimmte Anbaugebiete. *Quality wine of designated regions. The middle level of German wines to which sugar may be added (before fermentation) when grapes do not fully ripen. Subject to approval before the government quality control board.*

**QmP.** Qualitätswein mit Prädikat. *Quality wine with special attributes. The top 5 levels of German wines, made only in years when the grapes ripen fully and no sugar is added. In ascending order of quality and natural sweetness they are:*

**Kabinett.** *Driest of the QmP wines.*

**Spätlese.** *Late-picked, from grapes left on the vine to ripen further and develop higher sugars. Wines may be dry but are often lightly sweet, and good acidity makes them suitable with food, even such richly flavored dishes as game in Germany.*

**Auslese.** *Late-picked, selected bunches of grapes, affected by Botrytis cinerea (see Edelfäule). Naturally sweet but not heavy, can be excellent summer apèritif or just by itself. Auslese and the two following QmPs are only made in superior vintages.*

**Beerenauslese.** (BA). *Late-ripened selected berries. Only those attacked by Botrytis are used, resulting in small quantities of luscious sweet wines among the finest in the world.*

**Trockenbeerenauslese.** (TBA). *Selected dried berries—ultra-ripe Botrytised grapes left to dry until the sugars concentrate. Incredibly rich, honeyish wine with remarkable balance, depth, and longevity. The ultimate in German wine; a single bottle may cost several hundred dollars.*

**Tafelwein.** *Table wine; lowest classification of wines. It is ranked below QbA.*

**Trocken.** *Dry. By itself on a label, generally means safe for diabetics.*

**Weingut.** *Wine estate.*

**Weinkellerei.** *Winery.*

in Europe, on the same latitude as Newfoundland. More years than not, the grapes cannot develop adequate sugar on their own, and without added sugar, the wines would be hard, acidic, and unpleasant. At the QbA level, most of the sugar is converted to alcohol, leaving wines that are basically dry.

The next level takes a quantum leap—*Qualitätswein mit Prädikat* (QmP), quality wines with special attributes, those that have graduated "with honors," so to speak. They are made with naturally ripened grapes that develop higher sugars and thus can be made only in good years when weather permits. The great vintage years in Germany are those that result in the greatest number of QmP wines. There are five levels within this category. In ascending order of sweetness, they are *Kabinett; Spätlese; Auslese; Beerenauslese* (BA); and *Trockenbeerenauslese* (TBA). (See Glossary of Wine Terms.)

The latter three represent the pinnacle of German wines. Their exquisite balance of sweetness and acidity, never cloying, is the Riesling's response to unique combinations of soil and climate. They are wines of remarkable subtlety, elegance, and profound depth and are incomparably perfumed with the rich scent of honeyed fruit or hints of herbs, wildflowers, or exotic spices.

Some people find German wines too sweet to go with food. But do not be too quick to embrace that idea. In Germany, as well as among connoisseurs throughout the world, wines of Kabinett or Spätlese status are often superb choices with richly flavored dishes, particularly game. Many QbAs and Kabinetts are quite dry; Spätleses are usually lightly sweet or off-dry. There is a renewed trend in Germany toward drier wines, often labeled *Trocken* (dry) or *Halb-Trocken* (half-dry). The wines of Franconia (Franken), those that are sold in a *Bocksbeutel* (squatty green flagon), are also dry, for the most part.

As for the superior levels of naturally sweet wines, Auslese and above, they are most appropriate with dessert or just by themselves. They are wines for special moments.

# PRINCIPAL WINE REGIONS

**Ahr**    A tributary of the Rhine north of Koblenz, known mostly for red wines, rarely exported.

**Baden** (Bad.)    Southern Germany's wine region, bordered by Switzerland and Alsace and embracing the Black Forest. Districts such as Ortenau, Kaiserstuhl-Tuniberg, and Bodensee produce good, fresh wines and occasionally some that are more distinguished. Also a few red wines from the Spätburgunder grape.

**Bereich**    Subregion of a Gebiet, such as Bereich Niersteiner of the Rheinhessen; a Bereich may include several villages and vineyard sites (Grosslages) but no vineyard name appears on the label since wines may come from any part of the region.

**Einzellage**    Individual vineyard site, the smallest geographic designation to appear on a German wine label, usually producing the best wines.

**Franken, or Franconia** (FrK.)    Located in the upper Main valley either side of Würzburg. Mostly, agreeable wines made from Müller-Thurgau and Sylvaner that come in a flagon-type bottle known as a Bocksbeutel.

**Grosslage**    "Composite" site. A grouping of several vineyards within a Bereich. There are 11 Grosslages in Bereich Nierstein, for example, the most famous of which is Niersteiner Gutes Domtal.

**Lagename**    Vineyard name.

**Mittelrhein**    The "middle Rhine" from Bonn to Bingen, a lesser region of some 2,000 acres producing light wines that are mostly consumed by tourists in the region. Leading Bereich: Bacharach.

**Mosel-Saar-Ruwer** (M-S-R.)    The Mosel, leading tributary of the Rhine, produces some of Germany's most exquisite wines—paler, more acid than those of the Rhine regions but also more flowery and spicy—as well as huge quantities of very ordinary wines from large Bereichs like Bernkastel and Zell. Riesling is predominant but Müller-Thurgau is also grown. The best wines come from specific vineyards in the leading wine towns of Bernkastel, Piesport, Wehlen, Ürzig, Brauneberg, and Zeltingen, which make up the Mittel-Mosel. The Saar and Ruwer rivers, tributaries of

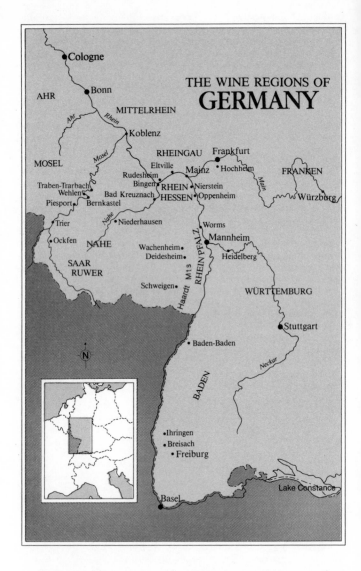

THE WINE REGIONS OF
**GERMANY**

the Mosel at Trier, also produce some wines with the distinctive floral aromas and spiciness of flavor that mark wines of the Mosel.

**Nahe** (Na.)   A tributary of the Rhine near Bingen producing very good wines from Riesling and a larger quantity of average to good wines from Sylvaner and Rulander. Best Nahe Riesling is fragrant and full-flavored. Principal wine towns are Bad Kreuznach and Schlossböckelheim (both also Bereichs).

**Rheingau** (Rhg.)   Acknowledged as Germany's premier wine region with vineyards facing south on the north bank of the Rhine between Hochheim and Rüdesheim. Excellent QbAs and some of the world's finest sweet wines from famed vineyards such as Schloss Vollrads, Steinberg, and Schloss Johannisberg, the best very long-lived.

**Rheinhessen** (Rhh.)   Large growing region on the south bank of the Rhine opposite the Rheingau and turning southward up the Rhine at Mainz. The best wines from vineyards in Nierstein, Nackenheim, and Oppenheim are made from Riesling and some Sylvaner. Müller-Thurgau predominates in the Hessen, however, and a great deal of Liebfraumilch, Germany's best-known blend, is made here. The greatest wines compare with those of the Rheingau, though tend to be somewhat softer and not as classically structured.

**Rheinpfalz** (RpF.)   Germany's largest wine region, over 50,000 acres of vineyards below the Rheinhessen on the upper Rhine's western banks. The vineyards are back from the river here, the best on low, east-facing slopes of the Haardt Mountains around the towns of Deidesheim, Forst, Ruppertsberg, Wachenheim, and Bad Dürkheim. Lesser wines have more earthiness and body than most German wines, but QmP wines such as AUSLESE, BA, and TBA show great noblesse and breed. Leading producers of the Pfalz, known locally as the "three Bs," are Bassermann-Jordan, Bürklin-Wolf, and von Bühl.

# VINTAGES

Because German wines taste so fresh and appealing within a few months of bottling, the refinements they acquire with maturity— nuance, harmony, elegance—are not always readily appreciated or explored. The fact is, however, that Germany's finest wines improve considerably with bottle age, and often require it to be at their best. An example is the 1976 vintage, which exhibits much more grace, balance and depth at present than it did earlier on. Vintages that yield wines of exceptional quality and ripeness, those of KABINETT status and above, invariably improve in bottle, particularly if acidity is in good proportion. The wines can then be extremely long-lived, up to ten years and beyond.

The following list of vintages indicates which vintages are best for keeping.

1981.   Short, but better than 1980, with nearly half production of QbA status, about one third KABINETT, which will age 3 to 5 years. QbAs show freshness and charm for drinking young.

1980.   A difficult vintage, drastically reduced in most areas by very late flowering and cold, wet growing season, especially in Mosel and Baden. Rheinpfalz most successful. Overall, QbAs are attractive for drinking young; some KABINETTS and SPATLESEN very good but few PRÄDIKAT wines beyond that.

1979.   Greatly reduced by frost in some regions, notably Mosel Saar-Ruwer, the Nahe, Franconia, and Rheinhessen. Bigger crops in the Rheingau (very good); Rheinpfalz; and Baden. Generally 70% QbA, 25 to 30% QmP wines, mostly KABINETT and SPÄTLESE, a few AUSLESE in the Rheinhessen and Mosel, which should prove good keepers.

1978.   A late warm harvest, also reduced by frosts the previous spring. Generally good; warmer on the Rhine that produced many KABINETT, SPÄTLESE. 80% was QbA.

1977.   Big, useful vintage, mostly QbAs now past youthful appeal; some KABINETTS, best in the Rheinpfalz.

1976.   Excellent quality but reduced quantity. High percentage of QmP wines with very high sugars, some extraordinary wines. Best from Rhine regions, rich though perhaps not as balanced as 1975. Twenty percent KABINETT, 30% AUSLESE, some BAS, TBAS. Needs time to develop, best will be very long-lived.

1975.   Excellent year for Rieslings, mostly KABINETT and SPÄTLESE of fine, austere balance on the Rhine, superb AUSLESEN on the Mosel, also the Rheinpfalz. Will improve further with time.

1974. Variable quality, most no higher than KABINETT level; not suitable for keeping.

1973. Large harvest, mostly attractive wines but low acidity, particularly among Mosels; most should be drunk now.

1972. Large harvest, average quality, now over the hill.

1971. Superlative. Perfectly balanced QmP wines that will continue to develop, though showing beautifully now.

Earlier great vintages whose wines are still fine: 1967, 1966 (Mosel); 1964, 1959, 1953, 1949, 1945.

# WINE GUIDE

Ⓡ **Ahr.** Ahr. 81 80 79 78 76 75 ★/★★
Major region for red wines from Spätburgunder grape, from towns along the Ahr River such as Ahrweiler, Bad Neuenahr, Walporzheim. Pale, some very agreeable but not distinguished.

Ⓡ **Assmannshausen.** Rhg. 81 80 79 78 76 75 ★★
Town along the Rhine famous for its red wine from the Spätburgunder grape.

**Auslese.** See Glossary of Wine Terms.

Ⓦ **Avelsbach.** M-S-R. 81 80 79 78 76 75 73 71 ★★★
One of the better wine villages near Trier, falls within the Grosslage Trierer Römerlay, but best vineyards are Hammerstein, Altenberg, Herrenberg.

Ⓦ **Ayl.** M-S-R. 81 80 79 78 76 75 73 71 ★★★
Leading village along the Saar in the Grosslage Scharzberg. Outstanding vineyards: Ayler Kupp, Herrenberg.

**Bad Dürkheim.** See Dürkheim.

**Badische Bergstrasse/Kraichgau.** A leading Bereich in northern Baden, supplies much local wine to Heidelberg.

**Bad Kreuznach.** See Kreuznach.

**Bassermann-Jordan.** Excellent producer along the Rheinpfalz at Deidesheim, with vineyards also in Forst (Forster Jesuitengarten) and Ruppertsberg. Highly regarded wines, especially of AUSLESE level or higher.

**Beerenauslese.** See Glossary of Wine Terms.

**Bereich.** See Further Regional Designations.

Ⓦ **Bernkastel.** M-S-R. 81 80 79 78 76 75 73 71 ★★/★★★★
The principal wine town of the Mosel, finest wines are among Germany's best from the famous Bernkasteler Doktor vineyard; others are Lay, Graben, Bratenhofchen, Matheisbildchen. Best Grosslage: Badstube; the other, Kurfurstlay, also produces good wine.

Ⓦ **Bernkastel, Bereich.** M-S-R. 81 80 79 78 76 ★★
One of Germany's largest Bereichs, includes wines from several towns along the Mosel between Zell and the Ruwer (Mittel-Mosel). Often ordinary. Very pleasant in ripe vintages but best when young and fresh.

Ⓦ **Bingen.** Rhh. 81 80 79 78 76 73 71 ★★/★★★
A leading wine town on the Rhine near its juncture with the Nahe. Best vineyards: Scharlachberg, Kirchberg, Rosengarten. Also a Bereich for the west Rheinhessen.

**Blauburgunder.** A clone of Pinot Noir, grown mainly in the Ahr.

Ⓦ **Blue Nun.** Largest selling Liebfraumilch from the firm of Sichel. Semisweet but generally fresh and well-balanced.

**Bocksbeutel.** Flagon-shaped bottle with flat sides used for Franken wines.

ⓦ **Bockstein.** M-S-R. 81 80 79 78 76 75 73 71 ★ ★ ★
   One of the best vineyards in Ockfen on the Saar, known as Ockfener Bockstein.

ⓦ **Bodenheim.** Rhh. 81 80 79 78 76 75 ★ ★
   Wine town in the Rheinhessen. Good wines for the most part, from Sylvaner grape unless otherwise labeled (some Riesling).

**Bodensee.** Minor district of Baden near Lake Constance.

ⓦ **Brauneberg.** M-S-R. 81 80 79 78 76 75 73 71 ★ ★/★ ★ ★
   Major wine town along the Mosel. Excellent, often rich sweet wines of top class from vineyards such as Juffer, Juffer-Sonnenuhr, and Klostergarten. Grosslage: Kurfurstlay. Good value.

ⓦ **Breisach.** Bad. 81 80 79 78 76 75 ★ ★ +
   Town in Bereich Kaiserstuhl-Tuniberg. Best-known vineyard, Vulkanfelsen, produces good Gewürztraminer.

**Breisgau.** Bereich, minor district in southern Baden near Kaiserstuhl.

**Buhl, von.** One of the three principal growers in the Rheinpfalz, extensive holdings in top vineyards of Deidesheim, Forst, Ruppertsberg; very fine wines, especially of KABINETT level and above.

**Bürklin-Wolf.** Another of the top three producers (with Bassermann-Jordan and von Bühl) in the Rheinpfalz, with excellent vineyards such as Hohenmorgen in Deidesheim, Gerumpel in Wachenheim, and Ungeheuer in Forst.

ⓦ **Crown of Crowns.** Langenbach's widely-sold Liebfraumilch.

ⓦ **Deidesheim.** Rpf. 81 80 79 78 76 75 73 71 ★ ★/★ ★ ★ ★
   Quaint, charming town in the Rheinpfalz. Rich, aromatic, full-bodied wines. Several top vineyards: Hohenmorgen, Paradiesgarten, Nonnenstück, Herrgottsacker, Leinhöhle, Langenmorgen, Maushöhle, and others known for outstanding QmP wines.

**Deinhard.** Large firm headquartered in Koblenz, with several quality vineyards in the Mosel (including part of Bernkasteler Doktor) and the Rheinpfalz; also Hanns Cristof Liebfraumilch.

**Diabetiker Wein.** Dry wines with minute residual sugar, safe for diabetics, and becoming something of a trend among medium-quality wines.

ⓦ **Dhron.** M-S-R. 81 80 79 78 76 75 73 71 ★ ★/★ ★ ★
   Wine town on the Mosel, falling within Grosslage Michalsberg (Piesporter), some wines sold as Neumagen-Dhron. Best wines from Hofberg vineyard.

ⓦ **Dienheim.** Rhh. 81 80 79 78 76 75 73 71 ★ ★
   Wine village south of Oppenheim producing moderately good wines in the Grosslage Krötenbrunnen or vineyards such as Falkenberg, Tafelstein and Kreuz.

**Dom.** "Cathedral," word seen on wine labels of certain church-owned properties.

**Domtal.** See Niersteiner.

ⓦ **Durbach.** Bad. 81 80 79 78 76 75 ★ ★ +
   Wine village in central Baden, producing mostly light, drinkable wines; the best are Rieslings, Ruländers okay. Best vineyards: Wolf-Metternich and Staufenberg.

⨂ **Dürkheim, Bad.** Rpf. 81 80 79 78 76 75 73 71 ★ ★/★ ★ ★
   Largest wine-producing town of the Rheinpfalz; considerable quantities of moderate reds; whites, especially Riesling, are best from such vineyards as Herrenmorgen, Hochbenn, and Spielberg. Three Grosslage: Feuerberg, Hochmess, Schenckenböhl.

**Egon Müller.** Top producer of the Mosel, with important holdings such as Scharzhofberger in Wiltingen.

**Eiswein.** See Glossary of Wine Terms.

ⓦ **Eitelsbach.** M-S-R. 81 80 79 78 76 75 73 71 ★ ★ ★
   Town on the Ruwer producing quite fine, fragrant whites from leading vineyards of Karthäuserhofberg and Marienholz; others included in Grosslage Trier Römerslay.

# VINEYARD NAMES

Vineyards in Germany often have amusing and colorful names that have special significance in the region. Among the more interesting ones are these:

**Apotheke:** apothecary
**Drachenstein:** the dragon's stone
**Engelsberg:** mountain of the angel
**Feuerberg:** fire mountain
**Gerumpel:** clutter
**Hasensprung:** hare's leap
**Hergottsacker:** God's acre
**Himmelreich:** heavenly domaine
**Honigberg:** honey mountain
**Hohenmorgen:** high noon
**Kirchenpfad:** church path
**Klostergarten:** cloister garden
**Königsfels:** the king's rock

**Kupfergrube:** copper pit
**Liebfraumilch:** dear lady's milk
**Maushöhle:** mousehole
**Nacktarsch:** naked bottom
**Nonnenstück:** the nun's plot
**Paradiesgarten:** paradise garden
**Pfaffenberg:** mountain of the friar
**Sandgrube:** sand pit
**Sonnenberg:** sun mountain
**Sonnenuhr:** sun dial
**Taubenberg:** mountain of the dove
**Ungeheuer:** monster
**Vulkanfelsen:** volcano rock

---

Ⓦ **Eltville.** Rhg. 81 80 79 78 76 75 73 71 ★★★/★★★★

Top wine-producing town of the Rheingau, producing classic, extremely fine, elegant wines from such estates as Schloss Eltz, von Simmern, and the Staatsweingüter (state-owned domain). Important vineyards: Sonnenberg, Langenstück, Taubenberg, Sandgrub.

**Eltz, Schloss.** A leading wine-estate in the Rheingau, with vineyards in Eltville, Kiedrich, Rauenthal, Rudesheim. The Schloss or castle and cellars are in Eltville. Generally superb wines.

Ⓦ **Enkirch.** M-S-R. 81 80 79 78 76 75 ★★ +

Small town on the middle Mosel producing fresh, very agreeable light wines. Grosslage: Ürziger Schwarzlay.

Ⓦ **Erbach.** Rhg. 81 80 79 78 76 75 73 71 ★★★/★★★★

Wines of great distinction, powerful, long-lived, intensely fragrant. Best estate: Marcobrunn, but also Steinmorgen, Honigberg, Siegelsberg, Schlossberg, Michelmark.

Ⓦ **Erden.** M-S-R. 81 80 79 78 76 75 73 71 ★★/★★★

Small village along middle Mosel; strong-flavored, very good wines from Treppchen, Busslay, Pralat, Herrenberg vineyards. Grosslage: Ürziger Schwarzlay.

**Erzeugerabfüllung.** See Glossary of Wine Terms.

Ⓦ **Escherndorf.** Frk. 81 80 79 78 76 75 ★★★/★★★★

Wine-producing town in Franconia, second to Würzberg in quality. Top vineyards: Lump, Geibach. Grosslage: Kirchberg.

**Feine, feinste, hochfeinste.** Quality terms formerly used to denote a producer's best wine. No longer legal.

Ⓦ **Forst.** Rpf. 81 80 79 78 76 75 73 71 ★★/★★★★

One of the best wine-producing towns of the Rheinpfalz, excellent wines that are intensely fragrant and complex of KABINETT level or above. Top vineyards are Kirchenstück, Jesuitengarten, Ungeheuer, and Pechstein. Wines of the Grosslage Mariengarten, such as Bürklin-Wolf's, are reliable. Good value.

**Franken.** See Principal Wine Regions.

Ⓦ **Geisenheim.** Rhg. 81 80 79 78 76 75 73 71 ★★/★★★

Famous for its wine school on the Rhine; includes also good Rieslings from Rothenberg, Fuchsberg, Kläuserweg, and other vineyards.

**Gewürztraminer.** The spicy traminer grape of Alsace, planted to small extent in Germany, mostly Baden and Rheinpfalz.

**Goldener October.** Proprietary names of St. Ursula Liebfraumilch and Moselblümchen.

(w) **Graach.** M-S-R. 81 80 79 78 76 75 73 71 ★★/★★★ +

One of the Mosel's leading wine towns; fragrant, quite fine wines from such estates as Himmelreich, Josephshofer, Abstberg. Some of the best properties belong to von Kesselstatt family.

**Grosslage.** See Principal Wine Regions.

**Gutedel.** Lesser grape variety known elsewhere as Chasselas, grown mostly in southern Baden.

(w) **Hallgarten.** Rhg. 81 80 79 78 76 75 73 71 ★★/★★★★

Excellent wines, among the most forceful of the Rheingau from vineyards upland, well above the Rhine, specifically Jungfer, Hendelberg, Schönhell, and Würzgarten. Hallgarten is also the name of a well-known wine firm in London.

(w) **Hattenheim.** Rhg. 81 80 79 78 76 75 73 71 ★★/★★★★

Consistently good to outstanding wines, including top vineyards Marcobrunn and Steinberg, whose names appear alone on label. Others: Nussbrunnen, Pfaffenberg, Wisselbrunnen, Mannberg. Also the Grosslage Hattenheimer Deutelsberg.

**Hessiche Bergstrasse.** Lesser region near Frankfurt, and Germany's smallest. Mostly average wines, little exported.

(w) **Hochheim.** Rhg. 81 80 79 78 76 75 73 71 ★★/★★★

Major wine town on the eastern edge of the Rheingau; elegant wines but rather softer than rest of Rheingau. Best vineyards are Domdechaney, Kirchenstück, Hölle. Also a Grosslage: Hochheimer Daubhaus.

**Hock.** Old English term for Rhine wine, anglicized from Hochheimer.

**Huxelrebe.** One of the newer, early-ripening, frost-resistant grape varieties grown in Germany, mainly the Rheinphessen, for very sweet wines.

(rw) **Ihringen.** Bad. 81 80 79 78 76 ★

Mostly average wines from one of best-known wine towns in Baden.

**Iphofen.** One of Franconia's best wine-producing villages, particularly wines from the Julius Echter-Berg vineyard.

**Jesuitengarten.** Forster Jesuitengarten in the Rheinpfalz is one of Germany's top vineyards, world-famous.

(w) **Johannisberg.** Rhg. 81 80 79 78 76 75 73 71 ★★/★★★★

Perhaps the Rheingau's top wine-producing vineyards dominated by the famous castle and vineyard, Schloss Johannisberg overlooking the Rhine. Graceful wines, the best have exquisite breed and bouquet; can be very long-lived. Other top estates: Hölle, Klaus, Schwartzenstein. Johannisberg Erntebringer is the Grosslage; the Bereich is simply Johannisberg and includes the entire Rheingau.

**Josephshofer.** Important vineyard in Graach owned by von Kesselstatt.

**Kabinett.** See Glossary of Wine Terms.

**Kaiserstuhl-Tuniberg.** Important region in Baden near Black Forest, dramatically terraced vineyards on slopes of extinct volcano. Strong, full-flavored wines.

(w) **Kallstadt.** Rpf. 81 80 79 78 76 75 71 ★★/★★★

Good to excellent wines with rich, sometimes earthy flavor. Best vineyards: Annaberg and Horn.

(w) **Kanzem.** M-S-R. 81 80 79 78 76 75 71 ★★/★★★ +

Important wine village near Wiltingen on the Saar with excellent vineyards: Sonnenberg, Altenberg, Schlossberg, Horecker; wines rank with those of Wiltingen or Ockfen but often more full-bodied.

(w) **Kasel.** M-S-R. 81 80 79 78 76 75 ★★

Leading wine village of the Ruwer, producing good but light fragrant wines. Good value. Grosslage: Trierer Römerlay.

**Kerner.** One of the newer grape varieties developed for earlier ripening and resistance to frost.

**Kesselstatt, von.** A leading wine-growing family of the Mosel owning some of the best vineyards in Graach, Piesport, Kasel, and Wiltingen.

(W) **Kiedrich.** Rhg. 81 80 79 78 76 75 73 71 ★★/★★★★
Small wine town set above the Rhine near Rauenthal, with wine often as good, especially from such vineyards as Grafenberg, Sandgrub, and Wasserros.

**Kloster Eberbach.** Famous 12th century monastery, once a center of German viticulture, now site of the German Wine Academy that holds seminars and tastings and conducts tours to German wine regions.

(W) **Königsbach.** Rpf. 81 80 79 78 76 75 ★★★
Small village near Diedesheim, with good wines from such vineyards as Idig, Jesuitengarten, Ölberg, and Reiterpfad.

(W) **Kreuznach, Bad.** Na. 81 80 79 78 76 75 ★★+
Principal town on the Nahe, also known as a spa for its mineral waters; several good vineyards include Hinkelstein, Brückes, Kahlenberg, Kauzenberg. Kreuznach is also the Bereich name for a large quantity of regional wines.

**Krov.** M-S-R. 81 80 79 ★
Town on the Mosel, most famous for its regional wine of the Grosslage Krover Nacktarsch, which is quite ordinary wine.

**Liebfrauenberg.** Grosslage of the Rheinpfalz.

(W) **Liebfraumilch.** A semisweet QbA blended from Riesling, Sylvaner, or Müller-Thurgau grapes grown in various Rhine regions such as the Rheinhessen, Rheinpfalz, Nahe, and Rheingau. Touted as the wine that "goes with everything"—but that only if you like rather sweet wines with food. Can be balanced and pleasant on its own.

(W) **Lieser.** M-S-R. 81 80 79 78 77 76 75 ★★
Small village near Bernkastel producing good but somewhat heavy-ish wines for the Mittel-Mosel. Grosslagen: Beerenlay, Kurfürstlay. Good value.

(RW) **Lorch.** Rhg. 81 80 79 78 77 76 75 ★/★★
Town on the Rhine at the northern end of the Rheingau, though wines not as typical of Rheingau and many based on Sylvaner, Kerner, some red Spätburgunder. Best vineyards: Pfaffenwies, Bodental-Steinberg.

(W) **Marcobrun.** Rhg. 81 80 79 78 77 76 75 73 71 ★★★★
Outstanding vineyard at Erbach (part of it lies also in Hattenheim) producing Rieslings of fine bouquet and elegance, very long-lived.

**Markgraflerland, Bereich.** A lesser district in Baden. The Gutedel, or Chasselas, grape is widely grown for wines best consumed young; little exported.

**Matuschka-Greiffenklau, Graf.** Owners of the outstanding Rheingau vinegard, Schloss Vollrads near Winkel.

(W) **Maximin Grünhaus.** M-S-R. 81 80 79 78 77 76 75 73 71 ★★★/
★★★★
Acclaimed estate on the Ruwer at Mertesdorf producing QmP wines of great delicacy and distinction. Three superb vineyards: Herrenberg, Bruderberg, Abstberg.

**Mittelrhein.** See Principal Wine Regions.

**Mittel-Haardt.** Best section of the Rheinpfalz, including towns of Diedesheim, Forst, Rüppertsberg, Wachenheim, and Dürkheim.

**Morio Muskat.** One of the newer, early-ripening grape varieties, a crossing between Sylvaner and Pinot Blanc. Yields wines with flowery, muscat bouquet, hence its name. Most vineyards in the Rheinhessen and Rheinpfalz.

(W) **Moselblümchen.** Literally, "little flower of the Mosel," the Mosel's Liebfraumilch, a blended TAFELWEIN that may come from anywhere in the region. Generally sweet, some better than others, but rarely of very good value.

**Mosel-Saar-Ruwer.** See Principal Wine Regions.

**Moselle.** The name of the Mosel in France, where it originates. Commonly used as alternate (though not strictly correct) name for wines from the Mosel-Saar-Ruwer.

**Müller-Thurgau.** Productive grape variety yielding fruity, slightly low-acid wines, often attractive and agreeable, now more widely planted than Riesling, especially in Rheinhessen and Rheinpfalz.

ⓦ **Münster.** Actually two towns on the Nahe, Bad Münster and Münster-Sarmshein, producing average to very good wines.

ⓦ **Nackenheim.** Rhh. 81 80 79 78 77 76 75 71 ★/★ ★ ★
Prominent wine village adjoining Nierstein that is noted for some of best wines from the Rheinhessen. Leading vineyards: Rothenberg, Engelsberg. Grosslagen: Gutes Domtal, Spiegelberg.

**Nahe.** See Principal Wine Regions.

**Neumagen-Dhron.** See Dhron.

ⓦ **Niederhausen.** Na. 81 80 79 78 77 76 75 73 71 ★ ★/★ ★ ★
One of the Nahe's best wine towns with superb wines from vineyards such as Hermannsberg, Hermannshöhle, Pfingstweide, Steinberg. Good value.

ⓦ **Nierstein.** Rhh. 81 80 79 78 77 76 75 73 71 ★/★ ★ ★ +
Principal wine town of the Rheinhessen and very large vineyard areas. Produces superb wines from vineyards such as Hipping, Kranzberg, Glöck, Bildstock, Pettenthal, Ölberg, Heiligenbaum, Hölle, often shipped under Grosslage Niersteiner Spiegelberg. Without vineyard name the wine may be ordinary, as from Bereich Nierstein and Grosslage Niersteiner Gutes Domtal, both of which produce large quantities. Wines labeled Riesling are best.

ⓦ **Norheim.** Na. 81 80 79 78 77 76 75 73 71 ★ ★/★ ★ ★
A leading wine village on the Nahe; best wines from Kafels, Klosterberg, Delichen, good wines from Grosslage Burgweg.

ⓦ **Oberemmel.** M-S-R. 81 80 79 78 77 76 75 71 ★ ★ ★
Wine town on the Saar near Wiltingen; good Rieslings of QmP level, flowery but subtle. Best vineyards: Rosenberg, Hütte, Karlsberg, and Altenberg. Grosslage: Wiltinger Scharzberg.

ⓦ **Ockfen.** M-S-R. 81 80 79 78 77 76 75 71 ★ ★/★ ★ ★ ★
Outstanding wine village on the Saar. Steep vineyards of Riesling producing some of Germany's most distinguished and highly perfumed wines—particularly AUSLESEN, BA, TBA. Vineyards: Bockstein, Herrenberg, Geisberg, and Heppenstein. In lesser years (1977, 1973) can be too acid. Grosslage: Scharzberg.

ⓦ **Oestrich.** Rhg. 81 80 79 78 76 75 ★ ★
Large village in Rheingau producing good but generally not outstanding wines. Best vineyards are Lenchen, Doosberg, Klosterberg.

ⓦ **Oppenheim.** Rhh. 81 80 79 78 76 75 73 71 ★ ★/★ ★ ★
Wine town below Nierstein known for good to superior wines, softer than Niersteiners but generally more reliable in quality. Best vineyards: Kreuz, Sackträger, Daubhaus, Herrenberg, and others. Grosslages: Guldenmorgen and Krötenbrunnen.

ⓦ **Ortenau.** Bad. 81 80 79 78 77 76 ★ ★ +
One of the best Bereichs in Baden, producing soft pleasing wines. Good value.

**Palatinate.** Alternative name for the Rheinpfalz (English).

ⓦ **Piesport.** M-S-R. 81 80 79 78 77 76 75 71 ★ ★/★ ★ ★ ★
Important town on the Mittel-Mosel famous for very fragrant, fruity wines, the best of which carry vineyard name such as Goldtröpfchen, Gunterslay, Falkenberg, or Schubertslay. Wines labeled Piesporter Michelsberg (Grosslage) dependable. Good value.

**Prumm, J.J.** Owner of fine vineyards along the Mosel at Wehlen, Graach, and Bernkastel. Major owner of Wehlener Sonnenuhr.

ⓦ **Randersacker.** Frk. 81 80 79 78 77 76 75 ★ ★ +
One of the best wine-producing towns in Franconia, most of it dry.

ⓦ **Rauenthal.** Rhg. 81 80 79 78 77 76 75 73 71 ★ ★ ★
Village on the Rheingau behind Eltville; excellent wines known for spicy bouquet and fruit, generally outstanding in top vintages. Grosslage: Rauenthaler Steinmacher. Best vineyards: Baiken, Langenstück, Gehrn, Wulfen. Good value.

**BRAUNEBERGER JUFFER.** Brauneberg is one of the leading wine towns along the Mosel River ("er" is commonly suffixed to village or vineyard names on wine labels). Juffer is the name of its best vineyard. Vineyard names on German labels generally signify superior wines. *Qualitätswein mit Prädikat* is the term for the highest quality level in German wines, and the word *Auslese* indicates that the wine is naturally sweet, made from late-harvested, very ripe grapes. *Erzeugerabfüllung* means estate-bottled (see Glossary). *Amtliche Prüfungsnummer* is the wine's identity number registered with the government testing bureau.

**Rheingau, Rheinhessen, Rheinpfalz.** See Principal Wine Regions.

**Riesling.** Germany's best grape, giving wines of excellent fruit, bouquet, and breed.

Ⓦ **Rüdesheim.** Rhg. 81 80 79 78 77 76 75 73 71 ★★/★★★+
Popular town in the Rheingau noted for excellent wines from better vineyards like Bischofsberg, Drachenstein, Kirchenpfad; also those west of town with Berg attached to vineyard name: Berg Rottland, Berg Roseneck, Berg Schlossberg. Grosslage: Burweg. Not to be confused with Rüdesheim on the Nahe that produces lesser wines.

**Ruländer.** The Pinot Gris grape in Germany; produces fresh, attractive wines in Baden, but rather dull ones elsewhere.

Ⓦ **Ruppertsberg.** Rpf. 81 80 79 78 77 76 75 73 72 71 ★★/★★★+
One of the four leading wine towns along the Rheinpfalz; good wines from better vineyards owned by Bassermann-Jordan, Bürklin-Wolf and von Bühl. Good value.

**Ruwer.** See Principal Wine Regions.

**Saar.** See Principal Wine Regions.

**Scharzberg.** Grosslage lying partly in Wiltingen, partly in Oberemmel on the Saar River. Not as good as formerly.

Ⓦ **Scharzhofberg.** M-S-R. 81 80 79 78 77 76 75 73 71 ★★★/★★★★
Distinguished vineyard in Wiltingen, largely owned by family of Egon Müller, others. Known for supremely fragrant, full-flavored but elegant wines; those from great vintages very long-lived.

**Scheurebe.** New variety developed by crossing Sylvaner and Riesling, producing full-bodied, aromatic wines; planted mainly in Rheinhessen, Rheinpfalz, and Franconia.

Ⓦ **Schlossböckelheim.** Na. 81 80 79 78 77 76 75 ★★/★★★
The town with the best vineyards on the Nahe, such as Königsfels, Kupfergrube, Felsenberg. Also now a Bereich that includes several villages producing only average wines.

**Schloss Johannisberg.** See Johannisberg.

(W) **Schloss Reinhartshausen.** Rhg. 81 80 79 78 76 75 73 71 ★ ★ ★
Important estate in the Rheingau between Erbach and Hattenheim, including portions of vineyards in both towns.

(W) **Schloss Vollrads.** Rhg. 81 80 79 78 77 76 74 73 71 ★ ★ ★ / ★ ★ ★ ★
Perhaps the most famous of all German estates (at Winkel) and one of the largest, producing dependably good to incomparable QmP wines in top vintages.

**Schmitt Söhne.** Large firm with vineyards in many regions; average to good wines, several in the TROCKEN style.

**Schoppenwein.** Wine served in restaurants by the glass or in pitchers.

**Schwarzwald.** The Black Forest, in Baden.

**Sichel Söhne.** Large producer of quality German wines, including Blue Nun Liebfraumilch.

**Simmern, Langwerth von.** Owners of fine vineyards in Hattenheim, Eltville, Rauenthal.

**Sonnenuhr.** "Sun-dial." Several vineyards so-named, the best and most famous at Wehlen on the Mosel.

**Spätburgunder.** Name for the Pinot Noir grape in Germany.

**Spätlese.** See Glossary of Wine Terms.

**Staatsweingut.** State wine domain. There are state-owned vineyards in several leading wine regions, including the Rheingau (Steinberg vineyard), Rheinhessen, Mosel, and Nahe.

(W) **Steinberg.** Rhg. 81 80 79 78 77 76 75 73 71 ★ ★ ★ / ★ ★ ★ ★
Celebrated state-owned vineyard and estate at Hattenheim in the Rheingau. Wines range from good QbA to QmP wines of unsurpassed quality, fine and powerful, impressive depth.

**Steinwein.** Commonly used term for Bocksbeutel wines that are from Franconia.

**Südliche Weinstrasse.** Bereich name for southern Rheinpfalz.

**Sylvaner.** Grape variety of lesser distinction than Riesling but producing fresh, clean, often softer wine; leading grape for Franconia.

**Tafelwein.** See Glossary of Wine Terms.

**Thanisch, Dr.** Prominent vineyard owners in Bernkastel, including a portion of the famous Doktor vineyard.

(W) **Traben-Trarbach.** M-S-R. 81 80 79 78 77 76 75 ★ ★
Two towns on the Mosel across the river from one another that share good vineyards such as Schlossberg, Hühnerberg, Ungsberg. Grosslage: Schwarzlay. Good value.

(W) **Trier.** M-S-R. 81 80 79 78 77 76 75 71 ★ ★ ★
Famous town on the Mosel near its confluence with Ruwer. Several important wine firms headquartered here; appellation also includes vineyards of Avelsbach and Eitelsbach.

(W) **Trittenheim.** M-S-R. 81 80 79 78 77 76 75 ★ ★ +
Light, appealing wines, best when quite young and fresh except in great vintages. Best vineyards: Apotheke, Altarchen, and Felsenkopf. Grosslage: Michelsberg. Good value.

**Trocken.** See Glossary of Wine Terms.

**TbA.** See Glossary of Wine Terms.

(W) **Ürzig.** M.S.R. 81 80 79 78 77 76 75 71 ★ ★ / ★ ★ ★
Little village on the Mittel-Mosel known for spicy, intensely fruity wines. Best vineyard is Würzgarten. Grosslage: Ürziger Schwarzlay, average quality. Good value.

(W) **Wachenheim.** Rpf. 81 80 79 78 77 76 75 71 ★ ★ ★ / ★ ★ ★ ★
One of the four top wine towns along the Rheinpfalz known for exceptional Rieslings in superior vintages. Vineyards Gerümpel, Böhlig, Rechbächel, Goldbächel, and Altenburg produce lovely wines, similar to but lighter than Deidesheimer or Forster. Grosslagen: Mariengarten, Schenkenböhl, Schnepfenflug. Good value.

(W) **Waldrach.** M-S-R. 81 80 79 78 77 76 75 ★ ★ +
Wine village on the Ruwer producing light, attractive wines. Vineyards: Krone, Ehrenberg. Grosslage: Trierer Römerlay.

1975

Bereich
Johannisberg Riesling

QUALITÄTSWEIN · RHEINGAU

A. P. Nr. 1 234 567 8 78
Alc. 10% by Vol.                         1 PT. 7.5 Fl. Oz.

Abgefüllt für:
FREDERICK WILDMAN and SONS, GmbH
Bingen · Germany

70cle

**BEREICH JOHANNISBERGER.** *Bereich* is the regional term covering a broad area and numerous vineyards within a given wine district, in this case the whole of the Rheingau. Johannisberg is a principal town of the region, and the wine is made from the Riesling grape. Qualitätswein is the middle level of quality in German wines. Bereich Johannisberger wines are generally above average and represent good value.

(w) **Walluf.** Rhg. 81 80 79 77 76 75 73 ★ ★ +
Previously Nieder-Walluf and Ober-Walluf, two villages now combined. Good Rieslings, generally less fine than best Rheingau.

(w) **Wehlen.** M-S-R. 81 80 79 78 77 76 75 71 ★ ★ ★/★ ★ ★ ★
Wine village on the Mittel-Mosel near Bernkastel with equally fine vineyards, many owned by J.J. Prum family. Sonnenuhr is best, followed by Klosterberg, Nonnenberg. Grosslage: Münzlay.

(w) **Wiltingen.** M-S-R. 81 80 79 78 77 76 75 71 ★ ★/★ ★ ★ ★
Best wine village on the Saar (and one of Germany's best altogether) from some of the steepest and best vineyards in Germany, including Scharzhofberger. Austere, complex, exceptional wines in good vintages, steely-edged in poor ones. Other good vineyards: Braune Kupp, Braunfels, Klosterberg. Grosslage: Scharzberg. Fair to good.

(w) **Winkel.** Rhg. 81 80 79 78 77 76 75 73 71 ★ ★ ★/★ ★ ★ ★
Home of Schloss Vollrads, Rheingau's most famous estate, but also generally superior wines. Top vineyards include Hasensprung, Jesuitengarten, Gutenberg, Schlossberg, and Bienengarten.

(w) **Wintrich.** M-S-R. 81 80 79 78 77 76 75 ★ ★ +
Lesser village along the Mosel producing light, fragrant, attractive wines, the best from Riesling. Grosslage: Kurfürstlay.

**Winzergenossenschaft.** Wine growers' cooperative. Also known as *Winzerverein.*

(w) **Worms.** Rhh. 81 80 79 78 77 76 75 ★ ★
Lesser town in the Rheinhessen, site of Liebfrauenstift vineyard, thought to be origin of name Liebfraumilch, of which a great deal is produced in the Hessen.

(w) **Württemburg.** Dry wines of average to good quality produced along the Neckar River around Stuttgart.

(w) **Würzburg.** Frk. 81 80 79 78 77 76 75 ★ ★ ★/★ ★ ★
Famous for beer as well as wine in traditional Bocksbeutel, called "Würzberger Stein." Good, flavorful wines from Riesling and Sylvaner mostly; among Germany's driest and good with food. Top vineyards: Stein, also Innere Leiste, Abtsleite, and Pfaffenberg.

(w) **Zell.** M-S-R. 81 80 79 ★/★ ★

Village on the Mosel best known for its wine, Zeller Schwarze Katz, the "Black Cat of Zell." More famous than good, but often agreeable, usually inexpensive. Also the name for the Grosslage. Zell is the Bereich.

(w) **Zeltingen.** M-S-R. 81 80 79 78 77 76 75 71 ★ ★/★ ★ ★ ★

One of the Mosel's most reputable wine villages (includes also village of Rachtig) and the largest on the Mittel-Mosel. Best wines comparable to nearby Wehlen; top vineyards: Sonnenuhr, Schlossberg, Himmelreich, Deutschherrenberg. Grosslage: Münzlay, also good, but simple regional Zeltingers are rather ordinary.

# THE WINES OF SPAIN & PORTUGAL

T he best wines of Spain and Portugal are the famous fortified wines—Sherry, Port, and Madeira—and these are treated in the chapter on "Fortified Wines." Spain and Portugal produce large quantities of red, white, and rosé table wines. Spain is, after Italy and France, the largest producer of wine in the world. Until recently, old-fashioned and often primitive techniques in some cases produced wines of mostly indifferent quality, particularly among white wines. But there have always been exceptions, however, notably among the reds, such as the Riojas of Spain.

The Rioja of northern Spain is an area of over 100,000 acres that often produces more than two million cases of wine, predominantly red produced in the style of traditional red Bordeaux. This is more than just coincidence, for when the vine pest phylloxera wiped out vineyards in Bordeaux in the 1880s, many Bordeaux vintners came to Rioja to start again. Though not all of them stayed, their influence on viticulture, winemaking techniques, and aging in wood remained and the region still has strong connection with Bordeaux today. Most Rioja white wines were usually heavy in character and often spent so long in wood that they lacked freshness. The use of new stainless steel fermenters and other modern equipment is bringing about improvements. Rioja wines are excellent value for the wine drinker, priced generally between $4 and $7. The best Riojas are labeled Reserva.

Other good wines are produced in Catalonia, particularly in the Panadés region near Barcelona. Torres is the leading producer in this region.

Portugal's fresh and lively rosés are widest known, but she also produces sound and agreeable red and white wines, particularly the sturdy Dão among reds and the very young whites known as *vinho verde*. Portuguese wines are becoming more popular because the better ones are such bargains in the current wine market of escalating prices.

## PRINCIPAL WINE REGIONS OF SPAIN

**Andalusia** (And.)  Southwestern coastal region of Spain best known for the fortified wines from Jerez de la Frontera—Sherry. Another fortified wine, Malaga, is produced in the coastal city of that name.

**Catalonia** (Cat.)  Northern Mediterranean region near Barcelona. Some very good reds produced around Tarragona and Panadés; producers of Spain's best sparkling wines also located in this region.

**La Mancha** (L.M.)  Large region in central Spain (land of Don Quixote) producing mostly bulk table wines of ordinary quality and some popular fruity and agreeable reds and whites from the Valdepeñas district.

**Rioja** (Rio.)   Spain's most important region for table wines, named for the Rio Oja, a tributary of the Rio Ebro that runs practically the entire length of the region. It is divided into three distinct sections: Rioja Alta, or upper Rioja, whose capital is Haro; Rioja Alavesa (also known as Alava), which produces 65 percent of total production and is considered the best; and Rioja Baja, or lower Rioja, to the east of the other two, which produces coarser, more alcoholic wines.

# PRINCIPAL WINE REGIONS OF PORTUGAL

**Alto Douro** (A.D.)   The upper Douro Valley in northern Portugal where steep, terraced vineyards supply the grapes for Port. (See chapter on "Fortified Wines.") The city of Oporto gave Port its name, and its suburb, Vila Nova de Gaia, is where most of the shipping firms have their warehouses, or lodges.

**Madeira** (Mad.)   Island in the Atlantic nearly 400 miles off the coast of Morocco, producing fortified Madeira wines (see chapter on "Fortified Wines") such as Bual, Sercial, and Malmsey.

Other wine-growing regions are scattered through Portugal from the north to the Algarve (Alg.), producing mostly everyday table wines of agreeable quality. The best wines are often named for the region where they are grown—Vinho Verde (V.V.); Dão; Colares (Col.); Ribatejo (Rib.); and Bucelas (Buc.); for example—and will be treated in the Wine Guide: Portugal.

THE WINE REGIONS OF **SPAIN & PORTUGAL**

# WINE GUIDE: SPAIN

(RW) **Age Bodegas.** Rio. ★ ★ ★
Producer of good, light- to medium-bodied red wines under the well-known label Siglo; the bottles wrapped in burlap bags. Good value.

(W) **Alella.** Cat. ★ ★
White wine from the village of Alella near Barcelona, rather sweet though one of the most popular Catalonian whites.

(R) **Alicante.** City on the Costa Blanca south of Valencia and the name for locally produced wines, mostly sweet red, some full-bodied and dry.

(RW) **Berberana.** Rio. ★ ★ ★
Firm in Logroño; label names to look for include Carta de Plata, Carta de Oro, and Gran Reservas. Good value.

(RW) **Bodegas Bilbainas.** Rio. ★ ★ ★
A leading Rioja producer, Viña Pomal red, Brillante rosé, and white wines, Cepa de Oro (dry). Good value.

(3) **Campo Burgo.** Rio. ★ ★ ★
Principal brand names for the red, white, and rosé wines of leading Rioja producer in Alfaro Rioja Baja de la Torre y Lapuerta. Good value.

(3) **Campo Viejo de Savin.** Rio. ★ ★
Producer in Logroño whose principal wines are exported under the Campo Viejo label; very good RESERVAS.

**Clarete.** Term used for light red wine; also brand name for a light Rioja by Cune.

(W) **Codorniu.** Cat. ★ ★ ★
Producer of good sparkling wine by the traditional French *méthode champenoise* in Catalonia at San Sadurnyì de Noya; largest such facility in the world. Blanc de Blancs is one of their best.

(RW) **Compannia Vinícola del Norte de Espana (CVNE).** Rio. ★ ★ ★
A leading producer of the Rioja Alta with several good brands, Cune Clarete and Vina Real Reservas, among the imperial reds, and the dry white Monopole. Good value.

(R) **Coronas.** Cat. ★ ★/★ ★ ★
Light but firm dry red from the Torres firm in Catalonia. Gran Coronas Reserva, made with a percentage of Cabernet Sauvignon and aged in oak cask, is more substantial and ages well. Good value.

(R) **Domecq Domain.** Rio. ★ ★
Rioja produced by Pedro Domecq, the famous Sherry and Brandy house in Jerez. Red now labeled Privilegio del Rey.

**Don Jacobo.** Brand name for the Rioja wines of Bodegas Corral, which is located in Logroño.

(RW) **Faustino Martinez.** Rio. ★ ★
Producer known mainly for reds labeled Faustino I, Faustino V, VII. Good value, particularly among jug wines.

(3) **Federico Paternina.** Rio. ★ ★ ★
Leading producer of the upper Rioja. Banda Azul is a popular light red, Banda Dorada a white, but the most impressive are Gran Reserva and Vina Vial, which are aged longer in wood and can be quite firm and full-bodied. Good value.

**Franco-Españolas.** Rioja producer; recommended labels are the red Sin Rival and white Diamante.

(W) **Freixenet.** Cat. ★ ★
Large producer of sparkling wines made by the traditional *méthode champenoise,* under such labels as Carta Nevada Brut or Semi-Secco, Cordon Negro Brut and Brut Nature.

(RW) **Jean Leon.** Cat. ★ ★ ★
Proprietor of excellent vineyards in the Panadés region of Catalonia (as well as owner of La Scala restaurant in Los Angeles). Pioneer producer of Chardonnay and Cabernet Sauvignon in Spain; the Cabernet is especially interesting.

# GLOSSARY OF WINE TERMS: SPAIN

**Año.** *Year. 4°, 6° indicates the age of the wine when bottled.*
**Blanco.** *White.*
**Bodega.** *Storage warehouse or above-ground "cellar"; in Rioja refers to the entire wine-producing facility; elsewhere in Spain, the name for a little wine shop.*
**Cosecha.** *Vintage, or harvest.*
**Criado y embotellado por. . . .** Phrase meaning "grown and bottled by. . . ."
**Dulce.** *Sweet.*
**Embotellado de origen.** *Estate-bottled. Wine bottled on the property where the grapes were grown.*
**Espumoso.** *Sparkling.*
**Medio-seco.** *Semidry.*
**Reserva.** *Term for best wines, set aside for longer aging. In Rioja, Reservas must spend two years in wood at minimum.*
**Rosao.** *Rosé.*
**Seco.** *Dry.*
**Tinto.** *Red.*
**Vendimia.** *Vintage, harvest.*
**Viño.** *Vineyard.*
**Vino de mesa.** *Table wine.*

**La Rioja Alta.** Rio. ★ ★ ★
Producer of very good Riojas such as Viña Ardanza and several well-aged RESERVAS.

**López de Heredia.** Rio. ★ ★ ★
One of the oldest and most reputable of Rioja producers in Haro, whose Viña Tondonia reds and whites are widely known and very popular. Good value.

**Lan, Bodegas.** Rio. ★ ★ / ★ ★ ★
New, large producer in the Rioja Alta making good reds, fresh whites, and rosés.

**Málaga.** See chapter on "Fortified Wines."

**Mallorca.** This Mediterranean island produces a few interesting reds mostly consumed locally.

**Marqués de Cáceres.** Rio. ★ ★ ★
One of the newer producers in Rioja Alta using modern techniques and generally less aging in wood. Very good RESERVA. A line of inexpensive wines is marketed under the Rivarey label. Good value.

**Marqués de Murrieta.** Rio. ★ ★ ★
One of the oldest and best Rioja producers. Distinctive reds, particularly the Reserva and Castillo Ygay. Murrieta whites have unique, intriguing flavor as well.

**Marqués de Riscal.** Rio. ★ ★ ★
Another of Rioja's most reputable producers, known for its deep, earthy reds aged long periods in oak, becoming rather elegant with time, like a well-aged Bordeaux.

**Montilla-Moriles.** And. ★ ★ ★
Superb, unusually full-bodied wine from two villages in Andalusia, south of Cordoba. Often reaches 14 to 17% alcohol, although it is not fortified; not to be confused with Sherry, fortified wines, and Amontillado.

**CUNE IMPERIAL GRAN RESERVA.** A red wine from one of the leading Rioja producers. As a *Reserva*, it is one of the best wines from this firm and has received longer aging in oak casks than regular Riojan reds that normally spend 2 or 3 years in oak. This wine is dry, smooth and shows considerable complexity that will continue to evolve in bottle over the next few years. 1970 is one of the best vintages for Rioja.

Ⓡ **Muga.** Red wine from producer of that name in the Rioja Alava; th[e] RESERVA is known as Prado Enea.

Ⓡⓦ **Olarras.** Rio. ★ ★ +
New, forward-looking BODEGA in Logroño, styling its wines after Bo[r]deaux. Most successful wines are the Cerro Anon, Tinto Riserva, an[d] Olarra Reservas. The whites and rosés are dry and fresh. Good value.

Ⓡⓦ **Palacio.** Large producer in the Rioja Alavesa. Best values are the reds[,] Nobella, and Glorioso.

**Panadés** (also Penedés). Specified region near Barcelona producing goo[d] red wines, including some made from Cabernet Sauvignon. Leadin[g] town is Vilafranca del Panadés.

Ⓡ **Penafiel.** L.M. ★ ★
Robust red wine from Valdepenñas, made near Valladolid southwest [of] Rioja, on the River Duero.

Ⓡⓦ **Priorato.** Cat. ★/★ ★ +
Sturdy, dark red wine from Tarragona, one of Barcelona's better tabl[e] wines, also a sweet, darkly white fortified wine.

Ⓡⓦ **Rioja Santiago.** Rio. ★/★ ★
Best known for Yago Santgria, but also a good Rioja Reserva known a[s] Yago Condal.

Ⓦ **Rueda.** White wines of high alcohol (up to 17%) that develop Sherry-lik[e] aromas from a special yeast (flor) that forms as the wine ferment[s] produced near Valladolid in Old Castile.

ⓡ **Sangre de Toro.** Cat. ★ ★
  Literally, "blood of the bull." Sturdy reds from the town of Toro in Catalonia, and the brand name for pleasant, everyday reds from the firm of Torres.

**Sangria.** Red wine punch (white wine occasionally used) made by adding citrus fruits, sugar, and brandy to the wine; serve chilled.

ⓡ **Sarria, Seniorio de.** Navarra ★ ★ +
  Reputable producer near Pamplona of balanced, fruity, occasionally elegant reds. Similar in style to Riojas.

**Torres.** Family-owned firm in Panadés making reds and whites, especially Gran Coronas Reservas, Gran Sangre de Toro, and Viña Sol.

ⓡ **Vega Sicilia.** Old Castile ★ ★ ★
  Excellent, long-lived, and very rare Spanish red wine produced near Valladolid: worth seeking out when in the area.

ⓡⱳ **Viña del Oja.** Rio. ★ ★
  Leading brand name for Rioja Producer in Rioja Alavesa, Vizcaina Rojas. RESERVAS appear under the Sommelier label.

ⓦ **Viña Sol.** Cat. ★ ★ +
  Fresh, dry white made by the Torres firm of Tarragona. Gran Viña Sol has more body and fullness.

# WINE GUIDE: PORTUGAL

**Algarve.** Southern coast of Portugal producing mostly ordinary table wines, often unbottled and referred to as *vinhos de consumo.*

**Aveleda.** Estate in northern Portugal producing one of the best-known VINHOS VERDES.

**Avelar.** Brand name for average to good red, white, and rosé wines of Caves Velhas.

**Bual,** See chapter on "Fortified Wines."

ⓦ **Bucelas.** Buc. ★ ★ ★
  Light, fragrant, dry white wines from a delimited area 25 kilometers north of Lisbon, often only 11% alcohol, very pleasant drinking.

ⓦ **Carcavelos.** Carcavelos ★ ★ ★
  Rich and generous sweet white wine, often reaching between 18 and 20% alcohol. Chilled, it makes a fine apéritif wine.

ⓡ **Cartaxo.** Rib. ★ ★ ★
  Popular red table wine from the Ribatejo region northeast of Lisbon, often the carafe wine in the city's restaurants.

ⓢ **Caves Aliança.** One of Portugal's largest wine companies, producing range of wines from many of the better regions, including Dão, Vinho Verde (Casal Mendes), rosé.

ⓦ **Casal Mendes.** V.V. ★ ★ +
  The VINHO VERDE produced by Caves Aliança; fresh, dry, and one of the best of the "green wines."

ⓦ **Casal Garcia.** One of the most popular and largest selling VINHOS VERDES from Sogrape, Portugal's largest producer.

ⓢ **Casaleiro.** Brand name for the wines produced by Caves Dom Teodosio, such as rosés, Dão, and VINHO VERDE.

ⓡⱳ **Cepa Velha.** Proprietary name for the wines of one of Portugal's quality producers, Vinhos de Monçao, among them the very good VINHO VERDE Alvarinho.

(R) **Colares.** Col. ★ ★

Mountainous region near Sintra to the west of Lisbon; formerly produced Portugal's most esteemed red wine, full-bodied and long-lived. Most is made much lighter today but occasionally older, impressive wines can be found; they are worth looking for.

(RW) **Dão.** Dão ★ ★/★ ★ ★

Portugal's best-known red wine, produced in north-central region. Robust, round, occasionally harsh when young but generally ages well. Good value. Full-bodied whites are also produced to lesser extent.

---

# GLOSSARY OF WINE TERMS: PORTUGAL

**Adega.** *Winery, or storage cellars.*
**Branco.** *White.*
**Colheita.** *Vintage.*
**Doce.** *Sweet.*
**Espumante.** *Sparkling.*
**Garrafeira.** *Producer's "private stock," or best wines.*
**Madura.** *Mature, used to distinguish regular table wines from the young "green wines,"* vinhos verdes.
**Quinta.** *Farm or estate.*
**Rosado, rosario.** *Rosé*
**Seco.** *Dry.*
**Selo de guarantita.** *Seal of guaranteed origin for wines from demarcated regions.*
**Tinto.** *Red.*
**Vinho verde.** *"Green," or young wine.*

---

(R) **Douro.**A.D. ★ ★

The river region of the north famous for Port but also the name for local table wines of ordinary to good quality.

(RO) **Faisca.** A best-selling sweetish sparking rosé from the large producer J. M. de Fonseca.

(R) **Grao Vasco.** Dão ★ ★ +

Widely known brand name for the very good Dão of Sogrape. Good value.

**Green wine (vinho verde).** Portugal's famous and unique young wines, mostly white, from grapes picked at earliest ripeness when acidity is high. Refreshing, giving a slight prickle on the tongue, and fragile; often delightful and should be consumed as young as possible. The whites are superior to red or rosé. All should be well-chilled.

**Lagosta.** Brand name for line of wines produced by Real Companhia Vinícola do Norte de Portugal. Widely known, generally good.

(RO) **Lancers.** One of Portugal's most popular carbonated rosés. This wine is sold worldwide.

**Malmsey.** See chapter on "Fortified Wines."

(RO) **Mateus.** Brand name for Sogrape's carbonated rosé and white wines. Mateus Rosé is one of the largest-selling wines in the United States.

(W) **Moscatel de Setúbal** ★ ★/★ ★ ★

Very good sweet muscat wines made at Setúbal, southeast of Lisbon. Two versions are made: a 6-year-old that is lightly sweet, fresh and well-balanced, and a 25-year-old wine that is much darker and more concentrated; both reach 18% alcohol.

(R) **Perequita.** Rib. ★ ★ ★

Robust red from the Perequita grape made by the firm of J. M. Fonseca. A very agreeable red. Good value.

**Ribatejo.** Growing region along the Tagus River in cental Portugal producing better than average red wines and some whites.

**Ribeiro & Irmao.** A leading producer of table wines, including Ribeiros, a sweet white VINHO VERDE.

**Sercial.** Seè chapter on "Fortified Wines."

**Serra & Sons.** Producer of quality table wines under the brand names of Justina and Serra.

(R) **Serradayres.** Rib. ★ ★

A good, solid drinkable red from the Ribatejo region in central Portugal. Good value.

**Sogrape.** Sociedad Comercial dos Vinhos de Mesa de Portugal, Portugal's largest wine company owned by the Guedes family. Some of its best include the VINHO VERDES Casal Garcia, Aveleda, Mateus, and Dão.

(R) **Terras Altas.** Dão ★ ★ +

Sound and reliable Dão from the firm of J. M. Fonseca. Good value.

(RO) **Villa Real.** A village north of the Douro and the wines from surrounding area, mostly light reds and a good quantity of rosé.

(W) **Vinhos Verdes.** The delimited region between the Minho and upper Douro rivers; the region where Portugal's famous "green wine" (VINHO VERDE) is made.

# THE WINES OF AUSTRIA

**A**ustria's wine industry has recently geared up for much wider export, and more of her pleasant, gentle, German-style white wines (a few reds of lesser quantity and quality are produced) are appearing in international markets. They range from dry and lively to quite sweet and luscious, using German-quality designations that indicate degree of natural sweetness in the wines: Kabinett; Spätlese; Auslese; Beerenauslese (BA); and Trockenbeerenauslese (TBA). See Glossary of Wine Terms in "The Wines of Germany."

The better wines for export come from the eastern provinces of Lower Austria (Wachau, Krems, and Langenlois) and Burgenland. Most wine labels bear the name of the grape variety, such as Gruner Veltliner, Rheinriesling, and Blaufrankisch, and usually names derived from the village of origin, such as Kremser, Ruster, and Gumpoldskirchener ("er" is always added to the town name).

Austria is also known for very fresh, young wines called *heurigen*, which are sold in cafes and taverns in Vienna and its suburbs.

## WINE GUIDE

ⓦ **Apetlon.** Burgenland ★ ★
One of the better wine villages on the shores of the Neusiedlersee in Seewinkel; agreeable dry whites, some very good sweet wines of Spätlese and Auslese level. Good value.

**Ausbruch.** An Austrian term for very sweet, rich wines that fall between the BA and TBA levels; the best are from Rust.

ⓦ **Baden.** Vienna ★/★ ★ ★
Town and surrounding region below Vienna producing spicy, fresh whites, some quite pleasant, especially those of Gumpoldskirchen.

**Blauburgunder.** Pinot Noir grape; also called Spätburgunder.

**Blaufrankisch.** Austria's name for a Gamay-like red grape, giving dry, fruity wines.

**Bouvier.** Native white grape variety producing soft, fragrant white wines.

**Burgenland.** One of the principal wine-producing regions in eastern Austria near Hungary with vineyards surrounding the large, shallow Lake Neusiedl (Neusiedlersee); produces some of Austria's greatest wines, including sweet noble Auslese, Ausbruch, and TBA. Most famous wine center: Rust.

ⓦ **Durnstein.** Wachau ★ ★ / ★ ★ ★

A leading village of the Wachau district west of Vienna along the Danube, known for fresh and charming white wines from mostly Gruner Veltliner and Rheinriesling. Good value.

🄬 **Eisenstadt.** Burgenland ★ ★ / ★ ★ ★

Important wine village in foothills above Neusiedlersee; site of the famed Esterhazy firm.

**Esterhazy.** Old Austrian family with excellent estates in Burgenland producing some of Austria's finest wines; headquartered in Eisenstadt.

ⓦ **Grinzing.** Vienna ★ ★ +

Vienna's suburb, famous for its lively young *heurige* wines sold in restaurant wine gardens.

ⓦ **Grüner Veltliner.** White wine grape used for Austria's most typical wines—young, fresh, fruity, often with a spicy zest and stylish appeal. Best when young, quite young.

ⓦ **Gumpoldskirchen.** Vienna ★ ★ / ★ ★ ★

One of Austria's most charming wine villages near Vienna, producing delightful whites from mostly Rotgipfler and Spätrot grapes. Good value.

**Heurige.** Young wines sold in taverns (also called *heurige*)following the vintage.

🄬 **Kloch.** Steiermark ★ ★

Best-known wine village of the southernmost province, producing some good Traminer.

🄬 **Klosterneuberg.** Vienna ★ ★ +

Famous monastery and town above Vienna that is now a viticultural school and still produces wines, such as Klostergarten, a soft, dry red. Good value.

ⓦ **Krems.** Wachau ★ / ★ ★ ★

Leading wine town of the Wachau district along the Danube west of Vienna, with wines mostly from Grüner Veltliner, Rheinriesling. Good value.

**Langenlois.** Town west of Vienna giving its name to surrounding area, producing some good whites from Grüner Veltliner and some unassuming reds.

**Lenz Moser.** Austria's largest private proprietor and a strong influence on the upgrading of Austrian wines. Good wines from several regions, including Krems, Apetlon; also brands such as Schluck, Malteser, Blue Danube.

🄬 **Mörbisch.** Burgenland ★ / ★ ★ ★

One of the leading wine towns of Burgenland; good, sweet wines, light but ordinary reds.

**Müller-Thurgau.** White wine grape yielding mild but fragrant wines.

**Muscat Ottonel.** A muscat variety common to eastern Europe; mostly sweet wines.

**Neuberger.** White grape variety used in some wines from Krems, Langenlois, Gumpoldskirchen, and sections of Burgenland.

**Neusiedlersee.** Large lake in Burgenland affecting the climate of surrounding vineyards; mists off the lake during harvest foster growth of the noble mold *Botrytis cinerea* for splendid sweet wines.

ⓦ **Nussdorf.** Vienna ★ ★

One of Vienna's suburbs popular for the young *heurige* wines.

🄬 **Oggau.** Burgenland ★ ★ / ★ ★ ★

Wine village near Rust on the Neusiedlersee producing outstanding Ausbruch and other sweet wines. Good value.

**Pinot Blanc.** Also known as Weissburgunder in Austria, a white variety producing dry, crisp, rather full-bodied wines, occasionally made sweet as impressive Ausbruch, Beeren, and TBA.

(W) **Podersdorf.** Burgenland ★/★ ★ ★

Wine village east of Lake Neusiedl in Burgenland that produces average dry whites but fine, sweet BAs and TBAs. Good value.

**Portugieser (Blau Portugieser).** A red wine grape producing dark, medium-bodied, rather bland wines.

(R) **Pottlesdorf.** Burgenland ★ ★

One of the few communities known in Austria for its red wines, light, drinkable quality.

**Qualitätswein.** Wine that has passed official examination for meeting specified standards of quality, noted on a seal that is affixed to the neck of the bottle.

**Retz.** One of the growing regions of Lower Austria just north of Krems and Langenlois, important for its white wines, mostly light, dry Grüner Veltliner or Müller-Thurgau.

**Rheinriesling.** The true German Riesling grape, not widely grown; the name Riesling by itself on a label usually refers to a quite different strain of the variety developed in Italy, sometimes called Welschriesling.

# HEURIGEN WINES

One of the most delightful aspects of Viennese life is the tradition of drinking Heurigen, or the new wines from the previous vintage. During spring and summer—sometimes drifting well into autumn— the wine taverns (also called *Heurigen*) of Vienna and suburbs such as Grinzing resound with the lilting music of zithers and violins. The gardens of each tavern are strung with lanterns and filled each evening by the local citizenry who come to enjoy wholesome food and quaff the fresh, fruity, slightly green and spritzy white wines—by the steinful or the pitcherful. Many of these young wines are too light and fragile to withstand travel; you must travel to Vienna to experience their special charm.

**Rotgipfler.** White wine grape used mainly in the wines of Gumpoldskirchen to give zestful, full-flavored fruity wines; often conmbined with another white grape such as Spätrot or Zierfandler.

**Ruländer.** White grape, also known as Pinot Gris, used in making soft whites, mostly in Styria.

(W) **Rust.** Burgenland ★/★ ★ ★

One of Austria's leading wine towns on Lake Neusiedl, producing some of her most outstanding sweet white wines, especially Ausbruch, a Rust specialty; fine Auslese also. Good value.

**St. Laurent.** Richly colored red wine grape with pronounced flowery fruity aroma.

(W) **Schloss Grafenegg.** Krems ★ ★/★ ★ ★

Wines from this well-known estate owned by the Metternich family are sound, reputable-quality dry whites, with some quite fine Auslese, mainly from Gruner Veltliner and Rheinriesling.

(W) **Schluck.** Wachau ★ ★

Fresh, dry white produced in quantity in the Wachau from the Welschriesling grape, best when quite young. Good value.

**Seewinkel.** Dry, sandy region east of Lake Neusiedl making mostly mild whites; name means "sea corner."

**Spätrot.** White grape variety often used in conjunction with Rotgipler to make the popular Gumpoldskirchener.

**Spitzenwein.** Term used to refer to the better table wines, higher level than Tischwein.

**Steiermark.** Southernmost growing region in Austria, known also as Styria. Mostly mild, pleasant wines, some good flavorful Traminer. Leading wine town is Kloch.

(w) **Thallern.** Vienna ★ ★ +

Small wine village near Gumpoldskirchen making similar wine; also famed for its old church and monastery, Heiligenstift. Good value.

**Tischwein.** Everyday table wine, below the level of Spitzenwein.

(RW) **Traiskirchen.** Vienna ★ ★

Another of the wine villages near Gumpoldskirchen that produces lively, spicy wines, mostly white and best when young.

**Veltliner.** See Grüner Veltliner.

**Vienna.** Austria's capital and an important wine center, with vines surrounding and within the city and its suburbs; famous for young wines of the most recent vintage sold by glass or pitcher in the popular and numerous *heurigen*, or wine taverns.

(RW) **Vöslau, Bad.** Baden ★ ★

Resort town south of Vienna and below the town of Baden producing dark, soft, agreeable reds, some quite full-bodied, made from Portuguesier and Blaufränkisch, and a lesser amount of whites.

**Wachau.** One of Austria's most famous wine districts along the Danube west of Vienna, producing good whites from Grüner Veltliner and Rheinriesling, among Austria's best. Leading wine towns: Durnstein, Loiben, Stein, Weissenkirchen, and Krems on its eastern edge.

**Weinviertel.** "Wine quarter," a large growing region north of Vienna toward the Czech border, including towns of Retz, Falkenstein, Mailberg, Eggenburg, and others; known mostly for whites.

**Weissburgunder.** Pinot Blanc grape.

**Welschriesling.** A lesser strain of Riesling developed in Italy yielding light white wines without the finesse of true German Riesling.

**Wien.** Vienna.

**Zierfändler.** Zestful white grape (also known as Spätrot) used in Gumpoldskirchener; native to Austria.

# THE WINES OF SWITZERLAND

S witzerland produces mostly dry white wines and some light to medium-bodied reds. The best of both have a briskness about them that is often as bracing as the alpine air of the surrounding countryside. The Swiss drink a lot of wine and import far more than they produce (about 28 million gallons) with only limited quantities available for export.

The principal wine-producing cantons, or districts, are the Valais along the Rhône River Valley in the south, the Vaud above Lake Geneva, and the slopes above Lake Neuchatel. Whites are made mostly from the lesser Chasselas grape that here gives crisp, dry wines known as Fendant, Dorin, or Neuchatel. Reds are made from Pinot Noir or Gamay, often a blend of the two; Ticino, the section bordering Italy to the southeast, produces Merlot. Wines are also made in the northern and eastern parts of Switzerland bordering Germany and Austria but are rarely seen outside the region.

## WINE GUIDE

ⓦ **Aigle.** Vaud ★ ★
  Town in the Chablais region east of Lake Geneva producing good dry whites known as Dorin.

**Amigne.** Old white grape of the Valais making pleasantly scented but rather heavy, dry white wines.

**Arvine.** Another old-time white of the Valais but produces dry wines rather livelier than Amigne.

**Chablais.** Region between the Vaud and Valais cantons south of Lake Geneva. Best wines are Dorin from villages of Aigle, Bex, Yvorne.

**Chasselas.** Leading white grape of Switzerland known by different names such as Dorin (the Vaud); Fendant (the Valais); and Neuchatel.

ⓡ **Cortaillod.** Neuchatel ★ ★
  Light red from the village of Cortaillod made from Pinot Noir; also a pale rosé made here called Oeil de Perdrix.

ⓦ **Dezaley.** Vaud ★ ★ ★
  Good full-fruited Dorin from the slopes of Lavaux between Lausanne and Montreux, one of Switzerland's best whites.

ⓡ **Dole.** Valais ★ ★ +
  Usually considered Switzerland's best red, produced from Pinot Noir

with some Gamay blended in; medium but sometimes full-bodied and then powerful with rich fruit and fragrance.

(W) **Dorin.** Vaud ★/★ ★ ★

The name by which white wines from the Chasselas are known in the canton of Vaud; full, dry, fruity but generally lighter than the Fendant of Valais.

(W) **Ermitage.** Valais ★ ★

Sturdy, flavorful white wine that is made from the minor grape variety Marsanne.

(W) **Fendant.** Valais ★/★ ★ ★

Dry whites from the Chasselas grape from the Rhône River Valley. Fendant de Sion (wine center of the Valais) or Mont d'Or are often Switzerland's most potent, flavorful white wines.

(W) **Johannisberg.** Fragrant, soft white from Sylvaner or Müller-Thurgau in the Valais.

**Malvoisie.** Sweet, perfumed dessert wine from the Valais made from ripe Pinot Gris.

**Merlot.** Red grape of Bordeaux fame used to make reds in Ticino, the Italian-speaking section of Switzerland. The best is labeled Viti.

(3) **Neuchatel.** Neuchatel ★/★ ★ ★

Reds and rosés from Pinot Noir; dry whites from the Chasselas, some sparkling or semisparkling. They are referred to as "the star wines of Switzerland."

**Nostrano.** Red *vin ordinaire* of Ticino.

(RO) **Oeil de Perdrix.** Neuchatel ★ ★

The light rosé from Pinot Noir from around Lake Neuchatel; name means "eye of the partridge" and refers to the wine's color.

**Perlan.** Another name for the Chasselas grape for the dry white wines of the Mandement district west of Geneva.

(W) **St.-Saphorin.** Vaud ★ ★

Crisp dry white from the Lavaux area.

(R) **Salvagnin.** Vaud ★ ★

Dry reds from the slopes overlooking Lake Geneva, made from Pinot Noir and/or Gamay; lighter than Dole of the Valais.

**Spätburgunder.** Name for the Pinot Noir red grape in Germany and Switzerland; Blauburgunder is occasionally used also.

**Ticino.** Southeastern section of Switzerland bordering Italy, known mostly for reds: Merlot, Viti, Nostrano.

**Valais.** One of Switzerland's most important wine regions along the Rhône River Valley between the cities of Brig and Martigny. Known mostly for dry white Fendant and red Dole, both among the country's best wines.

**Vaud.** Largest wine region in Switzerland bordering northern shores of Lake Geneva with vineyards on steep slopes above Lausanne and Vevey. The dry white Dorin is its best wine; some dry reds (Salvagnin) also made.

(R) **Viti.** Ticino ★ ★ +

Name for the best quality Merlot of the Italian-speaking Ticino region.

(W) **Yvorne.** Vaud ★ ★ ★

Firm, full-bodied white wines from the village of Yvorne in the Chablais region east of Lake Geneva.

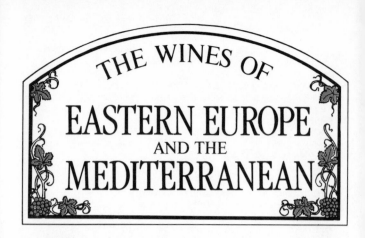

# THE WINES OF
# EASTERN EUROPE
## AND THE
# MEDITERRANEAN

T he wines of eastern Europe that we are most likely to see come from Hungary, Romania, Bulgaria, and Yugoslavia, all of whom produce tremendous quantities of wine, and have done so for centuries. Relatively few wines are exported to the West. But those that are in many cases represent each country's best. Because of expanded plantings of Cabernet Sauvignon and some Pinot Noir, red wines seem to be the most interesting. The labels, with some exceptions as noted, generally show place name and grape variety.

The wide variety of wines produced around the Mediterranean don't really have much in common other than the fact that their growing regions are, for the most part, hot and dry, a climate shared by Sicily and other parts of southern Italy. Only Greece, Cyprus, and Israel export to any great, or identifiable, extent. The wines of Algeria, Tunisia, Morocco, and other countries of the Middle East are mostly sold locally or exported in bulk for blending.

# Hungary

Hungary's most famous wine, the gloriously sweet Tokaji Eszencia (Tokay), was well known in Europe during the Crusades. Made in the northeast part of the country near the USSR-Czech border, its intense, concentrated sweetness, comparable to the finest Sauternes and Trockenbeerenauslesen (TBAs), was prized for centuries by European royalty. Legend has it that Catherine the Great deployed a special troop of Cossacks to guard her supply of it. Today it is extremely rare.

Hungary's red and white table wines come largely from the western half of the country on the Great Plain of the Danube, Somlo near the Austrian border and around the shores of Lake Balaton. Another important region is north of Budapest around the town of Eger. On wine labels place-names end in "i," thus Debrö becomes Debröi, Eger becomes Egri. Native grapes such as Furmint (Tokay), the red Kadarka, and white Leányka are the main varieties, though Olasz Riesling is also widely grown. Cabernet Sauvignon and Pinot Noir are becoming increasingly important.

# WINE GUIDE: HUNGARY

**Aszu.** The German equivalent of Auslese, signifying overripe grapes that make the sweetest, best Tokaji. Grapes often affected by noble rot (*Botrytis*).

(W) **Badacsony.** Balaton ★★/★★★
Some of Hungary's best white wines, both dry and sweet, come from this volcanic hill on the north shore of Lake Balaton from Welschriesling, Szürkebarat, and Kéknyelu grapes. Good value.

(RW) **Balaton.** Balaton ★★ +
Lake Balaton is known as "the Hungarian sea," and is Europe's biggest lake. Vines grow all around it, some of the best from Badacsony. Softer but still pleasing whites from Welschriesling, Furmint, and Sylvaner are made in other districts around the lake and Cabernet Sauvignon in some parts shows promise. Good value.

**Bársonyos Császár.** Northern hill country between Lake Balaton and the city of Budapest, best known for the dry whites of Mór.

(W) **Debrö.** Mátraaljai ★★ +
Town in the foothills of the Matra Mountains to the north, famous for its fragrant, semisweet wine Debröi Hárslevelü.

(RW) **Eger.** Mátraaljai ★★ +
Important wine town best known for its famous red Egri Bikavér, but also white Leányka and the thick fruity Médoc Noir (Merlot).

(R) **Egri Bikavér.** Mátraaljai ★★ +
Hungary's best-known dry red made from the Kadarka grape; "bikaver" means bull's blood and the wine was once stronger and darker than today; now mostly round, mellow, medium-bodied; ages fairly well. Good value.

**Eszencia.** The sweetest Tokaj, a concentrated elixir made practically drop by drop from raisined Furmint grapes to make the rarest of Tokaji wines; reputed to have miraculous healing powers but almost never seen now.

(W) **Ezerjó.** Mór ★★★
Móri Ezerjó, one of Hungary's finest dry white wines, comes from sandy hill vineyards of Mór; distinctive full aromas and flavor.

**Furmint.** The great white grape that makes Tokaji as well as some very good whites in Balaton.

**Hárslevelü.** White wine grape whose name translates as "lime-leaved," referring to the shape of the leaves. Most famous wine comes from Debrö, usually lightly sweet.

**Kadarka.** Hungary's most widely grown red grape, making mostly fullish dry, mellow reds, Egri Bikavér being the best known.

(W) **Kéknelyü.** Balaton ★★★
Interesting green-gold white wine made from the grape of the same name in the Badacsony district; heady, spicy aromas, bracing flavors.

(W) **Leányka.** Eger ★★
Delicate semidry white wine from a grape whose name means "young girl."

**Mátraaljai.** District in northern Hungary in the foothills of the Matra Mountains; best-known wine towns are Debrö and Eger.

**Mecsek.** Hilly region in southern Hungary known for its reds from Pinot Noir and Kadarka from Vilány and Székszard districts. Good Cabernet now coming from Hajós.

**Monimpex.** State-controlled export syndicate with headquarters located in Budapest.

**Mór.** Wine town in northern Hungary well-known for its dry white Móri Ezerjó.

**Nagyburgundi.** Hungarian name for Pinot Noir grape, which makes particularly good reds in the Vilány-Siklós district in southern Hungary (Mecsek).

**Olasz Riesling.** Italian or Welschriesling that makes moderate to good white wines.

Ⓦ **Pecs.** Mecsek ★ ★ +
Growing region in southern Mecsek region near Vilány that produces good, balanced whites from Furmint, Welschriesling, and Pinot Blanc.

**Puttonyos.** Term appearing on Tokaji Aszu labels that signifies the amount of sweet raisined grapes that were used to make the wine; one *putt*, or basket, added to the wine makes it lightly sweet; five *puttonyos*, the maximum, makes it intensely sweet.

Ⓦ **Somló.** Mt. Somló ★ ★ ★
White wine from an extinct volcano in northern Hungary; concentrated dry and sweet wines, highly regarded by Hungarians.

Ⓡ **Sopron.** Burgenland ★ ★
An extension of Austria's Burgenland into a small corner of Hungary, best known for its light reds made from Gamay.

**Szamorodni.** The driest of the wines from Tokaj made from normally ripened grapes; term means "as it comes."

Ⓡ **Szekszárdi Vörös.** Mecsek ★ ★
Dark red from the Kadarka grape in one of Hungary's growing regions in the south; robust wines that need aging to be palatable.

Ⓦ **Szürkebarát.** Balaton ★ ★
Hungarian name meaning "gray friar" given to Pinot Gris grape; makes rather heavy, rich dessert wine in the Badacsony district.

Ⓦ **Tokaji.** Tokaj ★ ★/★ ★ ★ ★
Hungary's splendid and famous white wine, especially Aszu, the sweetest (except for Eszencia, which is almost unobtainable today); produced in northeastern Hungary in foothills of the Carpathian mountains from the Furmint grape. Szamorodni is the drier version, Aszu the sweet, and the number of *puttonyos* indicates degree of sweetness.

Ⓡ **Vilány.** Mecsek ★ ★/★ ★ ★
Good reds from Pinot Noir known as Vilanyi Burgundi are quite good from this southern district, which makes reds from Kadarka also, though rather less impressive. Good value.

# Yugoslavia

Slovenian whites and Dalmatian reds jump first to mind among Yugoslavian wines because they were among the earliest and most widely seen outside the country. But Croatia and Serbia make the largest quantities of Yugoslavian wines, including well-balanced dry whites from Sauvignon Blanc and Traminer. Ljutomer whites from Slovenia near the Austro-Hungarian border are widely exported, made mostly from Rheinriesling, Sylvaner, and Pinot Blanc grapes. Numerous wines are made from native grapes such as Grk, Plavać Mali, Pošip, and Prokupac, among others. Yugoslavia's up and coming wines, however, are varietals based on Cabernet, Merlot, Gamay, Sauvignon Blanc, Traminer and Riesling, and Pinot Blanc.

# WINE GUIDE: YUGOSLAVIA

**Amselfelder.** Spätburgunder. Serbian red from the Pinot Noir grape, popular export to Germany where it gets its name.

**Bijelo.** Term for white wine.

**Cabernet Sauvignon.** Increasingly grown in various regions of Yugoslavia; average to good dry reds, the best from Istria.

**Crno.** Literally, "black," the term for red wine.

**Čviček.** Light red or rosé from native variety grown in Slovenia.

**Dalmatia.** The coastal province on the Adriatic between Rijeka and Dubrovnik, known for numerous reds, both sweet and dry, some quite potent.

**Dingac.** Heavy-bodied sweet reds from the Plavać Mali grape made along the Dalmatian coast.

**Grk.** Native Yugoslavian grape making mostly sweet, strong-flavored, full-bodied wines on the Dalmatian coast.

**Istria.** Peninsula jutting out from northern Yugoslavia above Dalmatia, producing some good Cabernet and Merlot.

**Kosovo.** Newly modernized wineries and vineyards in this region between Serbia and Macedonia may soon produce some of Yugoslavia's better wines; currently best known is Amselfelder.

**Laski Rizling.** Slavic name for the Italian Riesling.

**Ljutomer.** Source of Yugoslavia's best whites from Slovenia, mostly flavorful Riesling.

**Merlot.** The Bordeaux red grape now grown with some success in Istria and western Slovenia.

**Navip.** Large growers' co-operative in Belgrade producing a range of table wines including medium reds from Merlot, Prokupac.

**Plavać Mali.** The native grape responsible for reds of Slovenia and Dalmatia such as Dingac, Postup, and others.

**Posip.** Dry, full-bodied white made along the Dalmatian coast and islands just off it.

**Postup.** Popular sweet, strong-bodied red wine of the Dalmatian coast.

**Prokupac.** Another native red grape grown in Serbia and Macedonia to produce dark, robust reds and richly colored rosé.

**Prosek.** Potent dessert wine made from very ripe red grapes resulting in concentrated sweetness and high alcohol. A Dalmatian favorite.

**Ruzica.** A dark rosé made from Prokupac, Yugoslavia's best.

**Serbia.** Yugoslavia's largest grape-growing region producing the greatest quantity of table reds and whites.

**Sipon.** Actually Hungary's Furmint grape, small amounts grown in Slovenia, making good sweet wines.

**Slavonia.** District bordering Slovenia to the east, and northern part of Croatia, producing mostly white wines of middling interest.

**Slovenia.** Northern region whose capital is Ljubljana and whose Ljutomer whites are Yugoslavia's best.

**Tigrovo Mljeko.** "Tiger's Milk," a brand of sweet, white dessert wine, a local specialty of eastern Slovenia.

**Zilavka.** Flavorful, dry, aromatic white wine of Bosnia-Hercegovina in central Yugoslavia, around the town of Mostar.

# Greece

Birthplace of Dionysus, the god of wine, who according to legend passed on his precious knowledge of how to make it to the peoples of ancient Greece. Best-known survivor from antiquity is Retsina, the pungent resinated wine made around Athens in Attica. It is best served very cold. The greatest quantity of wine comes from the Peloponnese but wines are also produced in Macedonia, Thessaly, Hellas, Thrace, and most of the islands, notably Crete.

# WINE GUIDE: GREECE

**Achaia Clauss.** One of the two leading Greek producers headquartered in Patras on the Peloponnese peninsula. Best wines: Castel Danielis, Santa Helena.

**Attika.** The region around Athens that produces most of the country's Retsina.

**Cambas.** The other leading producer in Greece and largest exporter headquartered in Athens.

**Castel Danielis.** Vintage-dated dry red produced by Achaia Clauss. Varying quality but sometimes quite good.

**Crete.** Largest island of the Mediterranean that makes a considerable quantity of wine, the best being red Mavro Romeiko.

**Demestica.** Brand name for light, dry reds and whites of Achaia Clauss; moderately good and dependable.

**Hymettus.** Dry white wine made around Mt. Hymettus near Athens; also Cambas's line of dry red and dry white wines.

**Kokkineli.** Resinated rosé, sometimes called red Retsina, but generally more pink in color. Also best very cold.

**Lindos.** Agreeable white wine from the island of Rhodes.

**Malvasia.** Sweet wines from the ancient variety Monemvasia that appears to have originated in the southern Peloponnese; probably the fore-runner of Madeira's Malmsey.

**Mavro.** Greek word for black, signifying darker reds.

**Mavrodaphne.** Luscious sweet red wine from Patras whose name means "black laurel." A dessert wine taken at room temperature.

**Mavro Romeiko.** One of the best red wines, from the island of Crete; dry, dark and robust.

**Mavroudi.** Sturdy, dark red produced in Attica around Delphi.

**Naoussa.** Good dry red from the town of Naoussa in Macedonia.

**Peloponnese.** Large peninsula almost separated from the rest of Greece by the Corinthian gulf; the country's largest wine region.

**Pendeli.** Dry, full-bodied Attican red produced by the firm of Cambas.

**Retsina.** The famous resinated wine of Greece, mostly white, and best when very cold, a favorite with Greek food. Fully half the country's wine is resinated; the pink version is Kokkineli.

**Rhodes.** Famous island near the Turkish mainland producing dry white Lindos and Malvasia.

**Samos.** Luscious sweet Muscat from the island of Samos in the Aegean; widely exported.

**Santa Helena.** Pleasant, fresh, dry white of the northern Peloponnese.

**Santorin.** Island above Crete producing pleasant dry white and a potent sweet Vino Santo from sun-dried grapes.

# Cyprus

Winemaking traditions on Cyprus are among the oldest in the world, but the island has lately boosted exports of dry, full-bodied table wines that are finding ready acceptance in the world market. While not particularly distinguished, they are sound, well made, and inexpensive. Commanderia, a dessert wine of 14 to 15% alcohol, was legendary as far back as the Crusades for its intense, concentrated but uncloying richness. Though obviously lighter today than centuries ago, it can be a pleasant and lighter alternative to fortified wines, brandy, or liqueur.

Cyprus also produces the full range of sherries, long popular in Europe, the best of which are aged in outdoor soleras, as in Spain. Most of the Cypriot wine names have historic associations.

# WINE GUIDE: CYPRUS

**Afames.** Dry red table wine made by the co-operative in Limassol, Sodap.

**Amathus.** Full-bodied dry white made with some Muscat from the smallest of the four leading producers, Loel.

**Aphrodite.** Dry, full-bodied white wine from the Keo firm, named after the goddess said to have been born out of the sea off the southern coast.

**Ambrosia.** Average dry table red produced by Etko, known in Cyrus as Olympus.

**Arsinöe.** Sodap's crisp, dry white wine with a slightly bitter aftertaste.

**Bellapais.** Slightly *pétillant*, or semidry, white named for the historic abbey at Kyrenia.

**Coeur de Lion.** Sturdy, dry coral-colored rosé, the island's best.

**Commanderia.** Cyprus's famous dessert wine named for the command headquarters (Grande Commanderie) of the Knights Templars in the time of the Crusades; dark, burnished amber wine of rich, balanced sweetness made from red and white grapes dried in the sun in the Troodos Mountains.

**Domaine d'Ahera.** Wood-aged dry red from the firm of Keo; lighter than Othello.

**Etko.** One of the four leading producers of Cyprus, owned by Haggipavlu of Limassol. Olympus Red, Muscat, dry and cream sherries.

**Hermes.** Light, dry red from the firm of Loel.

**Keo.** A leading producer in Limassol with a full range of wines, especially Othello, Aphrodite, and Commanderia.

**Limassol.** Cyprus's largest coastal city and the center of the wine industry.

**Loel.** Smallest of the four top producers producing Hermes, Amathus, and Negro, a dry red blended from recently imported varieties such as Grenache and Carignane. Chateau de Lusignan Commanderia.

**Mavron.** The dark red grape native to Cyprus.

**Nefeli.** Fresh, dry white named after a sister of Bacchus, from Etko.

**Olympus.** The tallest mountain in the Troodos range in central Cyprus; also a brand name of table wines and sherries from Etko.

**Othello.** One of the island's best reds, dry, full-bodied, well balanced; made by Keo.

**Paphos.** Historic and picturesque port on the southwest coast; also a wine-gowing region in the low hills surrounding it.

**St. Panteleimon.** Assertive semisweet wine named after a charitable saint.

**Sherry.** Cyprus's full range of fortified wines in the sherry style, from dry fino to sweet cream, some quite good, such as Keo's Fino and some of the sweeter ones; others quite bland and characterless.

**Sodap.** The growers' co-operative at Limassol and largest of the island's producers. Arsinöe, Afames, St. Barnabus Commanderia.

**Troodos.** Mountains in the central part of Cyprus west of Nicosia; cool climate and annual rainfall make it the best for growing wine grapes, especially Commanderia and certain white wines.

**Xynisteri.** The white grape native to Cyprus.

# Romania and Bulgaria

These iron curtain countries ship very few wines to the West as yet, but those they do export are quite good. Romania, lying on the same latitude as France, has modernized her ancient traditions of wine-making over the last two decades. The best wines come mainly from the foothills of the Carpathian Mountains and the southern plains of the Danube bordering Bulgaria and the Black Sea. Cabernet Sauvignon and Pinot Noir are the most successful red varieties—they are dry, mellow, and easy to drink. Italian Riesling is the leading white, along with Chardonnay and Aligoté. Native varieties such as Feteasca, Perla, and Cotnari are also quite popular in Romania.

Bulgaria is more modern still. Its now-thriving wine industry was not created until halfway through the twentieth century, following World War II. The wines of Bulgaria come from broad flat plains in the north and central parts of the country (mostly reds) and east toward the Black Sea (mostly white varieties) with scattered vine-yard regions in the south and west. Most of Bulgaria's sizable production (sixth in world production) is exported to Russia, some to Germany and England. Presumably we soon will get more in the West since Bulgaria's robust, vigorous Cabernet has been so well received. The Chardonnay is also good, with surprising varietal character and body in a wine so inexpensive.

The wines of both countries represent good value for everyday table wines.

# Israel

Israel's flourishing vineyards were started in the 1800s by Baron Edmond de Rothschild, who sent a staff of experts and vine cuttings from his own vineyards in Bordeaux to get production underway. Today there are over 15,000 acres under cultivation in four principal areas: the slopes of Mount Carmel, some of which are at elevations of nearly 3,000 feet; the Judean hills from Hebron to Jerusalem; upper Galilee near the Jordan River; and along the Mediterranean from Haifa to Natanya.

More than 800 growers belong to the principal co-operative that markets wines under the brand name Carmel. Kosher wines, mostly sweet reds and whites, were major exports until recently, but expanded plantings of European varietals such as Cabernet Sauvignon, Sauvignon Blanc, Chenin Blanc, Grenache, and French Colombard show promise of better wines to come. These are the wines to look for from Isreal. Other leading producers are Askalon, Benyaminah, Eliaz, Israeli Distillers, and Richon-le-Zion.

# Lebanon

Unusual though it may seem, an interesting wine is made in Lebanon that has attracted international attention: Chateau Musar, a 300-acre wine estate on the slopes of Mt. Lebanon 20 miles north of Beirut. The Hochar family, which founded the estate in 1930, grow Cabernet Sauvignon, Cinsault, Syrah, and Merlot to make a robust red called Chateau Musar. The wine, aged in French oak from 9 to 24 months, has achieved some acclaim in Europe and the U.S. in the last decade. Also produced is a simpler red called Cuvee Musar, which has a greater proportion of Cinsault and is not aged in wood.

# Algeria

This North African country once supplied France with enormous quantities of red wines for blending. Algeria is one of the few countries in the world where vineyards have actually decreased in the last decade. Most of her dark, sturdy red wine is now exported to the USSR and Germany, as well as to other African nations. Typical hot country wines, they are, for the most part, low in acidity and high in alcohol. Sound, more balanced wines come from the hill vineyards of Medea, the Haut-Dahra, Mascara, and Zaccar, all west of Algiers.

# Morocco

Morocco produces the smallest quantity of the North African countries and its wine industry is the youngest, begun only in the last 50 years. The grapes are largely the same as in Tunisia, with sturdy red varieties such as Alicante Bouschet, Carignane and the Cabernets predominating. Reds and rosés from Cabernet Franc are often agreeable, especially with the country's spicy cuisine. They are most likely to be encountered only while traveling there, however, as most of the wine for export is shipped in bulk to European markets where it is used for blending.

# Tunisia

In ancient Carthage, viticulture and winemaking were well established centuries before Christ. The leading grape varieties today are Alicante Bouschet, Cabernet, Carignane, Pinot Noir, Grenache, and Muscat. Some of the reds, such as Coteaux de Carthage, are considered reasonably good examples of sturdy, hot-country reds. New efforts at quality control have been undertaken recently, and Tunisia is increasing its exports to European countries such as Switzerland, West Germany, and Great Britain.

# THE WINES OF THE UNITED STATES

**A**merica's wine regions are concentrated mainly in coastal areas just inland from the Atlantic and Pacific oceans. The earliest immigrants to both places attempted to grow wine grapes from vines they brought with them from their homelands in France, Spain, Italy, Germany, and other parts of Europe. Severe winters and native diseases defeated these efforts in New England, Virginia, and elsewhere along the east coast, so the settlers developed native varieties such as Concord, Niagara, Delaware. California, however, was more accommodating to the European vine, *Vitis vinifera*, especially varieties like Cabernet Sauvignon and Riesling. By the second decade of the twentieth century, the California wine industry was flourishing, but it virtually halted in 1919 because of Prohibition.

Over the last two decades, a dramatic revolution has taken place in America's wine industry. Consumption increased from half a gallon per capita annually in 1960 to some two gallons per capita today (still tiny in comparison to France or Italy, where 25 gallons is more like it). Vineyards have expanded east, west, and in between. California is by far the most important region with over 70% of production, and increasing quantities of wine are exported to England, France, and Germany. New York State and the Pacific Northwest regions follow in terms of size, but several other states are making serious attempts at winegrowing so that one day America's *vins du pays* may be quite widespread.

# GLOSSARY OF WINE TERMS

**Blanc de Blancs.** *White wine blended from white grapes.*

**Blanc de Noir(s).** *White wine made from red grapes, sometimes pink in color.*

**Botrytis cinerea.** *Beneficial mold that attacks ripening white grapes—mostly Riesling, Gewürztraminer, Sauvignon Blanc— under moist, warm harvest conditions, concentrating sugars and flavors to give a unique honeyed character and aroma.*

**Brix.** *Term of measurement referring to degrees of sugar in harvested grapes.*

**Carbonic maceration.** *Technique developed in Beaujolais region of France that ferments clusters of whole grapes instead of crushing them first. Yields light, fruity, NOUVEAU-style wines meant for early consumption; some have a light spritz from presence of carbon dioxide gas.*

**Generic.** *Nonvarietal wines, usually blended from several grape varieties, labeled Burgundy, Chablis, Claret, Rhine, and so on, and some proprietary names, such as Classic Red or Vino da Tavola.*

**Late harvest.** *Wines made from very ripe grapes, often an indication of Botrytis; usually sweet, as in Riesling, or very full-bodied, as with Zinfandel.*

**Made and bottled by.** . . . *Legally means that as much as 90% of the wine has been bought in bulk. "Cellared and bottled by" also used.*

**Magnum.** *Equivalent of two bottles; the metric magnum contains 1.5 liters, or 50.7 ounces.*

**Nouveau, or Nuevo.** *Term indicating light, fruity style of wine fermented quickly, bottled and released soon afterward; mostly Gamay Beaujolais or Zinfandel.*

**Produced and bottled by.** . . . *Legally means that at least 51% of the wine was fermented at the winery.*

**Residual sugar.** *Amount of sugar naturally remaining in wines that are not fermented completely dry. One percent is noticeably sweet.*

**Selected late harvest.** *See Late harvest.*

**Total Acid (TA).** *A term for natural fruit acids in finished wine; proper acidity gives crispness, balance, vitality. Reds normally range between 0.5 to 0.7, whites often higher, up to 1.0.*

**Varietal.** *Wine named for the principal grape variety used. New laws require that as of 1983 the wine contain a minimum of 75% of the grape variety named on label.*

# California

California's dynamic wine industry is at an exciting stage of growth, change, and expansion. It is a young industry, having started virtually from scratch in the years after Prohibition, a 14-year hiatus that brought winemaking (except for sacramental wines) to a standstill. Progress in the 1940s and 1950s was sluggish, with dessert and other sweet, fortified wines dominating production. It accelerated dramatically in the mid-1960s, however, with the infusion of a group of new winemakers who created much excitement with wines of intense varietal character and complexity, particularly those from Cabernet Sauvignon, the leading red grape variety, and Chardonnay, the leading white grape. California's unique red grape, Zinfandel, also moved to premium status during this time.

The key to quality in California is varietal labeling—wines named for grape variety, such as the three named above, Pinot Noir, Chenin Blanc, and so on—and the reputation of the winery. A listing of California Grape Varieties appears on pages 94–95, followed by a listing of individual wineries (Wine Guide: California).

The industry is in such a period of flux that quality ratings in many cases can be only tentative. Not only do new wineries constantly appear, seemingly overnight, but there are sometimes tremendous changes within the wineries themselves—winemakers come and go, ownership changes hands, certain types of wines may be added or dropped from a winery's product line, particularly those that purchase grapes instead of (or, in addition to) growing their own. Even the style of a given wine may change from year to year, being rather sweet in one vintage but totally dry the next, or vice versa. New growing regions are emerging as well, all of which leads to some confusion for the consumer. In the end, it means that the only way to keep up is to taste the wines frequently. Fortunately, California wines are generally so good—and improving—that such a task is not only useful but a very pleasurable pastime indeed.

The wineries included in the Wine Guide are those with a reasonable chance of national distribution and a few whose reputations have stretched well beyond the boundaries of California, even if the wines have not. Wines named in each entry are those for which the winery is particularly known. Those in **bold** type are especially recommended.

# PRINCIPAL WINE REGIONS OF CALIFORNIA

Geographic appellations are becoming increasingly important in California as knowledgeable consumers become familiar with regional distinctions. As yet, however, changing styles of winemaking and new and expanded plantings make it difficult in many cases to pin down specific regional character. Some areas, to be sure, have established enough of a track record for consumers to know what they can expect from the wines. We know that classic Cabernet Sauvignon of a certain style is produced in central Napa around Oakville and Rutherford; the fiercest Zinfandels seem to originate in Amador, and other areas with strong geographic identity are beginning to appear. In this decade regional characteristics will become much more defined, as young vineyards mature and winemakers extract the maximum from soil and climate factors.

Stating on the label where the grapes were grown is now common practice instead of merely a trend as it was a few years ago. For grape origin to appear on a vintage-dated VARIETAL (as in Napa Valley Zinfandel), the law requires that 95% of the grapes come from the area named and 75% for nonvintage wines. Following is a discussion of the principal growing regions, running from north to south.

## North Coast Counties

**Lake County** (L.C.)   Inland county north of Mendocino and Napa, recently expanded and planted mostly in red varieties. So far, sound but simple wines—no blockbusters yet.

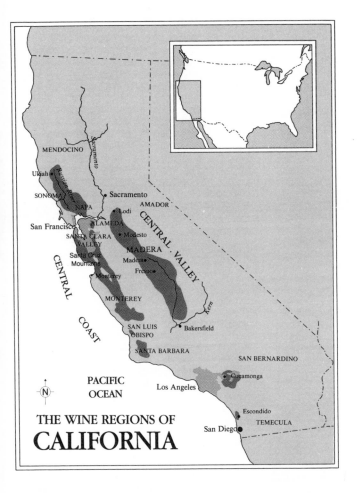

THE WINE REGIONS OF
# CALIFORNIA

**Mendocino** (Men.)   Mountainous region north of Napa and Sonoma famous
  for pears and apples, now becoming known for wine grapes. Fairly warm,
  though cool at night in places, and planted mostly in red varieties to date,
  though Chardonnay, Riesling, and Gewürztraminer from Anderson Valley, west of Ukiah, are promising. Chenin Blanc and French Colombard
  also do well. Largest producers here are Fetzer and Parducci. Other
  regions: McDowell Valley, Potter Valley.

**Napa Valley** (Napa)   California's most famous wine region, mostly because
  of the concentration of old, well-established names like Beaulieu,
  Beringer, Christian Brothers, Inglenook, and Martini and a growing number of newer ones that continue to add luster to the name. Small and
  compact, the narrow valley curves northward between two mountain
  ranges for about 35 miles, only 7.5 miles at its widest. Over 25,000 acres of
  vineyards cover the valley floor and pockets of hillside or mountaintop.
  Most plantings are of noble varieties, such as Cabernet Sauvignon, Chardonnay, Riesling, Pinot Noir, Zinfandel, and Chenin Blanc.

  The central part of the valley around Oakville and Rutherford yields
  outstanding Cabernet Sauvignon found in the Reserves of Beaulieu, Inglenook, Robert Mondavi, Heitz Martha's Vineyard, and Freemark Abbey
  Bosché. East of the Silverado Trail above the town of Napa is another good
  region for Cabernet, the Stag's Leap area.

89

The cool Carneros region in southern Napa—fog-bound hills overlooking San Pablo Bay—yields excellent Pinot Noir and Chardonnay. The northern end of the valley, bounded by the town of Calistoga, is the warmest, but produces some very good Zinfandel, Cabernet, Sauvignon Blanc and Chenin Blanc. Mountain vineyards in the ranges bordering the valley produce some of Napa's most intense wines, mainly Cabernet and Chardonnay. To the east of the valley proper are Pope Valley and Chiles Valley. Other subdistricts include Spring Mountain, Mt. Veeder, Pritchard Hill, Diamond Mountain.

**Sonoma** (Son.)   Separated from Napa Valley by the Mayacamas Mountains, its grape-growing industry is older than Napa's, but the lay of the land is very different—a broad, sprawling terrain of plains, valleys, and rolling hills that accommodates cattle ranches and fruit orchards as well as vineyards. The first grapes were planted in the south around the town of Sonoma that Jack London made famous as the "valley of the moon." Sebastiani and Buena Vista are here. In northern Sonoma, Alexander Valley is becoming known for its Cabernet, Zinfandel, Gewürztraminer, and Chardonnay, as is nearby Dry Creek. The cool, foggy reaches of the Russian River Valley, often attended by morning fog, yield fine Riesling, Chardonnay, and Pinot Noir. Kenwood, between Santa Rosa and Sonoma, is another important region, and Bennett Valley is just starting to emerge, south of Santa Rosa.

# San Joaquin Valley (S.J.V.)

**This inland** central valley stretches from Lodi to Bakersfield, a hot wide plain between the ridges of the coastal range and the Sierras—nearly 300 miles of over half a million acres of grapes. The giants are located here: Gallo, United Vintners, Guild, Franzia, and others. Table grapes are grown, but the region supplies most of California's wine grapes, including hybridized varieties developed to suit the climate—Ruby Cabernet, Emerald Riesling, Carnelian. Mid-VARIETALS like Chenin Blanc, Zinfandel, Petite Sirah better of late, especially from northern area around Lodi and the Delta region of Sacramento River. Grapes for dessert wines also come from here.

# Central Coast

**Alameda County (Livermore Valley)** (Alameda)   The Livermore Valley southeast of San Francisco is known mostly for white grapes like Chardonnay, Sauvignon Blanc, and Riesling, which do well in gravelly soil that gets very little rain. Wente Bros. and Concannon were pioneers here, both of whom tout it as a good region for reds too, especially Petite Sirah.

**Amador** (Ama.)   In the foothills of the Sierras east of Sacramento, Amador can hardly be considered coastal, yet its climate and wines are more nearly like those of the coastal counties. Hilly country and high plateaus make rich, full-bodied wines: hefty Zinfandel, Cabernet, even Sauvignon Blanc; small lots of Barbera and Nebbiolo, too. Place-names like Fiddletown, Sutter Creek, and Shenandoah Valley gauarantee very concentrated wines.

**Monterey** (Mon.)   Mainly, the valley floor of the broad Salinas Valley, once the "salad bowl" of the U.S., replanted in early 1970s with wine grapes. Main vineyard areas run from Gonzales down to Greenfield and King City, but also include pockets elsewhere such as Carmel Valley. High up on the Gavilan benchlands overlooking the valley above Soledad are Paul Masson's Pinnacles Vineyard and Chalone Vineyard. Monterey's climate, cooled by morning fog and strong Pacific breezes, gets little rainfall. White varieties seem to do best; Riesling, Gewürztraminer, Sauvignon Blanc, Chenin Blanc, Chardonnay show intense fruit and VARIETAL character. Reds occasionally plagued by vegetal flavor, due possibly to young vines and climatic factors. Mist during harvest promotes heavy BOTRYTIS at times, for interesting Riesling, Sauvignon Blanc, even Chardonnay. A still-evolving region.

**San Benito** (S.Ben.)   As vineyard acreage in Santa Clara decreased, wineries had to search elsewhere for it. Of the 4,500 acres in San Benito County, 95% belong to Almadén at Paicines and Cienega near Hollister. All types of varieties are planted, but Cabernet and Chardonnay predominate.

**San Luis Obispo** (S.L.O.)   One of California's newer and very promising wine regions with vineyards around Paso Robles, Edna Valley and Santa Maria; appears good for all varieties, especially Zinfandel, Cabernet, Merlot, Chardonnay, Chenin Blanc, and unusual Pinot Noir.

**Santa Barbara County** (S.Barb.)   The cool plateaus of the Santa Ynez Valley produce good reds and whites with distinctive regional character; early-ripening varieties like Pinot Noir, Merlot, Riesling, and Chardonnay are especially good. A growing region and one to watch.

**Santa Clara**   South of San Francisco Bay, this large area was one of California's earliest wine regions. Almadén planted vineyards in the 1850s, as did Paul Masson and Mirassou a bit later—all today among the largest of California's premium wineries. There are only pockets of vineyards left in most of Santa Clara Valley, as urban sprawl overtook most of the prime vineyard land in the 1950s and 1960s. Mirassou still has an important vineyard in San Jose. To the west, the vineyards of Mount Eden, Martin Ray, David Bruce, and Ridge (also considered part of the Santa Cruz Mountains) produce some of the state's most intense and interesting wines. In the south around Gilroy there are a number of wineries growing mostly Zinfandel and Cabernet and a bit of Pinot Noir.

**Santa Cruz Mountains** (S.C.M.)   North of the town of Santa Cruz, this lush, green mountainous region once boasted 40 wineries that dwindled to almost none. New, small operations have cropped up recently and the cool climate and soil composition have lured those in quest of Pinot Noir, some of which is formidable; also good Chardonnay and Cabernet.

# Cucamonga-San Bernardino (Cuc.-S.B.)

**This region** east of Los Angeles was the earliest wine-growing region, planted with mission grapes brought by the Spanish friars in the late eighteenth century. The region was best known for dessert varieties, including some astonishing Angelica. The tentacles of urban Los Angeles have enveloped most of the vineyards, though a few stands of Zinfandel, Grenache, Mission, and Palomino survive in patches.

# Temecula (Tem.)

**A microclimate** east of San Diego, cooled by Pacific breezes and sheltered from desert heat by Palm Springs mountains. Callaway is the best-known vineyard here. The most successful varieties appear to be whites: Riesling, Sauvignon Blanc, and Chenin Blanc. Very intense Zinfandel and Petite Sirah.

# VINTAGES: CALIFORNIA

Contrary to what you may hear, vintages in California are quite different from one another. While the region rarely suffers dismal or catastrophic years, as happens in the northern regions of Europe, complications can occur. Rain during the harvest is always unfortunate; if excessive, it tends to dilute the quality and flavor of the grapes. Too much heat can also be a problem, causing grape sugars to soar too fast while simultaneously reducing the acidity that gives vitality and balance to a wine. Following is a discussion of recent California vintages in the coastal counties.

1981.   Good, probably for early drinking. Earliest harvest in living memory, following early summer heat wave. Smaller crop than expected; some wines low in acidity and light in color for reds, making fruit maturity questionable. Considerable BOTRYTIS along Central Coast counties should yield good sweet wines.

1980.   Mostly good to excellent. A very late harvest following a cool growing season that brought intense fruit and VARIETAL character. High grape sugars were balanced with high acidity, resulting in many powerful, long-lived wines. Many whites—Chardonnay, Sauvignon Blanc, Riesling—showing superbly now. Reds are harder, less generous but the best will be long-lived.

1979.   Biggest crop in history but problems in some areas due to rain. Napa and Sonoma particularly hard-hit by storms following heat spells, throwing the grapes into a state of arrested development. Some Cabernet in the north coast counties never ripened sufficiently. Early-ripening varieties, such as Pinot Noir, Chardonnay, Riesling, and Merlot, did quite well in most regions, benefiting from warm, dry weather in August and early September. Overall, somewhat uneven but a few intense Chardonnays and, when not diluted, balanced Cabernets.

1978.   Until 1979, the biggest crop to date. Superb white wines, especially Chardonnay and Sauvignon Blanc. Vines seemed to recover quickly and healthily from previous two years of drought. High sugars for reds make the vintage somewhat similar to 1974; most regions report superb wines. Reds well structured for aging.

1977.   Second year of drought. Somewhat variable but extremely good in many instances, mostly reds. Reduced quantity, down as much as 50% from drought conditions and some frost in spring. Uneven ripening required successive pickings in some areas with different parts of the vineyard reaching desired sugar levels at different times. Chardonnays not as rich as 1978, nor as balanced as 1976, but many Cabernets, Zinfandels, and Pinot Noirs are excellent, especially along the central coast from the Santa Cruz Mountains to Santa Barbara County.

1976.   First year of drought, quantity reduced by half but some Cabernets of great intensity from small berries loaded with flavor and extract, particularly Napa and Sonoma; also full, balanced Chardonnay, the best holding nicely. Biggest reds need more time.

1975.   A cool year, with some uneven ripening, overshadowed by big, powerful 1974s. Reds were dark and tannic but lower in alcohol and generally more austere, but capable of achieving great elegance in time; Zinfandel richer in fruit than Cabernet. Good Chardonnay in Napa Sonoma, but some now losing fruit.

1974.   Considered by many the best vintage of the 1970s; big, powerful wines, especially among reds (Cabernet, Zinfandel), which are very high in alcohol. Very concentrated reserve wines whose value is now realized and they are correspondingly expensive; some will be very long-lived. Best whites holding but should be consumed now.

1973.  Cool growing season, rainy during harvest. Somewhat thinner wines but some elegant Cabernets drinking extremely well now.

1972.  Cool, rainy, generally quite poor, though a few pleasant reds from warmer regions.

1971.  Generally weak, but some Cabernets from central Napa still impressive.

1970.  A great year for reds, particularly Cabernet, which is still growing in bottle and showing very well; will last several more years.

1969,  Both great years for Cabernet, some Zinfandel, Pinot Noir, Chardon-
1968.  nay. 1969s surprisingly strong.

**HEITZ CELLARS.** The better California wines are varietals, made predominantly of a single grape variety, such as the Cabernet Sauvignon above. Varietal wines currently must contain 51% of the grape variety named (75% as of 1983), but for top producers such as Heitz the amount is always considerably more—in this case 100%. Martha's Vineyard in Napa Valley is the specific plot of land where the grapes were grown. Such vineyard designation calls attention to wines with a consistently distinct regional character.

93

# GRAPE VARIETIES: CALIFORNIA

**Alicante Bousche.** Deeply colored red grape grown mostly in the central valley for blending with paler reds; Papagni Vineyards makes a sturdy VARIETAL of it.

**Barbera.** Red wine grape from the Italian Piedmont. Widest plantings in San Joaquin Valley yield soft, mild wines, but tart, somewhat astringent fruit in young wines from the cooler coastal counties that develop rich warmth and roundness with age; best at 3 to 6 years old.

**Cabernet Sauvignon.** Leading variety of the Médoc in Bordeaux. California's best red grape and the single most widely produced VARIETAL; styles range from mellow fruitiness to classic elegance to darkly tannic with intense, concentrated fruit; ages extremely well. Best and most famous come from Napa Valley.

**Carignane.** Prolific and widely grown in warmer regions like San Joaquin for its dark, paunchy fruit; used mostly for blending but occasionally made as an interesting VARIETAL.

**Charbono.** Red grape similar to Barbera, making dark, thick, densely fruity wines that age nicely. Limited plantings in Napa, mostly at Inglenook and Franciscan; also by Papagni in Madera.

**Chardonnay.** California's noblest white grape, yielding dry wines ranging from crisp, apple-like freshness to more pronounced VARIETAL character and complexity, often with added dimension from aging in small oak barrels; the best are comparable to fine white Burgundy.

**Chenin Blanc.** Productive, widely-grown white wine grape. Usually off-dry or lightly sweet, but increasingly popular drier versions are full-flavored, racy, stylish, and best when young and fresh.

**Emerald Riesling.** Hybrid white grape developed in California with rather faint Riesling character but good acidity, fruity, and occasionally rather tart, though some are lightly sweet; popular with seafood.

**Flora.** Cross between Sémillon and Gewürztraminer; flowery, delicate white with a touch of spice and light sweetness; not widely known (or grown) as yet.

**Folle Blanche.** Clean, crisp, rather acidic white, produced as a VARIETAL only by Louis Martini; elsewhere used for blending.

**Franken Riesling.** See Sylvaner.

**French Colombard.** Very productive white, widely grown for GENERIC blends but newly popular as a VARIETAL: bracing acidity usually modified by a touch of sweetness; often fresh and appealing, especially those from Mendocino.

**Fumé Blanc.** Another name for SAUVIGNON BLANC.

**Gamay.** Also known as Gamay Noir or Napa Gamay. The French Beaujolais grape or a near relative, but tends to be heavier and more "serious" in California. Whole berry fermentation (CARBONIC MACERATION) often used for lighter, fruitier wines.

**Gamay Beaujolais.** Misnamed, actually a clone of Pinot Noir though the name is legal to use. Most is made in a light, fruity style but wines thinner and lighter than Napa Gamay.

**Gewürztraminer.** Good, spicy white grape; very fragrant, usually lightly sweet; most drier styles often excellent with more intense VARIETAL character and aroma.

**Green Hungarian.** Minor white grape for ordinary but occasionally zesty wines; popular mostly for its romanitc name, but not Hungarian in origin.

**Grenache.** A variety from the Rhone Valley and widest grown red grape for rosé, most rather sweet; occasionally also a red VARIETAL of no particular note.

**Grey Riesling.** Not a true Riesling but a lesser white variety yielding agreeably fruity wines; best when very young and fresh.

**Johannisberg Riesling.** Also known as White Riesling and the true Riesling of Germany. One of California's best white grapes; ranges in style from fresh and off-dry to richly sweet and complex LATE-HARVEST styles, comparable to Germany's fine Auslese and TBA (see "The Wines of Germany").

**Merlot.** Excellent red grape, often used for softening Cabernet but increasingly a VARIETAL on its own, making sound, solid reds of suppleness and grace.

**Monterey Riesling.** See Sylvaner.

**Muscat (Moscato).** White grape for light, sweet, fragrant, and often delectable white wines named for various muscat varieties, such as Canelli, Frontignan, Alexandria; some wines also labeled Moscato Amabile.

**Petite Sirah.** Dark, purple red grape, not the true Syrah of great Rhône reds but a minor variety known as Duriff. In warmer regions, yields soft, fruity wines of mild character but dense, tannic, more complex ones from cooler regions near the coast, also Livermore Valley.

**Pineau de la Loire.** Another name for Chenin Blanc.

**Pinot Blanc.** White grape yielding full-bodied dry whites, more austere than Chardonnay and much less known, though recently more popular.

**Pinot Noir.** The great red grape of Burgundy seems to have lost something in translation (or transplantation), yielding rather pretty, light wines in California but lacking richness and depth; a few achieve it, so the quest, fortunately, continues, mostly in cooler regions like Carneros, Santa Cruz Mountains, and Santa Ynez.

**Pinot St. George.** Sturdy variety, grown mostly by Christian Brothers and Almadén makes reds of rather distinctive robust flavor.

**Ruby Cabernet.** A cross of mostly Cabernet Sauvignon bred for the warm central valley where it is very successful, with reasonable hints of Cabernet character. More intense versions occasionally made in cooler, mountainous regions.

**Sauvignon Blanc.** White grape, excellent for dry, fruity white wines also called Fumé Blanc either in style of the Loire or fuller bodied dry Graves.

**Sémillon.** Mostly blended with Sauvignon Blanc, also seen as Dry Sémillon making a mild, rather stony white, crisp and fresh, at best. A few efforts at sweet wines (affected by BOTRYTIS) are interesting, with several experiments in the works, particularly in Monterey.

**Sylvaner.** Also known as Franken Riesling, Monterey Riesling. Sharper, and similar to, Riesling though of secondary rank and used frequently for blending. Can be quite good and fresh.

**Syrah.** The true Syrah of the Rhône, first made by Joseph Phelps in Napa Valley. Dark, sturdy, attractive; different from Petite Sirah.

**Zinfandel.** California's most popular red VARIETAL with a wide range of styles from light and fruity to heavy, LATE-HARVEST types. In between are medium styles of ripe, berryish, or spicy aromas and more concentrated fruit, as well as more classic, complex claret styles that age well.

# WINE GUIDE: CALIFORNIA

**Acacia.** Napa ★ ★ ★
New winery in Carneros producing **Pinot Noir** and **Chardonnay** from Carneros vineyards. 1979 and 1980 wines impressive, especially Pinot Noirs from Lee and St. Clair vineyards.

(RW) **Ahern.** Los Angeles ★ ★
Small operation in San Fernando Valley that buys grapes up north, including Zinfandel and Sauvignon Blanc; available mostly in Los Angeles.

(RW) **Ahlgren.** S.C.M. ★★/★★★

Small, new winery near Boulder Creek making good, chewy **Cabernet**, Chardonnay, and big Zinfandel.

(RW) **Alexander Valley Vineyards.** Son. ★★/★★★

New winery in Alexander Valley with 250 acres of VARIETALS making 7,200 cases annually. **Chardonnay**, **Cabernet Sauvignon**, dry Chenin Blanc, Riesling.

(3) **Almadén.** Santa Clara ★/★★ +

One of California's oldest wineries and largest of the premium producers making full range of table, sparkling, and dessert wines; reasonably priced. 6,000 acres in San Benito and Monterey. Charles Le Franc is top line but best values are regular **Cabernet**, **Merlot**, Gewürztraminer, Gamay Rosé, **Blanc de Blancs** champagne. Good value.

(RW) **Balverne.** Son.

Large vineyard holdings near Healdburg with early emphasis on crisp, dry whites like Chardonnay, Riesling, Gewürztraminer, Sauvignon Blanc and German variety Scheurebe. Good proprietary white called Healdsburger. Also Cabernet, Zinfandel.

(RW) **Bandiera.** Son. ★★

Small, new winery in northern Sonoma; purchases most grapes for Zinfandel, Cabernet, some whites; plans for jug wines in future.

(3) **Barengo.** Lodi ★/★★

Large, old winery in central valley making good table reds, Ruby Cabernet, Zinfandel, and port-like dessert wines.

(3) **Bargetto.** S.C.M. ★/★★

Large winery at Soquel known mostly for fruit and berry wines (pomegranate, olallieberry) but also creditable Chardonnay, Riesling; reds less interesting.

(RW) **Beaulieu Vineyard (BV).** Napa ★★/★★★★

Classic estate now owned by Heublein famed for premium table wines, especially **Georges de Latour Private Reserve Cabernet**; also Rutherford Cabernet, Pinot Noir, Sauvignon Blanc, Brut champagne.

**Bella Oaks Vineyard.** Fine Cabernet vineyard at Oakville, identified as of 1976 on Heitz label. Same owner planted Martha's Vineyard nearby, later sold it.

**Bell Canyon Cellars.** Second label for Burgess Cellars.

**Beltane Ranch.** Vineyard at Glen Ellen in Sonoma; formerly sold Chardonnay and Cabernet to Chateau St. Jean; now seen on Kenwood labels.

(3) **Beringer.** Napa ★★/★★★

One of Napa's oldest wineries owned by Nestlé producing average to good table wines and a good line of jugs, Los Hermanos. Lemmon Ranch Cabernet, Fumé Blanc.

**Berkeley Wine Cellars.** Berkeley ★★ +

Home winemaking supply company in heart of Berkeley known as Wine and the People. Produces good Zinfandel, some Pinot Noir and Port under above label.

(RW) **Boeger.** Placerville ★★

New, small winery in Gold Rush country (El Dorado County near Amador) making Zinfandel, Chardonnay, Chenin Blanc, very good **Cabernet** and a generic, Hangtown Red. Good value.

**Brander.** Santa Barbara ★★

New winery in Santa Ynez Valley founded by Fred Brander, who is the winemaker at Santa Ynez Valley Winery nearby. Early Sauvignon Blancs quite good.

(3) **Brookside.** Cuc.-S.B. ★/★★

Large, old winery making most dessert and fortified wines; table wines from Temecula, Chardonnay, Petite Sirah, bottled under Assumption Abbey label.

(RW) **Bruce, David.** Santa Clara ★★★

Small winery in northern Santa Cruz range known for sometimes quirky but intense, full-bodied wines, particularly **Chardonnay** and **Pinot Noir**.

Ⓡ︎Ⓦ︎ **Buehler.** Napa ★ ★ +
Growers near Conn Valley above Rutherford now making their own wines—Cabernet, Zinfandel, Pinot Blanc, Sauvignon Blanc.

③ **Buena Vista.** Son. ★ ★ / ★ ★ +
Oldest winery in Sonoma, founded by Agoston Haraszthy, now mostly show room and storage. New facility in Carneros producing full line of table wines, average to good quality but improving recently, with Cask Cabernet, Fumé Blanc, Riesling.

Ⓡ︎Ⓦ︎ **Burgess Cellars.** Napa ★ ★ ★
On site of the old Souverain winery, about 15,000 cases of top VARIETALS: **Cabernet**, **Chardonnay**, **Zinfandel**, Petite Sirah.

**Burgundy.** GENERIC term used for many blended reds, which may consist of any grape varieties. May be dry and fairly robust or fruity and off-dry, as in those from San Joaquin.

**BV.** Beaulieu Vineyards. See Beaulieu (BV).

Ⓡ︎Ⓦ︎ **Cakebread Cellars.** Napa. ★ ★ ★
Small winery at Rutherford specializing in Cabernet, **Chardonnay**, and Sauvignon Blanc.

Ⓡ︎ **Calera.** S. Ben. ★ ★ +
New, small winery near Hollister making impressive **Pinot Noir** from mountain vineyards (Reed, Jensen, Selleck) and robust Zinfandel.

Ⓡ︎Ⓦ︎ **Callaway.** Tem. ★ ★
Pioneers in southern California; inky, intense overpowering reds, better whites. Style of wines somewhat controversial. Lightly sweet Fumé Blanc, Chenin Blanc.

Ⓡ︎Ⓦ︎ **Carey, Richard.** A.C. ★ ★
Small winery in San Leandro that purchases grapes for Cabernet, Blanc Fumé, Chardonnay.

Ⓡ︎Ⓦ︎ **Carneros Creek.** Napa ★ ★ ★
Carneros-based winery dedicated to Burgundian-style **Pinot Noir** (Carneros District P.N. superb), rich Chardonnay, Cabernet, and hefty Zinfandel.

Ⓡ︎Ⓦ︎ **Cassayre-Forni.** Napa ★ ★ ★
Promising young winery at Rutherford making firm-structured **Cabernet** and dry, fruity Chenin Blanc.

Ⓡ︎Ⓦ︎ **Caymus.** Napa ★ ★ ★
Some 70 acres at Rutherford producing estate-bottled **Cabernet**, **Pinot Noir**, Fumé Blanc. Purchased grapes and/or blended nonvintage wines form second label, Liberty School, the Cabernets especially good value.

Ⓡ︎Ⓦ︎ **Chalone.** Mon. ★ ★ ★
Miniscule property in the Gavilan range 2,000 feet above Salinas Valley, noted for Burgundy-style **Pinot Noir** and **Chardonnay**, fine Pinot Blanc, and French Colombard. Chaparral labels are from younger vines.

Ⓡ︎Ⓦ︎ **Chappellet.** Napa ★ ★ ★
One of Napa's best mountain vineyards to the east on Pritchard Hill, producing intense, full-bodied wines of vigorous VARIETAL character: **Cabernet**, **Chardonnay**, **Chenin Blanc**, interesting Gamay Riesling.

Ⓡ︎Ⓦ︎ **Château Chevalier.** Napa ★ ★ +
Old château and estate on Spring Mountain restored in the 1970s, producing dark, tannic **Cabernet** and intense **Chardonnay**.

Ⓡ︎Ⓦ︎ **Château Montelena.** Napa ★ ★ ★
Winery in northern Napa at Calistoga with 100 acres plus purchased grapes; noted for Cabernet, Chardonnay, J. Riesling, Zinfandel.

Ⓡ︎Ⓦ︎ **Château St. Jean.** Son. ★ ★ ★ +
Growing operation at Kenwood famous for full-blown **Chardonnays** and luscious sweet **Riesling** and **Gewürztraminer** in the Auslese or TBA style (see "The Wines of Germany"). Dry Gewürztraminer, **Fumé Blancs** also good; from 1979 on, the only red is the intense Wildwood **Cabernet**. Increasing quantities of sparkling wines by méthode champenoise.

③ **Christian Brothers. Napa** ★ ★ / ★ ★ ★
Old, established winery run by the religious brotherhood; sound,

blended VARIETALS, GENERICS, and fortified wines; some VARIETALS now vintage-dated. Zinfandel, Pinot St. George, Fumé Blanc, and Cabernet are best. Also good brandy. Good value.

(RW) **Clos du Bois.** Son. ★ ★ / ★ ★ ★

Young winery in Dry Creek area of northern Sonoma; fine **Chardonnay**, **Cabernet**, Pinot Noir, Gewürztraminer. Also special vineyard appellalations such as Marlstone (Cabernet-Merlot) (Pinot Noir), Cherry Hill.

(R) **Clos du Val.** Napa ★ ★ ★ +

Excellent, small French-owned estate making well-structured **Cabernet**, **Merlot**, and elegant, claret-style **Zinfandel**; also a tiny amount of **Chardonnay**, Pinot Noir.

(3) **Concannon.** Alameda ★ ★ / ★ ★ ★

Founded in 1883 and owned by Irish family of Concannons, but recently sold. Known for very good **Sauvignon Blanc, Petite Sirah, Zinfandel Rosé.** Good value.

(RW) **Congress Springs.** S.C. ★ ★ +

Very young winery on hillsides near Saratoga, tiny production but plans to grow; good **Sauvignon Blanc**, Chardonnay.

(RW) **Conn Creek.** Napa ★ ★ / ★ ★ ★

Relatively new winery begun by a Napa Valley grower, producing several varieties, excellent **Cabernet**, good Riesling and Chardonnay.

(3) **Cresta Blanca.** Men. ★

One of California's oldest names, originally begun in Livermore Valley, now revived at Ukiah, but owned by Guild of the central valley. Average wines, should be better.

(RW) **Cuvaison.** Napa ★ ★ ★

Medium-sized winery at northern end of Napa, now owned by a Swiss firm; rich, full-bodied **Chardonnay**; big, spicy **Zinfandel**; and forceful Cabernet.

(RW) **Davis Bynum.** Son. ★ ★ +

Medium-small winery near Healdsburg making several above-average VARIETALS, attractive Pinot Noir.

(RW) **Dehlinger.** Son. ★ ★ ★

Young winery in northern Sonoma near Sebastopol, with promising beginning for Cabernet and **Chardonnay**, Pinot Noir, **Zinfandel**.

(RW) **DeLoach Vineyards.** Son. ★ ★ ★

New, family-owned winery near Santa Rosa with 150 acres Zinfandel, Pinot Noir, Chardonnay; first releases of all quite good. Rich, chewy reds.

(R) **Diamond Creek.** Napa ★ ★ ★

Very small vineyards on Diamond Mountain in northern Napa making only **Cabernet** under three excellent appellations: Volcanic Hill, Red Rock Terrace, Gravelly Meadow.

(W) **Domaine Chandon.** Napa ★ ★ ★

Showplace sparkling wine facility at Yountville owned by French firm of Moët-Hennessey. Excellent sparkling wine by true French méthode champenoise: Napa Valley Brut, Blanc de Noirs. Excellent restaurant at the winery. Good value.

(RW) **Domaine Laurier.** Son. ★ ★ +

New winery in Russian River area of northern Sonoma making laudable efforts with Pinot Noir, Chardonnay, Cabernet. Promising.

(RW) **Dry Creek.** Son. ★ ★ ★

Small, individualistic winery in Dry Creek area of northern Sonoma making quite fine VARIETALS, Cabernet, Chardonnay, **Fumé Blanc**, Zinfandel, Chenin Blanc.

**Duckhorn Vineyards.** Napa ★ ★ ★

Young winery at St. Helena owned by Duckhorn family, producing lush, chewy **Merlot**, Cabernet, and soon, Sauvignon Blanc. One to watch.

(RW) **Durney.** Mon. ★ ★ / ★ ★ ★

Young winery in Carmel Valley owned by rancher turned winegrower; 60 acres for well-balanced **Cabernet**, also Riesling, Chenin Blanc.

**Dutton Ranch.** Vineyard in Russian River Valley noted for Chardonnays produced by such wineries as Burgess, Martin Ray, Kistler.

(3) **East-Side.** Lodi ★

Huge central valley winery making full range of table and dessert wines under the Royal Host and Conti Royale labels. Best values: Ruby Cabernet, Grey Riesling, Chenin Blanc, Tinta Port.

(RW) **Edmeades.** Men. ★ ★

Small winery in Anderson Valley west of Ukiah; good Zinfandel, Gewürztraminer, French Colombard, and crisp proprietary brands like Rain Wine, Opal and Whale Wine.

(RW) **Edna Valley Vineyard.** S.L.O.

New winery at Edna Valley under direction by principals at Chalone. Outstanding Chardonnay to date, with Pinot Noir forthcoming, both looking to Burgundian models.

**Eisele Vineyard.** Vineyard in hills above Calistoga noted for fine Cabernet, sold mostly to Joseph Phelps.

(RW) **Estrella River.** S.L.O. ★ ★ ★

Very large property near Paso Robles with 700 acres of vineyards and recently improved VARIETALS like **Chardonnay**, Muscat Blanc, Zinfandel.

**Far Niente.** Napa

New owner renovating historic greystone winery at Oakville. 1979 and 1980 **Chardonnay** (made in Sausalito from Napa grapes) quite good, Cabernet to come. Winery's name means "without a care."

(RW) **Felton-Empire.** S.C.M. ★ ★ +

The old Hallcrest winery and vineyards revived in 1976. Fine sweet Riesling in the German style; BOTRYTISED Gewürztraminer.

(3) **Fetzer.** Men. ★ ★ +

Good sized winery making broad range of VARIETALS and GENERICS of somewhat variable quality; good values in **Zinfandel**, Petite Sirah, Cabernet, Premium Red.

(RW) **Ficklin.** Madera ★ ★ ★

Small family firm producing superb ports, one vintage-dated, another known as Tinta Port. Also limited bottlings of Emerald Riesling and Ruby Cabernet sold only at the winery. Good value.

(W) **Field Stone.** Son. ★ ★

Young winery built into hillside near Healdsburg, specializing in field-crushed Riesling, Gewürztraminer, also Chenin Blanc and Cabernet Rosé.

(3) **Firestone.** S.B. ★ ★/★ ★ ★

Pioneers of the Santa Ynez Valley with 300 acres of VARIETALS planted in 1972. Very good **Riesling**, **Gewürztraminer**, **Pinot Noir**, also Merlot, Cabernet, Chardonnay. Bears watching. Good value.

(RW) **Flora Springs Wine Co.** Napa ★ ★ +

New winery with over 200 acres in western hills at St. Helena; early Chardonnay and Riesling show great charm. Also producing Cabernet Sauvignon. Bears watching.

(3) **Foppiano.** Son. ★ ★/★ ★ +

Longtime growers near Healdsburg, recent VARIETALS, including dry **Chenin Blanc**, Fumé Blanc, Cabernet, and Petite Sirah. Generic line called Riverside Farm red, white, rosé, is good value.

(RW) **Forman Winery.** Napa

First wines appear in 1982. Owner Ric Forman, formerly of Sterling, grows 50 acres of mainly Merlot and Sauvignon Blanc in newly carved-out vineyard on Spring Mountain. High expectations for this one.

(RW) **Fortino.** Santa Clara ★/★ ★

Italian family making Italian-style, robust wines at Gilroy; earthy, full-bodied reds like Zinfandel, Cabernet, Barbera, Petite Sirah.

(RW) **Franciscan.** Napa ★ ★ +

Large winery at Rutherford now under new ownership, known for good-value Cabernet and Chardonnay, also Zinfandel and Riesling.

1980

# ROBERT MONDAVI WHITE

*California White Wine*

PRODUCED AND BOTTLED BY ROBERT MONDAVI WINERY
OAKVILLE, NAPA VALLEY, CALIFORNIA, U.S.A. 94562
ALCOHOL 12% BY VOLUME • B.W.- CA-4802

**ROBERT MONDAVI WHITE.** Generic wines such as this one are blended from several
grape varieties to a style chosen by the producer. Robert Mondavi White, a
vintage-dated dry white wine, shows only a California appellation, which means the
grapes may have come from anywhere in the state, including the central valley.
Generics come in fifths, magnums or multi-liter size bottles, often referred to as "jugs."
Other generic wines bear such names as Red Table Wine, Vin Rosé, Burgundy,
Mountain Claret, or Chablis.

③ **Franzia.** S.J.V. ★
Third largest producer in California, producing table, dessert, and
Charmat-process sparkling wines under several brands, all originating
from Ripon (near Modesto). Inexpensive, reliable Burgundy.

⟨RW⟩ **Freemark Abbey.** Napa ★ ★ ★
Medium-size winery at St. Helena specializing in very fine VARIETALS from
Napa grapes; notable **Cabernet Bosché**, **Chardonnay**, sweet Riesling
known as **Edelwein**.

③ **Gallo, E. & J.** Modesto ★/★ ★ +
World's largest winery, pacesetters for quality jugs like Chablis Blanc,
Hearty Burgundy, and recently good, moderate-priced VARIETALS. Best
are Sauvignon Blanc, Gewürztraminer, Barbera; wood-aged Chardonnay is newest addition to line, Cabernet and Zinfandel in 1982. Good
value.

⟨RW⟩ **Gemello.** Santa Clara ★ ★
Old family winery, well known for hearty, Italian-style reds: Barbera,
Cabernet, **Zinfandel**, Petite Sirah. Good value.

③ **Geyser Peak.** Son. ★/★ ★
An old name that keeps trying with moderately good VARIETALS, including Gewürztraminer, Fumé Blanc, and more recently, champagne.

③ **Giumarra.** S.J.V. ★/★ ★ +
Bulk producer of dessert wines at Bakersfield, upgrading image with
large quantities of premium and mid-VARIETALS like French Colombard,
Zinfandel, Ruby Cabernet, and Petite Sirah. Good value.

⟨RW⟩ **Grand Cru.** Son. ★ ★/★ ★ ★
Small winery at Glen Ellen making aromatic Gewürztraminer, both
sweet and dry and fresh, fruity Chenin Blanc; also good Cabernet and
Zinfandel.

⟨RW⟩ **Grand Pacific.** Marin ★ ★
New, small winery at San Rafael in Marin County that purchases grapes
to make Merlot, Cabernet, Riesling, and rosés priced rather grandly for
good but not distinguished wines.

**Gran Val.** Second label from Clos du Val. Good value.

(RW) **Grgich Hills.** Napa ★★/★★★
Flowery, fragrant **Riesling** and Chardonnay from this new winery at Rutherford. Also good Zinfandel.

(3) **Guild.** S.J.V. ★
Winegrower' co-op in the central valley; full range of VARIETALS, GENERICS, dessert wines, and brandy. Owns Cresta Blanca, Cribari, Roma; most famous brand is Vino da Tavola and new Winemasters VARIETALS.

(RW) **Gundlach-Bundschu.** Son. ★★/★★★
One of Sonoma's oldest names now revived on original site in the Valley of the Moon. Good **Cabernet, Gewürztraminer, Chardonnay**, others.

(RW) **Hacienda.** Son. ★★/★★★
Immaculate little winery in the town of Sonoma making fine **Chardonnay**, clean, fresh Gewürztraminer, balanced **Cabernet**, Pinot Noir.

(W) **Hagafen.** Napa ★★
A kosher Johannisberg Riesling, suitable for more than Passover. Owners procure grapes from Winery Lake Vineyard in Carneros.

(RW) **Hanzell.** Son. ★★★+
Important pioneer of using oak cooperage for Burgundy-style **Pinot Noir** and Chardonnay in the 1950s; both continue to be superb, big, intense though not always Burgundian.

(RW) **Harbor Winery.** S.J.V. ★★★
Small operation at Sacramento making small quantities of rich **Chardonnays** from Napa Valley and ripe Amador Zinfandels.

**Hawk Crest.** Second label of Stag's Leap Wine Cellars.

**Haywood.** Somona
New winery begun by Charles Haywood with good first effort on Chardonnay; other VARIETALS to come. Bears watching.

(RW) **Heitz.** Napa ★★/★★★★★
Pacesetter for intensely concentrated Cabernet, best from **Martha's Vineyard** and Bella Oaks near Oakville; lush, buttery **Chardonnay**; and an interesting range of other VARIETALS as well as excellent **Angelica** dessert wine.

(RW) **Hill Winery, William.** Napa ★★★
Hill and partners own 600 acres on Mt. Veeder and project 100,000 cases of Cabernet and Chardonnay. Early Cabernets intense, superbly balanced, deep.

(RW) **Hoffman Mountain Ranch (HMR).** S.L.O. ★★/★★★
Family-owned estate at Paso Robles making good **Zinfandel**, Chardonnay, and unusual **Pinot Noir** from hill vineyards. One to watch.

(RW) **Hop Kiln.** Son. ★★/★★★
Small producer housed in converted hop kiln in the Russian River Valley near Healdsburg; big Sonoma Zinfandel, good dry **Gewürztraminer**, Petite Sirah.

(3) **Inglenook.** Napa ★/★★★
One of Napa's oldest wineries now owned by Heublein, making full range of VARIETALS and expanded line of jug wines (Navalle); somewhat variable quality but still excellent **Cask Cabernet**, good Fumé Blanc, delightful **Charbono**. Good value.

(W) **Iron Horse.** Son. ★★★
One of Sonoma's newest wineries in the Russian River Valley; notable Chablis-like **Chardonnay**, fresh Pinot Noir Blanc; fruity Cabernet and Pinot Noir, sparkling wines in 1983.

(3) **Italian Swiss Colony.** Son.; S.J.V. ★/★★+
Large old winery founded in last century in northern Sonoma, now owned by Heublein with most wines from grapes in the central valley. Good value Chenin Blanc, Zinfandel; wide range of jugs and fortified wines under Lejon label.

(RW) **Jekel.** Mont. ★★/★★★
Quite new winery at Greenfield in Monterey making very promising **Chardonnay**, delightful Riesling of orange-blossom aroma.

(RW) **Johnson's of Alexander Valley.** Son. ★ ★
Young estate in Alexander Valley with 45 acres planted in **Chenin Blanc**, Zinfandel, and other varieties.

(R) **Jordan.** Son. ★ ★ ★
Ambitious new undertaking near Healdsburg modeled after Bordeaux estate and aiming at Bordeaux-style **Cabernet**; first vintage 1976 promising subsequent vintages more intense. Limited amount of Chardonnay made also.

(RW) **Keenan, Robert.** Napa ★ ★ ★
Small estate on Spring Mountain producing excellently balanced **Chardonnay**, good Cabernet, intense Pinot Noir.

(RW) **Kenwood.** Son. ★ ★/★ ★ ★
Located at Kenwood between Sonoma and Santa Rosa; makes full range of VARIETALS, best are **Cabernet** and dry **Chenin Blanc**; also good Zinfandel, Beltane Ranch Chardonnay.

(RW) **Kistler Vineyards.** Son.
Ambitious undertaking on ridge between Napa and Sonoma in Mayacamas range; 1979 Chardonnays from Dutton and Winery Lake impressive, 1980s somewhat disappointing. Pinot Noir and Cabernet to come. Bears watching.

(3) **Konocti Cellars.** L.C. ★ ★
Relatively new grower-owned winery in Lake County producing Cabernet Sauvignon, Cabernet Franc, White Riesling, Zinfandel, others. Projects 100,000 cases at full capacity.

(W) **Korbel.** Son. ★ ★ ★
One of earliest producers of good California champagne: Brut, Natural (the driest), Blanc de Noir (all Pinot Noir) and **Blanc de Blancs**.

(W) **Kornell, Hanns.** Napa ★ ★ ★
Good sparkling wines in the German style, from Riesling mainly but made by the méthode champenoise. **Extra Dry**, **Sehr Trocken** (driest). Good value.

(3) **Krug, Charles.** Napa ★ ★ +
Founded in the last century at St. Helena, consistently above-average table wines with clean, straightforward VARIETAL character; rarely extraordinary but good **Cabernet**, Chardonnay, sweet Chenin Blanc. Jug line: CK Mondavi, inexpensive but uninteresting.

(RW) **La Crema Viñera.** Son.
Very young operation in Petaluma going after Burgundian-style Pinot Noir (from Winery Lake) and Chardonnay (from Winery Lake and Ventana); Steiner Vineyard Cabernet. One to watch.

(RW) **Lambert Bridge.** Son. ★ ★ +
Young winery in Dry Creek area of northern Sonoma, attractive barrel-fermented **Chardonnay**, balanced Cabernet.

(RW) **M. Lamont.** S.J.V. ★
Brand name for wines of Bear Mountain growers' co-op at Bakersfield; now owned by Labatt Brewery. Huge quantities sold also in bulk; decent mid-VARIETALS such as French Colombard, Ruby Cabernet are best values.

(RW) **Landmark.** Son. ★ ★ +
Young winery at Windsor in the Russian River Valley specializing in white wines, Chenin Blanc, **Chardonnay**, Gewürztraminer; also good Cabernet and Pinot Noir.

(3) **Lawrence Winery.** S.L.O. ★/★ ★
Winery founded in 1979 with large acreage near Edna Valley, emphasizing straightforward, fruity VARIETALS in a light style, including Cabernet, Chardonnay, Pinot Noir, Gewürztraminer, others. Recently sold but original direction continues.

**Le Fleuron.** GENERIC and second label for Joseph Phelps Winery of Napa Valley.

**Liberty School.** Second label of Caymus, used for nonvintage Cabernets and Zinfandels identified by Lot numbers; also red and white table wines. Good value.

**Llords and Elwood.** Los Angeles ★/★★
Old-style winery based in L.A. but purchases North Coast grapes and ferments in leased space. Best known for sherries and ports.

(W) **Long Vineyards.** Napa ★★★
Very promising Chardonnay, LATE-HARVEST Riesling from tiny vineyard on Pritchard Hill; first efforts rich, intense, and well-balanced. Cabernet to come.

(R) **Lytton Springs.** Son. ★★★
Tiny property on Lytton Springs Road in Alexander Valley making blockbuster Zinfandel (grapes formerly sold to Ridge) with rich, spicy fruit and aromas. 1979 Zinfandel lighter.

(W) **Mark West Vineyards.** Son. ★★ +
Russian River Valley estate making good Chardonnay, Gewürztraminer, Pinot Noir Blanc.

(RW) **Markham.** Napa ★/★★
Recently founded winery in St. Helena with 200 acres in various parts of Napa Valley—Cabernet, Chardonnay, Muscat, Riesling. Wines from bought grapes under Vin Mark label.

**Martha's Vineyard.** Notable Cabernet vineyard in Napa Valley at Oakville, designated on Heitz Cellar's top Cabernet Sauvignon.

(RW) **Martin Ray.** S.C. ★★★
Small mountaintop property above Saratoga founded by legendary and eccentric wine figure Martin Ray; soil and climate produce intriguing Cabernet. Wines now made by Ray's son.

(3) **Martini, Louis.** Napa ★★/★★★
One of Napa's older, most distinguished names with a full range of VARIETALS and GENERICS: good Cabernet (Special Selections very fine), Pinot Noir, Zinfandel, Barbera; Mountain jug wines reliable. Luscious Moscato Amabile, but very limited availability. Good value.

(RW) **Martini & Prati.** Son. ★★
Large producer of table and GENERIC wines in southern Sonoma, extensive use of redwood cooperage for mostly Italian-style wines.

(3) **Masson, Paul.** Santa Clara ★/★★ +
Large premium producer with full line of table, sparkling, and fortified wines, founded by Burgundian Paul Masson and famous for his champagnes. Moderately good VARIETALS and Souzao ports. Top line of vintage-dated wines: Pinnacles Selections. Good Emerald Riesling.

(RW) **Matanzas Creek.** Son. ★★★
Young winery in Bennett Valley; small but impressive start with Gewürztraminer, Chardonnay, Pinot Blanc; reds to come, Cabernet and Merlot planted.

(RW) **Mayacamas.** Napa ★★★ +
Small, mountaintop estate in the Mayacamas range making Cabernet and Chardonnay of big, intense character, very long-lived. Made LATE-HARVEST Zinfandel famous; some Zinfandel occasionally produced.

(RW) **McDowell Valley Vineyards.** Men. ★★/★★★
Young solar-operated in McDowell Valley of Mendocino producing fresh, attractive whites like French Colombard, Chenin Blanc, Chardonnay. Also red VARIETALS. Bears watching.

(RW) **Mill Creek.** Son. ★★★
Young, small winery near Healdsburg with good Cabernet, Merlot, and Chardonnay; worth watching.

(3) **Mirassou.** Santa Clara ★/★★ +
The fifth generation at Mirassou first produced wines for the family label, formerly large producer of VARIETALS sold to other wineries. Pioneers with mechanical harvesting and field-crushed grapes in Monterey.

(3) **Mondavi, Robert.** Napa ★★/★★★★
Dynamic, energetic family winery started from scratch in 1966, now over a million cases annually. Constant experimentation results in often brilliant wines, but some less so. Outstanding Cabernet Reserve, also fine regular Cabernet, Fumé Blanc, Chardonnay, sweet Rieslings.

Ⓡⓦ **Monterey Peninsula.** Mon. ★★/★★★
Fruit-jammed **Zinfandel** and **Barbera** and good Cabernet from this winery on the edge of Monterey; also Petite Sirah.

Ⓡⓦ **Monterey Vineyard, The.** Mon. ★★/★★★
Part of Coca-Cola's Wine Spectrum, a huge facility at Gonzales scaled down from original 1974 projections. Good, sweet **Riesling**, Gamay Beaujolais, Gewürztraminer, and BOTRYTISED **Sauvignon Blanc**.

Ⓡⓦ **Montevina.** Ama. ★★★
Excellent property in the Shenandoah Valley making passionate **Zinfandel**, potent Sauvignon Blanc, and good Cabernet and Barbera; experimenting with Nebbiolo. Zinfandel Nuevo is a light, fruity treat. Good value.

Ⓡ **J. W. Morris Port Works.** Oakland ★★★
Small operation specializing in very good vintage-dated port and dense, fruity Pinot Noir, Cabernet, big Chardonnay.

Ⓡⓦ **Mount Eden.** Santa Clara ★★★ +
Formerly part of Martin Ray estate, now owned by multiple partnership. Spectacular vineyard on mountain overlooking Santa Clara Valley above Saratoga gives superb **Pinot Noir** and **Chardonnay**; again under direction of Richard Graff and looking more stable.

Ⓡⓦ **Mount Veeder.** Napa ★★★
Tiny mountaintop estate in the Mayacamas range producing intense **Cabernet** from own vineyard; other VARIETALS from purchased grapes.

Ⓡⓦ **Napa Wine Cellars.** Napa ★★★
New winery near Yountville in southern Napa Valley making very good Chardonnay, Cabernet, Zinfandel. One to watch.

Ⓡⓦ **Navarro Vineyards.** Men. ★★ +
Specialist in white VARIETALS from Anderson Valley; good Gewürztraminer, Riesling, and Chardonnay; produces Cabernet as well.

Ⓡⓦ **Nichelini.** Napa ★★
Small, family winery in hills east of the valley, with tasting and sales at the winery. Good Chenin Blanc, Sauvignon Vert. Good value.

Ⓡ **Niebaum-Coppola.** Napa
The old Niebaum manor house and Cabernet vineyard purchased from Inglenook by the movie director. 110 acres in vines; mostly Cabernet, some Charbono, Zinfandel, Cabernet Blanc. Ambitious projections, wines due in 1984; expensive.

③ **Novitiate of Los Gatos.** Santa Clara ★★
An old winery known mostly for fortified dessert wines; Black Muscat, Dry Malvasia. Recent emphasis on VARIETALS, Pinot Blanc, Petite Sirah, others.

Ⓡⓦ **Obester.** S.C.M. ★★ +
Small new operation at Half Moon Bay making VARIETALS from purchased grapes (mostly North Coast Counties); good Cabernet.

Ⓡⓦ **Papagni.** Madera ★★ +
Sizable grower in the central valley with new winery for VARIETALS, sherry, and dessert wines; Barbera, Alicante Bouschet, Zinfandel, excellent **Moscato d'Angelo**. Also bottles Rancho Yerba Buena Cabernet and jugs. Good value.

Ⓡⓦ **Parducci.** Men. ★★/★★★
Old-style producer at Ukiah known for round, fruity Zinfandel, good Petite Sirah, Chardonnay, moderately priced. Top line is Cellarmaster. Some wines labeled "not aged in wood." Good value.

Ⓡⓦ **Pecota, Robert.** Napa ★★★
Very small vineyard near Calistoga with good Gamay Beaujolais and delicate, spicy Flora, Petite Sirah, Sauvignon Blanc.

③ **Pedroncelli.** Son. ★★
Old, family-owned winery at Geyserville producing good standard VARIETALS; earthy, medium-bodied reds; pleasant whites at good value. Zinfandel, Chenin Blanc, Chardonnay.

(3) **Perelli-Minetti.** San Joaquin ★
Large bulk producers in the central valley, also market own VARIETALS, GENERICS, and brandy under various labels, including Eleven Cellars. Ambassador, Guasti.

(RW) **Phelps, Joseph.** Napa ★ ★ ★ +
Deluxe small winery in eastern hills above St. Helena; notable **Chardonnay**, late-harvest **Rieslings**, and fine **Gewürztraminer**; powerful reds as well, including Cabernet, Pinot Noir, Syrah. **Insignia** is top-label red; second line of table wines, Le Fleuron.

**Philip Posson.** Brand name for a Dry Flor sherry produced by the large Sierra Wine Company in San Joaquin.

(RW) **Pine Ridge.** Napa
Specialist in Cabernet and Chardonnay in recently established winery at Yountville in southern Napa Valley. The 1978 Cabernet is meaty and ripe; objective is 50,000 cases of these two VARIETALS.

(RW) **Pope Valley Winery.** Napa ★ ★
Young winery in Pope Valley, a small area in the eastern hills of Napa County, making wide range of VARIETALS in small amounts. Best so far are Sauvignon Blanc, Zinfandel.

(RW) **Preston.** Son. ★ ★ ★
Young winery at Dry Creek with first-rate Sauvignon Blanc, good Cabernet; bears watching.

(R) **Quady.** Madera. ★ ★ ★
Small producer in central valley making good vintage-dated port solely from Zinfandel, Portuguese varieties recently planted.

(R) **Rafanelli, A.** Son. ★ ★ +
Very small operation in Dry Creek area making good, berryish Zinfandel, Cabernet, and Gamay Beaujolais.

(RW) **Raymond.** Napa ★ ★ ★
Newly launched winery at St. Helena with sound, balanced **Cabernet** and Zinfandel, plus Riesling and **Chardonnay**.

(R) **Ridge.** S.C. ★ ★ ★/★ ★ ★ ★
Top-flight winery on ridge of northern Santa Cruz range; pacesetters for Zinfandel in all styles, from smooth, round Coast Range to powerful LATE HARVEST; excellent, intense Cabernet (Monte Bello, York Creek), Petite Sirah, Ruby Cabernet; occasional fine whites.

(3) **River Oaks.** Son. ★ ★
Large new winery at Healdsburg with extensive vineyards; attractive Chardonnay, Riesling, rosés, good value GENERICS.

(RW) **Roudon-Smith.** Santa Clara ★ ★ +
Small winery in hills above Santa Cruz, concentrating on powerful Zinfandel, including LATE HARVEST, fruity Cabernet. Best Zinfandel: Chauvet vineyard.

(RW) **Round Hill.** Napa ★ ★ +
Home winemaker now selling commercially from purchased grapes; medium-style Cabernet, Chardonnay, Chenin Blanc at good prices. Very good value.

(RW) **Rutherford Hill.** Napa ★ ★ +
New winery owned by valley growers and partners in Freemark Abbey. Good quality, especially Gewürztraminer, Chardonnay, Merlot.

(RW) **St. Clement.** Napa ★ ★ ★
Winery at the foot of Spring Mountain with fine, oaky **Chardonnay**, well-balanced classic Cabernet. One to watch.

(RW) **Sanford & Benedict.** S. Barb. ★ ★/★ ★ ★
Young winery and vineyards near Lompoc above Santa Barbara; Pinot Noir, Cabernet, and Merlot packed with extract, intense Chardonnay. Promising, but harsh young reds need time to develop.

(3) **San Martin.** Santa Clara ★ ★/★ ★ ★ ★
Large winery at Gilroy producing very creditable VARIETALS, especially Zinfandel (Amador), attractive Chenin Blanc, also light, low-alcohol whites: soft Chenin Blanc, soft J. Riesling. Good value.

ℝⓦ **San Pasqual Vineyards.** Escondido ★ ★ +

30,000-case winery near San Diego owned by a group of partners growing Napa Gamay, Chenin Blanc, **Sauvignon Blanc**. Red table wine a blend of Cabernet, Petite Sirah, and Gamay—good value.

ⓇSanta Cruz Mountain Vineyard.** S.C.M. ★ ★ ★

Very small property making intense, powerful, hill-grown Pinot Noir and stalwart Cabernet, Petite Sirah from purchased grapes. To watch.

ℝⓦ **Santa Ynez.** S. Barb. ★ ★ / ★ ★ ★

Promising new winery in the Santa Ynez Valley—lovely 1978 Sauvignon Blanc, delicate Chardonnay; somewhat vegetal Cabernet so far.

ℝⓦ **Sausal Winery.** Son. ★ ★ +

Growers in Alexander Valley with 150 acres, mainly in Zinfandel and white varieties. Recently began making their own wines, including full-bodied Zinfandel and an excellent dry white, Sausal Blanc (Colombard blended with 10% Chardonnay); very good value.

ⓌSchramsberg.** Napa ★ ★ ★ ★

California's finest champagnes, especially fresh Blanc de Blancs, rich **Blanc de Noir**, charming Cuvée de Pinot Noir sparkling pink; at revived Schramsberg estate in hills near Calistoga.

③ **Sebastiani.** Son. ★ ★ / ★ ★ ★

One of the largest family-owned wineries at Sonoma, making full range of table, sparkling, and dessert wines. New directions of late as well as traditional Italian-style reds like fine, well-aged Proprietor's Reserve **Barbera, Cabernet, Pinot Noir**, and **Zinfandel**. Good value.

**Setrakian.** San Joaquin ★

A California Growers' brand, large producer of bulk wines, plus average table, dessert and sparkling wines.

Ⓡ **Shafer Vineyards.** Napa ★ ★ ★

First releases of Cabernet Sauvignon and Merlot from this new winery off the Silverado Trail at Yountville are quite good. One to watch.

Ⓡ **Shaw, Charles F.** Napa ★ ★ ★

New small producer above St. Helena aiming at cru-style Beaujolais; first efforts very close. Small amount of Zinfandel by 1982.

ℝⓦ **Shown & Sons.** Napa

A well-known grower near Rutherford now making his own Cabernet, Riesling, Chenin Blanc from vineyard of 75 acres.

Ⓡ **Silver Oak.** Napa ★ ★ ★

Limited production from small winery at Rutherford. Producing only Alexander Valley Cabernet, given 5 years aging before release.

③ **Simi.** Son. ★ ★ ★

Old winery at Healdsburg now owned by Moët-Hennessey, producing good, sound VARIETALS, especially graceful Cabernet, Zinfandel, **Chardonnay, Gewürztraminer**.

ℝⓦ **Smith-Madrone.** Napa ★ ★ ★

Small winery on Spring Mountain making Chardonnay, Cabernet, interesting Spätlese-style **Riesling** (see "The Wines of Germany").

Ⓦ **Smothers.** S.C.M. ★ ★ / ★ ★ ★

Smashing first Gewürztraminer, recently back on form, in transition from Santa Cruz vineyards to Sonoma near Glen Ellen.

ℝⓦ **Sonoma-Cutrer.** Son.

Extensive vineyards in Sonoma Valley now geared up for making own wine; noted to date for intense Chardonnay. One to watch.

③ **Sonoma Vineyards.** Son. ★ ★ / ★ ★ ★

Large, modern winery at Windsor in the Russian River Valley; full range of VARIETALS, GENERICS, new sparkling Piper-Sonoma. Good Chardonnay (Chalk Hill Vineyard) and Cabernet from estate-owned vineyards, especially **Alexander's Crown Cabernet**. Good value.

ℝⓦ **Sotoyome.** Son. ★ ★

New small winery at Healdsburg emphasizing unfiltered Cabernet, Petite Sirah, Zinfandel.

(RW) **Souverain.** Son. ★ ★ / ★ ★ ★

Handsome winery in Alexander Valley and an old name revived with sound, attractive VARIETALS, good value Cabernet, Colombard Blanc, Zinfandel, Pinot Noir.

(RW) **Spring Mountain.** Napa ★ ★ ★

Showcase estate on Spring Mountain producing very fine **Cabernet**, **Chardonnay**, Sauvignon Blanc, also Pinot Noir.

(R) **Stag's Leap Vineyard.** Napa ★ ★ +

Longtime grower at estate near the crag known as Stag's Leap, now producing robust, reasonably priced reds like Burgundy, Petite Sirah, light red Barboza.

(RW) **Stag's Leap Wine Cellars.** Napa ★ ★ ★ / ★ ★ ★ ★

Small but growing producer in lower Napa with notable **Cabernet**, very good **Merlot**, good Chardonnay and Riesling; well-made wines that receive meticulous attention.

(RW) **Sterling.** Napa ★ ★ / ★ ★ ★ ★

Magnificent gleaming winery set on knoll at north end of the valley, now part of The Wine Spectrum of Coca-Cola. Superb **Cabernet**, especially Reserve, Merlot, Sauvignon Blanc, **Chardonnay**.

(RW) **Stevenot Vineyards.** Calaveras ★ ★ +

Young winery in Sierra foothills producing attractive Sauvignon Blanc, Chenin Blanc, Chardonnay, also reds. Whites delicate and appealing.

(RW) **Stonegate.** Napa ★ ★

Small winery in northern Napa, generally attractive but variable quality Sauvignon Blanc, Chenin Blanc, Pinot Noir.

(W) **Stony Hill.** Napa ★ ★ ★ ★

Notable small estate on top of mountains above St. Helena; very limited quantities of fine, crisp Chardonnay, Riesling, Gewürztraminer, and sweet Sémillon du Soleil. Hard to find, but worth seeking.

(3) **Stony Ridge.** Alameda ★ ★

Medium-sized winery in Livermore Valley, best known for reds; also fair whites such as Sauvignon Blanc, Chenin Blanc, good dry **Riesling**.

(R) **Story Vineyards.** Amador ★ ★ +

Big, punchy Zinfandel is main thrust at this young winery, located on the edge of Amador's Shenandoah Valley.

(RW) **Sutter Home.** Napa ★ ★ +

Known for stalwart, hearty Zinfandels from Amador; also a fresh, dry white Zinfandel and sweet Moscato Ambile. Good value.

(R) **Swan, Joseph.** Son. ★ ★ ★

Tiny estate at Forestville making very big, rich Pinot Noir and Zinfandel from intense ripe fruit. Most sold out to regulars on mailing list.

**Taylor California Cellars.** Mon. ★ / ★ ★

A brand owned by Coca-Cola's Wine Spectrum, producing large quantities of GENERICS (Burgundy, Chablis, Rhine) and inexpensive nonvintage VARIETALS; also dry white and red table wines. Good value.

(RW) **Trefethen.** Napa ★ ★ ★

Large estate at Yountville that sells most of its grapes but also produces notable, stylish **Chardonnay**, **Cabernet**, and quality table red and white under the Eschcol label.

(RW) **Trentadue.** Son. ★ ★ +

Long-established growers and bulk producers in northern Sonoma, now making recently upgraded VARIETALS like **Zinfandel**, Chenin Blanc, Cabernet, good red GENERICS.

(RW) **Turgeon & Lohr.** Santa Clara ★ ★ / ★ ★ ★

Small winery in San Jose with sizable holdings in Monterey; wines appear on J. Lohr label, include Chardonnay, aggressive Cabernet, and Gamay Noir.

(RW) **Veedercrest.** Napa ★ ★ +

Winery on Mount Veeder in the Mayacamas range, variable quality reds and whites such as White Riesling, Chardonnay, Chenin Blanc.

(RW) **Ventana.** Monterey ★ ★ / ★ ★ ★
Young winery in Soledad with 600 acres, sells most of its grapes;
Sauvignon Blanc, Chardonnay quite good, reds somewhat light.

(RW) **Villa Mount Eden.** Napa ★ ★ ★
Small estate at Oakville making good, elegant **Cabernet**, full, oakish
Chardonnay, dry **Chenin Blanc**, elegant Pinot Noir.

(3) **Weibel.** S.C.M. ★
Large, old winery at Mission San Jose making broad range of average
wines, both table and dessert; sparkling wines from Sonoma.

(RW) **Wente.** Alameda ★ ★ ★
One of the oldest names in California wine, pioneer with VARIETALS. Best
known for fresh, balanced whites like **Chardonnay**, Chenin Blanc,
**Sauvignon Blanc** and blends like **Blanc de Blancs**, **Grey Riesling**; good
Petite Sirah, straightforward Pinot Noir. Good value.

(RW) **Wine and the People.** See Berkeley Wine Cellars.

(RW) **Yverdon.** Napa
Still-evolving winery on Spring Mountain; vineyards there and near
Calistoga planted to Cabernet, Merlot, Riesling.

(RW) **Zaca Mesa.** S.Barb. ★ ★ +
Young winery in the Santa Ynez Valley making interesting Zinfandel,
**Sauvignon Blanc**; also Cabernet, Chardonnay, Pinot Noir.

(RW) **ZD.** Napa ★ ★ ★
Small winery transplanted from Sonoma to Rutherford in Napa Valley;
big, tough **Pinot Noir** promising; good Amador Zinfandel; reasonably
good Chardonnay.

# The Pacific Northwest

The vineyards of Washington, Oregon, and Idaho are on the same
latitudes as Bordeaux and Burgundy in France, a fact that has
fostered a tremendous surge in plantings over the last decade. The
state of Washington has the most acreage, most of it in the Yakima
Valley 190 miles southeast of Seattle, and some near the Oregon
border in Hood River Valley.

Oregon has a sprinkling of small but growing wineries, principally
in the Willamette Valley west and south of Portland but also in the
Umpqua Valley in southwest Oregon. Idaho's small vineyards lie in
the western part of the state between Boise and the Snake River.

Though a fair amount of Concord grows in the northwest, particularly Washington, and both states produce fruit and berry wines; but
excitement centers on such early-ripening vinifera varieties as Chardonnay, Sauvignon Blanc, Pinot Noir, and Merlot; excellent White
Riesling is made in Oregon, also promising for Pinot Noir and
Cabernet.

# WINE GUIDE: THE PACIFIC NORTHWEST

**Adelsheim Vineyards.** Small operation in Oregon's Willamette Valley, producing good Merlot and Semillon (from Yakima grapes); also Chardonnay, Riesling, Pinot Noir from own vineyard. Graceful wines.

(RW) **Amity.** Small winery southwest of Portland in Oregon's Willamette Valley emphasizing whites, especially Riesling, and Pinot Noir.

(RW) **Associated Vintners.** A group of professors in Seattle whose jointly owned vineyards in Yakima Valley produce notable Gewürztraminer, Sémillon, Chardonnay, also promising Pinot Noir and Cabernet Sauvignon.

**Big Fir Winery.** Specialist in berry wines near Oregon's northern border in the Cascade foothills. Other wines from vinifera grapes forthcoming.

**Bjelland Vineyards.** Small winery in southern Oregon making Cabernet Sauvignon, Chardonnay, Riesling, other varieties, plus berry wines.

**Château Benoit.** Small winery in Willamette Valley in Oregon named for its owners; good **Riesling**, also Chardonnay, Pinot Noir, Muller-Thurgau.

(3) **Château Ste. Michelle.** Large winery headquartered in Seattle with large vineyards in Yakima Valley. Good Cabernet, Sémillon, Riesling, sweet Chenin Blanc. Sparkling wines from Chardonnay and Pinot Noir grapes are very good.

(RW) **Cote de Colombe.** 20-acre vineyard and winery in northwest Oregon hills producing Chenin Blanc, Riesling, Chardonnay, Pinot Noir, and Cabernet (from Washington grapes). Name means "hill of doves."

(RW) **E.B. Foote Winery.** Young winery in the Yakima Valley, best known for good home-grown Riesling.

(RW) **Elk Cove Vineyards.** Tiny Willamette Valley winery producing fine Yakima Valley Merlot, good estate-grown Pinot Noir; also Chardonnay and other varieties.

(RW) **Eyrie Vineyards.** Quite small winery and vineyard in the Willamette Valley near Dundee, Oregon, making fine Pinot Noir and other varieties.

**Forgeron Vineyard.** Small winery established in 1976 near Eugene, Oregon. Very limited production but noted for White Riesling.

(RW) **Hillcrest.** One of the first wineries in the Umpqua Valley at Roseburg, Oregon, emphasizing White Riesling and other white varieties; some Pinot Noir, Zinfandel.

(RW) **Hinzerling.** Small winery in the Yakima Valley near Prosser, Washington, making sweet and dry Gewürztraminer, some Cabernet; expansion planned.

(RW) **Knudsen-Erath.** Partners in a growing winery at Dundee, Oregon, in the Willamette Valley making impressive Pinot Noir, Chardonnay, some sparkling wines. One to watch.

**Oak Knoll Winery.** Oregon winery west of Portland noted mostly for fruit and berry wines, especially Loganberry, Raspberry, unusual Gooseberry. Also produce Pinot Noir, Zinfandel, other VARIETALS.

(RW) **Ponzi Vineyards.** Small, lively winery near Portland growing Riesling, Pinot Noir and Chardonnay; Riesling is best to date.

(RW) **Preston.** Small but growing winery in eastern Yakima Valley near Pasco; quite good Chardonnay, Sauvignon Blanc, Chenin Blanc; also making Cabernet and Merlot.

**Sagemoor Farms.** Large vineyard in the Yakima Valley producing good **Merlot** and Cabernet Sauvignon—no winery but sells grapes to several Oregon and Washington wineries.

(RW) **Shafer Vineyard Cellars.** 20 acres in Gales Creek Valley of northwestern Oregon. First releases of Chardonnay, Pinot Noir, and Sauvignon Blanc appeared in 1981.

(RW) **Siskiyou Vineyards.** Young winery and 12-acre vineyard in highlands of southwest Oregon, producing Riesling, Pinot Noir.

Ⓡⓦ **Ste. Chapelle.** Idaho's foremost winery so far, located at Sunny Slope west of Boise; named for the famous Paris chapel and making promising Rieslings, austere Fumé Blanc. Excellent Chardonnay.

Ⓡⓦ **Sokol Blosser.** Young winery in the Willamette Valley at Dundee, Oregon, making fine Riesling, good Sauvignon Blanc, and big plans for Pinot Noir. One to watch.

Ⓡⓦ **Tualatin.** Growing winery due west of Portland producing excellent Riesling, Gewürztraminer; oak-aged Pinot Noirs beginning to appear. Bears watching.

Ⓡⓦ **Valley View Winery.** An old vineyard property in southern Oregon replanted with Chardonnay, Gamay, Gewürztraminer, and Cabernet, now equipped with modern winery.

# New York and Other States

New York and other states east of the Rockies have traditionally produced wines from two types of grapes: (1) those developed from native varieties, such as Concord, Catawba, and Niagara, or (2) from French-American hybrids, crossings of native American grapes with French species bred to survive the colder climates of the Northeast. The native American grapes have a distinct grapiness about them that is quite different from wine grapes grown anywhere else, a flavor sometimes characterized as "foxiness." The French-American hybrids were developed to ameliorate this character; they are much closer in style and flavor to the European grape species *Vitis vinifera* that is grown in wine regions around the world.

New York State's wine industry is the second largest in the nation. Its principal growing regions are the Finger Lakes district west of Albany and toward the Great Lakes, Erie and Ontario; and the Hudson River Valley, a burgeoning region 50 miles north of New York City gaining attention for its hybrid varietals like Seyval Blanc and Chancellor. European varieties are grown in the state's newest region on the eastern tip of Long Island; there is also growing interest for them in the Finger Lakes region.

Important vineyards are also to be found in Ohio, Michigan, Virginia, Maryland, Missouri, Pennsylvania, Arkansas, and Texas.

## GRAPE VARIETIES: NEW YORK AND OTHER STATES

**Aurora.** One of the top white French-American hybrids developed by Seibel, producing crisp dry white wines and quite good sparkling ones.

**Baco Noir.** Forceful red French-American hybrid; gives deeply colored wine and is often blended with other red varieties (such as Chancellor) to soften its impact.

**Cascade.** Early-ripening, pale red French-American hybrid used for reds and rosés.

**Catawba.** Native light red grape with strong grapy flavor used to make pink or white wines and a great deal of sparkling wine (New York).

**Cayuga.** A cross between Riesling and Seyval Blanc that makes a soft, fragrant, pleasing white wine.

**Chambourcin.** Increasingly popular French-American hybrid red.

**Chancellor.** French-American hybrid red that produces sound, medium-bodied dry reds.

**Chelois.** French-American hybrid for round, fruity reds of some richness but often hints of native grapiness.

**Concord.** The great American jam grape that produces grapy, usually sweet red wine, or white if juice is pressed leaving color-rich skins behind. Widely planted in New York, strong grapy flavors.

**Cynthiana.** A red grape native to the Ozark Mountains in Arkansas and Missouri; full-bodied, usually sweet, but without the "foxy" flavor.

**De Chaunac.** Good, rich, red French-American hybrid; excellent color and body, but lacks tannin.

**Delaware.** One of the best of the native white grapes—crisp, clean wine with less of the native grapiness. Dry versions can be quite pleasant.

**Dutchess.** Native grape found mostly in New York, similar to but not quite as good as Delaware.

**Foch (Marechal Foch).** Vigorous French-American hybrid red producing fullish, Burgundy-style wines.

**Isabella.** Deep red native American grape with pronounced grapy flavors; pale juice used in New York sparkling wines.

**Leon Millot.** French-American hybrid producing red wines similar to Foch.

**Niagara.** One of the oldest American grapes used for sweet, grapy whites, sometimes quite pleasant.

**Ravat.** Crisp white hybrid, increasingly planted for dry, Chablis-like wines and late-harvest sweet wines.

**Seyval Blanc.** Possibly the best and certainly most popular of French hybrid whites, making fine, fruity, full-bodied dry wines.

**Verdelet.** Excellent white hybrid producing fragrant, delicate dry white wines; promising future.

**Vidal.** A white hybrid that is gaining popularity in the New York wine regions for dry and LATE-HARVEST wines.

# WINE GUIDE: NEW YORK AND OTHER STATES

③ **Benmarl.** Forward-looking property in the Hudson Valley at Marlboro with increasingly good wines from French-American hybrids, notably Marlboro Village White, Red, Seyval Blanc.

⑭ **Boordy Vineyards.** Vineyards owned by Philip Wagner who pioneered with French-American hybrids in the United States. Sound red and white table wines from vineyards in Maryland near the Potomac.

③ **Brotherhood.** One of the oldest wineries in the East (Hudson Valley) with a wide range of mostly sweet table wines, fortified wines, some hybrid VARIETALS such as Chelois, Chancellor.

③ **Bully Hill.** Small property in the Finger Lakes district of New York making good reds and whites, some sparkling wine from French-American hybrids. Bully Hill Red, Bully Hill White, Chancellor, as well as fanciful proprietary labels like Space Shuttle White.

③ **Canandaigua.** Old firm in the Finger Lakes region of New York producing under the Virginia Dare label.

③ **Cascade Mountain.** Small property near Poughkeepsie in the Hudson Valley region of New York producing good dry reds, white, rosé.

(RW) **Chadwick Bay.** An ambitious young winery in the Lake Erie district of western New York near Fredonia. Promising hybrids, Chardonnay.

(RW) **Chateau Esperanza.** New winery in the Finger Lakes on a bluff over-looking Lake Keuka making a name with Chardonnay and Riesling. One to watch.

(3) **Chateau Grand Travers.** Ambitious producer in Michigan; grows French-American hybrids and imports vinifera wines from California.

(3) **Chicama.** Family-owned winery on Martha's Vineyard pioneering with vinifera such as Chardonnay, Riesling, Pinot Noir, Zinfandel.

(W) **Clinton Vineyards.** Small but important estate near Poughkeepsie, N.Y., producing superb Seyval Blanc.

(RW) **Commonwealth.** Young winery in Plymouth, Massachusetts that buys grapes from the Finger Lakes to produce Vidal Blanc, Cayuga, and other hybrids.

(W) **Fenn Valley Vineyards.** Winery established in early 1970s in Fenns-ville, Mich. with plans for expansion; hybrids and some vinifera vari-eties well-received to date, especially Riesling.

(3) **Glasscock Vineyards.** Texas' newest winery and most promising with vineyards in west Texas on cool plateaus of the Davis Mountains. Good Sauvignon Blanc and Chenin Blanc to date, Zinfandel, Cabernet, Pinot Noir to come. Best vineyard: Blue Mountain. Winery is in San Antonio.

(RW) **Glenora.** Young winery in the Finger Lakes at Dundee, N.Y., producing good hybrid VARIETALS such as Seyval Blanc Cayuga, Chardonnay.

(3) **Gold Seal.** Old leading firm in the Finger Lakes region of New York strongly influenced by Frenchman Charles Fournier who encouraged work with vinifera varieties. Best wines: **Chardonnay**, Charles Fournier Blanc de Blancs champagne.

(3) **Great Western.** Long-standing sparkling wine producers in New York's Finger Lakes, now owned by Coca-Cola's Wine Spectrum. New wine-maker, new directions seem promising, especially with Vidal Blanc, Verdelet, de Chaunac Rosé. Superb 1981 Vidal Ice Wine.

(RW) **Haight Vineyards.** Connecticut's first bonded winery at Litchfield, producing French-American hybrids, prize-winning Riesling.

(3) **Hargrave Vineyards.** Pioneering young winery at Cutchogue on the eastern tip of Long Island, with good Chardonnay, Cabernet-Merlot, Whole Berry Pinot Noir; promising future.

(W) **Herman Wiemer.** New winery well-situated on Seneca Lake in the Finger Lakes, already noted for fine Chardonnay and Riesling.

(W) **Heron Hill.** New small winery in the Finger Lakes region at Hammonds-port, New York; interesting Riesling, Chardonnay, Seyval Blanc, Dela-ware.

(RW) **Johnson Estate.** Small winery near Lake Erie that sells most of its native American grapes and hybrids but makes small amounts of Seyval Blanc, Chancellor, Ives Noir.

(RW) **Lenz Vineyard.** New plantings on Long Island's North Fork that will eventually produce Merlot, Sauvignon Blanc, Chardonnay. Look for it.

(RW) **Markko.** Very small property in Ohio near Youngstown producing very fine **Chardonnay**, good Riesling, some Cabernet. Quantity too small to go very far but quality has far-reaching impact.

(3) **Meredyth.** Virginia's foremost winery, with plantings in mostly hybrids, some vinifera. Foch, Seyval Blanc, Johannisberg Riesling, others.

(RW) **Montbray.** Carefully tended vineyards of French hybrids and vinifera at Silver Run, Maryland. Good Seyval Blanc, Foch, Chardonnay, Riesling.

(3) **Nissley.** Young winery in Bainbridge, Pennsylvania making wine in a converted, century-old barn; 30-acre vineyard is in French-American hybrids, including Aurora, de Chaunac. The Susquehanna White is dry and fresh.

(3) **Royal Winery.** Large family-owned winery in the Hudson Valley pro-ducing broad range of kosher wines under the Kedem label; also some hybrids and vinifera: Chenin Blanc, Grenache rosé.

(RW) **Sakonnet.** Small winery making a name in New England for Rhode Island Red and America's Cup White, which are based on French hybrids.

(3) **Tabor Hill.** Well-estabished winery in Michigan becoming more widely known for its Vidal Blanc, Baco Noir; also some Chardonnay.

(3) **Taylor.** New York State's largest winery with vineyards in the Finger Lakes region and a new line of wines, California Cellars; still produces wines from native grapes, some hybrids for table wines (Lake Country Red, White, Gold), sherries, New York State champagne.

(RW) **Vinifera Wine Cellars.** Owned by Dr. Konstantin Frank, pioneer with vinifera wines (Chardonnay, Riesling, Muscat Ottonel) in the Finger Lakes region of New York. Only vinifera VARIETALS.

(RW) **Wagner.** One of New York's most promising young wineries with vineyards on the east bank of Seneca Lake in the Finger Lakes district. Fine Chardonnay, Seyval Blanc and fruity reds.

(3) **Widmer.** Large old firm in the Finger Lakes region producing wide range of table wines from native grapes, hybrids, and vineyards in California. Lake Niagara, Delaware, Cream Sherry.

(3) **Wiederkehr.** The South's largest winery with extensive vineyards in the Ozark Mountains at Altus, Arkansas. Mostly native varieties, including good Cynthiana; earnest experiments with Riesling and other vinifera varieties.

**SEYVAL BLANC.** This wine is made of 100% Seyval Blanc, one of the French-American hybrid grape varieties that does well in cold climates such as that of New York State. The grapes were grown on the Clinton estate in the Hudson River region near Poughkeepsie, N.Y., and the wine was made and bottled by the owner.

# THE WINES OF AUSTRALIA

I t is only fairly recently that the world has discovered some of the fine wines of Australia. Though the industry got its start about the same time as that of California (wine grapes were planted by the first immigrants in 1788 near Sydney), production and export have increased steadily and impressively in the last 20 years. Credit for the first major plantings of the 1830s goes to a schoolteacher named James Busby, who planted vineyards in the Hunter River Valley of New South Wales. The success of wines from those vineyards encouraged plantings throughout southern Australia, though today they are in widely disparate areas ranging from Perth on the western coast to Coonawarra in the south, and as far north as Roma in Queensland.

Today, Australia has roughly 200,000 acres under vine at latitudes roughly corresponding to the northern coast counties of California around San Francisco (Napa, Sonoma, Santa Clara), as well as those of central Chile. Most of Australia's wine-producing regions are in hot, dry climates that produce full-bodied wines and a large quantity of dessert and fortified wines such as Sherry. The better table wines come from cooler growing regions, such as Hunter Valley in New South Wales, the Barossa Valley of northwestern Victoria, the Southern Vales near Adelaide and Coonawarra of South Australia's southernmost portion.

Principal wine grapes were, until recently, the Shiraz for red wines and the Sémillon for white, and they are still the dominant premium varietals. The German Riesling (here known as Rhine Riesling) and related varieties have also accounted for many of the lighter, fruitier white wines. In the last decade, however, there has been much interest in such grape varieties as Cabernet Sauvignon and Chardonnay, with the result of many new plantings of these varietals as well as increases for Pinot Noir and Sauvignon Blanc.

Nomenclature is varied and somewhat confusing to those unfamiliar with Australian wines. Many wines are labeled as generics, such as Claret, White Burgundy, or Hermitage (actually considered another name for the Shiraz grape), but varietal names are increasingly used, as in Cabernet Sauvignon, Shiraz, or often a combination of the two, as they are frequently blended. There are numerous proprietary names as well, such as Chateau Tahbilk or McWilliam's Lexia. The most informative labeling, however, gives regional designation and grape variety, as in Watervale Shiraz Cabernet, a red blended from these two varieties from the Watervale district of Southern Australia.

In the last decade tremendous modernization has taken place within the industry. New technology, such as the use of stainless steel fermenting tanks and cold fermentation techniques, has resulted in fresher, more delicate and fragrant white wines, for example. While Australia has long been known for its robust, full-bodied, and long-lived red wines, it is now producing a great many light fruity reds, increasingly popular for everyday consumption, at very reasonable prices.

Vintages in Australia are rather like those in California since the two climates are relatively similar. Although some years are definitely superior to others, such as 1980, catastrophes across the board are rare. Poorer vintages in some regions are usually offset in other areas.

# PRINCIPAL WINE REGIONS

## New South Wales (N.S.W.)

**Corowa**   South of Sydney near the Murray River; known chiefly for fortified wines and Brandy.

**Hunter Valley**   One of the oldest and most important wine-producing areas for claret-style reds based mostly on Shiraz and dry whites made from Sémillon, also known as Hunter Riesling. Principal areas are Pokolbin and Rothbury, both often seen on labels. Famous individual estates include Lindemans' Ben Ean, Lake's Folly, The Rothbury Estate, Brokenwood, Drayton's Bellevue, and Penfold's Dalwood.

**Mudgee**   Climate similar to Hunter but on higher ground. Principal plantings are Cabernet, Shiraz, Sémillon, Rhine Riesling, Chardonnay, and Traminer. Excellent reds are made here.

**Riverina**   Also known as MIA, Murrumbidgee Irrigation Area. Hot, flat country formerly known mostly for fortified wines. Cold fermentation techniques now account for lighter, fruitier table wines, increased emphasis on better varietals.

**Rooty Hill**   Just west of Sydney and best known for its sparkling wines, namely, Minchinbury Champagne.

## Queensland

**Roma**   Australia's northernmost, and warmest, wine region. Mostly fortified and dessert wines made here.

## South Australia (S.A.)

**Barossa Valley** (Eden Valley, Springton)   Famed for fruity whites from the Rhine Riesling, Barossa is Australia's most famous wine region, located about 35 miles north of Adelaide. Settled by German immigrants, the region reflects this heritage in the white wines, cuisine, and music. Most major wineries have vineyards here, including Seppelt's, Lindeman, Penfold, Thomas Hardy, Henschke, Gramp, and the cooperative, Kaiser Stuhl. Also small prestigious producers like Wolf Blass. In addition to fruity whites, Barossa is known for Shiraz and classic reds from Cabernet Sauvignon.

**Coonawarra**   Small but excellent region for red wines based on Cabernet and Shiraz, also Rhine Riesling. Aboriginal name means "wild honeysuckle." Coolest and southernmost growing region where grapes ripen slowly and late. Wynns, Redman, and Lindeman are important producers here.

**Keppoch**   Adjacent to Coonawarra on the north, with similar climate and possibilities for future expansion. Reds and whites similar to Coonawarra though perhaps more intense.

**Southern Vales** (McLaren, Morphett)   Longhorne Creek, South of Adelaide. Cool regions producing fine reds and whites that are among Australia's best. Hardy's Tintara vineyard is here, Kay Bros.' Amery, as well as Reynell, Ryecroft, and Seaview.

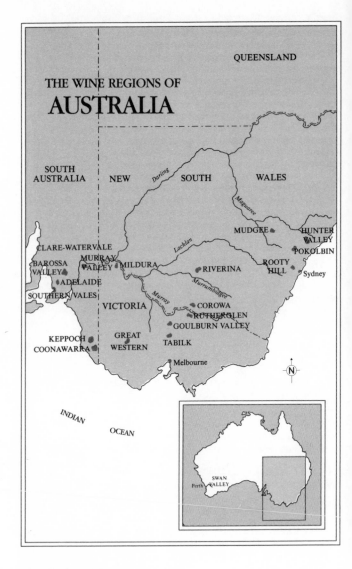

THE WINE REGIONS OF
# AUSTRALIA

# TASMANIA (Tas.)

**This island** off the southeastern coast is too cool and damp for most
varieties, but limited experimental vineyards of Pinot Noir, Cabernet and
Rhine Riesling show promise for future.

## Victoria

**Glenrowan-Milawa** (Wangaratta)    Green valley of the Ovens River, producing interesting whites and reds. Leading vineyards are Bailey's Bundarra, Brown Bros.
**Goulburn/Tabilk**    Small area north of Melbourne producing good reds,
especially from Chateau Tahbilk.

**Great Western**  Westernmost slopes in Victoria at 1,000 feet above sea level. Known mostly for sparkling wines; dry reds and whites also produced. Seppelt's Arrawatta estate is here and Best's Concongella.

**Mildara** (Merbein, Red Cliffs, Robinvale)  Mostly fortified dessert wines and red/white blending wines here at another district along the Murray River. Crisp dry whites and good reds appear under Mildara Winery label. Robinvale is becoming known for its dryish whites such as McWilliams' Lexia.

**Rutherglen**  South of Corowa on the hot plains of the Murray. Known for Sherries, big, hearty reds from Shiraz, and more recently, lighter table reds and whites.

## Western Australia (W.A.)

**Margaret River**  New region south of Perth showing excellent promise for varietals like Sauvignon Blanc and Chardonnay.

**Swan Valley**  Near Perth, very hot climate producing very robust wines, from Sandalford's and Houghton's.

# PRINCIPAL GRAPE VARIETIES

## Red

**Cabernet Sauvignon.**  Gaining ground rapidly, second only to Shiraz in number of plantings; the two are often blended and prosper similarly in cooler regions. Several 100% Cabernets are extremely good and age well.

**Grenache.**  Fairly widely grown and produces some light wines under the grape name, but mainly used for blending in dry reds.

**Pinot Noir.**  Small acreage as yet but appears promising for cooler regions of Australia.

**Shiraz.**  Of Persian origin and similar to the Syrah of the Rhône Valley in France where it is used in Hermitage and Châteauneuf-du-Pape. In cooler regions of Australia, like Barossa, Coonawarra, or Mudgee, Shiraz produces big, interesting red wines, though somewhat lighter than those of the Rhône. Wines from the hot plains, however, are much heavier and less distinguished, but often pleasantly robust.

## White

**Chardonnay, Sauvignon blanc, Traminer (Gewürztraminer).**  These varietals, especially Chardonnay, are increasingly of interest in Australia, though only small quantities are produced.

**Rhine Riesling.**  The German Riesling. Produces light, aromatic wines, often dry and crisp as Alsatian Rieslings, though just as often fruity or sweet. Best often labeled Moselle, from the Barossa Valley.

**Sémillon.**  Australia's most important grape for dry whites, particularly from Hunter Valley (where it is known, confusingly, as the Hunter Riesling). Produces soft but full-bodied wines labeled by grape variety or as White Burgundy. Soon to be transcended by Chardonnay.

**Trebbiano.**  The Italian grape known elsewhere as Ugni Blanc; widely planted for everyday table whites; often blended with white varieties.

# WINE GUIDE

**All Saints.** Vic.
One of Australia's oldest; many vineyards in Rutherglen that produce their Clarets. Lyre Bird Claret, Estate-Bottled Claret, Cabernet Shiraz, Old Liqueur, and Muscat.

**Angove.** S.A.
Mostly blended table wines, a Cabernet Sauvignon and several dessert wines. Fino Sherry, Sauvignon Blanc, and Bookmark Riesling.

**Bailey's.** Vic.
Very old winery whose famous Bundarra vineyard produces long-lived Shiraz and Claret. Also many excellent dessert wines. Bundarra Hermitage, Bundarra Claret, and Muscat Liqueur.

**Berri's.** Vic.
This cooperative in the Murray Valley has Australia's largest winery, producing a full line of table wines, dessert and fortified wines, and Brandy. Rhine Riesling Selected Vineyard, Cabernet Shiraz, and Gordo Moselle.

**Best's.** Vic.
Owners of famous Concongella vineyard in Great Western district of Victoria. St. Andrew's Hermitage Great Western Claret No. 0, producing Claret-style reds, hock, and dessert wines.

**Bilyara, Wolf Blass.** S.A.
Small producer of blockbuster reds in Barossa Valley; also clean fresh whites. Bilyara Individual Vineyard Dry Red (often Langhorne Creek), Bilyara Rhine Riesling.

**Bleasdale.** S.A.
Old family winery in Langhorne Creek district known for quite good dry reds among a full line of table wines and fortified dessert wines. Shiraz, Cabernet Sauvignon, and Verdelho.

**Brand, Eric.** S.A.
Small dedicated winemaker in Coonawarra producing highly respected reds. Cabernet Sauvignon, Laira, and Cabernet-Shiraz.

**Brokenwood.** N.S.W.
Relatively new, small producer of fine reds in Hunter Valley. Hermitage/Cabernet Sauvignon, Cabernet Sauvignon.

**Brown Bros.** Vic.
Family-owned winery of high repute in Milawa producing good table reds and whites; the reds from Milawa are especially good. Milawa Cabernet Sauvignon, Bin Claret, Rhine Riesling, and Mystic Park Dry White. Also fine Muscat and liqueurs.

**Buring, Leo.** S.A.
Large producer of full range of table and dessert wines, Ports, and Sherries in Barossa Valley. Chateau Leonay, Rhine Riesling, and Chateau Leonay Vintage White Burgundy.

**Campbell's.** Vic.
Large producer of full range in Rutherglen, best are whites and dessert wines, including a crisp dry Trebbiano.

**Chateau Tahbilk.** Vic.
Very reputable producer in Tabilk area known mostly for big, well-made reds, some whites. Private Bin Cabernet Sauvignon.

**Chateau Yaldara.** S.A.
Large producer of mostly white wines and good sparkling wines in southern Barossa Valley. Good but not outstanding quaffing wines.

**Craigmoor.** N.S.W.
Sizable winery in Mudgee, producing good table red and white, Port, and Muscat. Cabernet Shiraz, Mudgee Shiraz, Sémillon Chardonnay.

**d'Ahrenberg.** S.A.
Producer of very robust reds in McLaren Vale, as well as some white wine and Port. Aggressive Cabernets, generous full-bodied reds labeled Burgundy.

**De Bortoli.** N.S.W.

Very large producer of over 50 different products, including a line of everyday table wines mostly from the Riverina.

**Drayton.** N.S.W.

Long-established producer in Hunter Valley, owners of famous Bellevue estate. Bellevue Hermitage, Bellevue Riesling.

**Elliott's.** N.S.W./

Quality producer of red and white table wines in Hunter Valley, traditional full-flavored Hunter-style wines. Hunter Valley Riesling Private Bin (Belford) and Dry Red "Tallawanta."

**Hamilton's.** S.A.

Family-owned winery in south Adelaide producing fresh whites, light reds, and more durable reds from MacLaren Vale and Langhorne Creek. Ewell Vineyards Cabernet, Nildottie Hermitage and Springton Riesling.

**Gramp's.** S.A.

Large firm in Barossa producing good Rieslings and dry reds under the Orlando label. Best wines contain minute label information. Moorooroo White Burgundy, Miamba Riesling, and Orlando Hermitage.

**Hardy's.** S.A.

One of Australia's largest wineries with vineyards in Barossa, Hunter Valley, and Southern Vales; best known for reds but produce full line. St. Vincent Chablis, Nottage Hill Claret.

**Henschke.** S.A.

Barossa Valley winery best known for white wines, and one fine red, Hill of Grace; also Rhine Riesling, White Frontignac.

**Hollydene.** N.S.W.

Small new winery in northern Hunter Valley making creditable varietals. Sémillon. Shiraz Cabernet.

**Houghton.** W.A.

Leading vineyard in the Swan Valley, known for White Burgundy, robust reds, and full-flavored dessert wines. Owned by Hardy's.

**Hungerford Hill.** N.S.W.

New Hunter Valley winery, modern, trend-setting with lighter-style reds and fresh, fruity wines. Pokolbin Shiraz and Pokolbin Sémillon.

**Kaiser Stuhl.** S.A.

Large cooperative in Barossa Valley recently purchased by Penfold's, producing broad range of quite good table wines, mostly white. Individual vineyard selections often outstanding. Rhine Riesling and Special Reserve Bin Claret.

**Karrawirra.** S.A.

Large grower in Barossa who has recently begun to produce and bottle his own wines, good solid reds based on Cabernet and Shiraz.

**Kay Bros.** S.A.

Owners of well-known Amery vineyard in McLaren Vale; good Cabernets and dry whites, especially Amery Rhine Riesling and Sauvignon Blanc.

**Lake's Folly.** N.S.W.

Dr. Max Lake's small winery and vineyards in Hunter Valley produce highly individual reds of interesting complexity and long life. Lake, a retired surgeon, is an influential force in the Australian wine industry. Cabernet Sauvignon, Hunter Valley Estate Dry Red.

**Leeuwin.** W.A.

A newly developed vineyard operation in the Margaret River region of Western Australia; Robert Mondavi of Napa Valley, California has an interest here.

**Lindeman.** N.S.W.

Large, old firm with vineyards in most of Australia's wine regions, originally Hunter Valley, site of the famous Ben Ean estate. Full-range production with excellent dry reds and whites. Ben Ean Moselle, Bin 23 Riesling, and Limestone Ridge Coonawarra Shiraz Cabernet.

**McWilliams.** N.S.W.

Large firm in Hunter Valley and Riverina producing full line. Better table wines often given such names as Ann or Elizabeth Riesling, Philip Hermitage. Private bin wines generally quite good. Rhine Riesling, Robinvale Lexia, and Riverina Cabernet Sauvignon.

**Mildara.** Vic.

Producer of dessert and fortified wines in the Murray River Valley but well known for its Reserve Bin Cabernets and Shiraz; many now from Coonawarra.

**Morris.** Vic.

Full-spectrum producers in Rutherglen. Blue Imperial Dry Red, Cabernet Shiraz.

**Norman's.** S.A.

Medium-sized producer of sound reds and whites. Angle Vale Claret, Angle Vale Gewürztraminer.

**Penfold's.** S.A.

Another of the largest wineries in Australia, with vineyards everywhere; wines from various regions often blended. Outstanding reds and whites, very good dessert wines. Autumn Riesling, Grange Hermitage, Coonawarra Claret, St. Henri Claret, and Grandfather Port.

**Pokolbin Estate.** N.S.W.

New small winery in Hunter Valley using modern techniques for quality red wines. Gold Medal Hermitage, Cabernet Sauvignon.

**Quelltaler.** S.A.

One of oldest wineries in Clare-Watervalle region above Adelaide. Best known for Sherries, Ports, and German-style whites; some sparkling wines. Granfiesta Sherry, Hock Bin 65.

**Redman.** S.A.

Winemaker Owen Redman makes outstanding Coonawarra Claret (from Shiraz and Cabernet Sauvignon).

**Reynell.** S.A.

The House of Reynell, famed for its Reynella line of reds and whites, is now owned by Hungerford Hill but still produces under its own label. Chateau Reynella Claret, Rhine Riesling, White Burgundy, Flor Sherry.

**Rothbury Estate, The.** N.S.W.

New modern winery in Hunter Valley whose aim is French-style classic red and white wines, with special lots of individual vineyard wines.

**Ryecroft.** S.A.

Producer of agreeable table and sparkling wines; emphasis on big, full-bodied reds from Shiraz and Cabernet. McLaren Vale Hermitage.

**Saltram.** S.A.

Barossa Valley producer of aromatic reds and good quality ports and sherries. Mamre Brook Cabernet and Rhine Riesling.

**Sandelford.** W.A.

New winery near Perth making interesting varietals from newly-developed Margaret River area.

**Seaview.** S.A.

A large old winery in the Southern Vales, noted for white wines, some sparkling, and an excellent Cabernet Sauvignon.

**Seppelt.** S.A.

Headquartered in Barossa, this huge firm has vineyards in all wine-producing regions for its full line of table wines, champagne, and dessert wines, some of which are outstanding, such as the 1972 Cabernet Sauvignon. Widely exported. Great Western Brut Champagne, Moyston Claret, and Arrawatta Riesling.

**Southern Vales.** S.A.

Cooperative marketing large range of reasonably priced whites, reds, and fortified wines. Certain lots of best wines are set aside from each vintage that is specifically labeled (such as Tatchilla Cabernet Shiraz or Langhorne Creek Dry Red); generally worth looking for.

**Stanley.** S.A.

Producers of good, sturdy reds in Clare-Leasingham west of Adelaide.

**Stonyfell.** S.A.

Sturdy, full-flavored reds from the Barossa Valley, several private bin Clarets and Burgundy made from Shiraz and/or Cabernet Sauvignon.

**Taltarni.** Vic.

Up-and-coming estate producing excellent Cabernet Sauvignon and Shiraz, both good, meaty reds with considerable elegance. Dominique Portet (brother of Bernard Portet of Clos du Val in Napa Valley) is the winemaker. Bears watching.

**Tolley.** S.A.

Old firm known mostly for dessert and sparkling wines but recently producing very good Cabernet. Pedare Cabernet Sauvignon, Pedare Rhine Riesling, and Pedare Red Hermitage.

**Tulloch.** N.S.W.

Old Hunter Valley firm notable for its fine reds and Hunter Rieslings (Semillon). Pokolbin Dry Red and Pokolbin White Label.

**Tyrell.** N.S.W.

Important Hunter Valley producer of long standing, known for good reds and whites; best given special vat numbers. Recently making Chardonnay and Pinot Noir.

**Wynns.** S.A.

Large, widespread producer, especially in Coonawarra, probably the first to bring that region into prominence back in the 1950s. Coonawarra Claret, Huntersfield Riesling, Coonawarra Estate Hermitage.

**Yalumba.** S.A.

Large producer in Barossa with full range of table wines, dessert and sparkling wines. Some good Cabernet and Shiraz. Galway Vintage Claret and Pewsey Vale Hock.

# New Zealand

The two islands of New Zealand lie on the same latitudes in the southern hemisphere as Bordeaux and Burgundy in the northern hemisphere, thus the country's future for wine production is being considered with interest. Very little wine is exported as yet, but expanded plantings on both islands, particularly in Chardonnay, Cabernet Sauvignon, and Pinot Noir, seem promising. Principal growing regions on the north island are at Hawkes' Bay, Henderson/ Auckland, and more recently Gisborne and Waikato. The northern part of the southern island at Blenheim has a high quantity of sunshine hours and is becoming known for dry, fruity whites.

Six companies dominate production: Cook's, Corbans, Glenvale, McWilliams, Montana, and Penfolds.

## WHITE WINES

**Chardonnay, Gewürztraminer.** New plantings from these European varietals promising but only small quantities so far.

**Chasselas.** Mostly sweet whites from this lesser grape.

**Palomino Hock.** Light, pleasant semidry whites from the Palomino grape.

**Riesling-Sylvaner.** Dominant white wine, actually from Müller-Thurgau, cross between Sylvaner and Riesling; both dry and sweet wines.

## RED WINES

**Cabernet Sauvignon.** Among New Zealand's oldest reds, especially those of Hawkes' Bay.

**Hermitage (Shiraz).** Medium-bodied reds from the Shiraz grape. Also Pinotage, cross between Pinot Noir and Cinsault.

**Pinot Noir.** Experimental but promising for future on south island.

# THE WINES OF
# SOUTH AFRICA

S outh Africa's wine industry dates to the seventeenth century when the land was settled by the Dutch. Her famed sweet wine, Groot Constantia, a rich and noble muscat, was well known to Europeans in the 1800s, as her fine sherries and ports came to be later on and are still today.

New technology and modern equipment, including stainless steel cold fermentation, are making a big difference in the quality of table wines, particularly the white wines, and the move to good varietals is growing rapidly. In 1972 the government set up controls for Wines of Origin and certified wines bear neck seals guaranteeing origin, vintage date, and grape variety.

Wines are made in the southernmost Cape Province in such districts as Constantia, Stellenbosch, Tulbagh, and Paarl; the coastal belt near Capetown; the drier, warmer region of the Little Karoo (Klein Karoo); and to the north, Piquetberg and the Olifants River area.

## WINE GUIDE

**Alto.** A leading estate in the Stellenbosch region noted for sturdy reds, Cabernet, and Alto Rouge.

**Backsberg.** Large estate between Stellenbosch and Paarl with recently upgraded wines, especially reds.

**Bergkelder.** Large commercial firm distributing several major brand lines such as Fleur du Cap, estate wines of Hazendahl and Meerendahl, Grunberger Steen.

**Boberg.** A regional designation for sherries and other dessert wines of Tulbagh and Paarl.

**Cabernet Sauvignon.** South Africa's best reds are made from this Bordeaux variety.

**Cinsaut.** Formerly known as Hermitage, a Rhône grape now made as a sound red varietal or blended with Cabernet.

**Colombard.** The white variety of French Colombard producing light fruity whites similar to those of California.

**Constantia.** Southernmost growing region below Capetown, known earlier for sweet muscat wines, today producing good varietals.

**Drostdy.** Large growers' co-op in the Tulbagh area producing wide range of table wines, sherries.

**Groot Constantia.** Famed estate outside of Capetown renowned for its sweet muscat of the nineteenth century; now state-owned and producing Cabernet and other very good reds.

**Kanonkop.** Private registered estate north of Stellenbosch noted for good Cabernet Pinotage.

**Klein Karoo.** Growing area to the east on warm, dry plains between the Drakenstein and Swartberg mountains, producing mostly fortified dessert wines and bulk wines for distilling into spirits.

**K.W.V.** South Africa's largest producers, a cooperative at Paarl making a wide range of table and dessert wines of good quality. Better lines include Cape Cavendish and Paarlsack sherries, Landskroon ports, Roodeberg Red, and varietals such as Cinsaut and Cabernet.

**Montagne.** New large estate in Stellenbosch region making impact with varietals like Cabernet, Chenin Blanc, and Riesling.

**Montpellier.** One of South Africa's old famous estates near Tulbagh, best known for varietal whites such as Riesling, Chenin Blanc, Gewürztraminer; also méthode champenoise sparkling wines.

**Muratie.** Old family estate near Stellenbosch producing solid red varietals, especially Pinot Noir plus Steen and Riesling.

**Nederburg.** Famous estate in Stellenbosch now owned by the Stellenbosch Farmers' Winery. Early producers of estate Cabernet and other fine wines; latest innovation: a sweet Botrytised Edelkeur Riesling.

**Olifantsrivier.** Northern section of the Cape Province, a warm, dry climate producing wines mostly for distillation but some table wines of late.

**Paarl.** Wine capital of South Africa and center for several co-operative producers known mostly for white wines and fortified wines, especially sherry.

**Pinotage.** A hybrid red varietal made from a cross of Pinot Noir and Cinsaut, increasingly a South African specialty for round, full-bodied reds that age well.

**Roodeberg.** A sound, blended red from K.W.V. producers.

**Rustenberg.** Estate-style red wines from Cabernet and Cinsaut, among South Africa's best, in Stellenbosch.

**Schoongezicht.** Registered estate in Stellenbosch region making popular Steen, Riesling, and other whites.

**Simonsvlei.** Large co-operative estate near Paarl noted for good reds and whites.

**Steen.** The name for Chenin Blanc in South Africa making both sweet and dry white wines; the country's leading white grape.

**Stellenbosch.** Town and region noted for excellent table wines, especially reds from Cabernet, Pinotage, Cinsaut.

**Stellenbosch Farmers' Winery.** Famous co-op with extensive estates and vineyards producing a wide range of good wines, including Chateau Libertas Cabernet, La Gratitude (white), Nederburg Cabernet and Steen, Oude Libertas Muscat, Tassenberg (red).

**Superior.** Government-regulated standard of quality for superior wines.

**Theuniskraal.** Famous estate in Tulbagh known for well-made whites from Riesling, Steen, Grewürztraminer, Sémillon.

**Tulbagh.** Important growing region for white wines north of Paarl.

**Twee Jongegezellen.** Very old famed estate at Tulbagh known for white wines made from Riesling, Steen, Sémillon; more recently, ambitious efforts with Cabernet Sauvignon.

**Verdun.** Registered estate near Stellenbosch producing good Gamay.

**Zonnebloem.** Brand name for a line of good varietals (Pinotage, Steen, Cabernet) from the Stellenbosch Farmers' Winery.

# THE WINES OF

# SOUTH AMERICA

T he best known wine-producers of Latin America are Chile and Argentina, both of whom are diligently working to expand and improve vineyard plantings in their respective wine regions. Experiments with varieties like Chardonnay, Chenin Blanc, and Pinot Noir are promising but of small scale as yet. In both countries the best reds are based on Cabernet Sauvignon. Though the wine regions of Chile and Argentina lie only 150 miles apart, they are separated by the Andes, with different soils, climates, and approach to winemaking.

# Argentina

Argentina jockeys with Russia for fourth place in wine production. Most of it stays in Argentina, however, for the country's per capita consumption is almost on a par with those of France and Italy. Most of Argentina's wines come from Mendoza, from vast flat plateaus that back up against the Andes. Glacial melt irrigates the hot, arid plains of vineyards, which are about the same distance from the equator as the vineyards of North Africa.

The Argentines like robust, full-bodied wines that go well with the hearty beef dishes that are the focal point of their cuisine. Modern techniques and equipment in recent years have improved the quality of the wines based on such varietals as Cabernet Sauvignon, Malbec, Merlot, Pinot Noir, Chardonnay, and Chenin Blanc. The whites especially are fresher and fruitier than before, though ripe, well-aged, rather heavy whites are still popular locally.

## WINE GUIDE: ARGENTINA

**Andean.** Brand name for the wines of five growers in Mendoza carefully developed for international markets; good Chardonnay, Chenin Blanc, and Cabernet Sauvignon.

124

**Arizu, Bodegas.** Large producer with wineries and vineyards in Mendoza planted principally in Cabernet, Merlot, Chardonnay, and Sauvignon. Also méthode champenoise Champagne Arizu.

**Bianchi, Bodegas.** One of the best-known producers of sound varietals, including Don Valentín, a robust red, Lacrado, and Bianchi 1887 (based on Cabernet and Merlot).

**La Caroyense Cooperativa.** Co-op with vineyards in Cordoba, best known for the robust red Vasija Mayor made from Pinot Noir.

**Carrodilla.** Red and white table wines based on Cabernet, Malbec, Pinot Blanc; also bottle-fermented sparkling wine from Pinot Blanc and Pinot Noir.

**Castell Chandon.** Sparkling wine facility owned by Moët-Hennessey of France, producing bubbly from Riesling and other varieties.

**Crillon, Bodegas.** Sparkling wine producer producing tank-fermented wines under the Crillon, Monitor, and Frederic Bastiat labels.

**Etchart.** Well-known producer in the Salta region north of Mendoza with popular line of table wines under the Etchart Privado label.

**Flichman, Bodegas y Vinedos.** Large Mendoza producer of several varietals, including the popular Caballero de la Cepa, a blend of Cabernet and Syrah.

**Furlotti, Angel.** Well-known and widely exported wines from Cabernet and Merlot among reds, whites from Riesling and Pinot Blanc.

**Greco Hermanos.** Large growers in eastern and central Mendoza producing reds from Malbec and Lambrusco, dry, full-bodied whites from Semillon.

**Lopez, Bodegas.** Old, family-owned winery well known for its full and long-lived Cabernet, Chateau Montchenot.

**Navarro Correas, J. Edmundo.** Reputable winery in the Maipu-Mendoza regions noted for robust reds and fine dry whites such as Chardonnay and Sauvignon.

**Peñaflor.** Giant producer of mostly fortified wines, including the well-known Tio Quinto sherry. Owned by the Pulenta family and markets also Andean and Trapiche brands.

**Santa Ana.** Mendoza producer with vineyards planted mostly in Italian red varieties such as Barbera and Pinot Blanc. Best-known dry white is White Pinot; also Santa Ana Burgundy (red).

**Suter, Bodegas.** Highly regarded firm producing sound reds and whites, including the popular Etiquetta Marron, dry white from Pinot Blanc, and Reserva reds.

**Toso, Pascual.** One of Argentina's best-known producers of Cabernet, Riesling, and sparkling wines.

**Trapiche.** Family-owned vineyards high in Mendoza producing good Cabernet, Malbec, Chenin Blanc, and Montana table wines in liters.

# Chile

Chile's best reds are very good indeed—Cabernets and Merlots handled in the Bordeaux style, a holdover from earlier days when Bordeaux vintners, fleeing the ravages of phylloxera in the vineyards of Bordeaux, came to Chile. The little bug that dines on vine roots never made it across the Andes. Chile's climate in the central valleys of the Aconcagua, Maipo, Cachapoal, and Maule rivers is ideal for Bordeaux varieties, including Sauvignon Blanc and Sémillon among the whites. Riesling also makes fruity, flavorful whites. If Chile can emerge from political difficulties long enough to organize her wine industry for export, we should see more of her good wines in the near future.

# WINE GUIDE: CHILE

**Aconcagua Valley/** Region north of Valparaiso and Santiago in central Chile with some of the best Cabernet and Merlot vineyards.

**Canepa, Jose.** One of Chile's modern, forward-looking firms with vineyards in the Maipo basin south of Santiago. Excellent Cabernet in the Bordeaux style and dry Sémillon.

**Concha y Toro.** Large old firm with wineries at Pirque and San Miguel in the Maipo River Valley; very good Cabernet, especially Casillero del Diablo Tinto and Sauvignon Blanc.

**Cousiño-Macul.** One of the oldest and most distinguished estates in the Maipo basin near Santiago; vineyards planted with cuttings from Pauillac and Graves. Excellent reserve Cabernet aged in French oak. Also good Sémillon and Chardonnay.

**Maipo River Valley.** Leading region south of Santiago for top varietals, such as Cabernet, Merlot, Chardonnay, and Riesling; several of the top wineries located here.

**San Pedro.** One of Chile's oldest producers in the Talca Province of the Maipo district. Claret-style Cabernet quite fine.

**Santa Carolina.** Popular reds and whites ranging from light, fruity style to aged, more mature Cabernet Estrella de Oro; Gran Porton red has more fruit and charm, is better value.

**Santa Rita.** Winery in the Maipo basin just south of Santiago with popular light reds and a good Casa Real Cabernet.

**Undurraga.** Large firm in Santa Ana, west of Santiago, producing Cabernet, Riesling, generic burgundy, and Pinot Noir. Sporadically exported to the United States.

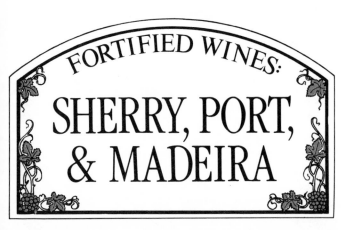

# FORTIFIED WINES:
# SHERRY, PORT, & MADEIRA

Fortified wines are those to which brandy is added, bringing their level of alcohol to between 18 and 20%. Both dry and sweet versions are made, the dry ones popular as aperitifs and the sweet ones as dessert or after-dinner wines.

The unique style of sherries from Spain, Porto from Portugal, and madeiras from Madeira, the island in the Atlantic off the northern coast of Africa, is imitated in many wine-producing countries around the world, including the United States, South Africa, Argentina, Australia, and Cyprus. None, however, has yet managed to achieve the distinctive character and finesse of the prototypes, steeped in centuries-old traditions of their respective countries.

The various types of ports, sherries, and madeiras are described in the Wine Guide that follows. The guide includes brief notes on the leading firms that produce them and the names of their best wines. Vintage years are those declared for vintage port.

## WINE GUIDE

**Amontillado.** A medium-dry, amber-colored sherry, richer and more full-bodied than fino or manzanilla but only slightly less dry. Name means "in the style of Montilla," a town and its wine near Cordoba.

**Amoroso.** A name occasionally used for sweet oloroso sherries.

**Barbeito.** Madeira shippers exporting under the Crown label—Malmsey, Rainwater, Bual.

**Bertola.** Sherry shippers owned by the conglomerate Rumasa, exporting mainly to the United Kingdom.

**Blandy.** Old firm of Madeira shippers at Funchal, principal city and port of Madeira. Duke of Clarence Malmsey.

**Bual.** Medium-sweet sherry, rich and dark but not as sweet as Malmsey.

**Calém.** 77 75 63 60 58 55 48 47 35
Family-owned firm of Portuguese port shippers that has recently widened exports. Full line of ports.

**Cockburn.** 77 75 70 67 63 60 55
A leading shipper of fine ports (British-owned), including a very good Special Reserve Ruby.

**Cossart Gordon.** One of the oldest shipping firms in Madeira; good, dry Rainwater Madeira and No. 92 Crown Bual.

**Cream Sherry.** An oloroso sherry blended with sweet wines made from Pedro Ximenes or Moscatel; can be richly dark or mellow amber in color.

**Croft's.** 77 75 70 66 63 60 55

Distinguished shippers of port and sherry; one of the oldest firms in Oporto now owned by Gilbey's. Croft's Distinction (Particular in Great Britain) is fine old tawny.

**Crusted port.** Port blended from two or more vintages but bottled within a few years; as it matures a "crust" of sediments forms in the bottle; like vintage port, it requires decanting.

**Delaforce.** 77 75 70 66 63 60 58 55

Port shippers with expanding world market. His Eminence's Choice is excellent tawny.

**Domecq, Pedro.** One of the largest sherry shippers, still family-owned. La Ina, excellent fino; Celebration Cream. Now also making Rioja under Domecq label.

**Dow.** 77 75 72 70 66 63 60 55

Vintage port sold mostly in England, the name retained when Dow merged with Portuguese firm of Silva & Cosens.

**Dry Sack.** Popular amontillado marketed by Williams & Humbert.

**Duff Gordon.** Old firm of sherry shippers now owned by Osborne. El Cid amontillado, Santa Maria Cream.

**Fino.** Lightest and driest of sherries, usually 15 to 16% alcohol. Bone-dry, crisp, distinctive almond aromas; a superb aperitif that should be served chilled.

**Flor.** A unique yeast that forms on the surface of certain sherries as they develop, giving the wines a particular character and aroma that set them apart as finos.

**Fonseca.** 77 75 70 66 63 60 55 48

Port shippers with an excellent range of ports, particularly fine ruby, Bin 27, and dark, full-bodied vintage port.

**Garvey.** Very old sherry storage and shipping firm in Jerez, several sherries and brandies. Fino San Patricio, Tio Guillermo Amontillado.

**Gonzalez Byass.** One of the largest, oldest shipping firms in Jerez, with one of the best finos, Tio Pepe; also a very good Alfonso Dry Oloroso, La Concha Amontillado.

**Graham.** 77 75 70 66 63 60 55 48

Best known for vintage ports popular in England and Scotland, also late-bottled vintage.

**Harvey's.** Widely known sherry shippers in Bristol, England; famous Bristol Dry, Bristol Milk, and Bristol Cream sherries. Also port shippers, good Ruby and Directors' Bin Tawny.

**Henriques & Henriques.** Shippers of fine madeiras, mostly to Europe.

**Jerez de la Frontera.** Center of sherry production in Spain near Cadiz. The name sherry derives from the town name that is pronounced "Hereth." Most of the leading *bodegas*, or storage and shipping warehouses, are located here and open to tourists.

**Kopke.** 77 70 66 63 60 55 48

Said to be the oldest port shipper, founded in 1630s.

**Late-bottled vintage (LBV).** Port of a single vintage kept in wood beyond the two-year limit for vintage port. Matures faster and is ready to drink sooner, often the equal of some vintage ports.

**Leacock.** One of the oldest and best-known Madeira shippers; excellent dry Sercial, rich Malmsey.

**Malmsey.** The sweetest madeira, rich, dark, luscious but finely balanced. The word is a corruption of Malvasia, one of the grapes that is used to make it.

**Manzanilla.** Dry fino-style sherry that is sent to seaside town of Sanlucar de Barrameda on the Spanish coast where it picks up a certain tang from the salt-sea air. A connoisseur's favorite. La Gitana is one of the best known.

**Martinez.** 77 75 70 67 63 60 58 55
   Old, distinguished port shippers now owned by Harvey's.

**Niepoort.** Dutch-owned port shippers, still family-owned. Good Ruby.

**Offley Forester.** 77 75 72 70 67 66 63 62 60
   One of the oldest port shippers, famous for vintage ports from the estate Quinta Boa Vista.

**Oloroso.** Dark, rich sherry, more full-bodied than fino or amontillado with a distinctive nutty aroma; completely dry but sweetened for cream sherries; dry oloroso also popular.

**Palo Cortado.** Dark-colored dry sherry, lighter than oloroso but richer in body than amontillado, appealing fragrance; serve chilled.

**Palomino.** Well-known sherry shippers best known for Palomino Cream, now owned by Rumasa.

**Port of the vintage.** Wood-aged port (usually tawny) mostly of a single vintage; not the power and character of vintage port as name implies.

**Puerto de Santa Maria.** Coastal town near Jerez with a number of important sherry shippers.

**P.X.** Abbreviation for Pedro Ximenez grapes that are dried in the sun to intense sweetness; used to sweeten olorosos, occasionally made into very sweet wine on its own.

**Quinta do Noval.** 77 75 70 67 66 63 60 58 55 31
   One of the great port estates famed for its vintage ports, particularly the 1931.

**Rainwater.** A style of madeira similar to Verdelho but a bit drier; seen mostly in the United States and Canada.

**Rebello Valente.** 77 75 70 67 66 63 60 55
   The vintage ports of the shipping firm of Robertson's, now owned by Sandeman.

**Robertson.** Port shippers now owned by Sandeman. Rebello Valente vintage ports, also a pleasant tawny called Dry Humour.

**Rozés.** Port shippers formerly owned by a French firm, now with Domecq; medium-quality white, ruby, tawny ports.

**Ruby.** Youngest style of port aged 2 or 3 years in wood; rich red color; bold, fruity character, some richness at best; lesser ones harsh, thin.

**Rutherford & Miles.** Old shipping firm in Madeira with famous Old Trinity Bual, good Malmsey, Rainwater.

**Sandeman.** 77 75 70 67 66 63 62 60 58 57 55
   Huge concern with large shipping houses for both port and sherry. Partners' Port is an excellent tawny, also big, full-bodied, long-lived vintage ports. Excellent sherries such as Dry Don Amontillado, Apitiv, Armada Cream. Recently sold to Seagram's.

**Sanlucar de Barrameda.** Seaside town on the Andalusian coast of Spain where manzanilla is aged.

**Sercial.** Driest of the madeiras and an excellent aperitif; serve chilled.

**Solera.** A system used for aging and blending sherries and madeiras to maintain quality and consistency of style. A number of barrels containing wines of various ages are grouped together; as wines are drawn from the oldest level, the barrels are topped up with younger wines. Average solera age is usually up to 20 years.

**Tawny.** Port aged a number of years in wood until it becomes tawny in color, though some lesser ones are mixed with white port. The best aged 8 to 15 years or more in wood are mellow, rich, and very fine.

**Taylor, Fladgate.** 77 75 70 66 63 60 55; LBV 72
   One of the great port houses best known for its very full-bodied vintage ports, intense ruby and No. 10 tawny.

**Tio Pepe.** Well-known fino sherry from Gonzalez Byass.

**Verdelho.** Semidry style of madeira, best when chilled and served as an aperitif; often sold as Rainwater in Canada and the United States.

**Vintage port.** The best port of a single vintage, bottled after 2 years in wood to mature in bottle. Powerful, intense, sweet, and extremely long-lived, requiring at least a decade to mature, often two. Throws heavy sediment and must be decanted. Vintages declared only when quality of grapes merits it. Important old vintages are 48 45 35 34 27 20 12 11 08 04 1900

**Warre.** 77 75 70 66 63 60 55

One of the more distinguished port shippers and one of the oldest; long-lived vintage port, excellent Warrior Ruby, Nimrod Tawny, LBV '69.

**Wood port.** Port aged in wood (rubies and tawnies) rather than bottle (vintage).

# WINE & FOOD

A strict code of rules for what wine goes with what food is out of place today. Most people feel free to choose according to personal preference. There are those who prefer to drink white wine with everything; others feel that a serious dinner without red wine is somehow incomplete. Certain time-honored pairings, however, that have evolved over the last century or so indicate how specific wines bring out the best in a particular dish, or vice versa. They are well worth investigating, if only to see whether or not you agree.

Wines should be avoided with certain foods. Foods that are overly spicy and pungent may overwhelm even the sturdiest wine, especially such condiments as pickles, chilis, citrus, mustard, Worcestershire or Tabasco sauce, and vinegar. Try using dry white wine or cognac in salad dressing instead of vinegar. Chocolate also throws off the taste of sweet wine, so save the mousse to serve with coffee.

## APÉRITIF

One of the most delightful choices to precede the meal is champagne or other sparkling wine. A glass or two sets things off on just the right note and it's a marvelous icebreaker. Wines that are too sweet will dull rather than stimulate the appetite, but lightly sweet ones such as German Moselle, California Chenin Blanc or Blanc de Pinot Noir, or Gewürztraminer are very good choices. Chilled Fino Sherry is a classic apéritif wine and goes particularly well with salty or smoked hors d'oeuvres.

The following suggestions are intended only as a general guide to traditional combinations and a few recommendations that have particularly interested me on occasion. There are so many wines available to us today that any number of substitutions can be made, so I urge you to be adventurous and extend your taste horizons with discoveries of your own.

## HORS D'OEUVRES AND FIRST COURSES

**Antipasto.** Crisp, dry white such as Pinot Grigio or Tocai; light, Italian red Chianti, Valpolicella, Côte du Rhône.

**Asparagus.** Saint-Véran, California Chardonnay.

**Avocado.** Stuffed with shellfish: Johannisberg Riesling; Grey or Emerald Riesling.

**Caviar.** Champagne, iced vodka.

**Crudités.** Dry white such as Sancerre or Sauvignon Blanc or light red such as Côte du Rhône, Gamay, Bardolino.

**Eggplant, stuffed.** Robust red such as Zinfandel, Barbera, Dão.

**Escargots.** White Burgundy or Rhône such as Hermitage (white).

**Fish, smoked (salmon, sturgeon).** Fino Sherry, Manzanilla, dry sparkling wine from California or Saumur, Kriter.

**Foie gras.** Sauternes is preferred in Bordeaux; champagne or dry Gewürztraminer also good.

131

**Pasta.** With fish or cream sauce, Pinot Bianco, Soave; with meat or vegetables Chianti Classico, Carema, Valtellina, Charbono, Beaujolais.

**Pâté.** Dry white such as Mâcon-Villages, Chardonnay, Sauvignon Blanc, Seyval Blanc.

**Pizza.** Inexpensive Chianti, Zinfandel, Sicilian red, Barbera.

**Prosciutto and melon.** Dry fruity white such as Mâcon, Pinot Blanc; or just off-dry Sylvaner, Mosel, Grüner Veltliner.

**Quiche.** Light red from the Rhône, Chinon, Cabernet, Chancellor.

**Salami, cold cuts.** Dry rosé like Tavel, Roditys, Zinfandel.

**Terrine.** Light red from the Côte de Beaune, Pinot Noir, Corbières.

# FISH

**Bass, striped.** White Burgundy such as Puligny-Montrachet if baked or poached with sauce, or California Chardonnay. If grilled: dry Chenin Blanc, Rhine Kabinett.

**Blue fish.** Full-bodied dry white or medium-bodied red such as Volnay, or other Côte de Beaune; Rioja.

**Salmon.** Full-bodied dry white or medium-bodied red Côte de Beaune.

**Shellfish.** Crisp, dry, tart white; mussels with Muscadet; oysters with Chablis Grand Cru; crab, lobster with Chardonnay; shrimp, scallops with Sauvignon Blanc, Gros Plant, Gavi di Cortese.

**Sole.** Same as striped bass.

**Trout.** Delicate white such as Mosel, Chenin Blanc, Lugana.

# MEAT

**Beef, roast.** Full-bodied Cabernet, Merlot, Hermitage, Shiraz, Dôle, Egri Bikavér, Chianti Classico, Gattinara, Rioja, Taurasi.

**Beef stew.** Hearty red such as Côte Rotie, Spanna, Zinfandel, Dão, Barolo, Vino Nobile di Montepulciano.

**Chicken, roast.** Medium-bodied Cabernet, Merlot, Rhône, Chianti, Rioja, claret-style Zinfandel.

**Chicken, sautéed, Provençal, etc.** Dry, full-bodied white or medium red such as Crozes-Hermitage, Perequita, Inferno.

**Chicken, white sauce.** Full-bodied dry white Graves, white Burgundy, Chardonnay.

**Chinese food.** Crisp or spicy white such as Tocai, Grüner Veltliner, Gewürztraminer, generic chablis.

**Curry.** Same as Chinese food; or beer.

**Duck, goose.** Rhine Spätlese, Alsatian Gewürztraminer; Bordeaux or red Burgundy.

**Game.** Sturdy red such as Côte de Nuits Burgundy, Côte Rotie, Vino Nobile, Barolo, Brunello di Montalchino, Napa Valley Cabernet.

**Ham.** Fresh dry white or rosé, light red; California champagne.

**Hamburger.** Beaujolais-Villages, Champigny, Napa Gamay, Zinfandel.

**Lamb.** Fine Bordeaux or California Cabernet, Merlot; Sassicaia, Australian Cabernet-Shiraz.

**Liver, kidney, sweetbreads.** Light to medium-bodied red Bordeaux or Cabernet from California, Chile, Australia.

**Paella.** Rioja, Gran Coronas.

**Pork, roast.** Medium-bodied red from Rhône, Barbaresco, Barbera. Riesling Spätlese from Rheingau or Rheinpfalz; Alsatian Gewürztraminer.

**Steak.** Firm, sturdy red such as young Cabernet, Hermitage, Shiraz, Gattinara, Chianti Riserva.

**Stews, cassoulet.** Hearty, robust red such as Zinfandel, Châteauneuf-du-Pape, Spanna, Barbaresco, Amarone, Fitou, or Cahors.

**Veal.** Smooth, light to medium-bodied red for chops and scallops; in cream sauce, white Burgundy or Chardonnay.

**Venison.** Rich, lusty red such as Burgundy from the Côte de Nuits, Vino Nobile, Côte Rotie; Riesling Spätlese, Auslese from Rheinpfalz Alsatian Gewürztraminer Reserve Exceptionnel.

# CHEESE

**Blues.** Medium-full red with Oregon, gorgonzola, and other light blues, such as Barbera, Valtellina, Nebbiolo d'Alba. Roquefort and Danish Blue need very big, full-flavored wines like late-harvest Zinfandel, Amarone, or sweet fortified wines.

**Creams, brie, camembert.** Mature Bordeaux or Cabernet; medium-bodied Rhônes.

**Cheddar.** Substantial, full-bodied red, especially Cabernet; also Corvo, Rhône, Dôle, Shiraz.

**Cheshire, Stilton, or other English cheeses.** Good ruby or tawny port; big reds such as Amarone, late-harvest Zinfandel.

**Goat cheeses.** Crisp, dry whites such as Sancerre, Sauvignon Blanc, Pinot Grigio; fine, mature Médoc or Côte de Nuits Burgundy, Gattinara.

**Parmesan.** Wines of the Piedmont: Barolo, Barbaresco, Fara, Ghemme.

**Soufflés.** Warm, medium-bodied reds like Moulin-à-Vent, Crozes-Hermitages, Corvo, Pinot Noir.

# DESSERTS

**Cakes.** German Auslese, Sauternes, Hungarian Tokay Aszu; Bual Madeira; Asti Spumante.

**Chocolate.** No wine goes with it.

**Creams, custards, puddings.** Barsac, sweet Vouvray, or other sweet white from the Loire.

**Fruit Bavarians, bombes.** Sauternes, Beerenauslesen (BAs); sweet Muscats.

**Fruit, fresh.** Pears or sweet apples paired with cheese can take red wines, but citrus or other acid fruits are difficult unless they are cooked in cakes or custard.

**Nuts.** Tawny port, vintage port, dry Oloroso sherry, Bual Madeira, or Verdelho Madeira.

**Sorbets, ice cream.** Liqueurs instead of wine.

**Strawberries, whipped cream.** Sauternes, late-harvest Rieslings, Gewürztraminer.

**Soufflés.** Sauternes, Beerenauslese (BA); Tokay Aszu; late-harvest Riesling.

**Note:** A glass of fine, sweet wine is often a perfect choice served by itself instead of, or after, dessert.

# STORING & SERVING ADVICE

## STORAGE

Improper storage can damage or destroy a wine, depriving you of the pleasure of fully enjoying what you paid for. Wines should be stored on their sides, for example, so that the cork will stay moist and firmly in place to keep air from getting to the wine. When wines are left upright for a couple of weeks or more, the cork will dry out and shrink, allowing air to reach the wine and spoil it. Heat and vibration can also be injurious to wine.

The most important thing to consider in storing wines is to place them in a stable atmosphere, free of vibration, fluctuations in temperature and away from light. The cellars of old houses were ideal in many respects, but today they are often the site of the boiler, washer, and dryer. Cool temperatures are best for wines—the ideal cellar temperature of yore was around 55° to 57°F (13° to 14°C). Normal household temperatures of 68° to 72°F (20° to 22°C) will not harm wines, as long as those temperatures are fairly constant year-round. In warmer atmospheres, however, the wines will tend to age faster, so keep that in mind.

It is useful to have a space to store wines so that you can stock what you need without having to rush out at the last minute to the wine shop or be caught short at a dinner party. Having a "cellar," even a small one, also allows you to take advantage of sales and special offers. After Christmas, for instance, odd lots of wines sometimes become available at special prices as close-outs for incomplete case-lots. It is also nice to be able to acquire wines that tend to disappear from the market soon after they appear—and often save money by doing so. Certain highly prized Cabernets from California are snapped up quickly or escalate in price within a few months. This is sometimes true of great Bordeaux and Burgundies, though consultation with a reliable wine merchant is your best guide here. You should get to know your wine merchant anyway and let him or her know the kinds of things you like. A good wine merchant will be quick to let you know about good buys that would interest you.

There is also the enjoyment one gets in being able to select a favorite wine at a moment's notice or contemplate the pleasures that lie ahead as good wines mature. Whether your storage space is large or small—the corner of an apartment, a closet, or a whole room—try to organize it by category so that you can find what you want easily. Keeping a cellarbook, or log, is also useful. It will enable you to know what you drank and when and what you need to replenish.

# Space for Storing

Storing wines can be done attractively in a variety of styles. Criss-cross bins can be constructed to hold as much as two cases each (all the same kinds of course, so you just remove the bottle on top as needed). Rectangular compartments can serve just as well, though perhaps should be smaller to hold fewer bottles so that they don't roll around. They can be built to your own design or specific space needs, or you can purchase ready-made wine racks that come in wide-ranging styles and sizes. Stackable racks that hold anywhere from eight to sixteen bottles allow you to expand your "cellar" at exactly the rate your wine collection grows.

# SERVING

**Temperature**. Room temperature, the traditional recommendation for red wines, can be a bit warm these days. I try to set my red wines in a cool place the day I plan to serve them so that they are around 65°F (19°C). Light reds such as Beaujolais-Villages, Gamay, or Côte du Rhône, even the lighter Zinfandels, are often enhanced by cooling—it makes them fresher. A half hour in the refrigerator puts them at a pleasing temperature. Fine white wines should not be overchilled or it will rob them of flavor, particularly white Burgundy and good California Chardonnays or Rieslings. About three hours in the refrigerator is sufficient for most, or 20 minutes in an ice bucket (half ice, half water—ice alone won't do the job) is best of all. Lesser white wines may benefit from more chilling, as the cold will mask certain deficiencies or overbearing flavors.

**Glasses**. Wine glasses come in a variety of sizes and shapes. The all-purpose glass of nine or ten ounces will suit most situations admirably. It should be made of clear, unetched glass (so you can enjoy the wine's appearance), preferably with no lip at the rim. Avoid glasses of less than eight ounces—there isn't room to swirl the wine to open up its bouquet and flavors. Fill each glass only half full so that you have plenty of room for swirling the wine about. Using glasses of different sizes is useful when you are serving two or more wines—it helps people keep them separate and it looks attractive and more festive.

**Breathing**. Wines "breathe" when they come into contact with the air. Oxygen opens them up and releases flavors and aromas. Pulling the cork and letting the bottle stand for an hour has virtually no effect on the wine. If you want to aerate wine quickly, pour it into a carafe. Or, once the cork is pulled, immediately pour the wine into glasses and allow it to breathe in the glass.

**Decanting**. Decanting a wine is nothing more than pouring it from the bottle into another container. Any vessel—a carafe, pitcher, or crystal decanter—will serve the purpose. Wines, generally only red, are decanted for two reasons:

1. To separate the wine from sediments that have formed during maturation. This is a natural occurrence, and most red wines over eight years old will have "thrown" some sediment; even younger ones occasionally will. The steps for decanting off sediment are illustrated below.
2. To aerate a young wine and loosen it up more quickly for pleasurable drinking.

# Glasses

ALL-PURPOSE
9–12 oz.

BALLON
12–14 oz.

CHAMPAGNE
FLUTE

RHINE/MOSEL

SHERRY

BRANDY

# Decanting

Decanting a red wine off its sediment can be done in three simple steps, leaving the wine crystal clear for your enjoyment.

1. Stand the wine upright for several hours or a day to allow the sediment to collect in the bottom of the bottle.

2. Place a candle or other source of bright light near the decanter so that you can see the sediment move toward the neck of the bottle.

3. Pour in one continuous motion from bottle to decanter. When you see the dark shadow of sediment appear in the neck, stop pouring. An inch or two of cloudy wine will remain in the bottle, and the wine that you drink will be clear and free of grit that would spoil its texture.

# ACKNOWLEDGMENTS

Numerous people and organizations have been helpful to me in the course of preparing this book. I want to thank the following in particular:

Sam Aaron
Gerald Asher
Martin Bamford
Phillip di Bellardino
Bill and Susan Blosser
Bordeaux Wine Information Bureau
Dr. Lucio Caputo
Jack Chambers
Champagne Information Bureau
Darrell Corti
Michael Coultas, Australian Trade Commissioner
Gerry Dawes
Neil Empson
German Wine Information Bureau
The Marquis de Goulaine
Louis Iacucci
Italian Wine Promotion Center, NY

Edmond Maudières
Daniel Mirassou
Robert Mondavi
Laurenz Moser
Kenneth L. Onish
Fenella Pearson
Dr. Richard Peterson
Bruno Prats
Rioja Wine Promotion Bureau
The Marquis de Roussy de Sales
Jean Sauvion
Sherry Institute of Spain
Steven Spurrier
Andre Tchelistcheff
Alfred G. Tesseron
Byron Tosi
Trade Commission of the Government of South Africa
Frederick Wildman & Sons
Wine Institute, San Francisco
Gallo Yello

# The Pocket Guide
# to Cheese

As a freelance wine journalist, Barbara Ensrud writes a weekly column for the New York *Daily News* and regular columns for *Vogue, The Wine Spectator,* and many other newspapers and magazines. She is the author of *The Pocket Guide to Wine* and has also contributed to several best-selling wine books, including *The Joys of Wine* and *The New York Times Wine Book.* A member of the New York Wine Writers Circle and the International Wine and Food Society, Ms. Ensrud has traveled extensively in many vineyard regions of the world and frequently lectures on wine.

# The Pocket Guide to
# CHEESE

## Barbara Ensrud

NEW ORCHARD EDITIONS

New Orchard Editions Ltd
Robert Rogers House
New Orchard
Poole, Dorset BH15 1LU

ISBN 1-85079-021-3

Printed in Great Britain by
Pitman Press Ltd., Bath

# CONTENTS

# INTRODUCTION

When I began this little odyssey through cheesedom, my enthusiasm for fine cheese had already developed quite nicely, right alongside my interest in wine. In the course of many months of concentrated research and tasting, however, something happened. While I have long enjoyed the mystery and luxury presented by numerous European cheese boards during travels abroad, suddenly, in the midst of *this* intensive journey, I developed a passion for the stuff.

Where before I was content to enjoy cheese as an occasional snack or after dinner with a fine wine (the wine chosen first and *then* the cheese to accompany it), I now find myself hooked, unable even for a day to be without a goodly cache in my refrigerator. There *must* be an excellent Cheddar available at all times, a fine, nutty Gruyère or a log of *chèvre,* and something from the soft-ripened family, be it Münster, Rollot or L'Ami du Chambertin. These, of course, supplemented fairly frequently by the brief-lived glory of a perfectly ripened Brie or Camembert.

Such an unexpected love affair is a fate that could befall anyone who undertakes a similar journey through the world's cheeses. And I suspect that those who do so will likely end up as I have, with admiration for the grand diversity of existing cheeses, the patient and painstaking artistry that certain ones entail, and the triumph of cooperation between man and nature.

Cheese is one of humankind's oldest foodstuffs. It has nourished, soothed, and satisfied the deepest of physical hungers, resuscitated flagging energies, and filled and fulfilled sensuous yearnings since the dawn of civilization. A superb cheese, once experienced and savored, lingers in memory the same way an extraordinary wine does, its afterglow of flavor coming back to spark a longing for its like again.

It was Clifton Fadiman—epic (and Epicurean) worksmith—who coined the phrase that best describes cheese as "milk's leap to immortality." The legend of how cheese was discovered has an appropriately exotic and romantic ring to it. Thousands of years ago, it is told, an Asian nomad set out on a journey by horse or camel, transporting milk in a leather pouch made from a calf's stomach. After many hours of rhythmic jogging in the warm sun, the rider grew thirsty and when he looked inside his saddlebag, the milk had turned into curds. The substance was not bad, he must have decided, for from that moment on, cheese became an important way to preserve surplus milk.

Today we know that it is the enzyme "rennin," which comes from rennet, a substance in the lining of calves' stomachs, that causes the solids in milk to coagulate. Little Miss Muffet's curds and whey were in fact very fresh cheese in its earliest stage of transformation.

The basic principles for making natural cheeses are much the same today as they have been for hundreds of years, though many of the steps have been highly mechanized. Bacterial "starter" cultures are added to fresh or pasteurized milk, which increases the acidity to a certain point. Then rennet is added, rapidly bringing about the curdling or clotting of the milk, separating it from the watery whey. The curds are then stirred with large forks or cut into cubes and heated to various temperatures to solidify them further or develop the proper texture.

After the draining of the curd, procedures vary somewhat for the different cheese types. Fresh cheeses are barely cooked at all, so as to retain their moist, loose-curd texture. The curds of Swiss cheese are gathered up in cheesecloth and lifted, dripping copiously, out of the whey and put into molds. Cheddar is cooked longer to hasten drainage of the whey, and then it is milled or cut into blocks and turned continuously in a process known as "cheddaring." Finally, it is put into cloth-lined molds and firmly pressed into the close, dense, satiny texture for which it is noted. Ripening times for cheeses also vary. Some ripen quickly, within a few days or weeks of production; others are cured for months, or even years.

One final word: while we are fortunate to be able to get so many cheeses heretofore unavailable, I urge those who travel abroad to try local cheeses whenever they present themselves. Better yet, seek them out. You may discover something quite fantastic—more immediately exciting and personally gratifying than the discovery of a new star.

# HOW TO USE THIS BOOK

The attempt with this volume has been to include the most important cheese classics, as well as certain newer cheeses—those of recent development and older cheeses that are nevertheless somewhat "new" to us through the advantages of modern transport.

The emphasis is on natural cheeses, and focuses more on authentic prototypes. Processed cheeses and imitations such as Swiss types produced outside of Switzerland, various semi-soft cheeses, and countless blues get less attention for the most part (and less enthusiasm from me unless they are exceptionally well done). Imitation in the cheese world is profligate, though not necessarily to be denigrated, as a burgeoning world demand encourages it. Rarely, however, do the imitations match the originals for depth of character and complexity of flavor.

Most of the important cheeses included here are preceded by specifications designed to give a quick indication of the cheese's character, flavor, and appearance, denoting *origin, type, taste, appearance,* and *availability* in the world cheese market. Each cheese is indexed, and cross-references are given throughout the text. Cross references appear in SMALL CAPS.

This book is intended mainly as a guide to selecting and serving cheese for the consumer. For more detailed information on the technicalities of making cheeses and in-depth discussion of *types*, please see "Further Reading" on page 137.

# ◆ CLASSIFYING CHEESES ◆

Categorizing cheeses has always been somewhat problematical because many of their characteristics overlap while other characteristics make them entirely different from one another. Technical experts and the cheese producers themselves tend to use terms that are arcane and convey very little to the consumer, who is, after all, primarily interested in flavor, appearance, and texture.

The most basic measure of the differences among cheeses is the degree of hardness, but categories such as hard, soft, and semi-soft are in many cases too broad to be of much use without further qualification. What I have tried to do here, under *type* in the specifications for each entry, is to use the term that best conveys the most distinctive characteristic of the cheese. Sometimes the chosen term will indeed refer to the degree of hardness, but at other times, the ripening method or type of rind or the origin of the milk is more indicative of character.

The method of production is important in certain cases, such as that of the *pasta filata* cheeses, where the curd is stretched and kneaded—a technique that is quite distinct from those used in the production of most other cheeses and the effect of which is immediately evident in the texture of Mozzarella, Provolone, or Caciocavallo. On the other hand, the most notable aspect of cheeses like Livarot or Liederkranz is their pungency of odor. Therefore, the term 'strong-smelling' may be used to type cheeses that might also be described as 'soft-ripened' or 'washed-rind' cheeses.

Despite the effort to categorize each cheese by its most salient feature, there are some overlaps that may be confusing, and certain cheeses will fall within two or more categories. Monastery cheeses, such as Port Salut, are generally semi-soft, but very ripe Münster could certainly be listed among the strong-smelling.

For those who wonder how I arrived at this particular system of classification (which doesn't differ radically from others except in a few instances), let me say that it is largely arbitrary but is based on conversations with some of the country's leading cheese vendors. I recognize that there are points to be made for other approaches, but it seemed burdensome to have too many categories and those I've used seemed to be the most useful for consumers. Following is an explanation of each category I've used under the *type* specification, together with "Buying and Storing Tips" and "Serving Tips" for each category.

## *Hard*
(SUB-TYPE: *Grana*)

The hard cheeses, the prototype of which is Italy's Parmigiano-Reggiano, are primarily used for grating. The word for such cheeses in Italian is *grana,* which means "grain" and denotes the grainy texture that results from long aging. They are also known, technically, as cooked, pressed cheeses because the curd is heated to between 125° and 140°F, then pressed into close-textured firmness. Most grating cheeses must be aged at least two years; four are better, and a few cheeses, such as Saanen or Sapsago, receive six or seven years. Twenty years' ripening is not unheard of, but it is rare, especially today.

The hard cheeses include Saanen, Sapsago, and Sbrinz of Switzerland; Parmigiano, Grana Padano, and Pecorino Romano of Italy; and Kefalotyri of Greece. Certain cheeses usually classed as semi-firm become harder with additional age and similarly suitable for grating. Among these are Aged Asiago, Dry California Jack, and Aged Gouda.

♦ **Buying and Storing Tips:** Hard cheeses obviously age well, but they should *not* be dried out, have cracked rinds, be too grainy or mealy in texture, or show heavy concentrations of white crystals. Nor should they be overly salty or bitter—try to sample before buying. *Parmigiano-Reggiano* is a strictly controlled cheese name and all authentic versions have it stencilled on the rind. The most flavorful seasoning comes from cheese you grate yourself; pre-grated cheese, even from specialty shops that use only the finest grades, loses its distinctiveness in a matter of hours. Whole cheeses of this sort, on the other hand, keep extremely well if securely wrapped in wax paper or foil and refrigerated or stored in a cool place.

♦ **Serving Tips:** Young versions of many grating cheeses (Parmigiano, Grana, Sbrinz) are closer to semi-firm than hard in texture and make excellent eating cheeses, accompanied by fresh fruit and sturdy red wines like Barolo, Barbaresco, Barbera, or Sfursat.

3

## *Semi-Firm*
( SUB-TYPES: *Swiss, Cheddar* )

This broad category includes cooked, pressed cheeses, rindless or with natural rinds, that are firm but not hard or brittle in texture. They may be close-textured, smooth, and slightly flaky like the Cheddars, Double Gloucester, French Cantel, Edam, Mimolette, or Aged Gouda; somewhat more open-textured like Cheshire or Lancashire; or very open like the "holey" cheeses, Swiss Emmentaler, Gruyère, Beaufort, Jarlsberg, Danbo, Samsoe, or Kanburra. The holes in cheese are formed by gases released during ripening.

Most cheeses of this category come in large, heavy wheels, or cylinders that weigh anywhere from 20 to 120 pounds. The numerous imitators of Cheddar and Swiss Emmentaler comprise much of this category, but there are other semi-firm cheeses with an individual character of their own, such as Fontina Val d'Aosta.

◆ **Buying and Storing Tips:** Beware of cracked rinds, a dried-out appearance, or an overly crumbly texture. Always taste the cheese if possible and avoid any cheeses that are bitter or rancid. Cheddars or Cheddar-relatives that are darker near the rind or at cut edges may not have been properly stored and may have hardened or dried out. Be specific about the origin of Cheddar (English, Farmhouse, New York, Oregon, Canadian) and of Swiss from Switzerland. The words "Imported Swiss" on the label do not automatically mean that the cheese was made in Switzerland—it may just as well have come from Finland, Austria, or Australia.

A sign of quality and maturity for Swiss-style cheeses is "weeping eyes"—the holes glisten with butterfat. The number of holes vary in number (Appenzell has few, Gruyère has many) and size (as small as peas or as large as walnuts), but they should be typical for the particular cheese as it is described in the Cheese Guide. Pre-cut, pre-packaged cheeses, such as those found in supermarkets, are convenient but have less flavor and character than portions freshly cut from whole cheeses. Semi-firm cheeses will keep very well for several weeks or longer if wrapped in plastic and refrigerated.

◆ **Serving Tips:** The semi-firm cheeses make fine after-dinner cheeses, especially in the company of cheeses with contrasting flavors or textures. They go well with balanced red wines such as Bordeaux, Cabernet Sauvignon, or Rioja. They are also fine for snacks or picnics with fresh fruit and lighter wines, cider, beer, or ale.

## *Semi-Soft*
( SUB-TYPE: *Monastery* )

This category, too, comprises a large group, embracing many of the so-called bland and buttery cheeses, such as Gouda, Bel Paese, Morbier, most Fontinas, Havarti, Samsoe, and the

Danish "bo" cheeses (Tybo, Fynbo, Maribo), Taleggio, and spiced cheeses such as Leyden or Nökkelost. They do tend to be mild-flavored and are higher in moisture content, with a smooth, sliceable texture that makes them very popular in sandwiches or for snacks.

Cheeses of the sub-type *monastery* (sometimes known as Trappist cheeses) are a little more complicated. The prototypes—Alsatian Münster, Swiss Tête de Moine, French Port-Salut—were indeed developed by Trappist monks in monasteries, some as far back as the Middle Ages. Most semi-soft cheeses, including many named in the preceding paragraph, as well as German Tilsit, French Saint-Paulin, American Brick, Danish Esrom, Canadian Oka, and others, derive from the early monastery types. Some have surface-ripened, washed rinds that continue ripening over time. Such cheeses as Pont-l'Evêque, Robiola Introbio, and Reblochon can become quite soft and develop a pungent flavor and aroma.

◆ **Buying and Storing Tips:** Semi-soft cheeses generally keep well for several weeks or longer if properly wrapped and refrigerated. The texture should be moist and smooth. With monastery types, especially those of the washed-rind variety, beware of rank odor, gummy rinds, sticky or discolored paper, and cheeses that have shrunk away from the container or wrapper.

◆ **Serving Tips:** Semi-soft cheeses make excellent snack or sandwich cheeses: the stronger-flavored monastery types are superb for cheese boards and can take sturdy, full-bodied red wines or crisp Alsace Rieslings.

## Soft-Ripened

( SUB-TYPES: *Bloomy rind, Washed rind* )

Surface-ripened cheeses are sprayed with or exposed to molds that cause them to ripen from the rind inward. The rinds are of two types: thin, white crusts that develop a velvety, white "bloom," known as bloomy rinds, and found on Brie, Camembert, or Carré de l'Est; and orange-hued "washed" rinds that are treated or cured with various solutions of brine, wine and spices, beer, or grape brandy such as Marc de Bourgogne. The soft-ripened cheeses have either a semi-soft consistency to begin with, or, like Brie, Camembert, or Coulommiers, firm, chalky centers that become soft and creamy as they ripen. Some of the soft-ripened cheeses fall into other categories as well. Many monastery and strong-smelling cheeses, such as Münster, Pont l'Evêque, Livarot, and Maroilles, also have washed rinds. Most of the double and triple creams such as Boursault, Brillat-Savarin, Chaource, and Caprice des Dieux, have downy white rinds.

The soft-ripened varieties are among the most delectable and popular of cheeses and some are capable of great nuance and complexity. Their lives are short, but often glorious. They ripen quickly and at their peak may last only a day or two, sometimes less, then tend to become ammoniated or rank. Factory-made versions (labeled *laitier* in France) generally have a somewhat longer life and more uniform consistency but are less distinctive in character.

♦ **Buying and Storing Tips:** Soft-ripened cheeses are considered ripe when they are plump within the rind, yielding, yet slightly springy to the touch. Once cut, they will not ripen further to any noticeable degree. It is necessary, then, to note carefully the texture of pre-cut Brie. For instance, if the center has a caky white line, the cheese may be quite good, but it is not fully ripe. Watch out for hardened or gummy rinds, darkened color, ammoniated aromas, or excessive runniness —these are sure indications that the cheese is past its prime.

Washed-rind cheeses should not have rank or "barnyardy" aromas. Avoid those with gummy rinds or those that are shrunken or misshapen.

Soft-ripened cheeses keep a short time once they are fully ripe. Wrap them in plastic and refrigerate in the vegetable crisper.

♦ **Serving Tips:** Soft-ripened cheeses are top choices for after dinner, especially as a contrast to blues, semi-firm cheeses, or *chèvres*. Remove them from the refrigerator two to three hours before serving. The strong odors of the washed-rind varieties will dissipate somewhat if they are allowed to stand in a well-circulated atmosphere. The rinds are edible, but eating them is a matter of preference and they should be trimmed if they are overly strong.

## Blue Vein

The blue-veined cheeses, marbled with bluish-green mold, are among the most intense and strong-flavored cheeses of all and include some of the most famous names in cheese— Roquefort, Stilton, Gorgonzola. Usually made from cow's milk (Roquefort is made from ewe's milk), they originally developed their mottled character spontaneously from spores of mold in the atmosphere where they were cured. Today nothing is left to chance, and most blue cheeses are innoculated or sprinkled with spores of *Penicillium glaucum* or *Penicillium roqueforti,* then skewered with holes to admit air, which encourages the mold. Most blues are dead white or pale ivory between the pockets or streaks of bluish (sometimes greenish) mold. The exception is Blue Cheshire, which is a rich orange-gold. The veining may be light in a young cheese and become more dense with age.

The classic blues have been imitated by almost every cheese-producing country in the world. The greatest successes are modeled after Gorgonzola, piquant in flavor but slightly milder and similarly creamy in texture. Stilton and Roquefort, however, are still without rival. Other fine blues are the French Blue de Bresse, Pipo Crem', and Bleu d'Auvergne; Danablu of Denmark; Oregon Blue and Maytag Blue of the United States; and Queso de Cabrales of Spain.

◆ **Buying and Storing Tips:** Blue cheeses vary from piquant and creamy to sharp and tangy. Some have a faint bitterness that is entirely characteristic. It is always best to sample before you buy to see if the taste is what you want. That is something you cannot do with pre-wrapped portions, so try to buy from stores where cheeses are sold in bulk. Good specimens should not be overly salty, bitter, or dried out. Blue cheeses keep very well for a few weeks if they are securely wrapped in plastic and refrigerated. Large portions keep much longer. Whole Stiltons or Roqueforts wrapped in damp cloth will keep for months if portions are cut as they are needed and the cheese is carefully re-wrapped.

◆ **Serving Tips:** Use a very sharp knife or a cheese wire for cutting blues so that they don't crumble. Wheels such as Stilton or Roquefort should be cut in half horizontally and then in wedges, starting at the top and moving down through the cheese in layers about two inches thick. Blues make an excellent contrast to other cheeses on the cheese board, but they are also superb with fresh apples, pears, or grapes and a sweet wine such as Sauterne, late-harvest Riesling, or Port.

## *Goat or Sheep*
( SUB-TYPE: *Chèvre* )

Ewes and goats give less milk than cows, but it is higher in fat and protein and richer and more concentrated in flavor. Both milks yield cheeses of a sharp, sometimes intense character. They are often described as having a sheepy or goaty tang that immediately sets them apart from cow's milk cheeses. Today goat's and sheep's milks are frequently mixed with cow's milk or with each other (which may be indicated by the term *mélange de lait* on some French cheeses. The addition of cow's milk makes these cheeses milder and, in the case of *chèvres,* creamier. Sheep cheeses range from semi-soft to very hard in texture, depending upon age, and the older ones are often used for grating. Goat cheese, which is generally ripened for shorter periods, is moist and smooth.

The sub-type *chèvres* is commonly used for goat's milk cheeses in France and there are dozens of them that come in various small shapes (see *Chèvres,* p. 37). The phrase *pur chèvre* (also the generic term) supposedly means that the cheese is made from 100% goat's milk, but there is no law to enforce this as yet. Increasingly, goat's milk is mixed with cow's milk because the latter is so much more abundant and is available year-round.

Goat and sheep cheeses are most widely produced in France, Italy, Spain, Greece, central Europe, and the Middle East. Roquefort is the most famous cheese made from ewe's milk (see Blue Vein). Other famous ones are Pecorino

Romano, Fiore Sardo, and the Caciottas of Italy; Corsican Venaco; Spanish Manchego; Balkan Kashkaval. The most famous—and most widely imitated—goat cheese is Greek Feta. It is also one of the world's oldest and now commonly includes cow's milk

♦ **Buying and Storing Tips**: Taste before buying, if possible, since these cheeses generally have a pronounced flavor and vary seasonally, with the best usually available from early autumn to May. Very ripe *chèvres* may be potent and sharp, especially if the rind has toughened. The French often prefer them this way. *Chèvres* have a relatively brief life but may keep up to two weeks if carefully wrapped and refrigerated, although they lose moisture and become sharper with age. Feta should be stored in a bath of salty or plain water to keep it moist; a milk bath will mitigate the saltiness. Sheep cheeses generally keep very well for long periods if they are not allowed to dry out.

♦ **Serving Tips**: The extra punch of flavor in sheep and goat cheeses makes them highly desirable as after-dinner cheeses providing vivid flavor contrasts to other types. Dry, fruity white wines, mature Bordeaux or Burgundy, and Port make excellent accompaniments.

## Pasta Filata

*Pasta filata* are the stretched-curd cheeses of Italy and include Mozzarella, Provolone, Scamorze, Caciocavallo, and others. The term means "spun paste" and refers to the method of bathing the curd in hot whey, then kneading and stretching it to the desired consistency. They are also sometimes called "plastic curd" cheeses. The pliable texture, ranging from the softness of fresh mozzarella to the firm smoothness of Provolone or Caciocavallo, should not be rubbery or tough.

♦ **Buying and Storing Tips**: Fresh mozzarella is fragile and should be bought as fresh as possible and consumed within a day or two. Firmer cheeses last a good deal longer, up to several weeks or even months for aged Provolone, but they must be carefully wrapped or they will dry out and harden.

♦ **Serving Tips**: Mozzarella and Provolone are widely used in cooking, but also for snacking and in sandwiches or salads. Lightly smoked versions and Scamorze can be delicious with light red or white wines. Aged Provolone is sharp and assertive and calls for sturdy reds.

## Double and Triple Creams

These are cow's milk cheeses enriched with cream. Double creams must have at least 60% fat, triple creams, 75%. They may be fresh, like Boursin, or have bloomy white rinds, like L'Explorateur, Chaource, and Gratte Paille. Their alluring richness and seductive creaminess completely beguile beginning cheeselovers, but experienced turophiles find them irresistible as well.

**Buying and Storing Tips:** These cheeses should be plump and full inside the rind or wrapping and should not be hard or discolored. They will keep up to a week if wrapped in plastic and refrigerated.

▶ **Serving Tips:** Double and Triple Creams are often substituted for dessert, served with ripe pears, plums, or peaches; and lightly sweet Rieslings, Sauternes, Champagnes, or fruity red wines.

## Fresh

The fresh cheeses are uncooked and unripened. They include Pot Cheeses, Cottage Cheese, Cream Cheese, Stracchino, Ricotta, Gervais, and others. Some are rich and creamy (fresh double cream). They are commonly mild and very moist, with a pleasantly sourish tang or tartness; they should not be overly acidic, nor should they be bitter.

▶ **Buying and Storing Tips:** Fresh cheeses, it should go without saying, should be purchased as fresh as possible. They are fragile and rarely keep beyond a week or ten days—less for imported ones such as Ricotta, Stracchino, Crescenza, or the fresh Robiolas. Fresh double creams, such as Boursin, have longer life. They should be securely wrapped or kept in tightly capped containers and refrigerated.

▶ **Serving Tips:** Fresh cheeses are versatile choices for breakfast, lunch, and snacks, and are often topped with fresh berries or preserved fruit. They may also be mixed with herbs or other flavorings.

## Strong-Smelling

The chief feature of cheeses in this group, composed mainly of the washed-rind varieties, announces itself boldly or even overpoweringly. The word "Limburger" is virtually synonymous with pungency of aroma. Limburger's cohorts and rivals are many: Liederkranz, Livarot, Maroilles, Handkäse, Schloss, Hervé, Romadur. Their rinds all are washed or smeared with solutions that contribute to their *odeur puissant,* "stinky odor." Very ripe Münster or Pont l'Evêque could be included here also.

Though not for the faint-hearted, these cheeses need no apologists. Their fans are ardently enthusiastic and eagerly dive through the thick curtain of aroma to the delights of the cheese within. "What cognac is to wine," said one notable cheese-monger, "the washed rinds are to cheese." Oftentimes, their bark is worse than their bite; the assertive character of the cheese itself is surprisingly delicious, even to the uninitiated—intensely savory but milder than the aroma would intimate. For devotées, however, the stronger the better.

♦ **Buying and Storing Tips:** These cheeses will be fresh and resiliently plump inside the rind when ripe or nearly so. Underripe cheeses will be slightly firm to the touch. Hardened rinds, shrunken or mis-shapen cheeses, and ammoniated flavors indicate overripeness. Wiping the rind with a damp cloth or salty water will remove some of the odor and slow ripening a bit, but these cheeses must be well-wrapped to keep them from overpowering everything in their environment. If a smelly cheese is left uncovered for a few hours before serving, some of its odor will dissipate— but be sure the area is well-ventilated. Cover it with a cheese bell to contain the aroma.

♦ **Serving Tips:** Serve strong-smelling cheese separately from other cheeses (not on the same board or tray) so as not to overpower the more delicate types. It is also advisable to provide a separate serving knife. Assertive, full-bodied wines, such as Alsace Riesling Reserve or robust reds, are called for.

## *Whey*

Whey cheeses are those made from the watery, white, or yellowish liquid that separates from the curds when milk and rennet are heated together. Italian Ricotta is a fresh whey cheese. Norwegian Gjetost, which is caramel-colored and somewhat sweet in taste, is a cooked whey cheese.

♦ **Buying and Storing Tips:** Ricotta is very perishable and is best when very fresh. It will keep up to five or six days, but then begins to sour or become moldy. Gjetost will keep extremely well for several weeks or more if it is securely wrapped in foil or plastic and refrigerated.

♦ **Serving Tips:** See Ricotta page 71 and Gjetost page 96.

## *Processed*

Processed cheeses are made by mixing natural cheeses with emulsifiers, additives, and sometimes special flavorings to give them longer shelf life. Most are soft to semi-soft and rather elastic in texture, with mild flavors and not much character. They are designed to appeal to a wide audience, which in fact they do; tremendous quantities are sold in Europe and the United States. American processed cheeses are mostly Cheddar-based, while European ones make use of surplus Emmental or Gruyère. Some of the best-known brands are La Vache Qui Rit, Neufchâtel, Swiss Knight, Velveeta, Gourmandise, Kavli, Reybier, and Reybino.

♦ **Buying and Storing Tips:** Most processed cheeses are foil-wrapped and it is not possible to tell if they are fresh. They last very well, however, and are generally reliable when purchased from reputable marketers.

♦ **Serving Tips:** Processed cheeses are mostly used for snacks.

◆◆◆

# ◆ Nutrition in Popular Cheeses ◆

| CHEESE TYPE | Fat *(grams/oz)* | Protein *(grams/oz)* | Calories *(per oz)* |
|---|---|---|---|
| Speisequark *(no-fat)* | 0 | 3.9 | 21 |
| Cottage Cheese *(1% fat)* | 0.3 | 3.5 | 20 |
| Cottage Cheese *(creamed)* | 1.2 | 3.8 | 30 |
| Danbo *(10% fat)* | 1.6 | 9.8 | 55 |
| Ricotta *(part skim)* | 2.5 | 3.5 | 43 |
| Ricotta | 4.0 | 3.6 | 54 |
| Mozzarella *(part skim)* | 4.5 | 6.9 | 72 |
| Edam | 5.7 | 7.7 | 87 |
| Feta | 6.0 | 4.0 | 74 |
| Mozzarella | 6.1 | 5.4 | 79 |
| Parmesan | 7.3 | 10.1 | 111 |
| Provolone | 7.3 | 7.4 | 98 |
| Gouda | 7.7 | 7.0 | 100 |
| Limburger | 7.7 | 5.7 | 93 |
| Brie | 7.8 | 5.8 | 94 |
| Emmental | 7.8 | 7.7 | 104 |
| Port du Salut | 7.9 | 6.7 | 99 |
| Blue | 8.5 | 6.0 | 103 |
| Monterey | 8.5 | 6.8 | 105 |
| Cheshire | 8.6 | 6.5 | 108 |
| Fontina | 8.7 | 7.2 | 109 |
| Roquefort | 8.7 | 6.1 | 105 |
| Gruyère | 8.9 | 8.1 | 115 |
| Cheddar | 9.1 | 7.0 | 112 |
| Cream | 9.9 | 2.1 | 99 |

Fat in cheese is a complicated and confusing subject. A figure of 45% fat IDM on a cheese label refers to the percentage of fat "in dry matter" only, that is, the dry solids excluding water. Most cheeses on the average consist of 30 to 70 percent moisture (or water). Thus in certain instances high moisture cheeses such as Brie or Camembert may contain considerably less fat than the 45 percent figure would indicate.

The fat content of cheese depends upon the fat in the milk used to make it. But diet-conscious folk should be aware that so-called skimmed milk cheese may not be lower in fat in the end because cream is often added for texture and flavor. It is the fat in the final cheese that counts. Jarlsberg, for example, is made of partially skimmed milk, yet the final cheese contains 47 percent fat IDM, because U.S. standards require that minimum.

# AUSTRALIA & NEW ZEALAND

**L**ike other former British colonies, Australia and New Zealand began to manufacture cheeses in imitation of the mother country during the nineteenth century. Cheddars were, and still are, the chief variety, although both countries now produce very creditable versions of the world's most popular cheeses, from Swiss and Gouda to Limburger and Gorgonzola.

Cows and sheep alike flourish on the plains of southern Australia and the lush mountain valleys of New Zealand, but cheese is made primarily from cow's milk. Both countries have strong cheese industries, regulated by national boards with high quality standards and incentives for innovation. To date there are no extraordinary new creations, but the cheeses are of consistent quality and often offer good value.

◆

## Cheese Guide

### BLUE VEIN, NEW ZEALAND

A creamy blue cheese made from cow's milk in the soft spreadable style of Danablu from Denmark.

### CHEDDAR, AUSTRALIAN

| | |
|---|---|
| ORIGIN | *southern Australia/cow's milk* |
| TYPE | *Cheddar/50% fat* |
| TASTE | *mild to sharp* |
| APPEARANCE | *Cheddar-like but varies in color and firmness* |
| AVAILABILITY | *general export* |

Cheddar is widely produced in many parts of southern Australia. Some of the best comes from the Margaret River region in the West. Mild Cheddar is aged about three months, mature six to twelve months, and vintage Cheddar up to two years. Australians also like their Cheddars spiced up a bit, and many of them are flavored with garlic, cumin, bacon, or nuts.

Most medium-bodied red wines go well with these Cheddars, but they provide a good opportunity to try indigenous reds like Shiraz or Cabernet.

## CHEDDAR, NEW ZEALAND

Quota restrictions limit the export of New Zealand Cheddars for the most part, though some reaches the United States where it is sold as Cheddar or Colby. It is mild, not especially interesting, but very inexpensive and acceptable as a snack cheese.

In New Zealand respectable versions of English-style Cheddars are made, including Cheshires, Gloucesters, Wensleydale, and others, but they are not exported to the United States.

## CHEEDAM

| | |
|---|---|
| ORIGIN | *Australia/cow's milk* |
| TYPE | *Cheddar/45% fat* |
| TASTE | *mild* |
| APPEARANCE | *semi-firm, pale yellow interior; sold in cylinders or blocks* |
| AVAILABILITY | *limited export* |

A very popular "invented" cheese, developed as a cross between Cheddar and Edam. Much of it is exported to Japan, where mild cheeses are prized. Light fruity red wines or beer are suitable to drink with this cheese.

## EGMONT

A relatively new cheese developed in New Zealand as a cross between Cheddar and Gouda. Egmont is also popular in Japan, but will soon be more widely exported. A mild cheese, it is best accompanied by light, fruity wines.

## KANBURRA

An Australian Swiss-style cheese, very similar in flavor to good Norwegian Jarlsberg. Mild but appealing and inexpensive, Kanburra is increasingly exported. Its principal use is with snacks, light red wines or beer.

## MACZOLA

An Australian version of Italian Gorgonzola, smaller in size and lower in fat than the original.

◆◆◆

# BRITISH ISLES

T he wholesome and satisfying goodness of fine English Cheddar has made it one of the world's most widely imitated cheeses. Like most originals, however, it remains in a class by itself. But it is only one—though perhaps the most famous—of Britain's "magnificent nine," a group that includes the mighty Stilton (contender with Roquefort and Brie for the world title, "king of cheeses"), as well as Cheshire, Lancashire, Wensleydale, and others.

The British love their own cheeses and of the nearly 200,000 tons produced annually, fewer than five percent are exported. The sight of a squatty cylinder of Stilton, with its wrinkled, crusty, brownish rind and creamy, blue-veined interior, is enough to set a Britisher's palate watering—especially if there is the prospect of pairing it with its classic partner, a glass of well-matured Port.

Cheese of one sort or another has been made in England for nearly 2,000 years. Farmhouse Cheddar is one of the oldest. Farmers of the Middle Ages made Cheddar; by Elizabethan times it was frequently cited in the literature of the day. Probably it tasted not unlike the Cheddars manufactured today, although the distinction is still drawn between what is known as "factory Cheddar" and traditional Farmhouse Cheddar, with its subtle depth and long, clean aftertaste of richness.

Early farmers made "New Milk Cheese" or "Morning Cheese" from the morning's whole milk mixed with the rich cream skimmed from the previous evening's milk. The resultant golden yellow cheese was thought to be the finest in England. For their own use, the farmers made a skimmed-milk cheese—hard, friable, and whitish—from the evening's leftover milk.

14

England's cheeses go back much farther than the Middle Ages, however; Roman legions posted in County Cheshire no doubt enjoyed an early version of salty, crumbly Cheshire cheese, thought to be England's oldest. Legend claims that the Roman legions built the wall around Chester, the capital of Cheshire County, to protect the city's cheese industry. English cheeses, although it is not known for sure which ones, very probably were sold at the *velabrium,* or dairy market, of ancient Rome.

Most of the cheeses of early Europe were made by dairymaids, the strong and sturdy wives and daughters of farmers. They were responsible for the process and often saw the milk through its entire journey from cow's udder to ripened cheese. Once rennet had been added to the milk in the cheese vat and the curds and whey separated, the dairymaid

15

would scoop out the curds and place them in the primitive press. But first, since it was important that the curds be as dry as possible and mechanical presses were as yet unheard of, she would pre-press them by hand, often climbing on the lid of the cheese basket to apply her full body weight, whence the old English saying, "The bigger the maid, the better the cheese."

In the seventeenth century, cheese-making began to move off the farmstead and into the first dairy cooperatives. Farmers sent their milk to a central dairy where it was processed into cheese. Gradually, technical improvements and more efficient methods of production were developed. In the nineteenth century, for example, a cheese-maker named Joseph Harding helped relieve the milkmaids' burden when he standardized the "cheddaring" process. Under his system, still in use today, the curd is cut into blocks, turned, and folded at a temperature of 90°F to enhance the release of moisture. This procedure results in the tender texture for which British Cheddars are noted.

In spite of the increase in factory productivity, however, farmhouse cheeses are still made today on the farms that dot the meadows and moors of Somerset, Devonshire, Dorset, Cheshire, and Lancashire, although their number has dwindled from 1500 in 1939 to only 50 today. The appellation Farmhouse Cheese is rigidly controlled under quality standards set by the Farmhouse Cheese Association of England. Only a rough dozen or so British cheeses survive today, most named for the county or town where they originated or were first marketed. Cheeses are also made in Scotland and Ireland. Blarney is Ireland's answer to Swiss; Dunlop is Scottish Cheddar. Only four varieties are farm-produced: Cheddar, Cheshire, Blue Cheshire, and Lancashire, all of which are exported in very limited quantities. Farmhouse cheeses were first exported only to the west coast of the United States but now are available (to limited extent) in the East, mainly in New York, Boston, and a few specialty shops elsewhere.

◆

# Cheese Guide

## BLARNEY

| | |
|---|---|
| ORIGIN | *Ireland/cow's milk* |
| TYPE | *semi-firm, Swiss/48% fat* |
| TASTE | *mild, buttery* |
| APPEARANCE | *bright yellow interior with numerous eyes; sold in red paraffin-rind wheels* |
| AVAILABILITY | *limited export* |

A Swiss-style cheese, Blarney is one of the few cheeses still made in Ireland. Although it has Swiss-like holes and a golden color similar to Emmentaler's, it is milder and more buttery in texture and taste. It is rarely seen outside Ireland, although some is exported.

## CABOC

| | |
|---|---|
| ORIGIN | *Scotland/cow's milk* |
| TYPE | *double cream/62% fat* |
| TASTE | *nutty, slightly sourish* |
| APPEARANCE | *4-inch cylinder covered with oatmeal* |
| AVAILABILITY | *domestic only* |

This relatively new Scottish cheese holds the distinction of being one of the few double creams produced in the United Kingdom. Its outer coating of oatmeal gives it a somewhat nut-like flavor.

## CAERPHILLY

| | |
|---|---|
| ORIGIN | *Wales/cow's milk* |
| TYPE | *semi-firm/48% fat* |
| TASTE | *mild, fresh, buttermilk-like tang* |
| APPEARANCE | *sold in low cylinders or blocks; white interior with a smooth, moist, moderately firm texture* |
| AVAILABILITY | *general export* |

Welsh Caerphilly, named for the village in Wales where it was first made, is a young, fresh cheese popular with Welsh miners for its mild, easily digestible properties. It requires a much shorter aging period than traditional English Cheddar and for that reason was taken up by Cheddar makers in Somerset, for whom it has proven a lucrative sidelight. Cheddar is expensive and time-consuming to make; Caerphilly is cheap and quickly sold, ready for eating within a few weeks. Once made exclusively on farms in Wales, it is no longer made there but is produced in creameries, for the most part in Somerset.

As it ages, Caerphilly's mild tartness gets sharper and in England is considered past its prime after only a few weeks. For this reason, it should be bought fresh and eaten fairly quickly, especially when purchased outside Britain. Wrapping it in a damp cloth helps preserve its flavor. In an over-ripe state it is too salty and will have lost its sought-after mildness.

Caerphilly is delicious with fresh dark bread; celery, radishes, or other *crudités;* and salad. And it is well-suited to ale, dry, fruity white wines, or rosé.

## CAITHNESS

A soft, high-fat Scottish cheese made in northern Scotland and rarely seen outside its homeland.

# CHEDDAR

|  |  |
|---|---|
| ORIGIN | *Somerset/cow's milk* |
| TYPE | *semi-firm, Cheddar/48% fat* |
| TASTE | *distinctively rich and nutty with a clean, lingering finish* |
| APPEARANCE | *50- to 60-pound cylinders or blocks; semi-firm, close-textured, ivory yellow to amber interior* |
| AVAILABILITY | *general export* |

Cheddar, the most widely imitated cheese in the world, was first made in southwestern England near the village of Cheddar in the Mendip Hills of Somerset County. English Cheddar is made both in farmhouse and factory. Many people think that there is no other cheese so wholesomely satisfying as genuine Farmhouse Cheddar. Certainly it is the highest-quality Cheddar, particularly that portion that is still made from fresh, unpasteurized milk. At one time the milk for Cheddar came only from Shorthorn cattle, but today most of it is provided by Friesians, along with other breeds.

The best and most highly prized Cheddar is made between May and October, when the milk is at its most flavorful because the cows are feeding on fresh grass. Winter Cheddar is richer and, because the cows feed on hay and other dried grains, higher in fat content. Farmhouse cheeses are graded on appearance, body, texture, and flavor, with Superfine as the highest grade, followed by Fine, Graded, and No-grade.

Only 26 farms now produce genuine Farmhouse Cheddar. Most English Cheddar now is made in the creamery (or factory) and therefore is more plentiful. Creamery Cheddar is very good, although it is made from various milks year 'round and doesn't have quite the incisive distinction and individuality of Farmhouse. But it is more uniform, if somewhat blander, in flavor and is more widely available.

Cheddar is of two kinds: mild and mature. A mild Cheddar, aged up to eight months, is mellow rather than sharp and has a clean, wholesome aftertaste. It is fine with bread and sweet butter, a medium-bodied red wine or full-bodied ale, and perhaps apples or pears. A mature Cheddar, aged over nine months and sometimes as long as two years, is rich, savory, and full-flavored with a lingering aftertaste, but without the bitterness of many imitative Cheddars. A good English Cheddar stands by itself at the end of a meal, a noble companion for well-aged Burgundy or a good Ruby Port. Cheddar melts well and is frequently used for Welsh rarebit in English pubs and grills.

The availability of English Cheddar in the United States is severely limited by American import quotas designed to protect domestic Cheddar production. However, specialty cheese shops on the east and west coasts consistently stock small quantities, including genuine Farmhouse Cheddar.

# Ploughman's Lunch

Probably the most traditional way of serving English Cheddar is in Ploughman's Lunch, a lunchtime feature of most pubs in England. The ingredients are simple and must be fresh: a hunk of crusty bread, a piece of Cheddar, and perhaps some pickle, yet its delights prove that good ingredients need little adornment. The one accompaniment that no Englishman would forego, however, is a pint of bitter beer, which many would argue is the best companion for Cheddar at any time.

## CHESHIRE

| | |
|---|---|
| ORIGIN | *Cheshire/cow's milk* |
| TYPE | *semi-firm/48% fat* |
| TASTE | *mild, creamy, salty* |
| APPEARANCE | *pale yellow (White Cheshire), apricot (Red Cheshire), or blue-veined (Blue Cheshire) interiors; loosely textured and crumbly; sold in large cylinders or bricks* |
| AVAILABILITY | *general export; Farmhouse Cheshire: limited export* |

There are three types of Cheshire: Red, White, and Blue. The White and the Red are alike in flavor and texture, but Red Cheshire is colored with natural vegetable dye from the seeds of the annatto tree. Both have a mild but rich and appealing lactic flavor. Blue Cheshire is considered a great delicacy; it is richer, rarer, and more expensive than Red or White Cheshire.

Cheshire is one of England's most famous cheeses and its praises have been sung by the English literati, including Samuel Johnson. He and his cohorts were wont to sit about in a famous inn of the day, Ye Olde Cheshire Cheese on Fleet Street in London, happily sipping beer and ale and eating Cheshire cheese.

Red and White Cheshires are among the younger cheeses, ripening within a few weeks. If too old, they may turn bitter, although they are seldom aged longer than eight weeks in modern factory production. These "medium-ripened" Cheshires are remarkably consistent in quality, though not as delightful as the longer-ripened farmhouse variety. Farmhouse Cheshire, relatively rare, is richer and sometimes more intensely flavored than Cheddar; made during July and August from the richest milks of the year, it is aged eight to ten months.

Red and White Cheshires have long been considered ideal for Welsh rarebit and for the prototype of the grilled cheese sandwich. One seventeenth-century knight of the realm described Cheshire as a "quick, fat, well-tasted cheese to serve upon a piece of toast." Both versions are equally good served plain or with bread and butter or sliced tomatoes, and accompanied by beer and light red or dry white wines.

Blue Cheshire originated spontaneously when blue mold (*Penicillium glaucum*) developed on certain cheeses as they aged in the cellar. The first Blue Cheshires were considered spoiled and inedible, although they were sometimes used externally as ointments. When Yorkshire miners discovered that the rich, creamy, Cheshire taste was intensified by the blue mold, its distinctiveness soon became highly prized among cheese lovers. The mold seemed to develop most readily on summer-milk cheeses wrapped in cloth and stored in moist cellars. Today Blue Cheshire is stored in similar conditions and aerated with skewers to encourage the development of the mold.

A worthy rival of Stilton (though milder), Blue Cheshire is pale orange-gold in color with striking blue veins running through it. It is rich but crumbly-textured and makes an excellent after-dinner cheese paired with a full-bodied red such as Burgundy or a fine Rhône such as Hermitage or Gigondas.

## COTSWOLD

| | |
|---|---|
| ORIGIN | *Gloucester/cow's milk* |
| TYPE | *semi-firm/48% fat* |
| TASTE | *Cheddar base with herby, chive flavoring* |
| APPEARANCE | *rich gold interior flecked with green bits of chive; natural-rind cylinders or blocks* |
| AVAILABILITY | *general export* |

Cotswold is the United States' name for Double Gloucester flavored with chives. Its mellow, rich, Cheddar-like flavor is accented by the fragrant, wild-onion herbiness of chives. It goes very well with dark beer and makes a fine luncheon cheese, served on a good rye bread and with sausages or salad. Light red wines also suit it.

## CROWDIE

| | |
|---|---|
| ORIGIN | *Scotland/cow's milk* |
| TYPE | *fresh double cream/60% fat* |
| TASTE | *creamy, buttery* |
| APPEARANCE | *whitish-yellow creamy paste, white mold rind* |
| AVAILABILITY | *domestic only* |

Also called "cruddy butter," Crowdie is made by combining fresh curd with fresh butter, which gives it its mild, buttery flavor. It is very popular in Scotland as a breakfast food. Refrigerated, it will keep for months.

# DERBY

| | |
|---|---|
| ORIGIN | *Derbyshire/cow's milk* |
| TYPE | *semi-firm/45–48% fat* |
| TASTE | *mild* |
| APPEARANCE | *pale orange-gold interior; sold in large cylinders or bricks; natural or paraffin rind* |
| AVAILABILITY | *general export* |

A semi-firm Cheddar-style cheese, Derby is flaky in texture but milder in character and generally less interesting than other Cheddars. Those aged up to six months are more pronounced in flavor.

Sage Derby, generously marbled with sage leaves, has a vivid and attractive green color and is much more distinctive than plain Derby. It is a good snack cheese and, due to its herby flavor, is best with beer or ale.

# DORSET BLUE

| | |
|---|---|
| ORIGIN | *Dorset, West Country/cow's milk* |
| TYPE | *blue vein/20–40% fat* |
| TASTE | *sharp and salty* |
| APPEARANCE | *chalk-white interior with a single, prominent streak of blue; thin natural rind* |
| AVAILABILITY | *domestic only* |

Also known as Blue Vinney, this is a strange and very rare skim-milk cheese. "Vinney" comes from the Old English word "fyniz," meaning "mold." Its very special taste is strong, its smooth texture firm, and sometimes crumbly. Its mold is supposed to have been started in the old days by dipping a horse bridle in the milk! Health regulations did away with that practice and the cheese almost became extinct. Today it is made under modern, controlled conditions but remains rare. Its strong flavors call for robust red wines.

# DOUBLE GLOUCESTER

| | |
|---|---|
| ORIGIN | *Gloucester, Somerset, Dorset/cow's milk* |
| TYPE | *semi-firm/45–48% fat* |
| TASTE | *full, mellow, rich* |
| APPEARANCE | *pale to yellow-gold interior; sold in tall cylinders; natural rind* |
| AVAILABILITY | *general export* |

Double Gloucester is one of the great English cheeses. It used to be made on farms in small rounds known as "single" Gloucester; nowadays only Double Gloucesters are made. Originally the cheese was made exclusively from the milk of Gloucester cattle, a breed that now has almost died out. Today Gloucester is creamery-made, but its superb keeping qualities and rich, mellow flavors continue to ensure its popularity. It should be savory, never bitter, and the best is satiny and firm in texture.

Gloucester makes a fine luncheon or after-dinner cheese and may be served with beer or a light Bordeaux or Cabernet Sauvignon. The English sometimes wrap it in lettuce leaves or slice it for sandwiches to be served with pickles or jam and honey. It is also good with fresh pears or apples.

## DUNLOP

|  |  |
|---|---|
| ORIGIN | *Scotland/cow's milk* |
| TYPE | *semi-firm, Cheddar/45–48% fat* |
| TASTE | *mild and buttery when young, sharper when aged* |
| APPEARANCE | *ivory-colored interior; sold in cylinders* |
| AVAILABILITY | *limited general export* |

Moister and milder than Cheddar when it is aged up to two months, Dunlop has a flavor that deepens when it is aged up to four months. Although it grows sharper with age, however, it should remain mellow and is considered too old if bitter. It is especially good with Scottish ale and oatcakes and is also a good toasting cheese.

## LANCASHIRE

|  |  |
|---|---|
| ORIGIN | *Lancashire/cow's milk* |
| TYPE | *semi-firm/45% fat* |
| TASTE | *subtly rich, with lactic tang* |
| APPEARANCE | *white, close-textured interior; sold in cylinders or blocks* |
| AVAILABILITY | *limited export* |

Softer, moister, and quicker-ripening than Cheddar, Lancashire is the ultimate toasting cheese. At the age of three months, it is as spreadable as butter; aged longer, it becomes firmer and more crumbly in texture. Though mild, it is not bland and develops a richness with more maturity. Farmhouse Lancashire is the best, of course, but is not made in great quantities. It is excellent as a component of cheese sauces or a topping for soup and is considered the premier choice for rarebit.

By itself, Lancashire goes well with fruity red wines or medium-dry sherry.

## LEICESTER

|  |  |
|---|---|
| ORIGIN | *Leicester/cow's milk* |
| TYPE | *semi-firm/45–48% fat* |
| TASTE | *mellow, tangy, with a medium-strong aftertaste* |
| APPEARANCE | *deep orange interior, crumbly texture* |
| AVAILABILITY | *general export* |

The loose, flaky texture of Leicester is higher in moisture content than Cheddar, and the cheese melts in the mouth with a mellow tang. Although Leicester does not have the distinctive character of true Cheddar, it is a fine snack cheese, at its best after ripening for three to nine months, but over-ripe in a year. Its texture makes it difficult to slice without its crumbling, and when poorly stored it develops unpleasantly strong patches of flavor. If the cut edges of the cheese are white, don't buy it, for these are signs of bitterness.

## RED CHESHIRE *see* Cheshire

## SAGE DERBY *see* Derby

## STILTON

| | |
|---|---|
| ORIGIN | *Leicester, Derbyshire, Nottinghamshire/cow's milk* |
| TYPE | *blue vein/45% fat* |
| TASTE | *rich, piquant, with creamy Cheddar undertones* |
| APPEARANCE | *white to pale amber interior with evenly spread blue veins; sold in tall cylinders with crusty rind* |
| AVAILABILITY | *general export* |

England's royal blue combines the most distinctive virtues of blue and Cheddar cheeses—the mellow richness of Cheddar is appealingly accented with a moldy tang that is neither overly pungent nor salty. Its copyrighted name dates to the eighteenth century when it was sold to stagecoach passengers in front of the Bell Inn in the small village of Stilton, Huntingdonshire.

Made from rich, whole milk, Stiltons are not pressed, but are turned regularly for at least a week before being removed from stainless steel molds. It is at that time that the brownish crusty rind begins to form. A mild, sourish White Stilton is sold young, before the veins develop, but the blue-veined king is ripened four to six months in cool ripening rooms. The cheese is skewered 300 times or more to encourage the growth of the mold, which develops naturally in the presence

# A Homage to Stilton

"Of Stilton it is hard to speak without emotion. Its azure veins avouching noble lineage, it enthrones itself as the world's most regal Blue, exerting, like any true aristocrat, authority without aggressiveness. A Stilton's self-confidence springs from its past (the richest cream and milk) and its future, which can only be one of glory.... There's such divinity doth hedge a Stilton as aureoles no other cheese. It is magisterial."

from an essay by Clifton Fadiman,
*"In Praise of Cheese"*

of oxygen. In the eighteenth century, a Stilton was not considered ripe until it was crawling with mites. Today the rind is brushed or wiped to keep it clean as the cheese matures.

Stilton is best kept at a cool room-temperature, covered with a cloth. If it dries out, rub it with a cloth soaked in salted water. If you have to refrigerate it, wrap it in a damp cloth. Stilton has a tendency to dry out, but the practice of pouring port wine into the hollowed-out cavity to preserve moisture is *not* recommended and, in fact, detracts from the quality of both the wine and the cheese. A whole Stilton keeps best if cut horizontally and then sliced into wedge-shaped portions for serving.

Stilton stands by itself, accompanied only by a glass of port or full-bodied Burgundy and perhaps a biscuit or dried fruit.

## WENSLEYDALE

| | |
|---|---|
| ORIGIN | *Yorkshire/cow's milk* |
| TYPE | *semi-firm, blue vein/45% fat* |
| TASTE | *White is fresh and buttermilk-like, richer with age; Blue is rich with a creamy tang and fine aftertaste* |
| APPEARANCE | *white or blue-veined interior; sold in cylinders or blocks* |
| AVAILABILITY | *general export* |

White Wensleydale, made from a finely cut curd that is lightly pressed, has a high moisture content. Ripened only up to three weeks, it should be eaten when it is young and fresh. Its tangy flavor and chalky, smooth texture are superb with fresh apples, pears, and green grapes; it is the cheese *par excellence* with apple pie. When more mature its flavor becomes richer and faintly sweet, and it develops a very attractive aftertaste. Dry, fruity white wines make excellent companions to White Wensleydale.

Blue Wensleydale is considered a great delicacy. It is much more robust in flavor and needs at least six months to mature. Its smooth texture is creamier than Stilton and its flavor a bit milder. Many people prefer it for that reason, although it is harder to come by. Dry reds are its best accompaniment.

## WINDSOR RED

A variation of Cheddar, flavored with a red berry juice that gives its pale yellow interior a pink-marbled effect.

◆◆◆

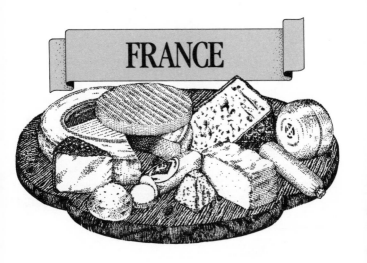

# FRANCE

**N**o one takes cheese more seriously—or treats it more lovingly—than the French, whether they are making it, buying it, serving it, or eating it. It is a staple of the everyday table. It can also be the *crescendo* of a great meal, a showcase for the principal wine of the evening. Annual per capita consumption is the largest in the world: On the average, nearly 38 pounds of cheese are consumed by each person every year.

The number and variety of French cheeses are astonishing. France produces some 400 cheeses. Most are produced from cow's milk, but there are numerous sheep's and goat's milk cheeses as well. Two of France's most famous cheeses—Brie and Roquefort—vie for the world title of *le roi des fromages.* So far, throughout their very long history the contest is a stand-off that awards the title to both!

Not only does France have cheeses that are individually famous; she has whole *groups* of cheeses that are eagerly sought after: the lush, rich double and triple creams like Brillat-Savarin, L'Explorateur, Boursault; the delectable soft-ripened Brie, Camembert, Coulommiers; the fragrant mountain cheeses like Beaufort, Gruyère, Tomme de Pyrénées; the tangy, piquant *chèvres,* or goat cheeses; the pungent and odiferous Livarot, Maroilles, Pont L'Evêque; the slightly milder monastery cheeses such as Munster or Port Salut; and, of course, *les bleus:* Roquefort, Bleu de Bresse, Pipo Crem', Fourme d'Ambert, and a number of others.

Cheeses are produced in every corner of France, with heaviest concentrations in the Auvergne (home of several blues and Cantal), the Loire Valley and Poitou *(chèvres),* the mountains of the Jura, the Vosges in Alsace and the Pyrénées, and the Ile de France surrounding Paris.

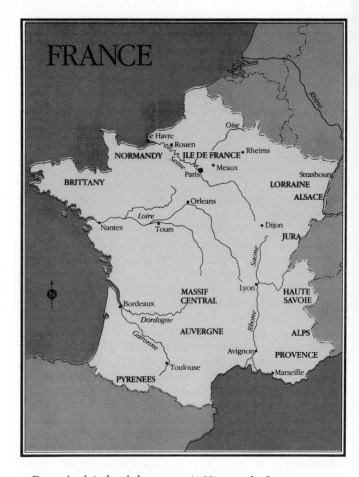

France's dairyland, however, is Normandy. Just as a wine road (Route des Grands Vins) winds through Burgundy, a "cheese road" wends its way through Normandy, connecting the towns that have fostered some of the country's most distinctive cheeses: Camembert, Livarot and Pont L'Evêque. Here, greener pastures give some of the richest cow's milk. Farm-made Camembert, produced from raw milk *(lait crû)* and ripened on straw mats, is a treasure Parisians constantly search out, but it is increasingly hard to come by.

Tourist travel to France has created a worldwide demand for French cheeses that has had a significant impact on cheese production in the last decade or so. It has spawned a factory industry that can better fulfill demand, though not without some sacrifice of quality and, in some cases, of the highly individual character for which certain cheeses are famous. The blandness of many factory-made Brie and Camembert are two examples. Genuinely original versions of each are now relatively rare. In addition, many new cheeses have been developed to satisfy the increasing clamor for popular types. Yet the demand for the French classics is unceasing and a whole cadre of specialty cheese shops has sprung up to bring them to us. Getting to know French cheeses is an adventure that demands something of you, rather like getting to know French wines.

In both cases, it's worth the effort.

# *Cheese Guide*

## BANON

| | |
|---|---|
| ORIGIN | *Provence/usually goat's milk* |
| TYPE | *chèvre/45% fat* |
| TASTETASTE | *mild and lactic to savory* |
| APPEARANCE | *4- to 7-ounce discs wrapped in green leaves and tied with rafia; white, creamy or chalky interior; natural rind* |
| AVAILABILITY | *general export* |

This natural-rind cheese is usually made from goat's milk, but sometimes from sheep's or cow's milk or a mixture of the two. Banon is cured in leaves and sometimes washed in *marc* over a period of two to eight weeks. It is most commonly either mild and lactic, or milky; as it ages it loses moisture and becomes more piquant. Leaves should not be dark, dried out, or mottled with mold when the cheese is purchased, and the cheese itself should be fairly firm. A hard texture is a sign that it is drying out.

Banon is a good summer luncheon cheese that goes well with dry, fruity whites such as Sancerre or Pouilly-Fumé, Tavel rosé, or light, fruity red wines.

## BEAUFORT (also Gruyère de Beaufort)

| | |
|---|---|
| ORIGIN | *Savoie/cow's milk* |
| TYPE | *semi-firm, Swiss/50% fat* |
| TASTE | *mellow, smooth, sometimes stronger* |
| APPEARANCE | *wheels up to 125 pounds with natural rough rinds; pale yellow interior with few holes* |
| AVAILABILITY | *general export* |

Similar to Swiss GRUYÈRE this cheese is made in the alpine regions of the Jura and Savoie of eastern France. It is mild and supple with Swiss-like flavors but very few small holes. *Beaufort haut-montagne,* which is made from the milk of cows that summer high in the alpine pastures and aged six months or longer, is richer in character and more flavorful. Avoid cheeses with cracked rind, too many holes, rubbery texture, or excessive saltiness.

Beaufort is fine as a snack cheese with fresh fruit and dry but fruity white or red wines.

## BEAUMONT

| | |
|---|---|
| ORIGIN | *Haut-Savoie/cow's milk* |
| TYPE | *semi-soft/50% fat* |
| TASTE | *savory, full-flavored* |
| APPEARANCE | *large discs with light ochre, firm rinds; yellow smooth interior* |
| AVAILABILITY | *general export* |

A supple-textured cheese similar to such monastery cheeses as Saint-Paulin, Beaumont is somewhat more vividly flavored and becomes earthier in flavor and darker in color as it matures. It will keep for a few weeks if well-wrapped and refrigerated. Avoid improperly cured ones with unnaturally bulging or cracked rinds.

Beaumont is enjoyed in France with wines of the Savoy such as Crèpy or Seyssel; Pinot Blanc is also a good choice, as are reds from the Côtes du Rhône.

## BELLE BRESSANE

| | |
|---|---|
| ORIGIN | *Bresse/cow's milk* |
| TYPE | *blue vein/50% fat* |
| TASTE | *mild and creamy, somewhat piquant but not sharp* |
| APPEARANCE | *cake-like cylinders with hole in center; whitish rind flecked with orange; ivory interior with blue veins* |
| AVAILABILITY | *general export* |

This is one of the milder blues from Grièges, a town in the alpine region of Bresse. The extra bit of richness makes it creamy and somewhat similar to PIPO CREM'. A good choice when you want a less piquant blue, and it goes well with sturdy red wines from Burgundy or the Rhône. Lightly sweet whites will also suit this cheese.

## BLEU

The French term for blue-veined cheeses injected with spores of *Penicillium glaucum*. Most French blues are made from cow's milk, except for Roquefort, which is made from sheep's milk. Generally, the region in which the cheese is produced is part of the name, as in BLEU DE BRESSE or BLEU D'AUVERGNE. Blues are often referred to as *persillé*, or parsleyed, because the network of blue-green veins resembles sprigs of parsley. The flavors range from creamy to very intense and piquant, and they require sturdy red wines.

# BLEU D'AUVERGNE

| | |
|---|---|
| ORIGIN | *Auvergne/cow's milk* |
| TYPE | *blue vein/45% fat* |
| TASTE | *salty, creamy, piquant* |
| APPEARANCE | *whitish yellow interior with well-developed blue mold; thin rind; sold in foil-wrapped, 4-inch-tall cylinders* |
| AVAILABILITY | *general export* |

This is one of the best and most intensely flavored French blues. When it is properly aged, the texture is creamy rather than crumbly, the flavors not overly strong or sharp. It originated in the nineteenth century as an imitation of Roquefort, with the distinction that it uses cow's milk instead of sheep's milk. Some Bleu d'Auvergne is still made on mountain farms; those that are particularly good carry the name of *Thiezac*. They are strong and densely blue but can be mellowed by mixing with sweet butter. Those from Laqueuille are milder. They are best with full-bodied Rhône reds such as Hermitage or *Gigondas*.

# BLEU DE BRESSE

| | |
|---|---|
| ORIGIN | *Eastern France/cow's milk* |
| TYPE | *blue vein/50% fat* |
| TASTE | *creamy, milder than most blues* |
| APPEARANCE | *small cylinders with whitish rinds; whitish interior with blue streaks or splotches; sometimes boxed or wrapped* |
| AVAILABILITY | *general export* |

A creamy, moist French blue with mild but savory flavors and a soft, spreadable texture, Bleu de Bresse is similar to Gorgonzola and Pipo Crem'. Exported cheeses are occasionally overripe with crumbly textures, heavy mold, and ammoniated flavors. Even these, however, have their fans among lovers of *bleu*. Bleu de Bresse is one of the most popular blues, especially prized in early spring in France when its consistency is very soft and creamy.

It is best with unflavored crackers, ripe pears, and rich wines such as Saint-Emilion or Sonoma County Cabernets.

# BLEU DES CAUSSES

| | |
|---|---|
| ORIGIN | *Auvergne/cow's milk* |
| TYPE | *blue vein/45% fat* |
| TASTE | *full, savory flavors* |
| APPEARANCE | *ivory interior with lacy blue veins; sold in rindless foil-wrapped cylinders* |
| AVAILABILITY | *limited export* |

A fine blue similar to Bleu d'Auvergne, though not quite as intense. Bleu des Causses should not be sharp, too strong in aroma, or dry and crumbly. Still, it is one of the more assertive cow's milk blues, made near the Roquefort region and aged in caves or humid cellars for two to three months.

Used in salads, as a snack, or as an after-dinner cheese, Bleu des Causses calls for robust reds such as Châteauneuf du Pape, Côte Rotie, or California Syrah.

## BLEU DE CORSE

A sheep's milk blue made on the highland plateaus of Corsica, Bleu de Corse is modeled after ROQUEFORT. Cured in caves, it is pungent and rich though sometimes only lightly veined. It is rarely exported.

## BLEU DU HAUT-JURA (also Bleu de Gex or Bleu de Septmoncel)

| | |
|---|---|
| ORIGIN | *Jura/cow's milk* |
| TYPE | *blue vein/45% fat* |
| TASTE | *tangy, savory, milder than most blues* |
| APPEARANCE | *sold in thick wheels with grayish rinds; ivory interior with blue streaks* |
| AVAILABILITY | *limited export* |

Bleu du Haut-Jura is the generic name for blues from Gex, Septmoncel and elsewhere in the region. *Bleu de Gex* is more commonly seen outside France. Slightly milder in flavor than most blue veins, it is said to be "the blue for people who don't like blues." This is true enough when the veining is light, but in its more mature versions it can be quite savory and faintly bitter. An appealing blue, it is good with Beaujolais, particularly one of the *crus* such as Fleurie or Saint-Amour, or with other fruity reds.

*Bleu de Septmoncel* is very similar to Gex; both cheeses are produced in the Jura mountains but in different areas.

## BONBEL

Brand name of exported, bland, semi-soft SAINT PAULIN.

## BONDON

Small cylinders of NEUFCHÂTEL.

## BOUILLE, LA

A small cylindrical double cream similar to MONSIEUR FROMAGE of Normandy, La Bouille has a white bloomy rind flecked with orange and a soft, creamy, savory paste.

## BOURSAULT

| | |
|---|---|
| ORIGIN | *northern France/cow's milk* |
| TYPE | *triple cream/75% fat* |
| TASTE | *rich, creamy, savory* |
| APPEARANCE | *small, paper-wrapped cylinders; soft, creamy interior with bloomy rind* |
| AVAILABILITY | *general export* |

One of the most popular of the triple creams, Boursault is

enriched with fresh cream. As a soft-ripened cheese it ripens inside its snowy rind to a luscious, salty paste with a consistency almost like whipped cream. Avoid those with discolored paper wrapping or sagging shape.

## BOURSIN

| | |
|---|---|
| ORIGIN | *Normandy, Ile de France/cow's milk* |
| TYPE | *triple cream/70–75% fat* |
| TASTE | *rich, savory, often herb-flavored* |
| APPEARANCE | *small foil-wrapped cylinders; rindless; white creamy paste, flecked with seasonings* |
| AVAILABILITY | *general export* |

Boursin is a triple cream, especially popular in versions flavored with garlic, herbs, or cracked pepper. It has a smooth, buttery texture and rich, creamy flavors often piquant with seasonings. It is good with dry white wines from the Loire Valley or Macon, as well as with fruity reds. In addition, Boursin is delicious as a breakfast cheese with bagels and black coffee.

## BREBIGNOL

A semi-firm sheep's cheese made in the Pyrénées region of southwestern France, Brebignol has the subtle but savory tang that characterizes many sheep's milk cheeses. It is mainly a snack or lunch cheese, best accompanied by fruity wines. Not widely exported.

## BREBIS FRAIS DU ROUERGUE

| | |
|---|---|
| ORIGIN | *Auvergne/ewe's milk* |
| TYPE | *sheep, fresh/45% fat* |
| TASTE | *fresh, rich, mild* |
| APPEARANCE | *chalky white, smooth interior; sold in containers* |
| AVAILABILITY | *limited export* |

Brebis Frais du Rouergue is a fresh sheep's milk cheese from the Roquefort region. Though quite rich, it has a delicate—and delicious—milky tang. A fine breakfast or luncheon cheese, Brebis Frais is good with fresh or preserved fruit, light wines, or black coffee.

## BRIE (also Brie de Meaux, Brie de Melun, or Coulommiers)

| | |
|---|---|
| ORIGIN | *Ile de France/cow's milk* |
| TYPE | *soft-ripened/45% fat* |
| TASTE | *creamy, savory with a fruity tang and rich aftertaste* |
| APPEARANCE | *round, flat discs of 2 or 4 pounds with white rinds flecked with gold or russet pigments; high-gloss, cream-colored paste* |
| AVAILABILITY | *general export* |

Specialty cheese shops claim to sell more Brie than any other cheese, so popular has this import become. There are Bries and there are Bries, however. The original, *Brie de Meaux,* was known at least as far back as the eighth century. One reference indicates that Charlemagne knew it, and in 1815, when the French diplomat Talleyrand introduced it at the Congress of Vienna, it was proclaimed by all present as the "king of cheeses."

Brie made from unpasteurized milk and produced on farmsteads around Meaux or Melun (famous cheese towns a few miles outside of Paris) counts, at peak ripeness, among the most sublime of taste experiences. The flavor was once described as "part mushroom, part cream, part cognac, part earth ... with a shade of truffle ... and something of the scent of ripe Anjou pears." Unpasteurized Bries are generally only available in Europe, and cannot be legally imported to the United States.

Most exported Bries are made from pasteurized milk by factories whose quality varies. At perfect ripeness they are still among the most delectable of cheeses. But a lot of them are bland or underripe. Learning to select a fine Brie takes practice and attention, and good ones may have to be searched out. When underripe, Brie has a hard, chalky core at the center. Such a cheese will never ripen fully. Look instead for an even, creamy color and a smooth paste that is plump inside its rind. When not fully ripe, a whole Brie will feel somewhat firm. If you buy Brie in this condition, store it in a cool place or in the warmest part of the refrigerator for a couple of days. Remove it to room temperature two hours before serving. A fully ripe Brie is somewhat yielding to the touch, perhaps even bulging a bit inside the rind, which will have begun to develop brownish edges and show coloration across the rind. Brie has a brief life, so if it has not softened and matured in a few days, you can be reasonably sure that it probably won't soften and mature at all. It will simply dry out and harden, the paste inside will darken, and the smell will become more ammoniated.

On the other hand, the best Brie will not be overly runny either. The French say that a good Brie should ooze, not run. Once cut, it does not ripen further, which is why it is critical to buy it at just the right moment and to serve it as soon as possible. One cannot buy much in advance. It is very perishable, especially when perfectly ripe, and therefore it is best to buy only the exact amount you are sure you will need for the occasion.

The bloomy rinds of Brie de Meaux and Brie de Melun, both of which come in thin, flat, pancake-like discs over a foot in diameter, show a reddish pigment dusted in the rind and sometimes the faint impression of the straw mats on which they were ripened. This is a good sign, especially if the cheese is plump and resilient to the touch. But if the rind is dry and tough, or gummy and sagging, or smells strongly of ammonia, it may be overripe—here your own taste preference must be your guide. Some people like them that way. The rind is edible, but don't hesitate to trim it off if you prefer. In France it is eaten both ways.

Rarest of the Bries is Brie de Meaux *fermier*—farm-produced, inimitably gorgeous, with the texture of rich honey. It is not widely available, even in France. Made solely of *lait crû* (raw milk), it has a subtle but penetrating and lingering savor that one must taste if one is to comprehend the difference between it and the mild, pleasant Bries we are mostly accustomed to.

Brie de Melun is a little deeper in color, slightly earthier in character and slightly less complex than Brie de Meaux, though some will argue it the other way round. Coulommiers is made in thicker rounds of smaller diameter than most Bries. It is milder than those from Meaux or Melun and more like Camembert.

Bries are classic after-dinner cheeses with red or white wines. Whole wheels make a dashing display for wine tastings or cocktail parties.

## BRILLAT-SAVARIN

| | |
|---|---|
| ORIGIN | *France/cow's milk* |
| TYPE | *triple cream/75% fat* |
| TASTE | *creamy, luscious, faintly sour* |
| APPEARANCE | *white, bloomy-rind discs of creamy white paste* |
| AVAILABILITY | *general export* |

A popular brand of triple cream, Brillat-Savarin is excellent as a dessert with Meedjol dates and German Spätlese or Auslese, or with Champagne biscuits and Champagne.

## BRIN D'AMOUR (also Fleur du Maquis)

| | |
|---|---|
| ORIGIN | *Corsica/goat's or sheep's milk* |
| TYPE | *semi-firm/45% fat* |
| TASTE | *subtle but savory, herby* |
| APPEARANCE | *blocks with thin, natural rinds; chalk-white, smooth interior* |
| AVAILABILITY | *limited export* |

This delectable (and expensive) "morsel of love" comes from the central plateau of Corsica where sheep and goats graze on wild thyme, rosemary, coriander, and other herbs. Most are made from sheep's milk, but some are made from a mixture of goat's and sheep's milk. Brin d'Amour is cured for three months with the same aromatic herbs that the animals feed upon and is shipped with the herbs clinging to the rind.

The delicate herby flavors and sheepy tang of this cheese are excellent with full-bodied white Burgundies or reds from the Rhône.

## BÛCHE LORRAINE

A small, loaf-shaped DOUBLE CREAM with a downy white rind and mild Brie-like flavors.

## BÛCHERON

| | |
|---:|:---|
| ORIGIN | *Poitou/goat's milk* |
| TYPE | *chèvre, soft/45% fat* |
| TASTE | *mild, savory tang* |
| APPEARANCE | *5-pound logs with white rinds, occasionally covered with black ash* |
| AVAILABILITY | *general export* |

A popular, soft, chalky CHÈVRE, Bûcheron is tangy but mild, rich, and sometimes quite spreadable. It should not be yellowed or dried out. It goes well with crisp, dry whites or light red wines.

## CABECOU see Chabichou

## CALVADOUX

| | |
|---:|:---|
| ORIGIN | *Normandy/cow's milk* |
| TYPE | *soft-ripened/45% fat* |
| TASTE | *assertive, with a raunchy tang* |
| APPEARANCE | *flat cylinder with orange-gold rind, ochre paste* |
| AVAILABILITY | *general export* |

A fairly new variety of surface-ripened cheese, Calvadoux is also similar to other monastery types such as PONT L'EVÊQUE, after which it is modeled. The name comes from the fact that it is produced in Calvados country. When very ripe, it oozes thickly and takes on pungent flavors and aromas.

## CAMEMBERT

| | |
|---:|:---|
| ORIGIN | *Normandy/cow's milk* |
| TYPE | *soft-ripened/45% fat* |
| TASTE | *creamy, Brie-like but milder* |
| APPEARANCE | *small discs; white downy rind with goldish-orange flecks; pale, creamy paste* |
| AVAILABILITY | *general export* |

A classic among world cheeses, Camembert is widely imitated in many countries. Fine Camembert, however, is exceedingly hard to come by. Just as Americans search for the perfect Brie, the French go after Camembert *à point*. It is a great coup at Paris parties to serve a farm-made variety that is at ripe perfection—a state that doesn't last beyond a day and a half at most. Like Brie, it should ooze thickly and creamily, or "exude," as one gastronome put it. But it is better to have faintly underripe than overripe Camembert, as it tends to become bitter and ammoniated to the point of rankness when overly ripe.

This cheese is said to have been invented by a farmer's wife named Marie Harel, to whom a statue was erected in her home town of Vimoutiers in Normandy. Camembert was christened by Napoleon. Stopping for lunch in the little town of Camembert near Vimoutiers, he is said to have leaped to his feet and kissed the serving maid who brought him the cheese.

Most Camembert today is factory-made and therefore fairly uniform in quality, but those made by small dairies or on farms can still be highly individual cheeses that vary subtly from season to season (look for *Le Rustique, La Normandie*). When perfectly ripe, Camembert will have a pronounced aroma, pleasantly piquant and redolent of its special mold *Penicillium camemberti,* and rich creamy flavors that end on a distinctive tangy note. Quite extraordinary. Supermarket versions are likely to be bland or bitter, especially those in cans.

It is best to buy the whole cheese since it is small, usually boxed in cardboard or chipwood. Like Brie, it should be plump and full inside its rind and soft to the touch. Those that have shrunk away from the box or have hardened rind edges may be overripe.

In Normandy, Camembert is usually accompanied by cider, since apples are as ubiquitous there as dairy cows. It is also fine with Bordeaux reds or California Cabernets and Merlots.

## CAMPAGNOLE

Developed rather recently, this goat's milk blue is made with *roqueforti* mold. It is tart, fresh, and chalk white, with a blue vein running through the center. It is not widely exported.

## CANTAL (also Fourme de Cantal)

| | |
|---|---|
| ORIGIN | *Auvergne/cow's milk* |
| TYPE | *semi-firm/45% fat* |
| TASTE | *mellow, nutty, smooth* |
| APPEARANCE | *large cylinders with greyish-beige rinds; smooth yellow interior* |
| AVAILABILITY | *limited export* |

This cheese is produced only in the department of Cantal in central France, its name protected under the laws of *appellation controlée.* One of France's oldest cheeses, it is somewhat like Cheddar in flavor. The texture of young cheeses aged three to six months is smooth and supple, rather like an American Colby Cheddar. Its mellow, nutty flavor begins to sharpen and deepen after that, and the texture becomes firmer and more crumbly. Its wholesome, milky flavors make Cantal an excellent snack cheese, but well-aged versions are superb with solid red wines after dinner, or with beer.

## CAPRICE DES DIEUX

| | |
|---|---|
| ORIGIN | *Haut-Marne/cow's milk* |
| TYPE | *double cream/60% fat* |
| TASTE | *rich, mild, creamy* |

APPEARANCE *flat, oval discs with downy white rind and pale, soft interior*
AVAILABILITY *general export*

One of the best known double creams, Caprice des Dieux is similar to Brie and Camembert, but is enriched with cream. When ripe, the paste should be resiliently soft; the rind tinged with light orange. Overripe cheeses have hardened rinds, distorted shapes, and the smell of ammonia. Caprice des Dieux is good with Bordeaux reds, wafers, and grapes.

## CAPRICETTE

Capricette is a creamy, fresh goat cheese (CHÈVRE) that comes in small, frosty white cakes that have mild flavors and a spreadable texture.

## CAPRICORNE

Made in the shape of a flat wheel, this *chèvre* has a downy white rind and a hole in its center. Inside the thin rind, the cheese has a dryish texture (it may be creamy near the rind) and sharp, salty flavors. It is very appealing with crisp white wines such as Sancerre or Chablis.

## CARRÉ DE L'EST

ORIGIN *northeastern France/cow's milk*
TYPE *soft-ripened/45–50% fat*
TASTE *mild, creamy, mushroomy*
APPEARANCE *small squares with downy rinds and soft, ivory paste*
AVAILABILITY *general export*

A French classic of the minor leagues, Carré de l'Est is made in Lorraine and the Champagne region. The name means "square of the East." It is similar to Camembert in flavor and texture but develops a light mushroom aroma when ripe. It makes an enjoyable snack or after-dinner cheese served with firm-textured dark breads and fruity red wines.

## CHABICHOU (also Cabécou)

ORIGIN *Poitou/goat's milk*
TYPE *chèvre, soft/45% fat*
TASTE *assertive goaty tang*
APPEARANCE *sold in small cones with bluish-grey rind, or small white logs with white rind; soft, chalk-white interior*
AVAILABILITY *limited export*

Chabichou (the name means "little goat") is a very tasty *chèvre* from the Loire Valley with a zesty tang that sharpens with age. Farm-produced Chabis have bluish rinds flecked with reddish-brown. Like all soft cheeses, it is considered overripe if it appears dark and shrunken. Chabichou is good with full-bodied reds such as Juliénas or Paso Robles.

## CHAMOIS D'OR

Almost a double crème (52% fat), this soft-ripened cheese has a bloomy rind. As a cross between Brie and Camembert it doesn't quite come off. It is modeled after Brie de Coulommiers but is rather lacking in interesting character. Creamy enough, it is a somewhat bland but agreeable addition to the cheese board and goes with a variety of red or white wines.

## CHAOURCE

| | |
|---|---|
| ORIGIN | *Champagne/cow's milk* |
| TYPE | *soft-ripened/45%–50% fat* |
| TASTE | *rich, very creamy, fruity* |
| APPEARANCE | *flat cylinders 5 inches in diameter with bloomy white rinds; ivory center* |
| AVAILABILITY | *general export* |

Chaource, named for a leading market town in the Champagne region, is very similar to Camembert or Coulommiers. Although it lacks the complexity of either, it is lusciously rich and creamy, and gets stronger and saltier as it matures, ultimately developing a pronounced mushroom aroma and an acidic edge. A popular choice for the after-dinner cheese tray, it goes well with light Burgundies; it is also good with Mâcon Blanc, Chardonnay, or other full-bodied white wines.

## CHAUMES

| | |
|---|---|
| ORIGIN | *France/cow's milk* |
| TYPE | *monastery/45% fat* |
| TASTE | *assertive, tangy* |
| APPEARANCE | *large, flat orange disc, soft yellow center* |
| AVAILABILITY | *general export* |

A soft-ripened cheese with a semi-soft texture and an assertive aroma like Munster, Chaumes comes in a flat, round, pancake-style disc with a deep orange, washed-rind surface. Numerous small holes dot the pale yellow paste. Its pronounced flavors have a richness and a faint edge of bitterness that turns to stinkiness when the cheese is very ripe. Chaumes needs a Pilsner-style lager beer or a very full-bodied red to stand up to it.

## CHÈVRES

*Fromage de chèvre,* or goat cheese, accounts for less than three percent of the total cheese production in France, yet it is one of the most popular types. A great many come from farms or cooperatives along the Loire River and Poitou to the south, but they are also produced in other regions. Cheese labeled *pur chèvre* is supposed to be all goat's milk, others may include some cow's milk, but all exhibit the fresh, tart zing common to goat cheese. They range in texture from soft, moist, and creamy to somewhat dry and sliceable, and

---

# Cheese and Herbs

One of the most appetizing ways to serve a fresh *chèvre* is gently bathed in fine olive oil and sprinkled with thyme. Use only fresh rindless cylinders of *chèvres* and just enough French or Italian olive oil to coat the cheese lightly, then sprinkle the herbs on top.

The herbiness of thyme provides the perfect accent for the dry tang of young *chèvres,* but Herbes de Provences may also be used. Do not refrigerate as the oil will solidify and discolor. Serve with crusty French bread.

Pont l'Evêque, Chaumes, Rollot, Vieux Pané, or other washed-rind cheeses are similarly herb-enhanced by sprinkling fennel or anise seed on the rind. Let stand a day or overnight to absorb the flavor and brush away the herbs before cutting and serving.

---

they are always chalk white. They are molded into numerous shapes: cones, pyramids, logs, cylinders, small discs. Some have bloomy white rinds, others are *cendré* (coated in edible vegetable ash that preserves moisture), still others are wrapped in leaves or sprinkled with pepper or herbs. Specialty cheese shops carry as many as 20 or 30 different *chèvres.* They will keep a couple of weeks if refrigerated, but after three weeks or so they become dried out and ammoniated. They are always tart and tangy to some degree but should not be overly acidic or biting, or too sour.

There are too many varieties to include in this volume but some of the better-known ones have their own entries: Banon, Lezay, Sainte-Maure, Géant, Bûcheron, Montrachet, Chevrette, Saint-Marcellin. Goat cheeses, with their mild or bracing zest, are excellent with dry, crisp white wines like Sancerre, Mâcon, Chablis, or with reds like Chinon, Santenay, Pinot Noir, or Beaujolais.

## CHEVROTIN

One of the milder CHÈVRE, or goat cheese, that comes in cones or small cylinders.

## CHIBERTA see Tourton

## CLOCHETTE CHAPUT

This small CHÈVRES is produced in the shape of a bell (*clochette* means "little bell"). It has a fleecy rind and a goaty, piquant tang. Best when very fresh and served with crisp, dry white wines.

# COEUR DE BRAY

A soft, creamy cheese similar to NEUFCHATEL, Coeur de Bray has a bloomy white rind and is shaped like a heart. It comes from the Pays de Bray in upper Normandy.

## COMTÉ (also Gruyère de Comté or French Gruyère)

| | |
|---|---|
| ORIGIN | *Franche Comté, Savoie/cow's milk* |
| TYPE | *semi-firm, Swiss/45% fat* |
| TASTE | *mellow, fruity, nutty* |
| APPEARANCE | *large cylinders with gold rind; pale ochre paste with scattered hazelnut-sized holes* |
| AVAILABILITY | *limited export* |

This cousin to BEAUFORT and EMMENTAL is part of the family of French GRUYÈRES. It has typically nutty, Swiss-like flavors but is a little more vivid and less sweet. Comté is widely used in cooking, for fondues as well as in omelets, quiche, and the French grilled sandwich known as *croque-monsieur.*

As a snack, lunch, or after-dinner cheese, Comté is well-suited to fruity wines, whether white, red, or rosé, and to beer.

# COROLLE DU POITOU

| | |
|---|---|
| ORIGIN | *Poitou/cow's milk* |
| TYPE | *double cream/60% fat* |
| TASTE | *rich, creamy, tangy finish* |
| APPEARANCE | *wheels with center hole, white bloomy rind; chalky center surrounded by creamy, ivory paste* |
| AVAILABILITY | *general export* |

This part of France (Poitou) is noted mostly for its goat cheeses, but the soft-ripened Corolle (named for its shape, which resembles a crown) is a new, cow's milk cheese, developed to capitalize on the popularity of Brie and double creams. Very rich and mild, it slices like angel-food cake—indeed, some would consider it angel's food.

## COULOMMIERS (also Brie de Coulommiers)

| | |
|---|---|
| ORIGIN | *Ile de France/cow's milk* |
| TYPE | *soft-ripened/45–50% fat* |
| TASTE | *creamy, Brie-like* |
| APPEARANCE | *flat cylinders 5 inches in diameter; white bloomy rind; creamy ivory interior* |
| AVAILABILITY | *limited export* |

From the town of Coulommiers near Meaux, this cheese is kissing cousin to BRIE DE MEAUX, although it is less fragile and not quite as distinctive in flavor. Often confused with small Brie, it is in fact thicker and tends to keep better, developing a nutty tang when ripe. It is a good bet for dinner parties where a large Brie would be too big. One of the best brands is *Le Fougerou,* whose rind is ornamented by a fern leaf. It should be soft and yielding to the touch; if not, it may show a hard, chalky core when cut. Avoid ammoniated, overripe cheeses with hard or smelly rinds.

This cheese is good with crisp French bread and most red wines.

## CROTTIN DE CHAVIGNOL

| | |
|---|---|
| ORIGIN | *Berry/goat's milk* |
| TYPE | *chèvre/45% fat* |
| TASTE | *dry and piquant to quite sharp* |
| APPEARANCE | *small, flat-bottomed balls; white rind splotched with brown; chalky interior* |
| AVAILABILITY | *limited export* |

Local farmers named this little cheese (*crottin* means "horse droppings") for its shape and the darkened color of well-aged versions. When young and fresh—as it often is in the town of Sancerre—it is deliciously goaty and tangy, delightful when spread on French bread and washed down with the local white wines, Sancerre or Pouilly-Fumé.

With age, however, it becomes quite sharp and strong and develops a dry, tough rind. Exported versions generally fall somewhere in between.

## CROTTIN POIVRE

| | |
|---|---|
| ORIGIN | *Pyrénées, Auvergne/cow's or ewe's milk* |
| TYPE | *semi-firm/45% fat* |
| TASTE | *savory, mildly salty, peppery* |
| APPEARANCE | *stocky cylinders with grooved black rinds; pale gold interior flecked with cracked pepper* |
| AVAILABILITY | *limited export* |

A rustic, savory close-textured cheese studded with pepper-corns, it has a zesty character and is sometimes hard enough for grating.

## CURÉ NANTAIS (also Fromage du Curé)

| | |
|---|---|
| ORIGIN | *Brittany/cow's milk* |
| TYPE | *monastery, soft/40% fat* |
| TASTE | *assertive flavor and aroma* |
| APPEARANCE | *small, rounded squares with orange-gold rind; soft yellow interior* |
| AVAILABILITY | *limited export* |

A washed rind-cheese, Curé Nantais becomes quite pungent in flavor and aroma as it ages, falling somewhere between Saint-Paulin and Pont l'Evêque. Developed by a parish priest near Nantes, it is also known as *Fromage du Curé*. Seldom exported, it is delicious with local wines such as Muscadet or Gros Plant du Pays.

## DOLMEN

This CHÈVRE comes in the shape of trapezoidal bricks from Poitou. It is rich, tangy, not overly sharp, and is sometimes ash-coated.

## DOUX DE MONTAGNE (also Pain de Pyrénées)

| | |
|---|---|
| ORIGIN | *Pyrénées/cow's milk* |
| TYPE | *semi-firm/45% fat* |
| TASTE | *mellow, sweet, fruity* |
| APPEARANCE | *sold in cylinders; pale yellow interior with irregular holes; dark rind* |
| AVAILABILITY | *general export* |

Doux de Montagne is a relatively recently developed cheese from the foothill region of the Pyrénées in southwestern France. Its name means "sweet of the mountain" and fairly describes its mellow nuttiness. Aged versions have a more interesting character, but exports for the most part are young, semi-soft, and have waxed rinds.

Country reds, such as Corbières, Fitou, Cahors, or regional Bordeaux, go well with it.

## EMMENTAL

| | |
|---|---|
| ORIGIN | *Franche Comté, Savoie/cow's milk* |
| TYPE | *semi-firm/45% fat* |
| TASTE | *mild, nutty* |
| APPEARANCE | *sold in large wheels with convex sides; gold rind; pale yellow interior with many large holes* |
| AVAILABILITY | *general export* |

The French version of Switzerland Swiss may have been made in the eastern mountains as early as the sixteenth century. Like the other French Gruyères, BEAUFORT and COMTÉ, it has mellow, nutty flavors and is widely used for snacks and cooking, as it grates well and melts easily.

Fruity red or white wines suit it well, as does cider or beer.

## EPOISSES

| | |
|---|---|
| ORIGIN | *Burgundy/cow's milk* |
| TYPE | *monastery, soft/45% fat* |
| TASTE | *mild with tangy finish to quite strong* |
| APPEARANCE | *small, thick cylinders; light orange to reddish rind; creamy-soft ivory paste* |
| AVAILABILITY | *limited export* |

One of the classic washed-rind cheeses, Epoisses is traditionally cured in salt water and *marc de Bourgogne* (*eau-de-vie*
from grape pomace). It has a fine character, tangy and faintly
acid when young, becoming very pronounced in flavor and
aroma with age, like Pont L'Evêque. The rind is sometimes
dusted with fennel or pepper. A cheeselover's cheese,
Epoisses is best with full-bodied red Burgundies from
the Côte de Nuits.

## EWE ROUERGUE

A lightly-veined blue cheese made from ewe's milk in the
south of France. Like most sheep cheese, it is tangy and
assertive but not widely exported.

## EXCELSIOR

| | |
|---|---|
| ORIGIN | *Normandy/cow's milk* |
| TYPE | *triple cream/72% fat* |
| TASTE | *mild, creamy, faintly nutty* |
| APPEARANCE | *small, fat cylinders with snowy rinds, soft ivory interior* |
| AVAILABILITY | *general export* |

Excelsior, enriched with cream, was invented nearly a
hundred years ago in a Norman dairy. Now factory-made, it is
one of the most popular triple creams, only slightly less rich
than EXPLORATEUR, but with a little more complexity of
character. Serve with red Burgundy, Champagne or other
sparkling wines.

## EXPLORATEUR

| | |
|---|---|
| ORIGIN | *Ile de France/cow's milk* |
| TYPE | *triple cream/75% fat* |
| TASTE | *unctuously rich, creamy* |
| APPEARANCE | *small, thick cylinders with white rinds, soft ivory paste* |
| AVAILABILITY | *general export* |

Although this cheese is sometimes described as a triple-
cream Brie, its rich creaminess masks the character that
might be present in a cheese of lower fat content.
Extravagantly rich and creamy, Explorateur has a faintly
piquant finish when perfectly ripe. When too old, its
ammoniated rind destroys its delicate flavors. It is best with
fruity, dry white wines or light reds.

## FEUILLES DE DREUX

| | |
|---|---|
| ORIGIN | *Ile de France/cow's milk* |
| TYPE | *soft-ripened/40–45% fat* |
| TASTE | *creamy, Brie-like but fruitier* |
| APPEARANCE | *flat discs of 6 inches in diameter wrapped in brown chestnut leaves; soft, creamy, yellow interior* |
| AVAILABILITY | *general export* |

Feuilles de Dreux is a fast-ripening, quickly perishable cheese made on farms or in small factories north of Chartres in the town of Dreux, sometimes from partially skimmed milk. It is an excellent alternative to Brie de Meaux or farm-produced Camembert. Watch out for an intense ammonia smell and dried out or rotted leaves, which indicates, of course, that the cheese is too old.

## FOL AMOUR

A brand of soft-ripened double cream produced in northern France. General export.

## FONTAINEBLEAU

A fresh cheese enriched with whipped cream, Fontainebleau is normally eaten with berries or preserved fruit. It should be as fresh as possible.

## FONTAL

French Fontina.

## LE FOUGEROU *see* Coulommiers

## FOURME D'AMBERT

| | |
|---|---|
| ORIGIN | *Auvergne/cow's milk* |
| TYPE | *blue-vein/45% fat* |
| TASTE | *assertive blue, faintly bitter* |
| APPEARANCE | *comes in tall slender cylinders; dense veining; whitish interior* |
| AVAILABILITY | *limited export* |

This is one of the more intense French *bleus*, distinguished by a salty, slightly bitter bite that appeals to many blue cheese *aficionados*. The texture is rich and softly crumbly and should not be dried out. It is similar to BLEU D'AUVERGNE but stronger and demands sturdy reds such as Châteauneuf-du-Pape.

## FOURME DE SALERS (also Salers)

| | |
|---|---|
| ORIGIN | *Auvergne/cow's milk* |
| TYPE | *semi-firm/45% fat* |
| TASTE | *mellow, nutty, with a Cheddarish tang* |
| APPEARANCE | *tall cylinders with natural grayish-beige rind, semi-firm interior of light yellow-orange* |
| AVAILABILITY | *limited export* |

Fourme de Salers is a mountain cheese, similar to CANTAL, produced on farms in the upland pastures in the Auvergne. One of the *appellation controlée* cheeses of France, its name is protected by law. Salers is an excellent eating cheese with wholesome, lactic flavors and good depth of character, especially in well-aged versions ripened six months or more. It keeps well and is excellent with mature full-bodied red wines such as Napa Gamay or Beaujolais.

# FROMAGE DES PYRÉNÉES

A generic term that denotes any of several cow or sheep cheeses made in the Pyrénées, such as DOUX DE MONTAGNE, Pain de Pyrénées, TOMME DE PYRÉNÉES, or TOURTON (Chiberta).

# FROMAGE FONDU

This is the generic term for French processed cheeses, which are generally foil-wrapped and often flavored with seasonings such as garlic, herbs and spices, nuts, cherry juice. *Fondu au Raisin,* mild and bland like most of these cheeses, is encrusted with dried grape seeds. *Gourmandise* is flavored with hazelnut and cherry. *Rambol* is often garnished with walnuts. Other brands are *Beau Pasteur, La Vache Qui Rit,* and *Reybier.* Most are based on Gruyère or other Swiss-like cheeses and processing gives them long shelf life. These are primarily snack cheeses and are popular with children.

# FROMAGE FRAIS

The French term for fresh, unripened cheese. *Fromage Frais* is rich and creamy like Cream Cheese but is often more tart or sour than American Cream Cheese. It is sometimes enriched with cream, bringing the butterfat up to 60% and 75%, the levels for double and triple creams such as PETIT-SUISSE or FONTAINEBLEAU. They are best consumed as fresh as possible and are often mixed with sugar and fresh or preserved fruit.

# GAPERON

| | |
|---|---|
| ORIGIN | *Auvergne/cow' milk* |
| TYPE | *semi-soft/30% fat* |
| TASTE | *rich, spicy with garlic* |
| APPEARANCE | *orange-sized balls tied with ribbon; dark natural rind; ivory interior* |
| AVAILABILITY | *limited export* |

Gaperon is a country cheese made from skimmed milk or buttermilk and flavored strongly with garlic. A fine snack or picnic cheese, it goes especially well with rough-textured breads, fresh fruit, and sturdy, simple wines such as Côte du Rhône, Petite Sirah, or Zinfandel.

# GÉANT DU POITOU

| | |
|---|---|
| ORIGIN | *Poitou/goat's milk* |
| TYPE | *chèvres, soft/45% fat* |
| TASTE | *creamy, tangy, very rich* |
| APPEARANCE | *9-inch flat wheels with bloomy rind; white interior* |
| AVAILABILITY | *limited export* |

One of the more luscious-textured *chèvres,* Géant du Poitou becomes as creamy as Brie when fully ripe but retains the tart tang of goat's milk. Often mixed with cow's milk, it is not as sharp as pure goat cheeses, but it is distinctive. Excellent with dry, full-bodied whites such as Chablis, Chassagne-Montrachet, or Chardonnay.

## GÉROMÉ (also Munster Géromé)

| | |
|---|---|
| ORIGIN | *Lorraine/cow's milk* |
| TYPE | *monastery, semi-soft/45% fat* |
| TASTE | *strong, spicy* |
| APPEARANCE | *small to medium-sized flat discs with orange rind; soft, yellow paste* |
| AVAILABILITY | *limited export* |

Strong, savory flavors that ripen to very pungent and pronounced aromas make Géromé similar to MUNSTER from Alsace. The cheese is of course milder when young, with a fruity tang, and it is sometimes flavored with anise, fennel, or cumin. The riper cheeses taste considerably better without the rind.

Flavored or unflavored, Géromé has the same uses as Munster and goes well with Alsace Gewurztraminer or Riesling.

## GERVAIS

The brand-name of a fresh double cream produced in great quantity in the factories of Normandy. It is sold in flat little squares with snowy white rinds, and is widely available.

## GOURMANDISE

This processed cheese is pale ivory in color and flavored with cherry juice (kirsch *eau-de-vie* in France). It is sold in cake form, sometimes adorned with nuts, or in foil-wrapped wedges. The flavor is mild and sweet.

## GRATTE PAILLE

A soft-ripened triple cream with a light, yellowish rind, Gratte Paille is made in small loaf shapes in the Ile de France region. Its flavors are mild, creamy, and faintly salty.

## GRUYÈRES

The generic term for French Swiss-style cheeses such as BEAUFORT, EMMENTAL, and COMTÉ. Gruyère is also the name of a Swiss-made cheese, also similar to Emmentaler.

## LA CHEVRETTE

The brand name for a log-shaped CHÈVRE that is made creamier and milder with the addition of cow's milk. These popular cheeses are usually flavored with herbs, cracked pepper, or olives.

## LA GRAPPE

A processed, flavored cheese covered with a dry crust of grape seeds. The seeds must be removed before eating.

## L'AMI DU CHAMBERTIN

ORIGIN *Burgundy/cow's milk*
TYPE *monastery, soft/50% fat*
TASTE *creamy, savory, salty*
APPEARANCE *small, boxed rounds with orange, washed rind; soft, cream-white interior*
AVAILABILITY *very limited export*

A favorite of the *cognoscenti,* this little cheese becomes quite strong when very ripe. It should be soft and smooth, but may have a firm chalky core in the middle—it should not be totally runny. The rind is washed in *marc,* which gives it a pleasantly pungent aroma. The cheese itself is milder than the rind's smell but still assertive. A mature Bordeaux or full-blooded Burgundy, such as Chambertin, complements it handsomely.

## LANGRES

ORIGIN *Northern Burgundy/cow's milk*
TYPE *monastery, soft/50% fat*
TASTE *earthy, sourish with lactic tang*
APPEARANCE *biscuit-shaped mounds with concave tops, soft, whitish-orange rind, often paper-wrapped; soft ivory interior*
AVAILABILITY *limited export*

Similar to EPOISSES in character, Langres has a strong aroma and rather sharp, pungent flavors. It is very agreeable in the stages from young to ripe, but when it is very ripe, verges on stinkiness. Stained paper, a darkened, shrunken rind, and an ammoniated smell are signs of overripeness or damage.

Langres is very good with crisp whites from Alsace, such as Pinot Blanc, or with full-bodied red wines.

## LA VACHE QUI RIT

"The Laughing Cow" brand of processed cheese. Its base is Gruyère and it is most often seen in small, foil-wrapped cubes, occasionally in larger sizes.

## LEZAY

Lezay are tangy logs of goat cheese from Poitou. They also come in trapezoidal bricks and may be coated with edible vegetable ash. Firm, smooth-textured, and chalky white, this CHÈVRE has a rich tang without being sharp or sour. Widely available and usually good value, it goes well with crisp, dry white wines like Sancerre or Sauvignon Blanc.

## LINGOT

A mild CHÈVRE from the Loire Valley, Lingot is sometimes ash-coated. It has a very limited import and is somewhat uneven in quality with varying texture—soft and moist or dryish and somewhat chalky.

# LINGOT D'OR

A Munster-style, washed-rind cheese from the Vosges Mountains in Alsace, Lingot d'Or comes in flat, orange rectangles. With 50% butterfat, it is a little milder and less complex in flavor than Munster. Trim the rind if it is strong-smelling. The cheese goes well with Alsace Gewurztraminer or Riesling.

# LIVAROT

| | |
|---|---|
| ORIGIN | *Normandy/cow's milk* |
| TYPE | *strong-smelling, monastery, soft/45% fat* |
| TASTE | *assertive with pungent aroma* |
| APPEARANCE | *small, thick cylinders with orange or reddish-brown rind and wrapped in sedge or reeds; yellow-gold soft interior* |
| AVAILABILITY | *limited export* |

Sometimes nicknamed "the Colonel" because of the five strips of grass in which it is wrapped, Livarot is often overpoweringly scented. Cured in unvented cellars that are incomparably odorous, the cheese itself is far less aggressive on the palate than one would expect, especially if the rind is removed (preferably away from the eating atmosphere altogether). Livarot is one of France's oldest and most esteemed cheeses, with a fine and surprisingly appealing flavor and character beneath its smelly exterior.

Some like it with cold, fruity white wines, but in Normandy it is often served with Calvados, an appropriately forceful match, or with strong black coffee.

# LOU PERALOU

A new Brie-style cheese produced from ewe's milk. Very creamy, it comes in seven-inch flat cylinders with bloomy rinds resembling COULOMMIERS. It is surprisingly delicate, with attractive tangy flavors and extravagantly creamy consistency, but tends to be overpriced.

# MAROILLES (also Marolles)

| | |
|---|---|
| ORIGIN | *Picardy, northern France/cow's milk* |
| TYPE | *strong-smelling/45–50% fat* |
| TASTE | *strong, similar to Livarot, potent aroma* |
| APPEARANCE | *flat squares, 5 inches in diameter; orange rind; soft yellow interior* |
| AVAILABILITY | *limited export* |

One of France's oldest monastery cheeses, Maroilles was first made during the tenth century by monks near Lille in northern France. It is similar to LIVAROT and very ripe PONT L'EVÊQUE in pungency of aroma (its nickname is *Vieux Puant*, or "old stinker") and the "thunderous savor" of its flavors has long been appreciated by notable gourmands. The rind is rinsed in beer during the curing process.

*Quart Maroilles* is a smaller-sized version of Maroilles. *Gris de Lille* or *Vieux Lille* are aged longer and are consequently more potent. Maroilles requires sturdy reds such as Côte Rotie and Amarone or full-bodied ale.

## MIMOLETTE

| | |
|---|---|
| ORIGIN | *northern France/cow's milk* |
| TYPE | *semi-firm/45% fat* |
| TASTE | *mellow, bland, faintly nutty* |
| APPEARANCE | *large balls with dark rind, usually waxed; vivid orange, smooth interior* |
| AVAILABILITY | *general export* |

Mimolette is a popular cheese that has flavors similar to Dutch EDAM or mild Cheddar, and a smooth, firm, sliceable texture. Generally mild-flavored and rather bland, the aged versions develop a more pronounced character. Mimolette is primarily a snack cheese and provides an interesting color contrast on the cheese tray. It is well-suited to light fruity or medium full-bodied red wines such as Beaujolais, Napa Gamay, or spicy Zinfandels.

## MONTRACHET

A brand of CHÈVRE from the Burgundy region that comes in logs or small containers. Its flavors are attractively sourish and tangy and its texture is usually moist and creamy. Ash-coated logs tend to be firmer, drier, and a bit sharper in flavor. This cheese is best when quite fresh and it is very good with white Burgundies, such as Puligny-Montrachet or others of the Montrachet family, or with California Chardonnay; fruity reds and Port are also suitable.

## MORBIER

| | |
|---|---|
| ORIGIN | *Franche-Comté/cow's milk* |
| TYPE | *semi-soft/45% fat* |
| TASTE | *mild, smooth* |
| APPEARANCE | *flat wheels with grayish-brown rind; smooth ivory paste with center streak of gray ash* |
| AVAILABILITY | *limited export* |

Morbier is one of the milder monastery cheeses. Supple in texture, with bland but pleasant flavors, it is immediately identifiable by the line of edible cinder that divides it. Originally the two layers were distinct cheeses made separately from the morning and evening milks and pressed together. Nowadays it is uniformly made from pasteurized milk.

Morbier is good with light red wines such as regional Bordeaux.

## MUNSTER

| | |
|---|---|
| ORIGIN | *Alsace/cow's milk* |
| TYPE | *monastery, semi-soft/45% fat* |

| | |
|---|---|
| TASTE | *mild and savory to pungent* |
| APPEARANCE | *small thick wheels with orange rind; yellow paste* |
| AVAILABILITY | *general export* |

One of the most widely imitated cheeses, Munster originated in a monastery in Alsace during the Middle Ages. Most imitations are bland and rather characterless, with the exception of German MÜNSTER, which is strong. Farm-produced Munster *(fermier)* has a distinct and assertive character and is sometimes quite potent in aroma. Its smooth, soft consistency is highly prized by cheese connoisseurs. Munster *laitier,* made in the creameries, tends to be less interesting but is nonetheless agreeable and consistent.

Young, full-flavored Munsters go well with Alsace Gewurztraminer; stronger ones are better suited to ale or well-hopped beer.

## NEUFCHÂTEL

A popular and widely copied soft-ripened cheese made in Normandy, Neufchâtel may be found in various small shapes: square, brick, cylindrical, heart-shaped (COEUR DE BRAY). It is creamy, mild, and somewhat salty (American versions are sweeter). This cheese is best when fresh; some uncured versions are available in France, and it varies from 20 to 45% butterfat. Try it with black coffee as a mid-morning snack.

## NIOLO

Niolo is a Corsican goat or sheep cheese from the central Niolo plateau. Cured in baskets, which leave their impression on the rind, it is sharp-flavored and firm-textured. This cheese is made on mountain farms and is only sporadically exported. Warning: Some versions have explosively fiery aftertaste.

## PAVÉ DE JADIS (also Pavé Gençay)

This CHÈVRE comes from Provence in ash-covered bricks with moist, sliceable texture and moderately tangy flavors, suited to dry white Burgundies or California Chardonnay.

## PELARDON DES CÉVENNES

Sold in small, sharp-flavored cylinders, this CHÈVRE hails from the Languedoc region of southern France. It is well-suited to Côte du Rhône reds.

## PETIT SUISSE

A soft, cream-enriched (60–75% fat content), fresh cheese made all over France, Petit Suisse is sold either in small cylinders or in plastic containers. Mild and creamy, it is generally served with berries or other fruits and accompanied by strong coffee. *Gervais* is the best-known brand.

## PIPO CREM'

| | |
|---|---|
| ORIGIN | *Ain/cow's milk* |
| TYPE | *blue vein/50% fat* |
| TASTE | *rich, savory, but milder than most blues* |
| APPEARANCE | *5-pound logs; thin whitish rind; ivory interior with blue veins* |
| AVAILABILITY | *general export* |

Pipo Crem' is milder than most blue cheeses and creamier in texture, with a salty, rich flavor. It should not be bitter or crumbly. A nice addition to the after-dinner cheese tray, Pipo Crem' is good with full-bodied reds from Burgundy.

## POIVRE D'ANE

| | |
|---|---|
| ORIGIN | *Provence/goat's milk* |
| TYPE | *chèvre/45% fat* |
| TASTE | *fresh, tangy, herby* |
| APPEARANCE | *sold in small discs covered with sprigs of savory* |
| AVAILABILITY | *limited export* |

This *chèvre* is similar to BANON and comes from the same region, but it is flavored with herbs such as savory (*sariette* in French) or pepper. It is sometimes made from mixed goat's and cow's milk, sometimes from cow's milk alone. Its aromas are pleasant and herby and the paste mild, flavorful, and smooth-textured.

## PONT L'EVÊQUE

| | |
|---|---|
| ORIGIN | *Normandy/cow's milk* |
| TYPE | *monastery, soft/45–50% fat* |
| TASTE | *rich with a fruity tang, complex* |
| APPEARANCE | *sold in boxed, 4-inch squares with orange-gold rind, grid-marked; soft yellow interior* |
| AVAILABILITY | *general export* |

This classic French cheese is from the famed Pays d'Auge region of Normandy and dates from the Middle Ages. Finding a perfectly ripened Pont L'Evêque is considered an achievement. *A point,* it will be plump and resilient inside the rind, oozing stickily rather than runny. It should not be dark or gummy, or bitter in aftertaste. Good ones are strong-smelling but not stinky; rich and creamy with a fruity, faintly sweet tang; slightly acid with a refreshing finish; of long-lasting flavor. They are delicious with fresh cider or assertive reds.

## PORT SALUT (also Port-du-Salut)

| | |
|---|---|
| ORIGIN | *western France/cow's milk* |
| TYPE | *monastery, semi-soft/50% fat* |
| TASTE | *smooth and savory* |
| APPEARANCE | *thick cylinders 9 inches in diameter; orange rind; smooth yellow interior* |
| AVAILABILITY | *general export* |

Widely popular for its mouth-melting texture and savory flavors, Port Salut was first made by Trappist monks in Brittany in 1815. An immediate success when it hit Paris in the 1870's, it is now widely copied and produced in factories. It is similar to SAINT-PAULIN, and the two are sometimes indistinguishable when factory-made. One of the best Port-Salut, and one of the most authentic, has "S.A.F.R." (the initials of the firm that makes it) stamped on the rind.

Port Salut is one of the better mild cheeses, although lesser versions are often bland in flavor and gummy or rubbery in texture. Fresh fruit goes well with it, as do fruity red wines.

## PRINCE DE NAVARRE

A sheep's milk cheese from the Pyrénées, Prince de Navarre is pale yellow with a hard, dark rind and rich, savory flavors reminiscent of good Cheddar or Parmesan. Hard enough for grating, it also serves as an after-dinner or snack cheese well-suited to full-flavored reds.

## PYRAMIDE

These pyramid-shaped cones of CHÈVRE are made in Poitou and the central Loire; they are sharp in flavor, chalk-white, and sometimes have bluish gray or ash-coated rinds.

## RAMBOL

A processed cheese, often covered with walnuts.

## REBLOCHON

| | |
|---|---|
| ORIGIN | *Savoie/cow's milk* |
| TYPE | *monastery, soft/45–50% fat* |
| TASTE | *creamy, savory* |
| APPEARANCE | *sold in small, firm discs with golden-brownish rind; light yellow paste with a few holes* |
| AVAILABILITY | *general export* |

One of the milder monastery cheeses, Reblochon is semi-soft when young and soft and spreadable when ripe. Deeply flavorful, it is stronger than Saint-Paulin or Port Salut, but not as pungent as Pont L'Evêque or very ripe Munster. It ripens steadily, however, even when refrigerated, and can become pungent and bitter. The rind should be removed before eating. This cheese is very good with rough-textured breads and fruity reds such as Beaujolais Brouilly or rustic ones like Barbera d'Alba or Zinfandel.

## RIGOTTE

Small biscuit-shaped CHÈVRES, now commonly made partially from cow's milk. Made mostly in the Auvergne, they have orangish rinds, are mild and pleasantly tangy.

## ROLLOT

Rollot is an assertively flavored monastery cheese from

northern France, similar to PONT L'EVÊQUE, that comes in small, flat, round or heart-shaped discs. It should be soft and resilient but not gummy or hard. You can expect a good depth of flavor and a fruity, tangy edge in the finish. Rollot becomes very strong-smelling as it ripens, but the interior is milder. It is best matched with hearty reds or beer.

# ROQUEFORT

|  |  |
|---|---|
| ORIGIN | *Aveyron/ewe's milk* |
| TYPE | *blue vein/45% fat* |
| TASTE | *pungent, rich, salty, long, piquant aftertaste* |
| APPEARANCE | *stocky cylinders that are foil-wrapped with emblem of red sheep clearly visible; white natural rind; white paste with blue marbling* |
| AVAILABILITY | *general export* |

Possibly the world's most celebrated cheese, Roquefort vies only with Stilton and Brie for the title "king of cheeses." It fairly well stands alone, however, as the most intense and individual of the blues. One of the oldest cheeses in existence, it was known in Roman times and referred to by Pliny the Elder. Charlemagne is said to have rejected it when it was presented to him but, upon tasting it, became an ardent fan.

Produced from the milk of sheep that graze on the high plateaus *(les causses)* of southern France near Rouergue (supplemented largely today by sheep's milk cheeses from Corsica) Roquefort is aged in the limestone caverns of Mount Combalou. Roquefort's unique flavors develop in the special air currents that move through the mountain's fissured depths. Long ago this unique atmosphere fostered the growth of a mold now known as *Penicillium roqueforti.* The cheeses, snow-white when they enter the caves, are skewered 36 times to aid the mold in its development and left to ripen at least three months. The rind is regularly scraped and the finished cheese wrapped in foil for shipping.

Roquefort is strictly protected and regulated by *appellation controlée* laws. No one may legally use the name or even the term "Roquefort-style." The red sheep emblem on the foil wrapper is assurance of authenticity.

Sublimely intense at its best, Roquefort should be rich and creamy-textured rather than crumbly, and not overly salty (as many exported Roqueforts are, unfortunately). Use it with a little fresh butter if you find it too powerful, although purists will eschew this practice. Roquefort overwhelms most wines, red or white, but it is a superb match for fine Sauternes (the best Roquefort and Chateau Yquem make a stunning contrast). It may also provide an opportunity to serve those powerful, late-harvest Zinfandels or Zin Essence.

## ROYAL PROVENCE

This is a mild, creamy CHÈVRE made into small white wheels, and flavored with pepper or crowned with sliced olives. It is not as tangy as some goat cheese because of the addition of cow's milk, but is quite popular.

## SAINT ANDRÉ

A widely-produced TRIPLE CREAM, beguilingly rich and luscious but lacking in character after the initial impact of richness.

## SAINT CHRISTOPHE

CHÈVRE from the Loire Valley, Saint Christophe has a white rind or is ash-coated and is sold in the shape of a small log.

## SAINT FLORENTIN

|  |  |
|---|---|
| ORIGIN | *Yonne/cow's milk* |
| TYPE | *soft/45% fat* |
| TASTE | *tangy, spicy, piquant* |
| APPEARANCE | *loose white curds, very moist; sold in containers* |
| AVAILABILITY | *very limited import* |

Some cheese books refer to this cheese as a soft-ripened variety similar to Epoisses, but today's exports are fresh, un-ripened cheeses with a salty tang—occasionally they are so fresh that they are still dripping with whey. In this state, the cheese, which is perishable to begin with, sours quickly, so examine each container carefully before you buy. It is a good spread on pumpernickel bread or bagels, with black coffee.

## SAINT MARCELLIN

|  |  |
|---|---|
| ORIGIN | *Isère/goat's milk, cow's milk* |
| TYPE | *chèvre, soft/45% fat* |
| TASTE | *fresh, creamy, piquant* |
| APPEARANCE | *sold in small white discs; chalk-white interior* |
| AVAILABILITY | *limited export* |

Once made of pure goat's milk on farms in eastern France, today Saint Marcellin is often only 50% goat's milk and the rest cow's milk. According to some authorities, Saint Marcellin is now all cow's milk, but its piquant tang and soft, moist texture suggest that a fair amount of goat's milk remains. It is often confused with BANON, but Banon is firmer in texture and may contain even less goat's milk.

Saint Marcellin also comes in small jars mixed with olive oil and herbs and is then referred to as *Le Pitchou*. But treatment with olive oil and herbs is one you can do yourself with a less heavy-handed effect (see page 38).

## SAINTE MAURE

| | |
|---|---|
| ORIGIN | *Touraine/goat's milk* |
| TYPE | *chèvres/45% fat* |
| TASTE | *fresh, mild to piquant* |
| APPEARANCE | *log-shaped, bluish or downy white rind, smooth white interior* |
| AVAILABILITY | *general export* |

One of the most popular *chèvres* from the Loire Valley, Sainte Maure is also made in Anjou and Poitou. Farm-produced goat cheeses of this name have natural bluish-gray rinds flecked with dark brown, whereas factory versions have bloomy rinds and develop a creamier consistency when ripe. Both are tangy and piquant, excellent with Loire Valley whites such as Sancerre or Pouilly-Fumé, Vouvray *sec,* or Loire reds.

## SAINT NECTAIRE

| | |
|---|---|
| ORIGIN | *Auvergne/cow's milk* |
| TYPE | *semi-soft/45% fat* |
| TASTE | *mild, savory, tangy finish* |
| APPEARANCE | *flat, thick wheels, eight inches in diameter, natural, light orange rind with some white-ish mold; pale yellow interior* |
| AVAILABILITY | *general export* |

This is one of the better semi-soft cheeses, similar to Saint Paulin but fruitier, with an appealing tang and a certain nuttiness of flavor. An old cheese, dating at least to the Middle Ages, it has long been popular in France as well as in export markets.

Saint Nectaire is a good choice for providing contrast on the cheese board. It is good with most reds, particularly fruity ones such as Beaujolais Brouilly, Fleurie or Chiroubles, light Burgundies like Mercurey, or California Pinot Noir.

## SAINT PAULIN

| | |
|---|---|
| ORIGIN | *France/cow's milk* |
| TYPE | *monastery, semi-soft/45% fat* |
| TASTE | *mild, savory* |
| APPEARANCE | *thick wheels, nine inches in diameter, thin orange rind; smooth, light yellow interior* |
| AVAILABILITY | *general export* |

Saint Paulin is a semi-soft monastery cheese modeled after the original Port-du-Salut. Produced in factories in Brittany, Maine, Anjou, and elsewhere, it is sometimes more bland in character than Port-du-Salut but is nevertheless an agreeable cheese that slices easily for snacks or sandwiches. Bonbel is the most common brand. Préclos and others from Brittany seem to have more robust flavor and character.

Like Port-du-Salut, it keeps very well when snugly wrapped in plastic and refrigerated. It is most suitable to fruity red wines, white wines, and beer.

## ST. SAVIOL

Trade name for several good and reasonably consistent goat cheeses (CHÈVRES) produced in the western Loire.

## SARRAZIN

Sarrazin is sold in flat wheels and has an orange washed rind and semi-soft yellow interior. It is similar to CHAUMES but is supple and more pliable in texture rather than soft. It is full-flavored and strong in aroma when fully ripe. Sarrazin is generally only available domestically, although it is occasionally exported.

## SELLES-SUR-CHER

|  |  |
|---|---|
| ORIGIN | *Touraine/goat's milk* |
| TYPE | *chèvres/45% fat* |
| TASTE | *bland to quite piquant* |
| APPEARANCE | *sold in flat-topped cones or cylinders, bloomy rind, some coated with cinders; chalk-white paste* |
| AVAILABILITY | *very limited export* |

Selles is a small town near Tours on the River Cher, a tributary of the Loire. This little goat cheese can be excellent, with a mildly piquant, goaty character and a dryish, chalky texture. Exports vary considerably, however; some are quite bland, others are overripe and excessively pungent, with darkened interiors and tough rinds. Look for the Jacquin label, and buy only the freshest specimens.

Serve Selles-sur-Cher with fresh fruit and crisp white or fruity red wines.

## SOUMAINTRAIN

This soft-ripened cheese from northern Burgundy is similar to LANGRES but yellower in color. When very ripe, Soumaintrain, which is not often exported, develops a crusty orange rind and flavor akin to Munster in full bloom.

## SUPRÊME

The brand name for one of Normandy's soft-ripened DOUBLE CREAMS.

## TAUPINIÈRE

A dome-shaped *chèvre* from the Loire Valley with a black-and-white bloomy rind, Taupinière has dry, tangy, and austerely musty flavors that grow sharper with age. The texture is moist, smooth, and firm, but gets drier as it ages. Taupinière is not heavily exported, but may be found in specialty shops. It is excellent with Sancerre.

## TOMME

This term generally refers to semi-firm or semi-soft mountain cheeses of rather simple character, such as those from the

Pyrénées or Savoie. But in some rural regions it simply means "cheese" and is used for many different types, such as *Tommes Arlsienne,* a soft ewe's milk cheese, and several farm-made goat cheeses from southern and eastern France.

## TOMME DE SAVOIE

| | |
|---|---|
| ORIGIN | *Savoie/cow's milk* |
| TYPE | *semi-soft/45% fat* |
| TASTE | *mildly savory, nutty* |
| APPEARANCE | *thick wheels, eight inches in diameter; ochre rind with whitish mold; yellow paste, few holes* |
| AVAILABILITY | *general export* |

One of the better mountain cheeses, *Tomme de Savoie* is somewhat similar to Saint Nectaire, with attractive nutty flavors and fruity fragrance. It keeps well if securely wrapped and refrigerated, but the aroma gets stronger with age— trimming the rind helps since the cheese inside rarely moves past mild savoriness.

This cheese is quite nice with sturdy, fruity reds like Morgon, Mercurey, and Crozes-Hermitage.

## TOMME DES PYRÉNÉES

Tommes des Pyrénées are medium-sized cylinders or wheels of semi-soft cheese with hard, sometimes waxed, rinds that are produced in the Pyrénées region of south-western France. Most are quite bland and without much character, although they are pleasant enough for snacks.

## TONNELAIT

This mountain-style *tommes* is in fact made on the grassy plains of Brittany from cow's milk and is sold in stocky cylinders. With its mild, smooth flavors and supple, semi-soft texture, Tonnelait is an agreeable, if not especially interesting, snack cheese.

## TOURTON (formerly Chiberta)

| | |
|---|---|
| ORIGIN | *Pyrénées/cow's milk* |
| TYPE | *monastery, semi-soft/45% fat* |
| TASTE | *mildly tangy* |
| APPEARANCE | *small, thick wheels; thin, orange rind; yellow paste dotted with holes* |
| AVAILABILITY | *general export* |

Tourton is one of the typical, supple-textured cheeses in the style of Bel Paese and Saint-Paulin that are made throughout the Pyrénées region. It has a bit more tang and character than Tomme de Pyrénées or Doux de Montagne but is basically a simple cheese with a mildly pronounced aroma.

Tourton is fine as a snack cheese or for picnics, with fruity red wines.

# VALEMBERT

A relatively new, factory-produced, semi-soft cheese similar to SAINT PAULIN but with a bloomy rind.

## VALENCAY (also Pyramide)

| | |
|---|---|
| ORIGIN | *Central Loire/goat's milk* |
| TYPE | *chèvre/45% fat* |
| TASTE | *tangy, sometimes quite strong* |
| APPEARANCE | *sold in flat-topped, pyramidal cones, either white or ash-coated; chalky white centers* |
| AVAILABILITY | *limited export* |

Valencay is one of the sharpest *chèvres*, especially in its bluish-black, farm-produced incarnation that is pure goat's milk but tends to be seasonal. The factory versions, with their white, downy rinds, are made year-round but are also variable in quality. When young and fresh, the little pyramids are mildly piquant and quite delightful, but they get strong, musty, and ammoniated when they are too old.

Valencay is especially good with ripe plums and dry, crisp white wines of the Loire, such as Sancerre and Savennières.

## VENACO

| | |
|---|---|
| ORIGIN | *Corsica/lait de mélange* |
| TYPE | *semi-firm/45% fat* |
| TASTE | *salty, sharp, swarthy* |
| APPEARANCE | *comes in small, thick blocks with foil-wrapped, washed rinds; pale yellow interior, irregular holes* |
| AVAILABILITY | *limited export* |

The term *lait de mélange,* which appears on the labels, indicates that the cheese was made from an unspecified mix of sheep's, goat's, or cow's milk. The sharp, salty tang and supple, somewhat oily, texture of most Venaco suggests that they are mostly sheep's milk. If not overly sharp, it has a vivid and appealing savoriness about it that provides an interesting contrast to other cheeses, after dinner or at a tasting. It requires sturdy reds to stand up to it.

## VIEUX PANÉ

| | |
|---|---|
| ORIGIN | *Aveyron/cow's milk* |
| TYPE | *semi-soft/45% fat* |
| TASTE | *mellow, nutty, smooth* |
| APPEARANCE | *large, flat squares with honey-orange, washed rind; yellow interior, few holes* |
| AVAILABILITY | *limited export* |

Although Vieux Pané looks like a large Pont l'Evêque, its aroma and flavor are milder and sweeter, with tinges of hazelnut and a lactic acidity that gives a very clean finish. It is good with Médocs or Saint-Emilion.

# ITALY

**T**ravelers to Italy discover with delight the diverse world of Italian cheese, until recently a world largely unto itself. No longer, however, are cheese-lovers confined to the harder, aged cheeses known for their keeping qualities. Air Express and specialty cheese shops now make it possible—at a price, of course—to enjoy some of Italy's delectable fresh and soft-ripened cheeses like Mascarpone, the Robiolas, Stracchino Cresczenza, Scamorze, and numerous others. The growing demand for fine cheese has also resulted in increasing export of Italy's classics—superbly aged Parmigiano-Reggiano, a variety of Gorgonzolas, the genuine and original Fontina from the Val d'Aosta, and the finest Provolone.

Many of Italy's cheeses were developed centuries ago, for cheese has been appreciated by the Italians since antiquity. Over a dozen cheeses were sold in the *velabrium* (dairy market) in ancient Rome, including varieties from Gaul, Helvetia, and even the British Isles. Legend attributes cheese-making to Romulus himself, who was said to have made Pecorino about the time he and his brother founded Rome. Argricultural writers of the Augustan Age were full of cheese-making tips. Columella advised using extracts of thistle, saf-flower, and fig bark as curdling agents. He also suggested pine seeds as a kind of rennet for goat's milk cheese. In *De Agricultura,* the oldest surviving Latin book of any kind, Cato provided recipes for cheese pastries called *Libum* and *Placcenta,* probably made with a kind of Ricotta. By the Renaissance, many modern cheese types were well established and were an important part of Italian cuisine. When

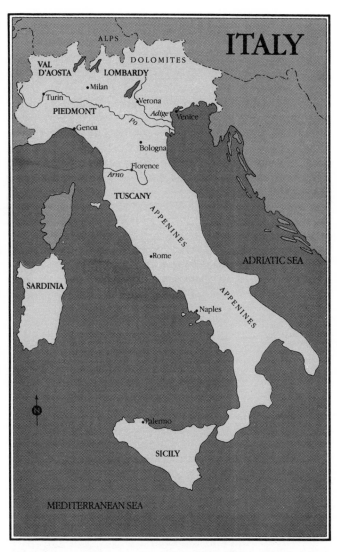

Catherine di Medici departed for France in the mid-sixteenth century, the glory of Tuscan cuisine, with its liberal use of Parmesan, went with her.

Italians appear to make cheeses from a greater variety of animal sources—and in a greater variety of ways—than any other people in the world. They use the milk of cows, goats, and sheep; some say Caciocavallo was once made of mare's milk. Water buffalo from the East were imported in the seventh century and vast herds of their descendants still graze in the marshes of Campania in order to supply the milk for Mozzarella and Scamorze. Cheeses are stretched and shaped into everything from egg-shaped balls to figures of saints and little pigs. They are whipped like cream, solidified into a soft mass by heating the whey, impregnated with mold, and ripened to a pliant consistency that is neither too soft nor too hard.

The great variety of Italian cheese is due in part to the landscape. Most of the rich cow's milk cheeses come from the fertile northern basin between the Alps and the Apennines, covering much of the Piedmont, Lombardy, and the Veneto. The smaller and more hilly central regions of Latium around Rome and Naples are the home of the *pasta filata* (plastic curd) cheeses like Mozzarella, as well as numerous goat and sheep cheeses. Southernmost, mountainous Sicily is the originator of many sheep cheeses and of the whey cheese, Ricotta.

◆

# *Cheese Guide*

## ANNABELLA

| | |
|---|---|
| ORIGIN | *Piedmont/cow's milk* |
| TYPE | *fresh/40–45% fat* |
| TASTE | *mild, creamy* |
| APPEARANCE | *soft, white, rindless cheese packed in square wooden boxes* |
| AVAILABILITY | *limited export* |

This *fresco formaggio,* or "fresh cheese," is similar to the milk-white cream cheeses made for early consumption. At the peak of freshness, it is mild creamy, rich but delicate, and very spreadable. Somewhat similar to fresh ROBIOLA, Annabella makes a lovely brunch or luncheon cheese and is excellent with crisp, white wines such as Pinot Bianco, Pinot Grigio, or Sauvignon Blanc. It is also superb with preserved fruit and black coffee.

## ASIAGO

| | |
|---|---|
| ORIGIN | *Vicenza/cow's milk* |
| TYPE | *semi-firm/30–45% fat* |
| TASTE | *rich and nutty to sharp and piquant* |
| APPEARANCE | *small wheels with flat sides; glossy rind, yellow interior with small eyes* |
| AVAILABILITY | *general export* |

Asiago, made principally in Vicenza, but also in other parts of the Veneto and Lombardy, is either a Cheddar-like table cheese or a grating cheese, depending on age. Aged up to a year, it is a fine eating cheese, with the nutty richness and sharp tang of Cheddar. At this age, it is a good companion for fruity reds such as Barbera d'Alba, California Zinfandel, or Petite Sirah.

Older cheeses aged up to two years become hard and brittle, suitable for grating. The sharper, aged Asiago can also be an after-dinner or snack cheese; it needs a brawnier red wine, however, such as Barbaresco or Barolo. Most Asiago is made from partially skimmed milk, but Asiago *grasso di monte,* a full-cream version aged six weeks, is sometimes found locally.

When buying Asiago look for even color throughout. There should be no dark spots in the paste or cracks in the rind. Asiago for grating should have a fine granular texture similar to Parmesan. Asiago keeps well in the refrigerator if it is wrapped securely in plastic wrap. It melts easily and is often used in cooking.

## BEL PAESE

| | |
|---|---|
| ORIGIN | *Lombardy/cow's milk* |
| TYPE | *semi-soft/50% fat* |
| TASTE | *mild, creamy, fruity* |
| APPEARANCE | *thick, foil-wrapped discs; pale interior with small irregular holes; sold in wedges* |
| AVAILABILITY | *widely exported, also produced in the U.S.* |

Bel Paese (the name means "beautiful country") is one of the world's most popular cheeses. Dependably consistent in quality, its mild but distinctive character makes it useful for snacks, sandwiches, or as a contrast to stronger cheeses on the cheese board. It is a fairly new cheese, developed in the 1920's by one Egidio Galbani, who wanted to make a soft cheese similar to French *Saint-Paulin.* It was modeled to some extent after FIORE DI ALPE, a mild, soft-textured cheese made in the Val d'Aosta.

Bel Paese is an ideal mild cheese for both producer and consumer. It ripens quickly, within four to eight weeks. Its creamy smooth texture and faint sweetness make it delicious with fruity white wines, rosés, or light reds. It melts easily and makes a flavorful topping for casseroles, soups, and even pizza.

A reasonably good imitation of Bel Paese is also produced in the United States, although it is somewhat blander and sometimes slightly bitter, as the best Italian cheese never is. The two versions have similar wrappings. Both show a priest (Father Stoppani, who wrote a popular children's book called *Bel Paese,* is on the Italian wrapper) and a map. But the imported version has a map of Italy, whereas the American version shows a map of North and South America.

## BRIGANTE

| | |
|---|---|
| ORIGIN | *Sardinia/sheep's milk* |
| TYPE | *semi-firm/45% fat* |
| TASTE | *tangy, salty* |
| APPEARANCE | *thick cylinders with grooved black rind, off-white interior, few holes* |
| AVAILABILITY | *limited export* |

A semi-firm sheep's milk cheese from Sardinia. Savory and rich with a sheepy tang, it has a supple, smooth texture and can be hard enough for grating.

## CACIOCAVALLO

| | |
|---|---|
| ORIGIN | *Campania/cow's milk* |
| TYPE | *pasta filata/45% fat* |
| TASTE | *mild but tangy, sharper with age* |
| APPEARANCE | *pear- or gourd-shaped; glossy, yellow-gold rind; semi-firm ivory interior* |
| AVAILABILITY | *general export* |

*Pasta filata* are drawn-curd cheeses made in a special way. The curds are bathed in hot whey until they become elastic. They are then stretched and shaped by hand; other *pasta filata* cheeses are Provolone and Mozzarella. Caciocavallo is an old cheese, dating at least to the fourteenth century, probably earlier. It is believed to have been brought to Italy from the eastern Mediterranean, for it resembles such cheeses as Bulgarian KASHKAVAL, Turkish KASAR PEYNIR, and others of Balkan origin. When aged about four months, it tastes somewhat like a young Cheddar, with a similar close, flaky texture, but more tang and bite. Aged longer it becomes sharper, more granular in texture, and very hard and is often used for grating.

The name is derived from *cacio a cavallo*—"cheese on horseback"—and suggests to some that it may originally have been made from mare's milk. More likely the name comes from the fact that, traditionally, two cheeses were tied together for drying and slung across a pole, saddle-bag style. The name may also refer to the symbol of the city of Naples—a galloping horseman—that was sometimes represented on the exterior. Caciocavallo keeps well if snugly wrapped and refrigerated. Correctly made, it will not be bitter or overly sharp. It goes very well with the wines of Tuscany, such as Chianti Riserva.

## CACIOTTA

Caciotta means "little cheese" and is a general designation for small cheeses made on farms in several regions. *Caciotta di Lodi,* from Lombardy, is a young, perishable cheese made from cow's milk, that is mild, creamy, and faintly sour. *Caciotta altopascio* from Tuscany, made from a mixture of cow's and sheep's milk, is stronger and firmer in texture.

Caciotta di Siena is made from sheep's milk and is richer and quite good. (However, watch out for overly ammoniated ones.) Others are made from goat's milk, and most have hard, natural rinds that often show mold. Younger ones are semi-soft, moist, and rather mild, but they become firmer and more pungent as they ripen.

## CAPRINO (also Caprini)

| | |
|---|---|
| ORIGIN | *northern Italy/goat's milk, cow's milk* |
| TYPE | *fresh/40–45% fat* |
| TASTE | *mild, creamy with pleasant tang* |
| APPEARANCE | *soft, white interior like cream cheese; sold in wooden boxes or 5- to 6-inch paper-wrapped cylinders* |
| AVAILABILITY | *mostly local, limited export* |

Caprino is a creamy, mild, fresh cheese, now mostly made from cow's milk, with an appealing tang or sourness. It is delicious with fresh fruit, fruit preserves, or with crudités, fresh tomatoes, olives, and dry white or fruity red wines. It is best when very fresh and moist, the *raison d'être* for this type of cheese. (Do not confuse Caprino with *Caprino Romano,* a hard grating cheese of the family PECORINO ROMANO.)

## CRESCENZA (also Crescenza Stracchino)

| | |
|---|---|
| ORIGIN | *Lombardy, Piedmont, Veneto/cow's milk* |
| TYPE | *fresh/50%+ fat* |
| TASTE | *delicate, creamy, mildly tart* |
| APPEARANCE | *soft-textured, ivory-yellow interior; sold in wooden boxes* |
| AVAILABILITY | *limited export* |

One of the most popular of the fresh, uncooked STRACCHINO cheeses. Ripe in ten days to two weeks, it is very perishable and does not travel well. Air Express, however, makes limited quantities available in export markets, and its delicious creaminess makes it a hot item at specialty cheese shops. Be sure it is fresh, moist, and plump when you buy, and eat it soon after purchase. At room temperature it becomes butter-soft and is, in fact, used like butter on its home ground in northern Italy.

## CROTONESE

| | |
|---|---|
| ORIGIN | *Calabria, Sicily/sheep's milk* |
| TYPE | *hard, Grana/32% fat* |
| TASTE | *sharp* |
| APPEARANCE | *small thick cylinders with tough natural rind; pale ochre, dense, granular interior* |
| AVAILABILITY | *limited export* |

This hard, Grana-style cheese of southern Italy has the sharp piquancy of a cheese made from sheep's milk, especially when it is mixed with goat's milk, as Crotonese sometimes is.

I'm told that in Sicily it is ripened with the aid of a certain species of worms and it is purchased only when the worms are alive and moving inside the cheese; imported versions however show no evidence of this.

## DOLCE LATTE (also Dolcelatte)

The brand name of one of the milder, factory-made GORGONZOLAS.

## DOLCEZZA

A fresh, skimmed-milk cheese with the texture and delicacy of sweet butter. It is rarely seen outside Italy and can be rather flavorless.

## FIOR D'ALPE

|  |  |
|---|---|
| ORIGIN | *Lombardy/cow's milk* |
| TYPE | *semi-soft/50% fat* |
| TASTE | *mild and bland* |
| APPEARANCE | *smooth, elastic texture, pale color* |
| AVAILABILITY | *mostly local* |

Similar to BEL PAESE, which was modeled after it, Fior d'Alpe is a pleasant enough snack or sandwich cheese. It slices easily but is not as flavorful as Bel Paese. The name means "flower of the alps."

## FIORE SARDO

|  |  |
|---|---|
| ORIGIN | *Sardinia/sheep's milk* |
| TYPE | *hard/45% fat* |
| TASTE | *rich, full-flavored, sharp when aged* |
| APPEARANCE | *thick wheels with yellow rind, pale yellow interior* |
| AVAILABILITY | *limited export* |

This Sardinian *pecorino* (or sheep's milk cheese) is a good table cheese when young, aged about two months or so, but it is more highly prized as a grating cheese, for the piquancy it adds to various dishes. It is often used in combination with grated Paramesan. For the younger version, which you will most likely encounter on Sardinia or in and around Rome, pick a robust Italian red such as Rubesco di Torgiano.

## FONTINA VAL D'AOSTA (also Fontina Valdostana)

|  |  |
|---|---|
| ORIGIN | *Piedmont/cow's milk* |
| TYPE | *semi-firm/45% fat* |
| TASTE | *nutty, delicately rich* |
| APPEARANCE | *dark gold, crusty rind; pale gold interior, scattered small holes* |
| AVAILABILITY | *limited export* |

The original and authentic Fontina made in the Val d'Aosta of the northern Piedmont, is so unlike most cheeses sold as Fontina that one wonders how the imitators ever came to use the name. The rich, but subtly distinctive flavor and firm, dense texture of the original are unique. (Look for the cooperative trademark stamped in purple on the rind.) Made from the milk of cows that graze high on the sub-alpine slopes, mature Fontina has a dry, slightly austere, but earthy character. A hint of white truffle (native to the Piedmont) is noticeable in mature Fontinas aged four months or more. Younger versions are less pronounced in character but still excellent after-dinner cheeses, well served by one of the balanced Nebbiolo wines such as Gattinara, Carema, or Inferno.

Fontinas made elsewhere in Italy (often called *Fontinella*) and throughout the world (Denmark, France, United States, Sweden) are made from pasteurized milk. While they can be quite good, they lack the depth of character of genuine Fontina. They are softer in texture, bland or strong-flavored depending on age, and tend to be more similar to one another than to the original Fontina Val d'Aosta. Still, they are pleasant (if not too rubbery in texture), and widely available.

## FORMAGELLE D'ARTAVAGGIO

| | |
|---|---|
| ORIGIN | *Lombardy/cow's milk* |
| TYPE | *soft-ripened/48% fat* |
| TASTE | *mild, creamy, salty* |
| APPEARANCE | *small thick cylinders; sticky rind; creamy, yellow interior* |
| AVAILABILITY | *limited export* |

A washed-rind cheese traditionally ripened in the caves of Sassina near Como in Lombardy, Formagelle d'Artavaggio is mild but savory when fresh. As it ripens, its saltiness becomes concentrated, and within a few weeks it verges on stinkiness, the stage at which some cheese-lovers find it glorious.

## FORMAGGIO

The Italian term for cheese.

## FORMAGGIO GRANDUCA

A rich, luscious triple cream, gorgeously full-flavored in its native territory (northern and northwestern Italy). Some exported versions are oddly flavorless, however. Exports are very limited; sample before buying, if possible.

## GORGONZOLA

| | |
|---|---|
| ORIGIN | *Lombardy/cow's milk* |
| TYPE | *blue vein/48% fat* |
| TASTE | *rich, savory, pungent* |
| APPEARANCE | *thick, foil-wrapped wheels; white or ivory interior with blue-green veining* |
| AVAILABILITY | *general export* |

One of Italy's finest cheeses and one of the world's most distinguished blues, Gorgonzola ranks with Roquefort and Stilton, but is creamier than either. Its veins, formed by the *Penicillium glaucum* mold, first developed when the cheese was aged for long months in caves outside the little town of Gorgonzola near Milan; they are more greenish than blue in color. Gorgonzola can be one of the most pungent and strong-flavored of the blues—spicy, piquant, with the earthy touch of the barnyard or dank cavern about it. As a result of today's economics and palates, curing times have been reduced to around six months, sometimes less, so that the cheeses are milder. White Gorgonzola (also called *Pannarone*) has no mold. *Dolcelatte,* a factory-made Gorgonzola, is white and mild with light veining. Aged Gorgonzola has very heavy mold and is quite strong and sharp; it is also drier and more crumbly than younger versions.

Gorgonzola calls for robust red wines like Barolo, Barbaresco, Amarone, or perhaps late-harvest Zinfandel. Mild to medium Gorgonzola is superb with fresh pears or peaches. Sometimes it is mixed with Mascarpone or herbs, as in TORTA CON BASILICO which consists of layers of Gorgonzola alternating with layers of basil. It adds zest when crumbled into salads or melted over potatoes or steak.

## GRANA PADANO

| | |
|---|---|
| ORIGIN | *Lombardy/cow's milk* |
| TYPE | *hard, Grana/32% fat* |
| TASTE | *similar to Parmesan but more delicate* |
| APPEARANCE | *medium-large cylinders; rough, brownish, natural hard rind; yellow-gold, flaky-textured interior* |
| AVAILABILITY | *limited export* |

*Grana* means "grain" and refers to the grainy texture of this Parmesan-like cheese, made in several parts of the Piedmont as well as in Lombardy. It can be excellent, both as an eating cheese and as a grating cheese. However, its production is not as strictly controlled as that of PARMIGIANO-REGGIANO, so the quality varies, depending on the season, the region, the producer, and the quality of the milk. While Parmigiano is usually aged at least two years, Grana Padano is often sold after a year. The younger cheeses are better for table use and are best accompanied by sturdy reds such as Grumello,

Sassella, or Inferno of the Valtellina or Nebbiolo d'Alba of the Piedmont.

Other regional Granas are Grana Lodigiano (made near Lodi) or Grana Lombardo.

## GRUVIERA (also Groviera)

The Italian version of Swiss GRUYÈRE, produced mostly in Lombardy and Piedmont. Quite good.

## MANTECA (also Burrino)

A *pasta filata* cheese, usually Mozzarella, that has a ball of sweet butter in its center. Manteca is very popular in many parts of Italy, especially the South where it was a useful way to store butter. Sometimes lightly smoked Caciocavallo is used. Sliced open, the smooth white cheese (with a darkened rind if smoked) makes an appealing contrast to the pale yellow knob of butter in the center. Usually the butter is scooped out, spread on a piece of bread, and then topped with a slice of cheese. It is well-suited to dry white wines or fruity reds and rosés.

## MASCARPONE (also Mascherpone)

|  |  |
|---|---|
| ORIGIN | *Lombardy/cow's milk* |
| TYPE | *fresh, double cream/60% fat* |
| TASTE | *rich, buttery, slightly acidic* |
| APPEARANCE | *soft, pale ivory mass, sold in containers* |
| AVAILABILITY | *limited export* |

This fresh, delicate cheese, now made all over Italy has been likened to the clotted cream known in England as Devonshire. Sometimes it is as light as whipped cream; at other times it has the consistency and delicate flavor of sweet butter, for which it is occasionally substituted. It can be lovely with fresh, ripe pears, or topped with fresh strawberries and Strega or brandy. It is quite versatile, however, and in the northeastern district of Friuli, it is often mixed with anchovies, mustard, and spices. It may also be mixed with Gorgonzola or spread between layers of Provolone.

It is very perishable and usually sells out quickly, so get to know your cheese vendor to find out exactly when it will be available.

## MONCENISIO

A mild, white GORGONZOLA with a light veining of blue mold, made in the Savoy mountains of western Piedmont.

## MONTASIO

A table or grating cheese similar to *Asiago* but closer to Swiss *Emmentaler* in flavor and texture, Montasio hardens with age and is then mostly used for grating.

## MOZZARELLA

ORIGIN  *Italy/buffalo's or cow's milk*
TYPE  *pasta filata/40–45% fat*
TASTE  *mild, delicate, sometimes smoked*
APPEARANCE  *varies—balls, ovals, rectangles, pear-shaped*
AVAILABILITY  *limited export*

An Italian original, Mozzarella is most famous in the United States as the "pizza cheese." It is one of Italy's *pasta filata* cheeses, which during production are dipped in hot whey and kneaded to the proper consistency. A fresh, mild, white cheese (yellowing is a bad sign) Mozzarella is most highly prized in Italy when it is fresh, even hours old. It is then sliced, sprinkled with olive oil, salt, and cracked pepper, and served on fresh white bread. The best is made from the milk of the water buffalo that were brought to Italy centuries ago. (Herds still graze on the plains of Campania and elsewhere.) Fresh Mozzarella from cow's milk is also good and is made daily in the Italian sections of many cities. It is delightful served with fresh tomatoes, anchovies, black olives, and dry white wines or rosés. *Mozzarella Affumicata* is lightly smoked and delectable, especially as an extra flavor-note in salads. MANTECA is Mozzarella with a knot of sweet butter implanted in the middle. *Boconccini* are little balls of buffalo-milk Mozzarella.

The delicate flavors of young Mozzarella won't keep beyond a week, so the fresher, the better. Supermarket varieties can be rubbery, flavorless, or overly salty and are better used for cooking. SCAMORZE is dried Mozzarella; it is firmer in texture, mildly salty, and quite tasty.

# Mozzarella in Carozza
("Mozzarella in a Carriage")

*Sliced Mozzarella Cheese*
1 *loaf medium-size of French or Italian bread*
1 *cup of milk*
1 *cup of breadcrumbs*
¼ *cup of milk beaten together with*
3 *eggs*
*Vegetable oil for deep frying*

Slice the loaf horizontally, cut into 3-inch sections and put slices of Mozzarella between each slice. Dip the sandwich in the milk, roll in the breadcrumbs then dip in the milk and egg mixture. Deep fry until slightly brown and crisp. Serve very hot.

Anchovies or Proscuitto may be added to the sandwich if desired.

# PAGLIETTA

Sold in small, flat discs, Paglietta is a soft-ripened cheese made from cow's milk in northern Italy. It is creamy ivory in color, with a soft, pliant, almost Brie-like texture. It is mildly rich with a faint ammonia scent from the surface mold and an excellent cheese when exactly, but not overly, ripe. Its fragility makes for very limited export and it is available only in specialty cheese shops.

## PANNARONE (also Gorgonzola bianca)

Fresh, white GORGONZOLA without the blue mold, Pannarone is tangy and slightly sharp and is found mostly in Lombardy. The name comes from *panna,* the Italian word for cream.

## PARMIGIANO-REGGIANO (also Parmesan)

| | |
|---|---|
| ORIGIN | *Emilia-Romagna/cow's milk* |
| TYPE | *hard, Grana/32–35% fat* |
| TASTE | *rich, spicy, sharp, but not biting* |
| APPEARANCE | *large cylinders (up to 75 pounds); oily, golden, hard rind; golden granular interior, sometimes crystalline* |
| AVAILABILITY | *general export* |

One of Italy's oldest cheeses, said to have evolved from an ancient Etruscan recipe, Parmigiano-Reggiano is one of the world's most famous and widely imitated cheeses. Although other Grana cheeses, such as Grana Padano, are similar and nearly as good, none equal its quality. It is known mostly as a grating cheese (what would pasta be without it?) and its subtle spiciness has enhanced and ennobled Italian dishes since the Renaissance. The making of Parmigiano is strictly controlled and it is aged with care like a fine wine.

Cheeses with the name Parmigiano-Reggiano stencilled on the rind are produced only in a designated area that includes Parma (whence its name), Modena, Mantua, and Bologna. It is produced only from mid-April to mid-November—never from winter milk—and aged at least 14 months, more commonly two years. *Stravecchio* is aged three years, *Stravecchione,* four years and sometimes the date is stamped on the rind. Its subtle richness, depth of flavor, and complex character combine for a pleasing sharpness without bitterness or bite in the aftertaste. Older cheeses develop tiny white crystals that are almost crunchy in texture yet melt quickly in the mouth. Younger cheeses are fine for after dinner, accompanied by fresh fruit and full-bodied red wines like Rubesco, Vino Nobile, Brunello di Montalcino, Taurasi, or similar robust wines.

Properly aged Parmesan is goldish-yellow; whitish ones may be too young and lacking in character. Look for an unbroken rind and evenly granulated texture when you buy. Sample if possible—good Parmigiano should not be bitter or too salty.

Parmesan cheeses are also made in Argentina, Australia, and the United States. The Wisconsin-made Stella brand is the most commendable American version for grating.

## PASTA FILATA

The term literally means "spun paste" and refers to plastic or stretched-curd cheeses such as Mozzarella, Provolone, Cacio-cavallo, and others. When they are made, they are covered in hot whey, then stretched or kneaded to a plastic consistency that can be molded or shaped.

## PECORINO ROMANO

|  |  |
|---|---|
| ORIGIN | *central, southern Italy/sheep's milk* |
| TYPE | *hard, Grana/35% fat* |
| TASTE | *sharp with sheepy tang* |
| APPEARANCE | *large cylinders with hard, yellowish rind; light yellow interior* |
| AVAILABILITY | *general export* |

All sheep's milk cheeses are known as *pecorino* in Italy. This one, made mostly in Latium, is best known as a hard, sharply piquant grating cheese. Young Pecorino Romano, known as *Ricotta Pecorino,* is white, soft, moist, and mild, but still flavorful, with an appealing "sheepy" tang. Rindless, it keeps well snugly wrapped and refrigerated; although it becomes drier, it doesn't lose its flavor.

Aged Pecorino Romano is hard, sometimes quite brittle, and sharper than other grating cheeses. It should not, however, be bitter or overly granular in texture. It is good with sausages, cured olives, rough-textured bread, and robust red wines. Sometimes mistaken for Parmesan when pre-grated, Pecorino Romano is a perfectly acceptable substitute; in fact, its extra tang is sometimes preferred over Parmesan. *Pecorino Siciliano* and *Pecorino Sardo* come from Sicily and Sardinia. *Pecorino Romano* is the oldest and considered the best.

## PROVATURA ROMANA

Provatura Romano refers to small cheeses similar to Mozzarella and made from the milk of the water buffalo. They are sold in egg-shaped spheres in and around Rome. Fresh and perishable, they are generally only available locally, although some are exported to specialty shops.

## PROVOLONE

|  |  |
|---|---|
| ORIGIN | *Campania, southern Italy/cow's milk* |
| TYPE | *pasta filata/about 45% fat* |
| TASTE | *mild to sharp, depending on age* |
| APPEARANCE | *sold in various shapes (salami, pear, cone, cylinder); gold to light brown glossy rind; whitish-yellow interior* |
| AVAILABILITY | *general export* |

Walk into an Italian delicatessen anywhere in the world and you're likely to be greeted by the sight of Provolone cheeses suspended from the rafters in all shapes and sizes, from the huge salami shapes that weigh up to 200 pounds to plump little piglets, all hand-molded.

Like Cheddar, Provolone sharpens with age. *Dolce,* aged about two months, is the mildest, with a smooth, even texture, and makes a good sandwich cheese. *Piccante* is aged four to six months, and some of the larger Provolones are aged a year or more. In the older cheeses the flavors are much more pronounced and have a bit of bite; the color is richer, and the texture often is flaky. The ripest ones are grainy and suitable for grating. Provolone is a good cooking cheese; you can stuff *ravioli* or *canneloni* with it or melt it on top of meat or bread. Sometimes smoked, it is a notable companion to ham and good Chianti Riserva.

One of the best brands of Provolone, known for being fine and well-aged, is *Auricchio,* not to be confused with a domestic brand of this name. The name or an "A" is stamped on the rind. It is also more expensive. Some Provolone Dolce is sold in logs, rolled with layers of prosciutto; these are ideal for salads or picnics and can be delicious for snacks with beer or light wines.

## QUARTIROLO

A mild, semi-soft cheese made in Lombardy from spring and summer milk, Quartirolo is similar in appearance to BEL PAESE but is sold in small rectangles.

## RICOTTA

| | |
|---|---|
| ORIGIN | *all Italy, especially Sicily/cow's milk* |
| TYPE | *fresh, whey/4–10% fat* |
| TASTE | *mild, fresh, and sweetish* |
| APPEARANCE | *white, fluffy or smooth interior; packed in containers* |
| AVAILABILITY | *limited export* |

This fresh, uncured cheese, delectably rich and creamy, is made from the whey, or milky liquid, that is drained from the curd in making Provolone, Mozzarella, or other cheeses. Lighter and smoother then whipped Cottage Cheese, not at all salty, with a mild flavor verging on sweetness. Up to 10% whole milk is added to American-made Ricotta, making it richer and creamier.

Ricotta is an important ingredient in many Italian dishes such as *lasagne, manicotti, canelloni.* It is also used in cheese cakes and other desserts. Dry Ricotta is pressed and sliceable like Farmer's or Cream Cheese. Dry or moist Ricotta is very perishable. It should be snowy white; yellowing indicates that it is too old.

In Italy, Ricotta is sometimes dried and used for grating or crumbled into salads. As a fresh Pot Cheese, it can be topped with fresh or preserved fruit and is very good with black coffee. Mixed with Gorgonzola it makes a savory spread and appetizer for dry white wines such as Pinot Bianco, Orvieto, or Trebbiano.

## RICOTTA PECORINO (also Ricotta Salata)

Not to be confused with fresh Ricotta, these are young, briefly cured, sheep's milk cheeses, similar to unaged PECORINO ROMANO. Mild but distinctive sheep flavors make it delicious as a snack cheese.

## ROBIOLA

| | |
|---|---|
| ORIGIN | *Piedmont/cow's, sheep's, or goat's milk* |
| TYPE | *fresh or soft-ripened/45–50% fat* |
| TASTE | *mild and creamy to pungent* |
| APPEARANCE | *small discs, sometimes boxed; creamy white to yellowish interior* |
| AVAILABILITY | *limited export* |

A family of mostly fresh, creamy cheeses produced mainly in the Piedmont and Lombardy from the milk of goats, sheep, or cows, sometimes in combination. All are soft-ripened and range from the mild *Annabella* made from cow's milk to the strong-smelling *Robiola Introbio.*

*Robiola Alba,* from cow's milk, is fragile with creamy, salty flavors and a fresh, soft consistency. *Robiola di Roccaverano* is made of sheep's and goat's milk and has a drier, chalkier texture and a pleasant tang. *Formaggio del Bek* shows a mountain goat on the label although goat's milk is mixed with cow's milk and/or sheep's milk to make it. It is sold in a small soft mound that is very delicate when fresh but becomes saltier as it loses moisture. *Robiola Introbio* is a washed-rind cheese with a more assertive aroma. At perfect ripeness, it is luscious and creamy, with a faint aroma of truffles hovering about it. It can quickly become slimy and strong-smelling, with the "dirty socks" smell associated with French *Pont l'Evêque* or very ripe American *Liederkranz.* Considered an exceptional cheese when perfectly ripe.

The leading dairies that produce Robiola cheeses are Osella, Mauri, and Carmagnola in the Piedmont and Lombardy.

## ROMANO *see* Pecorino Romano

## SAN BERNARDO DOLCE

This cheese comes in small, crusty mounds shaped rather like fat, homemade biscuits. It has a semi-soft, slightly elastic, ivory interior that becomes creamier and more assertive in flavor, but never really ripens. San Bernardo *piccante* is drier and does ripen, becoming saltier and more pungent with age. The *dolce* is good with light red wines such as the Cabernets and Merlots of Trentino; the stronger *piccante*, however, demands sturdier reds.

## SCAMORZE

| | |
|---|---|
| ORIGIN | *Latium/buffalo's milk* |
| TYPE | *pasta filata/44% fat* |
| TASTE | *mild, slightly salty* |
| APPEARANCE | *sold in white or yellowish apple-sized ovals, sometimes with a loop on top* |
| AVAILABILITY | *general export* |

Originally made in the Abruzzi exclusively of buffalo milk, this plastic-curd cheese is now more common to the hills around Rome. Basically it is dried Mozzarella, the best still from milk of the water buffalo, although much of it is now made from cow's milk. Mild and chewy, it is saltier than Mozzarella and sometimes lightly smoked, which gives it an appealing mushroom flavor reminiscent of a damp forest. Expensive but highly prized by Italian cheese connoisseurs, it becomes dried out when it is too old. Scamorze, fresh or smoked, is often sliced and covered with fresh Tuscan virgin or other fine olive oil.

## STRACCHINO

| | |
|---|---|
| ORIGIN | *Lombardy/cow's milk* |
| TYPE | *fresh/50% fat* |
| TASTE | *mild and delicate* |
| APPEARANCE | *white and smooth interior; rindless; sold in slabs or loaves* |
| AVAILABILITY | *limited export* |

Stracchino cheeses have a delicate, lactic flavor similar to American Cream Cheese but milder and somewhat more acidic. Usually ripened quickly—within two weeks—they tend to become drier, stronger, and more flavorful with age, but should not exhibit the bitter or metallic flavors that affect some cheeses.

The name comes from *stracca,* which means "tired," and refers to the condition of the cows as they made their way to winter pastures after summer grazing. This does not apply anymore, if it ever in fact did. Stracchino is sometimes mixed with herbs or other flavorings. Stracchino CRESCENZA is the richest, creamiest Stracchino.

## TALEGGIO (also Taleggio di Monte)

|  |  |
|---|---|
| ORIGIN | *Lombardy/cow's milk* |
| TYPE | *semi-soft/48% fat* |
| TASTE | *mild and piquant to quite pungent, depending on age* |
| APPEARANCE | *flattish cylinders with clear paraffin covering, thin surface mold, straw-yellow interior, semi-soft* |
| AVAILABILITY | *general export* |

Sometimes erroneously classified as one of Lombardy's *Stracchino* cheeses along with Gorgonzola, Taleggio actually has a family of its own. It is similar to the monastery cheeses because of its soft, smooth paste of pale yellow that darkens as the cheese ripens. Most factory Taleggio is bland and semi-soft, with a faintly acidic, mildly piquant finish that begins to sharpen within a few weeks. Taleggio di Monte, ripened in the caves of the Valsassina, matures quickly and becomes runny and quite pungent in aroma and flavor to the point of overripeness, a state which some cheese fanciers adore. *Formagelle d'Artavaggio* and *Tortalpina* are considered Taleggio relatives.

Taleggio is a fine after-dinner cheese with balanced red wines like Carema, Gattinara, or Valpolicella.

## TOMA DI CARMAGNOLA

A regional cheese of the Piedmont, semi-soft in texture with mild, somewhat salty flavors. Quite lovely when fresh, but very little is exported.

## TOMINO DEL MONFERRATO

A cow's milk cheese from the Piedmont with a mild, lactic flavor and pliant, semi-soft texture, Tomino del Monferrato is bland and pleasant, but not especially interesting. Although it is an old cheese, it has only recently begun to be exported.

## TORTALPINA

Flat, pancake-like cylinders of soft-ripened, washed-rind cheese of the Taleggio family. Rich and creamy but not sharp, Tortalpina is quite luscious when not overripe. It should be slightly springy and full inside its rind, not sticky or overly runny. Export is limited, and it is available only at specialty cheese shops.

## TORTAS

This is a fairly new genre of cheeses that have recently become very popular, though some consider them rather gimmicky. *Torta* means "cake" in Italian and these cake-like cheese loaves are composed of alternating layers of fresh cheeses and various flavorings of fruits, nuts, herbs, and the like. The basic *torta* mix is a combination of MASCARPONE, ROBIOLA, and sometimes fresh butter.

*Torta con basilico* is made of DOLCELATTE GORGONZOLA alternating with layers of basil and pine nuts. It is one of the best of the *tortas.* Others are composed of the basic *torta* mixture and alternate layers of such things as figs and bitter almonds, Scotch salmon, white truffles, walnuts, and green olives. Extravagant and luxuriant cheese treats, they are—not surprisingly—very expensive.

## VALFIORE

Valfiore is Italy's closest approximation to Brie. A soft-ripened cheese with a thin, velvety white rind, it is creamy like Brie when fully ripe, with a mild, buttery flavor. Very limited export.

## VECCHIO MULINO

Vecchio Mulino comes in a flattish cylinder with a bloomy white rind and is made in the Piedmont from cow's milk. Young versions have creamy, yellow paste and delectable, lightly salty flavors. The cheese gets stronger, and sometimes bitter, with age; it is best when young, clean, and fresh.

◆◆◆

# GERMANY

C heesemaking appears to have been underway in Germany over 1,000 years ago, mostly in the northern regions around the Baltic port cities of Hamburg and Bremen. The oldest style of German cheeses are the fresh *Sauermilchkäsen*—sour-milk fresh cheeses—that need no rennet. Still an important part of domestic production, these cheeses are rarely exported because they are so perishable.

In the Middle Ages, cheesemaking was fostered in the monasteries. By the fourteenth century the use of rennet made a wider variety of cheeses possible. In 1730 Frederick II of Prussia tried to encourage German cheese production by setting up a model farm with Dutch instructors, promising rewards to those who learned to make cheese from them. It worked—but resulted in the fact that most German cheeses have foreign origins: Limburger (Belgium), Emmentaler (Switzerland), Bavarian Blues (France and Italy), and others.

About 75% of German cheeses are produced today in Bavaria, where the mountain meadows of breathtaking Tyrol support a flourishing dairy industry. But cheese is also produced in other districts and the three principal ones are these: (1) The Northern Plain, stretching inland from the Baltic to just south of Hanover and Braunschweig. Most of the sour-curd cheeses, such as Handkäse, come from the area around these cities. (2) The Central Highlands, including the Rhineland and upper Bavaria. Sour-curd cheeses are produced around Frankfurt, German versions of Camembert and Brie and Edam around Nuremberg. (3) The Allgäuer Alps, in southwestern Germany near the Bodensee and the Swiss-Austrian border. Germany's best and most familiar cheeses come from here.

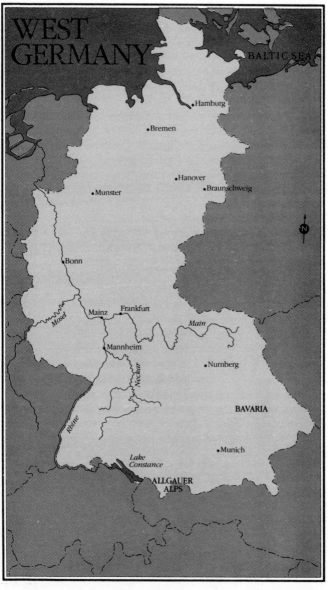

Although the potent-smelling Limburger and Romadur, Tilsit and, perhaps to *cognoscenti,* the Hand Cheeses, may seem most typical of the German style and preference, there is lately tremendous interest in the milder cheeses such as the Swiss-like Emmentalers from Bavaria, Münster, Brie and Camembert, and the Butter Cheeses (Butterkäsen). Smoked cheeses such as Bruder Basil and flavored cheeses are also enormously popular. Processed cheeses flavored with every-thing from mushrooms to bacon to herbs and spices account

77

for nearly half of the German cheeses exported to the United States. One of Germany's best groups of cheeses are the blues from Bavaria, marketed under such names as Bavarian Blue or Blue Bayou. Inspired mainly by the blues of France, they are higher in butterfat and creamier in texture, full and flavorful but less sharp and pungent than their prototypes.

In Germany, as in Scandinavia, cheese is very popular for breakfast, particularly the mild *Butterkäsen*. If you find yourself in Munich, pay a visit to the fabulous food emporium, Dallmayr's, where you will see an opulent array of gourmet food items and over 150 different cheeses.

♦

# *Cheese Guide*

## ALLGÄUER EMMENTHALER

ORIGIN *Allgäu/cow's milk*
TYPE *Swiss/48% fat*
TASTE *Swiss-like, perhaps milder*
APPEARANCE *light yellow interior with large eyes; dark yellow to brownish rind on wheels from 22 to over 200 pounds*
AVAILABILITY *general export*

Made in the traditional style of true Swiss, though milder in flavor, Allgäuer Emmenthaler is one of Germany's best cheeses. Emmenthalers for export are made from pasteurized milk, but in Germany one can find *Bergkäse* or *Alpkäse* (mountain cheese) that is more like Swiss Gruyère and made exclusively from raw milk. Made in the High Alps of the southern Allgäu, Bergkäse is rarely, if ever, exported. It may contain up to 60% butterfat, and it is well worth looking for in Germany.

Allgäuer Emmenthaler has the same uses as other Swiss-type cheeses—as an after-dinner cheese, for snacks or sandwiches, and accompanied by beer or medium-bodied reds.

## BAVARIAN BLUE

ORIGIN *Bavaria/cow's milk*
TYPE *blue vein/70% fat*
TASTE *rich, creamy, zesty*

APPEARANCE *white or ivory interior with blue veins or mottling; white bloomy rind*
AVAILABILITY *general export*

An excellent creamy blue so high in butterfat (70 percent) that it is almost a triple cream. This is one of Germany's newer cheeses, developed in the last several years as a combination bloomy-rind (soft-ripened) and blue mold cheese. It is soft, creamy, and mellow in taste with the sourish tang of blue mold. It is not as sharp as EDELPILZ, which has a more robust flavor and a crumbly texture. Though quite popular, Bavarian Blue does not have the highly individual character of the classic blues such as Stilton and Roquefort, which makes it a good choice for people who find those cheeses overpowering.

Bavarian Blue is very spreadable, excellent with fresh fruit, on French bread or neutral crackers, and with smooth, well-aged red wines.

## BIANCO

A mild-tasting, cream-enriched, semi-firm loaf cheese of the TILSIT family. It is 55% butterfat and its pale yellow interior has numerous small holes.

### BIAROM *see also* Caramkäse

A semi-soft cheese similar to Danish ESROM and sometimes called German Port Salut. Made in Bavaria, it comes in foil-wrapped loaves, plain or variously flavored with pepper-corns, onion, paprika or caraway.

### BIERKÄSE *see* Limburger and Weisslacker

Bierkäse means "beer cheese." It has been widely copied in the United States wherever there is a considerable German population and is similar to American BRICK.

## BLUE BAYOU

A German blue cheese sold in cylinders. Only 60 percent butterfat, it is not as rich as Bavarian Blue and is more slice-able than spreadable. It is an agreeable cheese but lacks the definition of character and flavor found in other blues.

### BRUDER BASIL *see* Caramkäse

## BUTTERKÄSE (also Damenkäse)

ORIGIN *West Germany/cow's milk*
TYPE *semi-soft/50% fat*
TASTE *mild, buttery*
APPEARANCE *pale yellow, smooth interior, sold in loaves or sausage shapes*
AVAILABILITY *general export*

The generic group known as Butter Cheeses are very popular

in Germany, where they are often called *Damenkäsen,* or "ladies' cheeses," because of their exceeding mildness. They are soft-textured and bland, with the consistency of sweet butter; the best are without holes of any sort. Their widest use is as a breakfast or sandwich cheese, or for snacks.

## CAMEMBERT

| | |
|---|---|
| ORIGIN | *Bavaria/cow's milk* |
| TYPE | *soft-ripened/45–50% fat* |
| TASTE | *creamy, faintly piquant or sour* |
| APPEARANCE | *creamy off-white interior with soft white rind* |
| AVAILABILITY | *general export* |

The attempt at French-style Camembert doesn't quite hit the mark, though it can be fairly flavorful and appealing at perfect ripeness. Even then, however, it tends toward bitterness. Try to buy it as fresh as possible. Germany also produces canned Camembert, which has a peculiarly cloying taste that bears little resemblance to genuine Camembert and is downright unpleasant when too old or ripe.

## CARAMKÄSE

| | |
|---|---|
| ORIGIN | *Bavaria/cow's milk* |
| TYPE | *monastery/45–60% fat* |
| TASTE | *mild, sometimes smoked* |
| APPEARANCE | *pale yellow, interior with semi-firm texture and few holes; smoked versions have brown rind* |
| AVAILABILITY | *general export* |

A popular bland cheese. Smoked versions are more aromatic and piquant in flavor, with a pronounced smokiness. *Bruder Basil* and *Biarom* are the best-known export brands. Bruder Basil is often flavored with caraway seeds or other spices.

## EDAM

German version of the Dutch EDAM but paler and milder, with a more pliant texture.

## EDELPILZ (also German Blue)

| | |
|---|---|
| ORIGIN | *Bavaria/cow's milk* |
| TYPE | *blue vein/45% fat* |
| TASTE | *rich, creamy, with pronounced moldy character* |
| APPEARANCE | *chalk-white mottled with blue pockets* |
| AVAILABILITY | *general export* |

A fine blue cheese of crumbly texture and assertive piquant flavors, Edelpilz is very rich but not sharp or overly salty. It is not as creamy as BAVARIAN BLUE but is an excellent after-dinner cheese, eaten with full-bodied Saint-Emilion or a sturdy Rhône like Hermitage.

## FRISCHKÄSE

ORIGIN *Germany/cow's milk*
TYPE *fresh/45–85% fat but some as low as 1%*
TASTE *fresh and tangy like cottage cheese*
APPEARANCE *loose white curds*
AVAILABILITY *general export*

This category includes a variety of fresh curd cheeses known by names such as *Zieger, Klatschkäse, Topfen, Luckeleskäse*. There are also several varieties made without rennet from soured milk and a lactic starter: *Buttermilchquark* is made from buttermilk; *Speisequark* from partially skimmed milk; *Rahmfrischkäse* is Speisequark enriched with cream; *Schichtkäse* has several layers of curd cheeses, one of skimmed curd alternating with another of full-fat curd. These cheeses are often served at breakfast or luncheon with fruit, raw vegetables, and spicy condiments.

## GAISKÄSLE

ORIGIN *Allgäu/cow's and goat's milk*
TYPE *goat/50% fat*
TASTE *red rind: strong and aromatic; white rind: milder*
APPEARANCE *flat discs of yellow paste interiors with reddish-brown or white rind*
AVAILABILITY *domestic only*

The red-rind version is similar to ROMADUR. Ripe within two to three weeks of making, it is pungent and smelly with a yellow, smooth paste. The white-rind variety is dipped in a solution of whey-Camembert culture to encourage the growth of its fleecy rind. It ripens in 11 days and is milder, with the moldy hint of mushroomy flavors. Both versions are made from raw goat's milk mixed with 20–40% pasteurized cow's milk. As they mature, they take on more of the sharpness of goat cheeses.

## HANDKÄSE (also Hand Cheese)

ORIGIN *Harz Mountains, Mainz/cow's milk*
TYPE *strong-smelling/10% fat or less*
TASTE *pungent*
APPEARANCE *various sizes and shapes, though usually round; hand-formed and irregular, soft*
AVAILABILITY *general export*

This is one of Germany's oldest cheeses made mostly from

skimmed sour milk. Its name, meaning "hand cheese," refers to the fact that the farmhouse variety is shaped by hand into flat discs, cylinders, or other shapes. Like all SAUERMILCHKÄSEN, even its mildest forms seem strong in flavor and odor to the uninitiated; some are startlingly pungent and overpowering, particularly at room temperature. Nevertheless Handkäse has its ardent adherents, who like it as a snack with raw onions, oil and vinegar dressing, and beer or cider. The Germans sometimes use it to flavor their beer, dropping in little bits of cheese that melt in the liquid.

Pennsylvania farmers of German descent made the first American Hand Cheese, and it is now also made in the Midwestern United States.

## HOPFENKÄSE

| | |
|---|---|
| ORIGIN | *Westphalia/cow's milk* |
| TYPE | *semi-soft/40% fat* |
| TASTE | *spicy, pronounced zest of hops* |
| APPEARANCE | *small, rindless, hand-molded spheres* |
| AVAILABILITY | *limited export* |

Hopfenkäse is similar to another hop-flavored cheese called *Nieheimer*—both are made without rennet, using sour milk and heating it before collecting the curd. Caraway seeds may be added to Hopfenkäse; salt, caraway, and sometimes beer or milk are mixed into Nieheimer after five to eight days of ripening. The cheeses are dried and packed in casks between layers of hops, which give the cheese its zesty flavor and aroma. Farmhouse versions often become hard enough to use for grating; factory-made cheeses are usually softer and sometimes flavored with cumin. They are best, of course, with a good lager beer such as Pilsener Urquell.

## LIMBURGER

| | |
|---|---|
| ORIGIN | *Allgäu/cow's milk* |
| TYPE | *soft-ripened, strong-smelling/20–50% fat* |
| TASTE | *strong, spicy, piquant, even gamy at times* |
| APPEARANCE | *smooth yellow paste, with yellow, brown, or reddish rind in rectangles or large blocks* |
| AVAILABILITY | *general export* |

The king of the smelly cheeses, Limburger actually originated in Belgium around Liège, but today most of it is made in Germany. As with all strong-smelling cheese, the taste for Limburger is an acquired one, but some people adore it. Like its cousin ROMADUR, Limburger is a surface-ripened cheese with a washed rind. It spends three months in a humid atmosphere acquiring its pungent aroma and soft texture. The export cheeses are often much riper by the time they reach their destination and can be devastating to the nostrils of the unprepared. Copies of these cheeses are now made in America and are especially popular in the northern Midwest.

Germans enjoy Limburgers mostly with beer. There is, in fact, a sub-type of Limburger called *Bierkäse* (Beer Cheese). Bierkase is aged five to six months and is firmer than Limburger; some say it tastes like bacon. There is another Limburger known as *Frühstückäse* or "breakfast cheese," which is barely ripened and slightly milder. Limburgers go with pretzels, dark breads, raw onions, radishes, and the like.

# MÜNSTER

| | |
|---|---|
| ORIGIN | *Germany/cow's milk* |
| TYPE | *monastery/45–50% fat* |
| TASTE | *mild to pungent* |
| APPEARANCE | *smooth, pale yellow paste, few holes; thin reddish-yellow skin* |
| AVAILABILITY | *general export* |

As with most European Münsters, German versions are generally more flavorful than American, especially when fully ripened. German Münster is not quite so highly flavored as the original cheese from Alsace, but it has a distinctive, often powerful aroma. Its texture is semi-soft and smooth. Young Münsters are milder, but robust red wines suit either type.

# NIEHEIMER *see* Hopfenkäse

# ROMADUR

| | |
|---|---|
| ORIGIN | *Bavaria/cow's milk* |
| TYPE | *monastery, surface-ripened/46% fat* |
| TASTE | *strong* |
| APPEARANCE | *white, semi-soft interior, few holes; smooth, honey-brown or reddish rind, sold in small foil-wrapped bars* |
| AVAILABILITY | *general export* |

Germany's cross between American LIEDERKRANZ and its own Limburger, Romadur is a creamy, surface-ripened cheese cured more briefly than Limburger—three to four weeks. Young Romadur is mild, plump, and resilient and ripens within a few weeks to the point of runniness. It is assertive and smelly, but not as strong as Limburger. Romadur that is too old is very runny and sticky, or hard and dried out.

Romadur is good with dark beer or ale, pumpernickel bread, and green onions and olives. Spicy, dry Gewurztraminer is a good wine choice.

# SAUERMILCHKÄSE

| | |
|---|---|
| ORIGIN | *Harz Mountains, Mainz/cow's milk* |
| TYPE | *strong-smelling/10% fat or less* |
| TASTE | *pungent flavors and aroma* |
| APPEARANCE | *generally small, sold in various shapes (discs, bars, spheres, etc.)* |
| AVAILABILITY | *limited export* |

The sour curd cheeses are widely popular in Germany. Powerful in flavor and aroma, they are based on *Sauermilchquark*, a sort of cottage cheese made without rennet or starter. They are low in fat (10% or less), high in protein, and specialized in taste—sharp, piquant, even rank. They are also very pronounced in aroma. Two of the best-known varieties are *Harz* and *Mainz*, named for the areas where they are made. Other varieties are named for shape or method of production: *Stangen* (bar), HANDKÄSE (hand-molded), *Korb* (basket), *Spitz* (pointed), *Kochkäse* (cooked cheese). Some are flavored with spices such as caraway or cumin.

In Germany they are most often eaten as a snack and accompanied by beer or cider.

## TILSIT (also Tilsiter)

| | |
|---|---|
| ORIGIN | *Germany/cow's milk* |
| TYPE | *monastery/30–50% fat* |
| TASTE | *full-bodied, pungent* |
| APPEARANCE | *ivory to yellow semi-soft interior; dark yellow rind, sometimes rindless* |
| AVAILABILITY | *general export* |

German Tilsit is another of those "accidental" cheeses. It was first made in East Prussia by Dutch farmers who were trying to make Gouda. A Dutch farmwife cured her cheese in too damp a cellar, so the story goes, and it became soft and sharp and developed cracks instead of the smooth, mild, and firm interior of Gouda. East Prussia is now a part of the Soviet Union, but Tilsit is made all over Germany, in both factories and farmhouses.

Farmhouse Tilsit, made from raw milk, is ripened for about five months and is by far the strongest version. Factory Tilsit is made from pasteurized milk and aged a shorter time and is therefore milder. But it is still rather pronounced in flavor and even more so in aroma, falling between a Danish Port Salut and a mild Limburger. Its numerous cracks are its hallmark, as is its slightly sourish aftertaste.

Germans like it with Spätlese whites from the Rhinepfalz, but sturdy reds can also accompany it.

## WEINKÄSE

Named "wine cheese," these are mild, round, usually soft cheeses whose creamy smoothness makes them good with the lighter Rhine and Moselle wines.

# WEISSLACKER (also Weisslacker Bierkäse)

ORIGIN *Bavaria/cow's milk*
TYPE *surface-ripened/3% fat*
TASTE *mild to pungent, depending on age*
APPEARANCE *thin, whitish, glossy rind; smooth, semi-soft, white interior, few holes; sold in 2- to 3-pound squares*
AVAILABILITY *limited export*

A popular cheese with Bavarian-style beer, Weisslacker (the name means "white rind") ranges from mild and moist as a young cheese, to pungent and strong-smelling when more mature. As it ages it becomes not unlike Limburger. The stronger ones, aged up to five months or more, are often called *Bierkäse* (beer cheese). Securely wrapped in plastic film and refrigerated, unaged Weisslacker keeps from two to four weeks, depending on how strong you like it. Bierkäse will keep considerably longer.

Both cheeses go best with dark breads, sausages, onions, and beer or ale.

# ZIEGER

ORIGIN *Germany/cow's milk*
TYPE *whey/under 10% fat*
TASTE *fresh, mild*
APPEARANCE *white, curdless mass*
AVAILABILITY *domestic only*

Originally Zieger was the name for Sauermilchquark in the Allgäu, but today it is properly used to describe a fresh whey cheese that resembles Ricotta.

# HOLLAND

C heese, much more than windmills, the Zuider Zee, or even Hans Brinker and his silver skates, is practically synonymous with Holland. Holland's yellow wheels of Gouda and red balls of Edam are the most well-known and widely exported cheeses in the world. The country's broad, flat expanses of rich pasturage, many below sea level, easily accommodate the large herds of sleek, velvet-coated, black-and-white Friesian cows native to northern Holland. Of the more than 600 million pounds of cheese produced annually, 450 million pounds are exported to over 100 countries.

Earliest records of cheese-making in Holland go back at least 800 years but the process probably was well underway before that. Cheese molds from the fourth century have been found and the court of the emperor Charlemagne enjoyed the fruits of the labors of dairymen from Friesland. By the Middle Ages the Dutch were important exporters, first by land and then by sea, to the far corners of Europe. As Holland's commercial empire grew, so did the importance of their two most dependable, long-keeping cheeses: Gouda (which the Dutch pronounce "howdah") and Edam. By the early seventeenth century they were being exported to the Americas. Because they lasted so well, they were good sailors' cheeses. Edam even came in handy in a sea battle in 1847, when the Uruguayan fleet, under U.S. command, defeated an Argentine fleet by using the well-ripened spheres as cannonballs!

Cheese-making began on private farms in Holland—there are still individual farmers who produce their own Gouda— but by the Middle Ages, cheese cooperatives began to appear and weekly cheese markets brought producers together to vend their wares. One of the oldest such markets is that of Alkmaar, in northwest Holland. Farmers transported their cheeses by barge to this medieval port town. There they were placed on wooden "cheese sleds" with red or green painted runners, brought to the central square, and laid out in neat, rectangular piles. Cheese producers still come to the Alkmaar cheese market each week from April through September to haggle over prices of various lots of cheese.

Edam and Gouda, Holland's two most famous cheeses, are very similar in taste and consistency, but Edam is firmer. It is the only cheese in the world, in fact, that can hold a perfectly spherical shape, largely because of its lower fat content. Traditionally, cows were milked twice daily on Dutch farms. The evening milk was kept overnight, skimmed the next morning, and mixed with the fresh, whole morning milk. From this mixture Edam was made. As a result, the smooth mellow cheese was firm enough to be formed into round balls, the shape in which it was cured and aged. Gouda, from southern Holland, was traditionally made twice a day from fresh whole milk. Higher in butterfat, it has a softer, creamier consistency than Edam, and is sometimes lighter in color. Both cheeses are popular in *broodjes,* delectable little sandwiches sold in *broodjewinkels,* Dutch sandwich shops. They can be found all over Amsterdam and feature sausages, roast meats, cheeses, hot little rolls with good Dutch butter, and beer—"fast food" Dutch-style.

Spice-flavored cheeses such as Leyden and certain varieties from Friesland, are less well-known than Gouda and Edam, both of which have been widely imitated throughout the world.

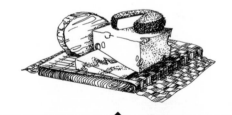

# ◆
# *Cheese Guide*

## EDAM

|  |  |
|---|---|
| ORIGIN | *northern Holland/cow's milk* |
| TYPE | *semi-firm/40% fat* |
| TASTE | *smooth, mellow, sharper with age* |
| APPEARANCE | *grapefruit-sized spheres coated in red or yellow wax; ivory to pale gold interior with few holes* |
| AVAILABILITY | *general export* |

Edam differs from Gouda in that it is made from partially skimmed rather than whole milk. It is less creamy in texture and the paste firms up quicker, allowing it to be molded into distinctive spheres. Originally its natural rind was rubbed with vermilion-dyed cloth. Today Edams produced for export are coated with red paraffin; in Holland, a yellow coating is more common.

Unlike Gouda, all Edam is factory-produced today. It is Holland's second most important cheese, after Gouda, and accounts for 16% of all cheese produced. Regular Edams generally weigh about four pounds. Baby Edams vary in weight from a pound and a half to just under two pounds. Edams in loaf shapes, weighing from five to eight pounds, are also available. Young Edam is mellow but savory; when too young it can be sourish. Mature Edam, aged up to a year, is drier, stronger and saltier. Its keeping qualities were demonstrated in 1956 when a tin of Edam was found by members of an expedition to the South Pole. The cheese was sharp but edible. It had been left there by the Scott expediton of 1912, 44 years earlier.

Edam is sometimes spiced with cumin, which adds an extra touch of flavor. It is a fine snack or luncheon cheese, easy to slice or dice for sandwiches and salads, and tastes best with dark beer or light-bodied red wines.

## FRIESE NAGELKAAS (also Friesian or Friesian Clove)

| | |
|---|---|
| ORIGIN | *Friesland/cow's milk* |
| TYPE | *semi-soft/20–40% fat* |
| TASTE | *tangy, spicy, but fairly mild* |
| APPEARANCE | *cartwheels weighing up to 20 pounds with brown-yellow rim* |
| AVAILABILITY | *general export* |

The aroma of clove is quite pronounced in Nagelkaas—the name comes, in fact, from the Dutch word *nagel,* or "nail," which the little club-headed clove resembles. Friesian cheeses are sometimes spiced with both clove and cumin, sometimes with one or the other. Skimmed-milk Friesians are harder than those made from whole milk. Fresh butter-milk is sometimes used with whole milk to add tang.

The best are aged about six months. Although a dry Gewurztraminer can perhaps handle them, Nagelkaas are too spicy for most wines, and work best with beer or ale.

## GOUDA

| | |
|---|---|
| ORIGIN | *southern Holland, Utrecht/cow's milk* |
| TYPE | *semi-soft/48% fat* |
| TASTE | *mild, buttery* |
| APPEARANCE | *cartwheels of various sizes with yellow (sometimes red) waxed rind; yellow interior with few small eyes* |
| AVAILABILITY | *general export* |

Mild and versatile Gouda owes its appealing texture to the double heating of the curd in the whey before draining off the liquid completely. Young or current-aged Gouda, on the market within a few weeks of making, is the mildest. Aged Gouda, particularly that aged a year or more, is firmer in texture and more developed in character and flavor.

Gouda is made in both factory and farmhouse. The farmhouse product is superior, especially for aging, as it is usually made from whole raw milk. Both whole and skimmed pasteurized milk are used in factory Gouda. Genuine farmhouse Gouda is marked *Boerenkaas* ("farmer cheese") on the rind, but little is exported. Particularly fine Boerenkaas is made in the Stowijk area near Utrecht.

Factory Gouda is a dependable bland cheese, but mature farmhouse Gouda is a true delicacy. Aged a year or longer, it develops sweet but full cheddar-like flavor without ever losing its smoothness. It turns a rich gold color and is saltier than young Gouda. Although the natural rind toughens considerably with age, the inner texture remains buttery and somewhat flaky. Some experts can identify the region, and sometimes the town, where an aged Gouda originated.

Gouda is sold plain or sometimes spiced with cumin or other spices (one popular version is known as Pompadour). Its versatility as a snack or table cheese gives it a variety of uses. It is good with pickles or jam, goes with almost any wine or beer, and is widely used in recipes. The Dutch make *kaasdoop* with it, a sort of fondue served with potatoes and dark bread.

## KERNHEM

| | |
|---|---|
| ORIGIN | *Holland/cow's milk* |
| TYPE | *double cream, monastery/60% fat* |
| TASTE | *full, rich, creamy* |
| APPEARANCE | *flat disc with red rind* |
| AVAILABILITY | *domestic* |

This cheese came about by accident, back in the days when Edam was made in the farmhouse. Sometimes a young, ripening Edam would collapse into a smelly disc. Though it was no longer Edam it tasted good, with rich flavors and a soft, creamy consistency. About 20 years ago, the Netherlands Institute for Dairy Research developed a way to make the cheese intentionally. Today though perhaps more potently flavored, it is comparable to traditional monastery-type cheeses such as French St. Paulin. Mature in four weeks, Kernhem makes a good after-dinner cheese but needs a full-bodied red wine to accompany it.

## LEYDEN (also Leiden)

| | |
|---|---|
| ORIGIN | *Leyden/cow's milk* |
| TYPE | *semi-soft/20–40% fat* |
| TASTE | *mellow, with spicy tang* |

APPEARANCE   *light yellow interior speckled with caraway*
*and/or cumin; natural rind cylinders*
AVAILABILITY   *general export*

One of the most venerable of spiced cheeses, Leyden (known in Holland as *Komijne kaas*) is peppered with seeds of caraway and cumin. Spiced cheeses from other countries are derived from the Leyden concept—Norwegian Nokkelost is a copy of it. Spiced layers of curd are sandwiched between two unspiced layers; the curds are then pressed together and ripened. Leyden is made both on farms and in factories. Farmhouse Leyden, made from partially skimmed milk plus buttermilk, is marked with two keys, symbol of the city of Leyden.

Leyden makes a flavorful sandwich cheese or snack. The Dutch often eat it with *jenever,* the juniper-flavored drink that evolved into gin. Stalwart reds such as Zinfandel can handle it, too.

## MAASDAMMER

A Swiss-type cheese modeled after Norwegian JARLSBERG, with medium to large eyes and mellow, nutty flavor, Maasdammer is not as well-defined as its prototype. The name comes from the River Maas, which bisects Holland and empties into the North Sea at Rotterdam. The best-known export brand is *Leerdammer.*

## MON CHOU

ORIGIN   *Holland/cow's milk*
TYPE   *double cream/73% fat*
TASTE   *rich, creamy, faintly tart*
APPEARANCE   *soft, white, rindless and foil-wrapped discs*
AVAILABILITY   *domestic only*

A very rich double cream (almost a triple cream) with a delicious, faintly sourish tang, Mon Chou was developed very recently in Holland and has not yet been exported.

## ROOMKAAS

ORIGIN   *Holland/cow's milk*
TYPE   *semi-soft/60% fat*
TASTE   *bland and buttery*
APPEARANCE   *wheels weighing 11 pounds with waxed*
*rinds; pale yellow, smooth interior*
AVAILABILITY   *general export*

*Roomkaas* means "cream cheese" and refers to the fact that this cheese is cream-enriched. Its smooth, sliceable texture and mild creamy flavors make it popular in Holland for sandwiches and as an appetizer with cocktails. Light, fruity red or white wines suit it very well also.

◆◆◆

# SCANDINAVIA

T he Scandinavians are the world's great cheese adaptors—most of the cheeses of Denmark, Sweden, Norway, and Finland are modeled after cheeses from other countries. The practice began during World War I, when imports from France, Holland, Switzerland, and Germany were interrupted. Ever lovers of good cheese, the Scandinavians were forced to develop their own cheese industry. This they proceeded to do extremely well, particularly in Denmark. Today some of the world's most popular and widely enjoyed cheeses are Scandinavian adaptations: the famous blues of Denmark, Jarlsberg of Norway, Danish Port Salut (Esrom), Samsoe, and Havarti.

Cheese-making in Scandinavia actually dates to the days of the Vikings. It was necessary in those rugged northern lands to set aside food for the long, dark winter. Cheese-making was a way of preserving the plentiful spring and summer milk for use in leaner times. Cheese by-products were also a basic part of the Viking diet. They ate curds and buttermilk and one of the earliest Viking drinks, referred to in the Sagas, was *skyr*, or curdled milk.

However, little evidence remains of the cheese-making of Viking days. It was the Cistercian Monks of the Middle Ages who fostered the first real interest in cheese. Since meat was forbidden them, they ate quantities of cheese instead and learned to substitute an extract of Venus Flytrap for animal rennet to separate the curd from the whey. This bizarre curdling agent must have done its work well. To this day, the Danes are particularly fond of the soft-ripening monastery-type cheeses, and they prefer cow's milk to goat or sheep cheeses—both inclinations inherited from the early monks. Cheese production, however, remained localized and

SCANDINAVIA

LAPLAND
•Kiruna

FINLAND

SWEDEN

NORWAY
•Bergen
•Oslo
Helsinki
Stockholm
North Sea
Goteborg
Gotland
Aalborg
Aarhus
Copenhagen
DENMARK
Baltic Sea

restricted in scope until the nineteenth century. Even then, expansion of the industry was hampered by the limited amount of grazing land in Scandinavia. Only 3% of Norway and 10% of Finland are arable. Denmark is the exception— 95% of its land is available for cultivation. The dairy industry thrives in northern Denmark and she is among the five largest exporters of cheese and butter in the world.

Denmark, like the other Scandinavian countries, produces its own versions of Brie, Cheddar, Swiss, Camembert, Fontina, and many other cheeses. But the Danish government, anxious to give certain cheeses their own identity, has recently succeeded in having Danish names adopted for many cheeses. Swiss-style Danish Emmentaler, for instance, still exists, but a whole range of similar cheeses—each with subtle variations in character—now carry the name of the town of origin plus the suffix -*bo:* Danbo, Fynbo, Tybo, Elbo, and so on.

Most of the Scandinavian imitations tend to be somewhat blander than the original and are sometimes thought of as lacking in character. They are, however, of consistent quality and relatively inexpensive, which explains why they are so popular in worldwide markets. Norwegian Jarlsberg is currently the single most popular Scandinavian cheese.

Although few are exported, indigenous cheeses are still available in Scandinavia. Goat cheeses may be found in the mountains; reindeer cheese is still made in Lapland, fresh sheep's milk cheese in Iceland. Scandinavia is also a huge producer and exporter of processed and flavored cheeses.

---

♦

# *Cheese Guide*

---

## AMBROSIA

|  |  |
|---|---|
| ORIGIN | *Sweden/cow's milk* |
| TYPE | *monastery/45% fat* |
| TASTE | *mild, buttery, faintly tart* |
| APPEARANCE | *pale yellow, semi-soft interior with scattered irregular holes; sold in thick wheels 10–12 inches in diameter* |
| AVAILABILITY | *general export* |

One of Sweden's most popular exports, Ambrosia is a mild, semi-soft cheese similar to German Tilsit or French Port Salut though not as strong in flavor or odor. It makes a good snacking or sandwich cheese, slices easily, and keeps reasonably well. Because it is generally sold young, after ripening for about two months, it lacks character as an after-dinner cheese.

## BLUE CASTELLO (also Blå Castello)

|  |  |
|---|---|
| ORIGIN | *Denmark/cow's milk* |
| TYPE | *blue vein/double cream/70% fat* |
| TASTE | *creamy, rich, tangy accent* |
| APPEARANCE | *soft, white interior with strips or splotches of blue mold; sold in small blue and white paper boxes* |
| AVAILABILITY | *general export* |

93

This soft, creamy blue cheese is one of the most popular Scandinavian cheeses. Its base is cow's milk enriched with cream and its spreadable consistency makes it very popular as a cocktail cheese on crackers or rounds of firm pumpernickel. The cheese is innoculated with both white and blue molds and ripened for as long as three weeks, during which time it develops a bloomy rind. When young it is mild with a piquant accent from the blue mold. As it ages, the edible rind becomes reddish-brown, and the cheese develops a stronger flavor and aroma. The young version is good with crisp, dry white wines like Sauvignon Blanc, Pinot Blanc, and Sancerre; the more mature cheese can handle a light Rhône red.

## CREMA DANIA (also Crema Danica)

| | |
|---|---|
| ORIGIN | *Denmark/cow's milk* |
| TYPE | *double cream/72% fat* |
| TASTE | *mild, richly creamy* |
| APPEARANCE | *creamy ivory interior with bloomy white rind; sold in 6-ounce rectangular boxes* |
| AVAILABILITY | *general export* |

A queen among double creams, Crema Dania is so rich that it is almost a triple cream (minimum 75% fat). Mild, very clean in taste, and well known for its even ripening, it is similar to Brie and Camembert but has a less distinctive flavor. Crema Dania was developed by Danish cheese-maker Henrik Tholstrup in imitation of the soft, creamy texture and subtle flavors of Brie.

Suitable as an after-dinner cheese, Crema Dania is best served on French bread with smooth, well-matured Bordeaux reds, California Cabernets, or Pinot Noirs.

## CREME ROYALE

A Danish double cream very like CREMA DANIA but sold in foil-wrapped cubes.

## DANABLU (also Danish Blue)

| | |
|---|---|
| ORIGIN | *Denmark/cow's milk* |
| TYPE | *blue vein/50% fat* |
| TASTE | *richer than most blues, but less piquant* |
| APPEARANCE | *white to ivory paste with deep blue veins; sold in 4-inch deep cylinders or rectangles* |
| AVAILABILITY | *general export* |

Danish Blue was developed just before World War I by a farmer named Marius Boel, who baked special loaves of barley bread to get the mold for his cheese. Modeled after Roquefort which is made from ewe's rather than cow's milk, Danablu is higher in butterfat and therefore richer in taste. Though not as piquant or salty as Roquefort, nor as complex, it has vivid, zesty flavors that make it one of the most popular of the blue veins. Its semi-soft texture slices and spreads easily, but it also crumbles nicely for use in salads. Although its flavors sharpen with age, it can be mixed with sweet butter to cut the salty edge. Excellent with dark bread and crudités or fresh fruit, Danablu needs a full-bodied red wine to stand up to it.

## DANBO

| | |
|---|---|
| ORIGIN | *Denmark/cow's milk* |
| TYPE | *semi-firm/45% fat* |
| TASTE | *bland, buttery* |
| APPEARANCE | *light yellow interior with holes and yellow or red wax rind* |
| AVAILABILITY | *general export* |

This is one of the Swiss-style, SAMSOE family of cheeses for which Denmark is famous. It has the mild, nutty, and faintly sweet flavors common to the numerous Swiss imitators. It is sometimes spiced with caraway seeds and marketed as King Christian IX. There is also a low-fat Danbo containing only 20% butterfat.

## DANISH CHEF

A brand of processed cheeses from Denmark containing various flavorings of herbs, salmon, and other piquancies.

## ELBO

One of the mildest of the Danish SAMSOE cheeses, Elbo's bland, buttery flavors and Swiss-like texture make it an ideal sandwich cheese for children's lunchboxes. Sold in loaf shapes.

## ESROM (also Danish Port Salut)

| | |
|---|---|
| ORIGIN | *Denmark/cow's milk* |
| TYPE | *monastery/45–60% fat* |
| TASTE | *mild when young, strong and earthy when mature* |
| APPEARANCE | *ivory to yellow interior with irregular holes; thin, yellow to tan rind; often foil-wrapped* |
| AVAILABILITY | *general export* |

Esrom, from the town of the same name, is often likened to French PORT SALUT, but its flavors are more pungent and its aromas—especially with age—are very pronounced, making it actually closer to German TILSIT. Current-aged Esroms are milder, but, because it is a surface-ripened cheese and continues to age within its thin, washed rind, exports tend to be strong. It is sold in large blocks or loaves and is sometimes flavored with caraway, peppercorns, or herbs.

Esrom is best accompanied by dark beer or full-bodied red wines.

## FONTINA (also Fontal)

ORIGIN *Denmark, Sweden/cow's milk*
TYPE *Swiss/45–50% fat*
TASTE *bland and buttery to faintly tangy to strong*
APPEARANCE *pale yellow interior with few holes; rind covered in red or yellow paraffin*
AVAILABILITY *general export*

Modeled after the Italian FONTINA D'AOSTA, Scandinavian Fontina is softer and more pliable in texture but tends to be fuller-flavored. The Danish version in particular is somewhat sharper than the subtler and more complex Italian original. The Scandinavian Fontinas are very popular as snack or sandwich cheeses.

## FYNBO

One of the sharper cheeses of the Danish SAMSOE family, Fynbo originated on the island of Fyn. In texture it resembles young Gouda. The thick, natural rind allows it to keep well for weeks if securely wrapped and refrigerated.

## GAMMELOST

ORIGIN *Norway/cow's milk*
TYPE *blue vein/5% fat*
TASTE *sharp, aromatic, strong mold character*
APPEARANCE *yellowish-brown interior; sold in tall cylinders with brownish rind*
AVAILABILITY *limited export*

This is one of the oldest Scandinavian cheeses. *Gammel* means "old"; *ost* means "cheese." The cheese itself is not old, but it is prepared in the traditional way from sour, instead of fresh, milk. It is both surface-ripened and has blue-green internal mold. During ripening it is stored on straw soaked with the juice of juniper berries. As it matures—four to six weeks in modern factories—furry tufts of mold cover the exterior and are worked by hand into the cheese. It is very low in butterfat—four or five percent—but nonetheless strong-smelling due to the mold. Grammelost is definitely an acquired taste but is quite popular in Norway. It is occasionally available in export markets around Christmas.

## GJETOST (also Getost, Ekte Gjetost)

ORIGIN *Norway, Sweden/goat's and cow's milk*
TYPE *whey/10–33% fat*
TASTE *buttery rich, faintly sweet and caramel-like*
APPEARANCE *brown paste sold in small, foil-wrapped rectangles*
AVAILABILITY *general export*

This is one of the most original Scandinavian cheeses, and also one of the oldest. Life was hard in earlier days and nothing was wasted if it was edible. Originally Gjetost was made from the whey of goat's milk. It was cooked till the sugars caramelized and it became a brown paste that was eaten on bread like butter. Today it is generally made from the whey of both goat's and cow's milk. When made from goat's milk alone, it is called Ekte Gjetost and is quite strong. The whey is heated slowly to evaporate the water, and lactose and brown sugar are sometimes added.

It is excellent as a breakfast cheese with strong, black coffee, but is generally considered an acquired taste because of its overtones of sweetness and consistency resembling peanut butter. It is best sliced thin with a cheese plane.

Swedish Getost is a goat cheese that may or may not be made from the whey. Norwegian Mysost is made in the same way as Gjetost, but entirely from cow's milk.

## GRADDOST

ORIGIN  *Sweden/cow's milk*
TYPE  *semi-soft/60% fat*
TASTE  *mild buttery*
APPEARANCE  *pale yellow interior with small, irregular holes; yellow or red paraffin-covered rind; sold in cylinders or blocks*
AVAILABILITY  *general export*

A popular butter cheese (*graddost* means "butter cheese"), it is mild in taste, but rich enough to be a double cream. Graddost slices easily for sandwiches and is good with fresh fruit. Beer and light, dry wines suit it well.

## HAVARTI

ORIGIN  *Denmark/cow's milk*
TYPE  *semi-soft, monastery/45–60% fat*
TASTE  *full-flavored with piquant finish*
APPEARANCE  *pale yellow interior with numerous irregular holes; sold in blocks or loaves, often foil-wrapped*
AVAILABILITY  *general export*

Originally known as Danish Tilsit, this distinctive cheese was developed by Mrs. Hanne Nielsen on her experimental farm called Havarti. It has a mild but piquant flavor and is semi-soft in texture after ripening for two to three months. As it ages it gets stronger in flavor and can become quite pungent. Low-fat Havartis are made but are available only in Denmark; the double cream versions have 60% butterfat and are more acid in taste. Light fruity reds go best with young Havarti, sturdier ones with the more mature cheeses.

## HERRGARDSOST

ORIGIN  *Sweden/cow's milk*
TYPE  *Swiss/45% fat*
TASTE  *rich, nutty, mellow*

APPEARANCE   *ivory to yellow interior with round holes;*
             *yellow paraffin rind*
AVAILABILITY   *general export*

Sweden's version of Swiss Emmentaler is consistently good but milder and less flavorful than the prototype. It is matured three to eight months. In Sweden a full-cream version is known as *Herrgard Elite.*

Herrgardsost is very popular in Sweden. A version called *Drabant* is a mild and popular breakfast cheese. A genuine and well-made Herrgardsost "weeps" when allowed to mature 12 months or more—the eyes become moist and glossy and the flavors well-developed. It enjoys all the uses of a good Swiss: as a snack, sandwich, or mild after-dinner cheese with light red wines.

## JARLSBERG

ORIGIN   *Norway/cow's milk*
TYPE   *Swiss/45% fat*
TASTE   *mild, delicate, faintly sweet*
APPEARANCE   *rich yellow with large eyes; yellow wax*
             *rind; sold in large wheels*
AVAILABILITY   *general export*

The Norwegians firmly deny that Jarlsberg is a copy of Swiss Emmentaler, which it strongly resembles in both appearance and flavor. It is more delicate and buttery, however, and doesn't have the nutty aftertaste associated with genuine Emmenthaler. It is also sweeter. Jarlsberg's enormous popularity has some cheese specialists wondering if all the milk needed to produce it can possibly come from Norway alone. Generally reliable in quality, Jarlsberg keeps well for weeks.

Dry white wines and fruity reds partner it best and it goes with a wide assortment of foods and snacks.

## KUMINOST   *see* Nökkelost

## LAPPERNAS RENOST (also Lapland)

ORIGIN   *Swedish Lapland/reindeer milk*
TYPE   *reindeer/high fat*
TASTE   *strong*
APPEARANCE   *unique dumbbell shape*
AVAILABILITY   *local only*

Made from the high-fat milk of reindeer, Lappernas Renost is the world's most northerly cheese The milk is so rich that it has very little whey; consequently the cheese has a naturally low moisture content. It is strong-flavored and so hard that the Lapps sometimes break off chunks and dunk them in their coffee. Since reindeer give less than 30 quarts of milk per year, the cheese is rare and seldom gets far from Lapland.

## LAPPI

Finland's pale ivory, Swiss-style cheese, very firm in texture.

# MARIBO ·

ORIGIN *Denmark/cow's milk*
TYPE *semi-soft/45% fat*
TASTE *mild to strong, depending on age*
APPEARANCE *yellow interior with many small irregular holes; sold in wheels or cylinders*
AVAILABILITY *general export*

Maribo is similar to, but not as strong as, Danish Port Salut, even though the riper versions are fairly pronounced in aroma and flavor. The Danes prefer the stronger Maribo, which is aged six to ten months and is firmer in texture than the commonly exported younger cheese. Maribo is sometimes flavored with caraway seeds and labeled King Christian IX (Caraway-flavored DANBO is also called King Christian IX).

# MOLBO

The Danish version of Dutch EDAM, Molbo has a similar flavor and is quite good.

# MYCELLA

ORIGIN *Denmark/cow's milk*
TYPE *blue vein/50% fat*
TASTE *mildly tangy*
APPEARANCE *rindless blocks or cylinders, white interior with greenish veining*
AVAILABILITY *general export*

This Danish blue is modeled after Italian Gorgonzola. It gets its name from the *mycelium* mold that is used instead of the bread mold common for other blues, including Danablu. The veins are more greenish than blue and the flavor is milder than Danablu. It is often exported in foil-wrapped wedges.

# NÖKKELOST (also Kuminost)

ORIGIN *Norway/cow's milk*
TYPE *semi-firm, spiced/20–40% fat*
TASTE *spicy*
APPEARANCE *smooth yellow interior dotted with seeds; natural- or waxed-rind cylinders or blocks*
AVAILABILITY *general export*

Nökkelost is the Norwegian copy of LEYDEN, the spiced cheese of Holland. Flavored with caraway, cumin, and clove, the basic cheese is semi-firm, mild, and somewhat oily like Leyden. Some are made from skimmed milk and are therefore lower in fat.

Nökkelost is versatile as a snack or sandwich cheese and is also used in cooking, where it lends its spicy flavors to quiche and other dishes. In Norway it is often served with beer or a shot of Aquavit.

## PORT SALUT, DANISH *see* Esrom

## SAGA BLUE

| | |
|---|---|
| ORIGIN | *Denmark/cow's milk* |
| TYPE | *blue vein, double cream/60% fat* |
| TASTE | *creamy, piquant* |
| APPEARANCE | *small cylinder with white bloomy rind; soft ivory interior with light veining* |
| AVAILABILITY | *general export* |

Saga Blue is a Danish Brie with blue mold, the only such combination existing to date. The delicate veining gives it a mildly piquant tang, but it is extremely rich and sometimes almost a triple cream with 70% fat. Fruity, lightly sweet wines go well with it, such as Riesling or Chenin Blanc.

## SAMSOE

| | |
|---|---|
| ORIGIN | *Denmark/cow's milk* |
| TYPE | *Swiss/45% fat* |
| TASTE | *Swiss-like, but milder* |
| APPEARANCE | *yellow interior with cherry-sized holes; yellow rind* |
| AVAILABILITY | *general export* |

This is the Danish national cheese, well-loved by the Danes for its mild, nutty character. Named for the island of Samsoe where it was developed, this cheese has spawned a number of the "-bo" cheeses that are similar in taste and texture but vary in shape and size; among them ELBO, FYNBO and TYBO.

All of the Samsoe cheeses lend themselves to a variety of uses because of their mild yet distinctive character. Mellow red wines are their best companions, but beer or ale goes well, too.

## SVECIAOST (also Svecia)

| | |
|---|---|
| ORIGIN | *Sweden/cow's milk* |
| TYPE | *semi-soft/30–60% fat* |
| TASTE | *bland, buttery* |
| APPEARANCE | *pale yellow interior with irregular small holes* |
| AVAILABILITY | *general export* |

Sweden's version of Dutch GOUDA is typically mild and bland with a smooth, semi-soft texture. Aged for 12 months, it takes on more pronounced flavors and aromas and develops a distinctive character of its own. Most of what is produced, however, is quite young. Sometimes it is spiced with caraway and/or cumin.

## TYBO

A loaf-style cheese of the SAMSOE family.

◆◆◆

# SWITZERLAND

**M**y earliest memory of Switzerland is of waking up on a frosty morning in a cosy billow of down to the sound of tinkling cowbells. Despite the chill, and the fact that I couldn't find my slippers, I was irresistibly drawn to the window just in time to see a line of dairy cows pass in single file below and head up the grassy incline toward the alpine meadows.

Cooking instructor and author Michael Field once wrote that Switzerland has "an almost mystical reverence for cows." Switzerland is so mountainous that there is very little arable land in this small country—and what exists is mostly covered in vineyards. Aside from the Alps themselves, Switzerland's greatest "natural resource" are cattle. They provide the endless supply of rich milk to produce her famous cheeses. Cheese-making is a proud local and communal affair in Switzerland. The lives of whole families revolve around the cow. In summer entire households move with their small dairy herds to the mountains so that the cows can graze with bovine abandon on the succulent grasses of the high meadows. The Alps are dotted with little wooden buildings known as *sennhütten* (cheese huts) that serve as alpine dairies.

The return to the valleys in autumn is often marked with festival and celebration. In the Oberland near Bern, the herders announce the descent of the herd from their lofty summer pastures by rolling blazing logs down the mountainside. The cows, festooned with garlands of wildflowers and with milking stools tied to their harnesses, are led down to winter in the valleys.

The best-known Swiss cheeses—Emmentaler and Gruyère —keep well over long periods of time, a quality important in

101

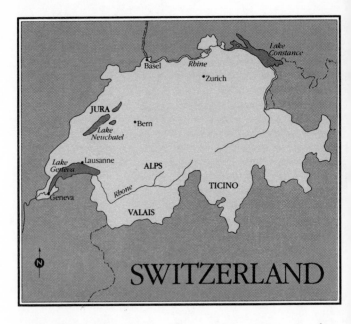

SWITZERLAND

a mountainous country where transportation is slow. Emmentaler, the "holey" cheese that is imitated the world over, has such good keeping quality that traditionally a single wheel of Swiss is given to a child at birth, to be eaten at christening, wedding and funeral! Another wheel might be buried with the dead to nourish them on their journey.

There are over 100 varieties of cheese produced in Switzerland, but most of them are available only locally. The dozen or so that are exported, however, generate a steady worldwide demand because of the high quality of genuine Swiss cheese. Although Swiss cheese has many imitators, none can quite match its special flavors, the effect of the unique climate and grasslands on the cows' milk. Swiss chocolate benefits from these conditions as well.

Sbrinz, Appenzeller, Raclette, Tête de Moine, Vacherin Mont d'Or—these and the other cheeses of Switzerland are produced in more than 1500 small dairies, each headed and supervised by a Master Cheesemaker under the regulation and strict controls of the Switzerland Cheese Association. Swiss regulations prescribe in detail the diet for dairy cows and absolutely prohibit the use of additives or coloring agents. The Swiss also make their own versions of several foreign cheese varieties, including Brie, Camembert, Limberger, Münster, various goat cheeses, and others.

All Swiss cheeses are labeled *Switzerland* on the rind. "Imported" Swiss does not necessarily mean you are getting Switzerland Swiss. It could be Finnish, Austrian, Swedish, or American, and although these cheeses can be quite good, they are not the same as genuine Swiss. Some of the worst

"Swiss" is the pre-sliced and packaged variety. Cheese without any natural eyes at all is sometimes stencilled to provide it with "Swiss" holes!

◆

# Cheese Guide

## ALPKÄSE (also Bergkäse)

| | |
|---|---|
| ORIGIN | *high Alps/cow's milk, some goat's milk* |
| TYPE | *Swiss/45% fat* |
| TASTE | *2 types, similar to Emmentaler: large wheels stronger in flavor* |
| APPEARANCE | *wheels of various sizes, 2 to 50 pounds* |
| AVAILABILITY | *local only* |

The term Alpkäse, which literally means "cheese made in the Alps," includes a wide variety of firm to semi-soft cheeses sometimes made from a mixture of cow's and goat's milk. Its flavors, particularly when made from whole or skimmed cow's milk, are similar to Emmentaler's—slightly sweet, nutty, and mellow. Large wheels of twelve to fifty pounds are generally stronger in flavor and sold under such names as *Hasliberger, Bündner, Justistaler, Piora;* smaller rounds of two to five pounds, such as *Mutschli, Tummeli,* and *Bratkäsli,* are softer in texture and aged for shorter periods.

Both are used as table cheeses, snacks, for melting, or in salads. In Switzerland, try with the red wine known as Dole.

## APPENZELLER

| | |
|---|---|
| ORIGIN | *All Switzerland, particularly Appenzell/cow's milk* |
| TYPE | *Swiss/45% fat* |
| TASTE | *mild to very fruity and faintly spicy* |
| APPEARANCE | *pale gold interior with small, sparsely scattered holes; sold in small cartwheels with convex sides; smooth brownish rind* |
| AVAILABILITY | *general export* |

*Appenzell,* also the name of a Swiss *canton,* or province, means "alpine cell" and refers to the mountain valleys occupied by families of dairy-herders in summer. Appenzeller is similar to both Emmentaler (Switzerland Swiss) and Gruyère but has a higher moisture content than either. It is much more highly flavored than Emmentaler and even tangier than Gruyère. That is because after it is made, Appenzeller is cured by washing it in a mixture of cider, white wine, and spices for four or five days. This adds an extra fillip of flavor that makes it a popular choice for fondue.

Appenzeller Räss, made from partially skimmed milk, is bathed for several weeks in the mixture and is therefore quite pungent, spicy, and sharp (*räss* means "sharp"). It is mostly available only in Switzerland.

Whole-milk Appenzeller goes well with fresh fruits, nuts, light red and white wines; it is fine for spicing up fondues or cheese sauces. Rässkäse calls for more full-bodied red wines.

## BELLELAY (also Tête de Moine)

| | |
|---|---|
| ORIGIN | *Bern/cow's milk* |
| TYPE | *semi-firm/45–50% fat* |
| TASTE | *rich, spicy, salty* |
| APPEARANCE | *sold in cylinders 5 inches high; pale gold, smooth-textured interior; brownish rind* |
| AVAILABILITY | *limited export* |

Originally produced in the Monastery of Bellaye in the Jura of Bern, Tête de Moine is a fall and winter specialty—made only from the rich milk of summer when the cows feed on fresh grass. Its name means "monk's head" and comes from the fact that a horizontal cut through the cylinder reveals a pale center surrounded by a darker ring and brownish rind that looks somewhat like the tonsured head of a monk.

A pressed cheese of firm texture, Tête de Moine is rich but subtly flavored and delicately spicy. It is an excellent dessert cheese, often served on crusty bread sprinkled with pepper. Serve it with crisp, dry white wines or full-bodied, fruity reds.

## EMMENTALER

| | |
|---|---|
| ORIGIN | *chiefly Bern/cow's milk* |
| TYPE | *Swiss/45% fat* |
| TASTE | *mellow, lightly rich, nutty* |
| APPEARANCE | *light yellow-gold with cherry-sized holes and natural rind; large wheels (up to 220 pounds) with convex sides; Switzerland is stamped concentrically over face of rind* |
| AVAILABILITY | *general export* |

Fifty-five percent of Switzerland's cheese production is Emmentaler, the original Swiss cheese. Of that 55%, more than 70% is exported worldwide. It is Switzerland's oldest cheese; one of its ancestors was probably the *caseus Helveticus* (cheese from Helvetia, or Switzerland) known in classical Rome. Although its production and distribution have been considerably modernized since farmhouse days, when it was made by alpine herdsmen called *sennen,* it is still made chiefly in small dairies and exclusively of raw milk.

Emmentaler is referred to as a "cooked" cheese because the curds are first separated from and then heated in the whey. It is ripened in three stages: first in a cool cellar where it is bathed in brine; then in a warm cellar where fermenting bacteria are added; then in a cool, humid room for five to ten months. The cheese gets its cherry-sized holes, or "eyes," from the gases that expand inside during fermentation.

When buying Emmentaler, make sure that there are not too many holes and that the rind is not unnaturally swollen.

An expert can tell when a cheese is of good quality simply by tapping the whole cheese and listening to it. A good sign of ripe Swiss is "weeping eyes,"—that is, the glistening of salt and butterfat in the holes.

The mildly rich, nutty flavors of Emmentaler make it delightful for a variety of uses—snacks, luncheon sandwiches, or after dinner with fruit and nuts. It is the basic cheese for Swiss fondue (often used in combination with Gruyère or Appenzeller) and is often grated as a condiment.

Many countries make versions of this cheese, including the United States, Finland, Austria, Australia, Argentina, Germany, Denmark, and Ireland, but none can match the sweet, distinctively nutty flavor of the original.

## GRUYÈRE

| | |
|---|---|
| ORIGIN | *Fribourg, Jura Alps/cow's milk* |
| TYPE | *Swiss/45–50% fat* |
| TASTE | *fruitier and sometimes saltier than Emmentaler, sweeter than French Gruyère* |
| APPEARANCE | *yellow-amber interior, with pea-sized holes spaced well apart; brownish wrinkled rind; sold in wheels at around 100 pounds* |
| AVAILABILITY | *general export* |

Swiss Gruyère, named for its village of origin in the canton of Fribourg, is moister than Emmentaler and more highly flavored. It has a similar sweet nuttiness about it but is stronger because of longer aging, usually for ten to twelve months. It is also sold after six months, but is considered to be too old if it is sandy in texture or if cracks have developed in the brownish rind. As with Emmentaler, weeping eyes are a sign of maturity and quality.

It is an excellent choice for fondue, but is also a fine after-dinner cheese with, perhaps, a mature Cabernet Sauvignon.

## RACLETTE

| | |
|---|---|
| ORIGIN | *Valais/cow's milk* |
| TYPE | *Swiss/50% fat* |
| TASTE | *mild, nutty, mellow* |
| APPEARANCE | *yellow to amber interior with small scattered holes; brown rind; sold in wheels* |
| AVAILABILITY | *general export* |

Raclette is made in all parts of Switzerland for local consumption but the Raclettes of the Valais are the best and most famous. Similar to Gruyère, it was originally used as a melting cheese in the dish it is named for. The word *racler* means "to scrape." The dish known as *raclette* is made by cutting the wheel of cheese in half and exposing it to an open fire. The melted cheese then is scraped onto a plate and served with boiled potatoes, gherkins, and pickled onions. It is a delectable dish, but Raclette is equally enjoyable in slices or as a soup topping or in sauces.

# Raclette

Making successful raclette is a matter of getting the right cheese. Dealers may try to sell you Appenzeller, Royalp, or Gruyère, but such cheeses are not for raclette. Only the cheese called "Raclette" has the correct combination of fat and moisture, producing a tasty, broiled specialty. Originally, raclette was made by cutting the wheel of cheese in half, exposing the cut surface to an open fire, and scraping off the melted cheese. This romantic method is not always convenient, since guests have to eat the servings one-at-a-time before the broiled cheese cools. Modern chefs prefer to slice the cheese, setting the slices under the broiler. Accompanied by black bread, boiled potatoes, pickled vegetables, and white wine, raclette makes a quick, delicious meal.

## ROYALP (also Swiss Tilsit)

ORIGIN *eastern Switzerland/cow's milk*
TYPE *monastery/15–50% fat*
TASTE *mild, fruity*
APPEARANCE *pale yellow interior with firm smooth texture and small holes; ochre rind; sold in small wheels*
AVAILABILITY *general export*

Similar to German TILSIT, Royalp is milder and not as strong smelling. It is one of Switzerland's newer cheeses, developed near the turn of the century. Made from whole or skimmed milk, its medium-firm texture and fullish, piquant flavors make it a good snack or after-dinner cheese, as well as a tasty garnish for salads. It is good with beer or dry rosé and dark bread.

## SAANEN

ORIGIN *Berne/cow's milk*
TYPE *Grana/45–50% fat*
TASTE *similar to Sbrinz when mature, milder when young*
APPEARANCE *smooth, hard, yellow interior; sold in thick cylinders or wheels weighing 40–90 pounds*

Saanen is very similar to Sbrinz, though harder and less subtly flavored, and is used primarily for grating. Sometimes aged as many as seven years, it is one of the hardest and most durable of cheeses. In the canton of Berne where it originated, it was the custom to make and dedicate a wheel of

Saanen for each newborn. At every birthday thereafter, a piece of it was eaten until the entire cheese was consumed.

As an appetizer, it is sometimes served in thin slivers shaved off with a cheese plane; it is good with crisp, dry white wines such as Fendant or Neuchatel.

# SAINT OTHO

ORIGIN *all Switzerland/cow's milk*
TYPE *Swiss/under 10% fat*
TASTE *mild*
APPEARANCE *ivory to pale yellow interior with small holes; orange rind; sold in small wheels*
AVAILABILITY *general export*

One of the best of the low-fat cheeses that are widely produced in Switzerland, Saint Otho is also one of the few exported. The fat content averages about 4%, as against 25–50% for most cheeses. Its mild flavor and soft texture make it a useful sandwich and snack cheese, especially for those on low-fat diets. Cheeselovers, however, may find it rather boring.

# SAPSAGO

ORIGIN *Glarus/cow's milk, skimmed*
TYPE *hard, Grana/under 10% fat*
TASTE *sharp, pungent, herby*
APPEARANCE *hard, greenish interior shaped into 4-inch cones*
AVAILABILITY *general export*

Sapsago, also known as *Schabzieger* in Switzerland, is a hard cheese made entirely from skimmed milk. Its unusual herb flavor and greenish color come from a specially-grown variety of clover that is added to the cheese to give it pungent flavor. It is used almost exclusively as a grating cheese because of its hard, dry consistency. It keeps indefinitely and makes a useful garnish for salads or a piquant condiment for spreads and dips.

# SBRINZ (also Spalen)

ORIGIN *Central Mountains/cow's milk*
TYPE *Grana/45–50% fat*
TASTE *very rich and mellow*
APPEARANCE *dark yellow interior; yellowish-brown rind; sold in flat cylinders*
AVAILABILITY *general export*

Sbrinz is principally a grating cheese. However, because of its smooth rich flavors, flaky texture, and mellow, lingering aftertaste, it can, like Italian Grana Padano, stand on its own. During World War II, in fact, when the Italians could not get Parmesan or Grana, they used Sbrinz. It is one of the oldest of Swiss cheeses and probably the one mentioned by Pliny. It is aged for two to three years and can be excellent with bold reds such as Barbera or Zinfandel.

A younger version, aged up to a year and a half, is known as Spalen and is used more as a table cheese, but also for flavoring in casseroles or pasta. It is also served as an appetizer with wine or cocktails.

## TÊTE DE MOINE  *see* Bellelaye

## VACHERIN FRIBOURGEOIS

| | |
|---|---|
| ORIGIN | *Fribourg/cow's milk* |
| TYPE | *monastery/45–50% fat* |
| TASTE | *mild, sometimes sourish and resiny* |
| APPEARANCE | *pale yellow interior of semi-firm texture; sold in wheels of 12 to 18 pounds* |
| AVAILABILITY | *limited export* |

This mountain cheese, considered a great delicacy by some cheese connoisseurs, has more a pronounced flavor than Gruyère, of which it is thought to be a predecessor. A specialty of the canton of Fribourg, it is often used to make strong fondues. It is also a fine after-dinner cheese with balanced reds from Pomerol or the Médoc. Fribourgeois is not easily found outside of Switzerland, but specialty cheese shops have it on occasion.

## VACHERIN MONT D'OR

| | |
|---|---|
| ORIGIN | *Swiss Jura/cow's milk* |
| TYPE | *monastery, soft/45% fat* |
| TASTE | *rich, creamy, subtle* |
| APPEARANCE | *flat 1-pound cylinders with thin beige crusty rind, pale creamy interior* |
| AVAILABILITY | *fall and winter, limited export* |

This delectable mountain specialty, highly prized by cheese connoisseurs, is more widely available than Vacherin Fribourgeois but only at certain times of year. A seasonal cheese, it is made from whole cow's milk taken in the last four months of the year. The rind is repeatedly washed with white wine, which results in a stiff, smooth beige crust. When fully ripe, Vacherin has a soft, creamy smoothness, runny enough to be eaten with a spoon. Its flavor has a delicate savor and fresh, appealing aftertaste, sometimes with slightly piney or resinous aromas from being wrapped in sprigs of spruce or balsam.

Its creaminess and subtle complex character make it greatly sought after in late fall and winter. It is delicious with fruity white wines such as Swiss Fendant and Rieslings from California or Germany, but it is equally fine with mature Bordeaux from the Médoc.

◆◆◆

# OTHER EUROPEAN COUNTRIES

S everal other European countries produce notable cheeses, some of which are ancient and famed. Greek Feta, widely imitated, is one of the world's oldest, probably a descendant of the ewe's milk cheese made by Polyphemus the Cyclops in Homer's *Odyssey.* The Greeks eat enormous quantities of cheese, some 33 pounds per capita annually. Kefalotyri, Haloumi, and Kasseri are also important cheeses in Greece and Cyprus.

Two other old world cheeses are Rumanian Bryndza and Bulgarian Kashkaval, both made from ewe's milk. Similar to Bryndza is Hungarian Liptauer, a fresh cheese flavored with spices, chopped onions, and other savories. It is popular in much of central Europe and in great demand for export.

Austria's best known cheese is Mondseer, a soft, strong-smelling monastery cheese. Austria also makes creditable Swiss, Gruyère, and Tilsit-type cheeses modeled after their prototypes. Belgium's claim to fame in cheesedom stems from the fact that pungent and smelly Limburger originated there, on farms near Liège. Limburger is no longer made in Belgium, having long since become a specialty of Germany, and more recently, the United States. Belgium's reputation for rank, aggressively flavored cheeses is nobly upheld, however, by Hervé and Remoudou.

Spain and Portugal have strong local cheese-making traditions, but neither country has yet managed to produce a much-sought after export cheese. Best-known is Spanish Manchego, a savory sheep's milk cheese that is widely made but sporadically exported. Highly esteemed locally are Queso de Cabrales, a goats milk blue made in Asturias, and Queso de Serra from Portugal, a mountain cheese.

◆

# *Cheese Guide*

## BRYNDZA (also Brinza)

|  |  |
|---|---|
| ORIGIN | *Rumania/ewe's milk* |
| TYPE | *sheep/45% fat* |
| TASTE | *tangy, rich, a bit sharp* |
| APPEARANCE | *white and soft, or firm like chèvre* |
| AVAILABILITY | *limited export* |

Bryndza, made from sheep's milk, sometimes mixed with goat's milk, is one of the world's oldest cheeses, originating in central Europe, and made throughout regions of the Carpathian Mountains (Poland, Czechoslovakia, Rumania, and Transylvania). It is salty in taste, from being cured in brine, but rich and creamy, not overly sharp. It can be soft, moist and spreadable or semi-firm and drier, rather like Feta. In Hungary soft Bryndza is often used as the base for Liptauer-like spread or dip, flavored with herbs and spices.

## FETA (also Telemes)

|  |  |
|---|---|
| ORIGIN | *Greece/sheep's or goat's milk* |
| TYPE | *sheep or goat, soft//45–60% fat* |
| TASTE | *rich, tangy, salty* |
| APPEARANCE | *white, matured or stored in whey and brine bath* |
| AVAILABILITY | *general export* |

Although Feta is widely available, the Greeks themselves consume so much of it on a day-to-day basis that much of what we actually import is made in Italy. Some of the imported Feta is also made from skimmed or partially skimmed milk. In Greece, Feta from whole sheep's or goat's milk, which is very rich and creamy, is preferred. Although it is traditionally made from sheep's milk (Polyphemus's cheese was probably a Feta), modern factory-made versions incorporate goat or cow's milk. Feta is at its best aged four to six weeks. It should be purchased right out of its brine bath, where it stays moist and flavorful. (Feta is often referred to as a "pickled" cheese because it is cured and stored in brine.) As it matures it becomes sharper and saltier but will stay mild and moist longer if stored in milk.

Feta has been made for centuries in Greece and the Balkans, but the growing international taste for it means that it is now made all over the world. American, Australian, and Danish Feta are made from cow's milk and are very sharp in flavor. The Danish version is crumbly and may have a harsh taste. German and Bulgarian Feta are milder and creamier.

Feta is an excellent snack cheese and gives delightful bite and zest to salads. It melts quickly and is often used for cooking in such dishes as *stifado,* a cinnamon-flavored beef stew. Ouzo and Retsina are the recommended drinks in Greece, but dry Italian whites like Pinot Grigio or Orvieto also go well with it.

## HALOUMI (also Haloumy or Halumi)

| | |
|---|---|
| ORIGIN | *Greece, Cyprus/ewe's milk* |
| TYPE | *sheep/40% fat* |
| TASTE | *savory, salty, tangy* |
| APPEARANCE | *ivory color, firm consistency; kneaded and rolled, sometimes mixed with mint leaves, sold in loaves or blocks* |
| AVAILABILITY | *limited export* |

Like Feta, Haloumi is cured in a brine solution and is therefore sometimes referred to as a "pickled" cheese. But Haloumi has a firmer, more pliable consistency, similar to the *pasta filata* of Italy, that comes from kneading and rolling the cheese while moistening it with warmed whey. Sometimes, in fact, it is quite stringy, and is generally creamier in color than chalk-white feta.

One of the best ways to eat it is the way they do on the island of Cyprus—it is cut into cubes or slices and sauteed in butter or grilled quickly over a fire. In a good Haloumi the savoriness is never sharp or biting, although it can be quite salty. The mint-flavored version (not often seen outside Greece) counters the saltiness and offers a fresh and unusual flavor of its own. Haloumi is also good in salads or melted on meat. The wines of Cyprus—red, white, or rosé—go well with it.

## HERVÉ

| | |
|---|---|
| ORIGIN | *Liège/cow's milk* |
| TYPE | *strong-smelling, monastery/45% fat* |
| TASTE | *pungent, tangy* |
| APPEARANCE | *soft, pale yellow cubes with reddish-brown outer rind* |
| AVAILABILITY | *general export* |

This Limburger-like cheese—a member of the genre known as "stinking cheeses"—comes from the city of Hervé but its origins go back to the Middle Ages when it was made by monks in the monasteries of Liège. It comes in several different styles, including a low-fat version made from partially skimmed milk. Repeatedly drained of its whey, the cheese is cut in cubes, dipped in brine and matured in a damp room for three months. As it ripens, a reddish-brown bacteria develops on the surface, giving the cheese its pungent aroma and flavor. One of the best Hervé cheeses is REMOUDOU. Hervé is sometimes flavored with chives, thyme, parsley, or other herbs. It needs a robust wine or strongly hopped beer to offset its strong flavors.

# KASSERI

| | |
|---|---|
| ORIGIN | *Greece/sheep's or goat's milk* |
| TYPE | *sheep or goat, hard/40% fat* |
| TASTE | *salty, savory* |
| APPEARANCE | *white to pale gold with Cheddar-like consistency, natural rind; sold in large blocks* |
| AVAILABILITY | *general export* |

Greek Kasseri is similar in appearance and taste to Feta, but is hard and often used, like Parmesan, as a grating cheese. It is sharp, salty, and savory, used a great deal in cooking, and, in fact, makes a delicious dish on its own called *saganaki:* slices of Kasseri are sauteed in a frying pan with a little butter. Very popular as an appetizer, the cheese is served sizzling hot with fresh lemon squeezed on it, and with pita bread.

An interesting American version of Kasseri is made in Wisconsin from cow's milk. It is pale gold in color and similar in texture to Cheddar, but sharper and saltier. It makes a good grating cheese and a snappy grilled cheese sandwich. Full-bodied red wines go well with it.

## LIPTAUER (also Brinza or Bryndza)

| | |
|---|---|
| ORIGIN | *Hungary/sheep's milk* |
| TYPE | *fresh/45% fat* |
| TASTE | *mild base, often flavored with spices, herbs, onions* |
| APPEARANCE | *basically white but commonly salmon-colored due to addition of paprika; sold in containers or small boxes* |
| AVAILABILITY | *general export* |

Hungarian Liptauer originally came from Liptó, a section of northern Hungary that is now part of Slovakia across the Czech border. Traditionally, this fresh, white Pot Cheese, made mostly from sheep's milk with cow's milk occasionally mixed in, was stored in wooden barrels and scooped out with wooden ladles. Mixed with paprika, chopped onions, and butter and spread on crusty white bread or caraway rye, it makes a delicious afternoon snack with beer or wine. Often other flavorings are added, such as mustard, anchovies, beer, capers, even a dollop of caviar. In German-speaking countries it is this flavored mixture that is called Liptauer, while in Hungary it is the name for the basic Pot Cheese itself. Romanian BRYNDZA is similar.

The fruity white wines of Austria and Hungary suit it well and it is often served with *heurigen,* the fresh young wines of Austria that become available soon after harvest.

## MANCHEGO

| | |
|---|---|
| ORIGIN | *La Mancha, Spain/sheep's milk* |
| TYPE | *semi-firm/50–60% fat* |
| TASTE | *rich, mellow* |

APPEARANCE   *light gold interior; low cylinders with dark or black rind*

AVAILABILITY   *general export*

Manchego is Spain's best-known cheese and was originally made from the sweet-scented milk of Manchego sheep that roamed the plains of La Mancha, the fabled birthplace of Don Quixote. Today it is widely made in several parts of Spain, in factories as well as by farmers. There are four stages of ripeness for Manchego: *fresco* (fresh), *curado* (aged three to thirteen weeks), *viejo* (aged over three months), and Manchego *en aceite* (cured up to a year in olive oil).

Manchego *curado* and *viejo* are the most widely exported; both are rich, flavorful, mellow cheeses. Some of them have up to 57% butterfat, making them practically double creams. Cheeses similar to Manchego are made in other parts of Spain and include *Grazalema* from Cadiz, *Oropesa* from Toledo or *Queso de los pedroches* from Cordoba.

Manchego is excellent with the full-bodied red wines of Spain—Rioja, Coronas, Cabernet Sauvignon, or Sangre de Toro.

## MONDSEER

ORIGIN   *Austria/cow's milk*

TYPE   *monastery/50% fat*

TASTE   *full, pungent flavors*

APPEARANCE   *yellow, semi-soft interior with a reddish washed rind; sold in small wheels, sometimes boxed*

AVAILABILITY   *limited export*

Mondseer, from the Lake Mond area of Austria near Salzburg, is a type of MÜNSTER but much stronger in flavor and aroma than the Alsace or German versions. It could even be described as Limburger-ish, though its consistency is more like Münster. It is made from skimmed and whole milk and is sometimes known as *Mondseer Schachtelkäse* when sold in boxes.

Like most strong-smelling cheeses, Mondseer is good with beer or full-flavored red wines.

## QUESO DE CABRALES

ORIGIN   *Asturias, Spain/sheep's and goat's milk*

TYPE   *sheep and goat, blue vein/50% fat*

TASTE   *sharp, piquant, and rich*

APPEARANCE   *low cylinder with crusty outer rind, crumbly blue-veined texture*

AVAILABILITY   *domestic only*

This cheese, considered a great delicacy, has the rich, sharp savor of combined goat's and sheep's milk, with some cow's milk added for smoothness. It is ripened for two to three months in limestone caves, where it develops blue mold and a flavor similar to Roquefort. Most of it is consumed in the region where it is made, but some may be found in the specialty food shops of Spanish cities, wrapped in leaves to retain its freshness and flavor.

## QUESO DE SERRA

| | |
|---|---|
| ORIGIN | *Portugal/ewe's milk* |
| TYPE | *sheep/40–50% fat* |
| TASTE | *creamy and mild to sharp and tangy* |
| APPEARANCE | *small cylinders or cakes, creamy whitish interior* |
| AVAILABILITY | *domestic only* |

Queso de Serra is the mountain cheese of Portugal, widely produced but tremendously varied because it is still made by shepherds and farmers in remote regions. Some are made in low cylinders and ripened to a style and flavor similar to Manchego. Others are formed in small cakes or cylinders the size of Camembert and are similarly creamy and faintly piquant. The name means simply "mountain cheese" and it is often further distinguished by a regional name. *Serra da Estrella* is thought to be one of the finest types. Estrella has a creamy white paste and is eaten young, at two to three weeks. Aged longer, the cheese takes on a sharper, more pungent flavor. Extract of thistle flower is sometimes used as a curdling agent instead of animal rennet, although today rennet is commonly added. Thistle continues to be used, however, for the distinctive flavor and texture it gives the cheese.

Portuguese red wines, including the simple, everyday carafe wines, are excellent companions for these cheeses.

## REMOUDOU

| | |
|---|---|
| ORIGIN | *Battice, Liège/cow's milk* |
| TYPE | *strong-smelling, monastery/45–52% fat* |
| TASTE | *similar to Limburger* |
| APPEARANCE | *sold in small blocks or cubes of butter-colored, semi-firm paste, foil-wrapped and boxed* |
| AVAILABILITY | *general export* |

One of the most distinctive of the HERVÉ cheeses, strong-smelling, even "stinky" when too ripe, although some prefer it this way. Its name means "after-milk," which is the milk taken from the cows just after lactation when it is richest in butterfat. It is sometimes referred to as a double cream, even though it is less than 60% fat. The history of Remoudou is preserved in a museum, converted from a former cheese factory in the town of Battice.

◆◆◆

# USA & CANADA

O ne way Americans reveal their diverse origins is through their love of cheese. The American taste for cheese has grown steadily since colonial days, when New Englanders tried to re-create the cheeses of their homeland. In trying to copy English Cheddars and Cheshires, early settlers in New York, Vermont, and elsewhere in New England, and eastern Canada set the stage for American imitations of Europe's famous originals—Emmentaler, Gorgonzola, Parmesan, Münster, Limburger, Roquefort, and others.

Some of these are very good, although they can scarcely be said to possess the distinctive—and mostly inimitable—character of their prototypes. The best New World cheeses, however—Canada's Black Diamond Cheddar, aged Sonoma Jack, Limburger, Canadian Oka, the Oregon and Iowa Blues, and a few others—deserve to be judged rather on their own merits than as imitations of something else. These are fine cheeses indeed. They are made by traditional methods, hand-tended and, though not widely available, are well worth seeking out.

Modern dairy technology in the United States has been something of a mixed blessing. While its vast production has made cheese widely available, it has at the same time fostered a taste for bland, characterless, packaged cheeses and processed varieties full of additives, emulsifiers, and artificial colorings and flavors. Subsequently, there has been a proliferation of imitation cheese products, some of which contain no dairy products whatsoever. These often find their way into partially pre-cooked "convenience" foods like frozen pizza and TV dinners.

America's technological prowess, however, has had its influence in the cheese world. As early as the mid-nineteenth century, production methods developed in the Herkimer County, New York, cheese factory were in demand in England, where American consultants helped the development of factory Cheddar. New York cheese-makers developed a successful, soft Cheddar relative called washed-curd cheese that could be ripened much faster than true Cheddar. And innovators in Wisconsin invented a stirred-curd cheese called Colby that was also distinctive and quick-ripening. Scientific research resulted in Canadian *Richelieu,* a monastery-type cheese similar to *Bel Paese.*

Two notable American originals are Brick, a Wisconsin-made, semi-soft, pungent cheese created in 1877, and Liederkranz, a creamy, soft-ripened cheese that becomes stronger as it matures. While Cheddar-style cheeses predominate in North America, there are also some excellent and distinctive blue-veins. The best are made in limited quantities and are available only in specialty cheese shops in the United States (Oregon Blue, Minnesota Blue) or by mail-order (Maytag Blue).

The Midwest—especially Wisconsin—is America's dairy-land, but cheese is produced in at least 37 of the 50 states. Fortunately, growing interest in truly fine cheese has prompted new experiments. Word comes from Petaluma, California, of an excellent new goat cheese, and from Graham, Washington, of fine Cheddar and Brie. The West Coast has also come up with respectable versions of Brie and Camembert (Rouge et Noir brand) and the triple cream known as Rondele. Scattered pockets of local cheese production still exist across the United States and Canada. The burgeoning demand for good cheese from increasingly knowledgeable consumers should encourage further experimentation and, with luck, the birth of a great American original.

# *Cheese Guide*

## AMERICAN CHEESE
ORIGIN *U.S.A./cow's milk*
TYPE *semi-firm, Cheddar/fat content varies*
TASTE *mild to sharp*
APPEARANCE *varies*
AVAILABILITY *domestic*

This umbrella term embraces all types of American Cheddar and Cheddar-style cheeses, but mostly it refers to the ubiquitous processed presliced sandwich cheese used in combination with ham, baloney, salami, or bacon and tomato. This along with other processed cheeses account for over half of American cheese consumption.

## BLUES

| | |
|---|---|
| ORIGIN | *U.S.A./cow's milk* |
| TYPE | *blue vein/50% fat* |
| TASTE | *varies from mild and creamy to salty and quite sharp* |
| APPEARANCE | *white with concentrated blue mold, usually crumbly-textured; mostly rindless; variously packaged* |
| AVAILABILITY | *domestic* |

American Blue Cheeses from large manufacturers have the sharpness and crumbly texture sought for garnishing salads or use in cooking. As dinner or snack cheeses, however, they are less satisfactory and do not compare well to the best blues from France, Germany, and Denmark. Three specialty blues do, however, and are worth the special effort to find them.

**OREGON BLUE:**

Produced in Central Point, Oregon, this blue is soft-textured, very savory, and not too salty and has an excellent blue-mold character. It is mostly available on the West Coast.

**MINNESOTA BLUE:**

Made in Fanibault, Minnesota, this is another fine American blue, ripened in sandstone caves in southwestern Minnesota. Produced by the Treasure Cave Blue Cheese Company, it is available to a limited extent in the Midwest or directly from the company in Fanibault (55021).

**MAYTAG BLUE:**

This blue is made from the milk of a prize herd of Holstein-Friesian cows that graze on 1600 acres of rolling grasslands in Iowa. Superbly marbled and aged six months, Maytag Blue is chalk white, soft, and creamier in consistency than Oregon Blue. It is also tangier and saltier. It comes in two- or four-pound wheels or singly-packaged wedges, but is available only at a very few specialty shops or by mail from Maytag Dairy Farms, Rural Route 1, Box 806, Newton, Iowa 50208.

## BRICK

| | |
|---|---|
| ORIGIN | *Wisconsin/cow's milk* |
| TYPE | *semi-soft, monastery/50% fat* |
| TASTE | *faintly earthy to quite strong* |
| APPEARANCE | *pale yellowish, semi-soft interior, usually sold in rectangles or bricks* |
| AVAILABILITY | *domestic* |

An American original, Brick was invented in Wisconsin in

1877 by John Jossi, an American of Swiss heritage. The cheese, which gets its name either from its shape or the fact that originally bricks were used to press out the whey and mold the curd, evolved from Mr. Jossi's production of Limburger. The basic procedure is the same but Brick cheese has less moisture than Limburger and is therefore firmer and more elastic.

When young, Brick is a mild, semi-soft cheese similar to other monastery-type cheeses such as French Saint Paulin. With age, however, it ripens into a very pungent cheese with a bitter rind. It is not quite as strong as Limburger and is best with dark breads, onions, and full-bodied beer or ale. Beer cheese is a variation similar to Brick and a descendant from the German Bierkäse. Beer cheese is popular in communities in the Midwest and the northeastern United States. The bitter rind on older beer cheeses should be removed before eating.

## CHEDDAR, AMERICAN

ORIGIN *U.S.A./cow's milk*
TYPE *semi-firm, Cheddar/45–50% fat*
TASTE *mild to sharp*
APPEARANCE *ivory to orange interior, sold in cylinders, wheels or blocks; natural or waxed rinds*
AVAILABILITY *general export*

Roughly 70% (over a billion pounds) of American cheese production are Cheddars. The first American Cheddar was produced in 1851 in Oneida County in upstate New York. New York Cheddar is still considered one of the best of American Cheddars.

Most American Cheddar is produced from pasteurized milk, but the best are still made from raw milk. (It is legal in the United States to use raw milk for cheeses aged over 60 days; the finest Cheddars are aged far longer.) The bitterness that some domestic Cheddars have is thought to be the result of pasteurization, or of what the cows feed on—silage in winter, bitter herbs or grasses in spring and summer. It's always best, if you can, to sample Cheddar before buying.

Cheddars labeled *mild* are aged two to three months; *mellow* indicates over four months; *sharp* means six to twelve months. Most pre-packaged supermarket cheeses receive minimum aging, although some are good values. Older Cheddars, those aged over a year, usually have the greatest character and flavor, but they are also scarcer and more expensive. They also keep the best. Uncut wheels of Cheddar keep several months in the refrigerator. Sharp Cheddar also keeps well if cut surfaces are securely protected with plastic wrap or foil. The color of Cheddar has nothing to do with its taste. Cheddars range in hue from almost white to pale yellow to bright pumpkin orange, usually determined by regional custom or preference. Vermont purists like their Cheddar white (yellow is also made), while in Wisconsin the preference is for deep orange-gold. Natural vegetable dye from the Latin American annatto bean is used to give color.

Mature Cheddar is excellent with apples, grapes, or other fresh fruit and with well-aged red wines such as Bordeaux or Cabernet Sauvignon. Cheddar is widely produced in the United States and some of the best have local identities or special names:

## COON CHEDDAR:

One of the sharpest American Cheddars, usually aged a year or more, Coon is crumbly-textured and darker in color than most because of the patented method of curing it at higher temperatures.

## GOAT'S MILK CHEDDAR:

A white Cheddar made in Iowa. Goat's milk Cheddar is not like other Cheddars, but has the rich and faintly sweet character of goat's milk. Not widely available.

## NEW YORK CHEDDAR:

One of the finest raw-milk Cheddars. *Herkimer* is white and sharp with excellent character and depth of flavor; its name should be specifically marked on it. *Cooper Cheddar* is another New York variety, a little mellower and softer than Herkimer, crumbly in texture, and yellow in color. Smoked Cheddar is also produced in New York.

## PINEAPPLE CHEDDAR:

A cheese first made in Litchfield County, Connecticut, Pineapple Cheddar got its name from the way it was suspended in netting during the curing process. The crisscross, diamond-shaped impressions on the rind resembled the exterior of a pineapple; it was also pineapple-shaped. Rarely seen now.

## TILLAMOOK CHEDDAR:

Yellow Cheddar from Oregon made exclusively from raw milk. It ranges from very mild to sharp. Well-aged Tillamook is highly prized by Oregonians but is generally available only on the West Coast and in a few specialty cheese shops elsewhere in the United States.

## VERMONT CHEDDAR:

Consistently one of America's best and most distinctive Cheddars, Vermont is rich, but sharp and assertive. It is usually the color of sweet butter but is sometimes yellow-orange or tinged with faint gold. *Crowley* is a Vermont original, a granular-curd Cheddar made by the Crowley family. It is more open-textured, softer, and has a higher moisture content than other Cheddars and becomes quite tangy with a year's aging. VERMONT SAGE is Cheddar flavored with sage.

## WISCONSIN CHEDDAR:

Cheddars from Wisconsin are produced in greater quantities than other American Cheddars and range from fair to very good in quality. *Colby,* named for the town in Wisconsin where it was created, is a mellow, soft-textured, Cheddar-style cheese made by the washed-curd process that eliminates the step of "cheddaring;" *Longhorn* is the name of another, usually mild, Wisconsin Cheddar. Smoked and flavored Cheddars are also produced in quantity in Wisconsin.

# The Big Cheese

The world's largest cheeses have been Cheddars. Queen Victoria was the honored recipient of one of the earliest mammoth Cheddars—a bridal gift that weighed in at about a ton. But it has been the North American cheese-makers who have produced the behemoths of cheese. A fourteen-hundred-pound Cheddar was given to Andrew Jackson in the White House. A four-ton Cheddar was displayed at the Toronto World's Fair in 1883. In 1937, a six-ton Cheddar graced the New York World's Fair. But this hefty fellow was dwarfed by a seventeen-ton giant displayed at the 1964 World's Fair in Flushing Meadow, New York. Largest in the world to date, the '64 Cheddar was made by fifteen Wisconsin and Canadian cheese-makers. It was subsequently displayed in England and eventually purchased by a London restaurant, where it was served with great ceremony.

## CHEDDAR, CANADIAN

| | |
|---|---|
| ORIGIN | *Canada/cow's milk* |
| TYPE | *semi-firm, Cheddar/45% fat* |
| TASTE | *savory to sharp* |
| APPEARANCE | *pale yellow, firm, close-textured interior; natural or black waxed rind* |
| AVAILABILITY | *general export* |

Canadian Cheddars as a group are of superior quality, and the best of them are surpassed only by genuine English farmhouse Cheddars. Two of the most respected brands are Black Diamond and Cherry Hill. Black Diamond, some of which is aged up to 30 months, is dependably excellent, a pale gold cheese of great character, a rich, satisfying texture, and fine aftertaste. Among American Cheddars, it is the best buy as an after-dinner cheese accompanied by fresh fruit and a mature red wine, such as Cabernet Sauvignon.

## CHEVREESE

ORIGIN *New Jersey/goat's milk*
TYPE *fresh/45% fat*
TASTE *fresh, acid, lactic, with a clean finish*
APPEARANCE *soft, white interior like whipped Cottage Cheese; sold in plastic containers*
AVAILABILITY *local only*

This pot-style goat cheese has an appealing tartness, lactic, rather acidic, flavors, and a wholesome, brisk aftertaste. It does not have as much individuality of character as older, similar cheeses from Europe, although it has made a promising start. Chevreese is produced by the LeComte family in Lebanon, New Jersey, from 100% goat's milk.

### COLBY *see also* Cheddar, American

A softer Cheddar named for the Wisconsin town where it was first made. Higher in moisture content and aged for only a month or so, it doesn't keep as well as other Cheddars but is very popular as a snack or a sandwich cheese.

## COLDPACK CHEESE

This popular specialty consists of two Cheddars ground together, sometimes with flavorings. The mixture is not heated and coldpack is therefore not a processed cheese. One of the most popular, and one of the best, Coldpack cheeses is Port Wine Cheddar, a soft, spreading cheese with a touch of sweetness from the addition of domestic port wine. A savory and tangy snack or appetizer, served on crackers, Melba toast, or dark breads, it is sold in small containers or crocks of various sizes.

### COON CHEDDAR *see* Cheddar, American

## COTTAGE CHEESE

ORIGIN *U.S.A., Canada/cow's milk*
TYPE *fresh/4–8% fat*
TASTE *smooth and bland or tangy*
APPEARANCE *loose or dense snowy white curds, in containers*
AVAILABILITY *domestic*

The curds of American Cottage Cheese are usually washed to cut the acidity, which makes it milder than the many acid-curd fresh cheeses produced abroad. An acid-curd Cottage Cheese is made in the United States, but sweet curd is far more common. Creamed Cottage Cheese has four to eight percent cream mixed with it. Brands vary in the size and density of the curds; "California-style" tends to have small curds, densely packed. Pot-style is usually whipped.

The life of Cottage Cheese is brief, so the fresher, the better. The best guide to freshness is the "pull date," or date

121

after which it should not be sold, that is printed on the carton. Best known as a diet food, Cottage Cheese is full of minerals and enzymes. It goes with a variety of fruits and is quite good with black coffee.

## CREAM CHEESE

ORIGIN *U.S.A., Canada/cow's milk*
TYPE *fresh/35% fat*
TASTE *fresh, creamy, appealingly sour*
APPEARANCE *snow-white bricks, foil-wrapped or whipped, in waxed containers*
AVAILABILITY *domestic*

Good Cream Cheese can be a singularly satisfying spread for sandwiches or bagels. Most contain emulsifiers, such as gum arabic, but the best do not. And the best are fresher, lighter, and more flavorful, but are also more open-textured and have a somewhat shorter keeping time. Cream Cheese mixed with jam or preserves is a treat; it also combines well with cucumbers, tomatoes, watercress, sliced olives, and, of course, lox and red onions.

Neufchatel, copied after French Neufchatel, has less butter-fat and more moisture than regular Cream Cheese. Unlike the French version, it is unripened and often mixed with flavorings such as minced fruit, vegetables, or spices.

## FARMER CHEESE

Farmer Cheese is basically Cottage Cheese pressed into a firm mass the shape of a flat brick. Fresh and mild, it is often a breakfast cheese, topped with fruit or salt, pepper, and a dollop or two of sour cream.

## GOAT'S MILK CHEDDAR *see* Cheddar, American

## HAND CHEESE

An American descendant of German HANDKÄSE, Hand Cheese was developed first in Pennsylvania and later in other German-American communities. Like its German counterpart, it is hand-shaped into small flat discs. It ripens in a yellow to reddish-brown washed rind and becomes creamy-soft, with pungent flavors and aromas. Such cheeses eventually become quite rank, in fact, and should be well-wrapped when stored. They are traditionally accompanied by dark beer.

# LIEDERKRANZ

ORIGIN *Ohio/cow's milk*
TYPE *soft-ripened/50% fat*
TASTE *mild to pungent and strong-smelling*
APPEARANCE *foil-wrapped, four-ounce bars; soft ivory interior*
AVAILABILITY *domestic*

Liederkranz is the most famous American original, invented in 1882 by a New York cheese-maker, Emil Frey. Frey was trying to imitate the German SCHLOSSKÄSE, a strong-smelling, soft-ripened cheese similar to Limburger. Frey named it after the Liederkranz Hall singing group in New York, because of their enthusiasm for the cheese.

Liederkranz is a good example of the complexities involved in making fine cheese. When the plant that made it first moved from New York to Van Wert, Ohio, the producers were unable to get the right flavor—even though they had taken precautions to insure that the production procedures remained the same. Somehow they hit upon the idea of smearing the walls with cheeses made in New York—Eureka! The air-borne bacteria from other New York cheeses had subtly affected the flavor of Liederkranz as it ripened.

Liederkranz is put on the market from four to six weeks from the date that appears on the package. When young, it is mild and semi-soft. As it matures in its foil-wrapped packaging, it becomes honey-colored, creamy-soft, and progressively stronger in aroma and taste; the rind turns from yellow to golden brown. Though pungent, it is never as strong or smelly as Limburger. When too old, however, it smells rank, even stinky, and feels dried out or sticky. Like other strong-smelling cheeses, it is good with dark bread, green onions, and dark beer.

## MAYTAG BLUE *see* Blues

## MINNESOTA BLUE *see* Blues

## MONTEREY JACK (also California Jack) *see also* Sonoma Jack

ORIGIN *California/cow's milk*
TYPE *semi-soft/50% fat*
TASTE *smooth and bland, Aged Jack sharp and flavorful*
APPEARANCE *very pale yellow to rich orange, depending on age; dark rind cylinders; sold as loaves or wheels*
AVAILABILITY *domestic (Aged Jack mainly California)*

Though Monterey Jack is classified as a Cheddar, young cheeses aged two to three weeks are as mild and pale as young Goudas. Some are blander, to the point of lacking much flavor at all, which is why flavored ones such as

Jalapeno Pepper Jack are so popular. As a high-moisture cheese, young Jack is good as a snack or sandwich cheese; it is often used as topping on Mexican dishes. The name is said to have come from David Jacks, who first marketed the cheese in Monterey County, California.

Quite different from young Jack is Dry or Aged Jack, which may be made from partially skimmed milk. Aged six months or more, it develops a tough brown, wrinkled hide and a firm, rich yellow interior. The aged version resembles Cheddar in texture and flavor, and it's rich, nutty, salty and sharp—excellent with Cabernet Sauvignon or Zinfandel. It is also used for grating.

Jack cheese has become quite popular nationwide and young Jack is produced by several large United States factories. The best, however, is still produced by small companies in California and specialties such as dill-flavored, rennetless versions (for vegetarians) and fine Dry Jack are only available in the West.

## MOZZARELLA

The American version of this fresh Italian cheese is made mostly in factories and sold in supermarkets. If not too old (and bitter) it is fine for cooking but not delicate enough to eat fresh. Mozzarellas made in Italian shops, often daily, can be excellent, however, especially when very fresh and dressed with olive oil, salt, and freshly ground pepper. Smoked Mozzarella has a delightful, lightly smoked flavor that makes a delicious snack and a unique garnish for salads.

## MÜNSTER (also Muenster)

Widely produced in America and generally reliable in quality, American Münster has a thin orange rind, a pale yellow interior, and resilient texture. Often quite bland, American Münster is never as strong in flavor or aroma as Alsatian MÜNSTER. At its most flavorful, domestic Münster is savory but simple in character. It is good with fruit, beer, or light fruity wines.

## NEW YORK CHEDDAR *see* Cheddar, American

## OKA

| | |
|---|---|
| ORIGIN | *Quebec/cow's milk* |
| TYPE | *semi-soft, monastery/45–50% fat* |
| TASTE | *smooth, flavorful, piquant* |
| APPEARANCE | *wheels with rounded sides* |
| AVAILABILITY | *limited export* |

One of the few genuine monastery cheeses in this hemisphere, Oka was originally made at *Fromagerie de la Trappe,* a Trappist monastery in Oka, Quebec, in the latter half of the nineteenth century. In 1975, the monks sold the company to a factory producer in Oka, but the old recipe is still used and the monks still oversee production methods. Highly regarded for its fine character—creamy, full-flavored, becoming stronger as it ripens—it is modeled after French PORT SALUT.

Today's version, aged about 30 days on cypress slats in the aging cellars, is said to lack the deep, penetrating flavors of the longer-ripened original made at the monastery. However, it is still considered one of the better cheeses produced in the Americas and demand usually outstrips supply. It goes well after dinner with full-bodied red wines.

## OREGON BLUE *see* Blues

## PARMESAN

American versions of Italian PARMESAN are either too salty or too sharp and almost always lacking in flavor. One exception is the Parmesan made by the Stella company in Wisconsin. Though somewhat uneven in quality, it is a cut above other domestic versions and is available in supermarkets. Pre-grated Parmesan is always second-rate and bears little resemblance to true Parmesan, as a single experience with Italian PARMIGIANA-REGGIANO will demonstrate.

## PINEAPPLE CHEDDAR *see* Cheddar, American

## RICHELIEU

| | |
|---|---|
| ORIGIN | *Canada/cow's milk* |
| TYPE | *soft-ripened/50% fat* |
| TASTE | *mild, creamy* |
| APPEARANCE | *soft Brie-like but loaf or brick-shaped* |
| AVAILABILITY | *domestic* |

Richelieu is a product of scientific research at Canadian universities and took over 20 years to develop. The efforts aimed for a monastery cheese similar to Bel Paese, but the result is more like factory Brie or Camembert. Though not truly notable, it is creamy, mild, and spreadable.

## RONDELÉ

An agreeable, though not truly distinctive, American version of the French triple cream BOURSIN. Rondelé is sometimes flavored with herbs and/or ground pepper.

## ROUGE ET NOIR

*Rouge et Noir* is the brand name for American Brie and Camembert made near Petaluma, California, by a small company founded in 1865 by Jefferson Thompson. These cheeses, like other imitations, do not have the rich, penetrating, unique character of the best French originals. Still, they are flavorful cheeses that, when perfectly ripe, have an appealing character of their own. They are very similar to one another, but the Brie has a more robust flavor. Pull dates are printed on the bottom of the package to give the consumer some idea of freshness. The cheeses ripen to full creaminess within three to four weeks of that date. When too old they are dry and hard and smell strongly of ammonia. The company maintains that when fully ripe and creamy throughout, the cheeses will freeze well without the texture changing.

Two other cheeses are also produced: Breakfast Cheese, a small soft-ripening cylinders with savory, dry flavors and a slightly grainy texture; and Schloss, salty, soft-ripened little bricks that are ripened 45 days. Their pungent, garlicky aromas and flavor will appeal to lovers of strong cheeses.

## SONOMA JACK

| | |
|---|---|
| ORIGIN | *California/cow's milk* |
| TYPE | *semi-soft/45% fat* |
| TASTE | *mild and smooth, sometimes flavored* |
| APPEARANCE | *sold in pale yellow bricks or wedges with thin natural rinds, or rindless* |
| AVAILABILITY | *local only* |

This cheese is a high-moisture, semi-soft cheese very similar to Monterey Jack and made in the town of Sonoma, California. Produced in two local, family-owned firms, the cheeses are hand-turned daily while being cured in a brine solution. The cheese is basically mild and bland, but there are several versions flavored with garlic, spices, hot peppers, and other seasonings. It is popular as a snack and sandwich cheese, being of very sliceable texture, but is more limited in distribution than Monterey Jack.

Wheels of Dry Jack, aged several months, are occasionally available. These are superb, firm-textured cheeses with tough, dark brown rinds, a flaky, dry texture similar to Cheddar, and rich, salty flavors. Dry Jack keeps well for many months and is hard enough for grating.

## TELEME

A soft cheese similar to domestic Brie, Teleme has a little more bite and tang. Aged about 21 days and hand-turned daily, it has up to 50% butterfat and a creamy consistency. Riper Teleme is runnier in texture and more pronounced in flavor. It is mainly available in northern California.

## TILLAMOOK *see also* Cheddar, American

Very good Cheddar made in Tillamook County, Oregon.

## VERMONT CHEDDAR *see* Cheddar, American

## VERMONT SAGE *see also* Cheddar, American

VERMONT CHEDDAR flavored with sage or sage flavoring. The best are the farm-produced varieties with bits of the herb worked into the curd, but they are made in small quantity and are only available locally.

## WISCONSIN CHEDDAR *see* Cheddar, American

◆◆◆

# SERVING CHEESE

A fine cheese needs no embellishment, yet cheese of any kind is never eaten just by itself. The simpler its accompaniments, however, the better, especially when it occupies center stage—as a lunch, a snack, or a course on its own. Cheese goes with a variety of things, but by time-honored tradition bread, fruit, and wine are its classic companions. Local breads and cheeses often complement one another superbly—the dark breads of Scandinavia, for example, Danish pumpernickel, Swedish limpa, caraway rye, are fine with the semi-soft varieties so prevalent there; crusty french baguettes are unbeatable for Brie, Camembert or other soft-ripened cheeses.

Quite a fuss is made in England over crackers to go with cheeses, according to an English friend of mine. There is heated discussion on the subject, he says, and something of a ritual involved in pairing the right crackers with certain cheeses. For some, it must be hard, large-ish biscuits known as Bath Olivers with Stilton. Others won't do without their tin of Romary's, which are a little sweeter and very good with Cheddar, or Cornish wafers, or Carr's Water Biscuits. Whatever the type of cracker, unsalted ones are best for most cheeses because most are often quite salty already.

What is it about fruit that sets off cheese so superbly? Perhaps it is the refreshing contrast of crisp acidity and juicy sweetness. Few would eschew the pleasures of ripe pears and Gorgonzola, apples with Cheddar or Wensleydale, summer berries with Petit-Suisse or the creams, ripe plums with *chèvres,* or fresh figs with young Parmigiano.

Although cheese is good with ale, beer, cider, and in some instances, strong black coffee, wine most often partners it best. Wine and cheese are boon companions that seem to bring out the best in one another. There is a saying in the wine trade: buy on apples, sell on cheese. The natural acidity of apples points up defects in a wine, but cheese makes any wine taste good. The milky proteins and richness of cheese take the edge off a harsh wine and tame rampant tannins or acidity. Some wine and cheese marriages seem preordained on high so sublime are they: Stilton with Port, Roquefort with Sauternes, ripe Camembert and mature Bordeaux, Dry Jack with Zinfandel.

Cheeses served on home ground are often excellent with the local drink. Never have I enjoyed the goaty tang of *chèvre* more than in the little hilltop town of Sancerre in the Loire Valley, sitting in the sun-dappled square, munching away on a pair of crusty Crottins washed down by the crisp wine that is also called Sancerre.

Cheese is appropriate served at all times of day or night—for breakfast, lunch, dinner, and snacks in between. In parts of Europe, like Holland and Scandinavia, it is commonly a breakfast food. In London, the Ploughman's Lunch of cheese, ale, bread, and sometimes chutney is a pub classic. In America, cheese is most widely used for sandwiches, snacks, or cooking, and most of the cheese products, unfortunately, are suitable for little else, certain well-aged Cheddars being the exception.

Cheese is a popular food for large cocktail parties, where people need more substantial nourishment to sustain them for long periods, or to soak up alcohol. It is ideal for wine tasting (for serious blind tastings, however, the cheese should *follow* the tasting so as not to interfere with fair judgment of the wines).

Cheese increasingly has an important part to play in the principal meal of the day, but because it is so adaptable it is often abused. It is, for example, commonly served as an appetizer with cocktails before dinner. With certain exceptions, this doesn't seem suitable to me. Most cheeses are fairly dense or heavy, sometimes quite cloying, often leaving a sharp aftertaste. Cheeses are so tasty, moreover, that guests may be tempted to eat too much at this stage and spoil their appetites for the meal to come.

Interesting exceptions do exist, however. In Spain, it is customary to serve bits of Manchego and salted nuts with Fino or Dry Oloroso Sherry. Here the body of the fortified wine nicely cuts through the savory richness of the cheese. The Spanish are wise enough not to overdo it, serving only a few bits of cheese before going into dinner. Other exceptions for before dinner are fresh double creams such as Boursin or creamy blues such as Blue Costello or Gorgonzola Dolcelatte, which can be spread on light wafers. These may be quite acceptable with the ubiquitous glass of white wine that is so boringly popular now, or with the best aperitif of all—Champagne.

# Cheese and Beverage Pairings

| CHEESE | TYPE |
| --- | --- |
| Appenzeller, Blarney, Beaufort, Emmental, Gruyère, Jarlsberg, Samsoe (Swiss types) | Swiss |
| Beer Cheese, Bierkäse, American Brick, German Tilsit | Monastery |
| Bel Paese, Saint-Paulin, Port-Salut, Saint-Nectaire, Tourton | Semi-soft |
| Blues, creamy blues | Blue vein |
| Brie, Camembert, Paglietta | Soft-ripened |
| Cheddar, Cheshire, Double Gloucester, Dunlop | Semi-firm |
| Chèvres, Feta | Goat |
| Crema Dania, Chaource, Explorateur, Corolle, Saint-André, Boursault, Vacherin Mont-d'Or | Soft |
| Esrom, Fontina, Port-Salut, Taleggio, Tilsit | Semi-soft |
| Gouda, Harvarti, Danish Muenster, California Jack, Tomme des Pyrénées | Semi-soft |
| Liederkranz, Limburger, Hervé, Handkäse | Monastery |
| Parmesan, Grana, Sbrinz, Asiago, Fiore Sardo | Hard |
| Pont l'Evêque, Chaumes, Maroilles, Rollet, Vieux Pané, Taleggio di Monte, Livarot | Surface-ripened |
| Provolone, Scamorze, Mozzarella | Pasta-filata |
| Aged Gouda, Dry Monterey Jack | Hard |

To my mind, the best time for cheese is after dinner, as a course of its own. At formal dinners and the best restaurants, cheese is served as a separate course following the entrée or salad and preceding dessert and coffee. In France it is sometimes served at the same moment as the salad. This is fine, certainly, but since I generally want wine with cheese, I prefer to serve the salad first and then the cheese. Cheese can also serve *as* dessert. People are eating more lightly today, so the cheese course sometimes serves as dessert, accompanied by fresh fruit.

Selections for an after-dinner cheese board should include cheeses with a variety of flavors and textures, ranging from mild to assertive, soft to firm, young and fresh to more mature. There should be at least one mild and popular cheese for the less adventurous or inexperienced, and a variety of shapes and colors that make a visually attractive presentation. You don't want to serve several semi-soft or firm cheeses, or all blues or *chèvres* (unless the group is into tasting the fine subtleties among them). Remember that strong-smelling cheeses like Livarot, Limburger, Handkäse, or ripe Münster will overpower more delicate ones, so place them well apart and provide separate serving knives for them.

**BEVERAGE**

Fruity reds, Beaujolais, Chinon, Barbera, Gamay, Zinfandel, Chelois

Beer or full-bodied reds, Petite Sirah, Dão, Zinfandel

Fruity whites or reds, Chenin Blanc, Napa Gamay, Beaujolais, Côte du Rhône

Full-bodied reds, Sauternes or Port, Barolo, Hermitage, Nuits-St.-Georges, Chambertin, Shiraz, Riesling, Mâcon Blanc, Champagne

Mature reds, Bordeaux, Cabernet Sauvignon, Burgundy, Pinot Noir

Mature, balanced reds, Bordeaux, Burgundy, Ruby Port, bitter beer

Crisp dry whites, fruity or mature reds, Retsina, Sancerre, Sauvignon Blanc, Chardonnay, Cabernet Sauvignon, Burgundy, Ruby Port

Dry whites, mature reds or Champagne

Beaujolais, Rhone, light Cabernet, Valpolicella

Light Bordeaux or Cabernet, Beaujolais, Côte du Rhône

Beer or ale

Barolo, Chianti Riserva, Vino Nobile di Montepulciano, Rubesco, Brunello di Montalcino, Taurasi

Assertive, vigorous reds, Saint-Emilion, Hermitage or Côte Rotie, Cabernet or Zinfandel

Chianti, Valpolicella, Cabernet del Trentino

Zinfandel

# Glossary of Cheese Terms

**Acid, acidity**: a description of a pleasant tang; it can be a defect if too PRONOUNCED.

**Affiné**: from the French *affiner,* meaning "to finish, or refine." WASHED-RIND cheeses, for example, may be *affiné au marc de Bourgogne*—the rind has been washed with *marc* during CURING.

**Ammoniated**: a term describing cheeses that smell or taste of ammonia, a condition that afflicts the rinds of overripe cheeses, primarily those with bloomy rinds such as Brie, Camembert, CHÈVRES. A hint of ammonia is not necessarily objectionable.

**Annatto**: a yellow-orange dye extracted from the seeds of a South American plant and used to color such cheeses as Cheddar, Mimolette, Double Gloucester, Edam, and many others.

**Aroma**: the smell or odor of cheese, which can vary from very faint to over-poweringly STRONG. Aroma is an excellent guide to personal preference in cheeses, though sometimes the smell is stronger than the taste on the palate, as with French Münster, Pont l'Evêque, Liederkranz, where the odor is mainly in the rind.

**Assertive**: term referring to pronounced taste or aroma.

**Barnyardy**: a term used to describe aromas or flavors associated with a stable or barnyard. The description is not necessarily negative, but it can refer to an excessively goaty, EARTHY, or even dirty character.

**Beestings**: a term for colostrum, the first milk a cow gives after calving. Very high in protein, its only known use is in Spain for a strong, semi-firm cheese known as Armada.

**Bleu**: the French term for "blue."

**Bloomy rind**: the white fleecy rind that develops on certain surface-ripened cheeses like Brie, Camembert, double or triple creams, and some CHÈVRES. It is formed by spraying the surface of the cheese with spores of *Penicillium candidum* mold (see Pencillium) while it is curing.

**Blue vein**: cheeses that develop bluish or greenish veins of mold throughout their interior. Veining generally gives cheese an ASSERTIVE and PIQUANT flavor. See p. 6.

**Body**: the "feel" of a cheese, on the palate or to the touch; it may be firm, SUPPLE, SPRINGY, elastic, chewy, GRAINY, etc.

**Brine**: a salt-and-water solution in which some cheeses are washed or dipped during curing. (See "Washed rind.")

**Brushed**: To keep the rinds moist, WASHED-RIND cheeses are "brushed" during curing with various liquids, such as brine, beer, or brandy.

**Casein**: the principal protein in milk that solidifies it into cheese through the action of RENNET.

**Chalky**: a positive term, referring either to whitest of white color or smooth, fine-grained texture, primarily for CHÈVRES. Not a reference to taste.

**Cheddaring**: the process used in making Cheddar, whereby the CURDS are cut, or milled, and repeatedly turned to knit the fibers together.

**Chèvres**: the French term for goat cheeses. See p. 7.

**Close**: a term describing a smooth, dense texture with no holes; cheeses with more OPEN texture may have large or small holes.

**Cold pack**: cheeses ground or mixed together into a soft, spreadable paste without heating or cooking. Port Wine Cheddar is an example.

**Cooked**: part of the cheese-making process during which the cheese is heated to help solidify the CURD. Most cheeses are heated somewhat, but Cheddar- or Swiss-types are heated to fairly high temperatures.

**Creams, Double or Triple**: a classification of cheese. See p. 8.

130

**Creamy:** a term describing texture or taste. Creamy texture is soft and even runny in some cases; creamy flavors are rich and associated with cream-enriched cheeses such as double or triple creams. Creamy may also describe a cream-colored appearance of the PASTE.

**Crumbly:** a descriptive term for texture that may be positive or not, depending on whether it is typical of the cheese. Blues may be somewhat crumbly, but if they are too much so, they are dried out.

**Cryovac:** vacuum-plastic wrapping commonly used for cheese portions sold in supermarkets. Large factory-made cheeses are sometimes cryovacked also. This method of packaging has the advantage of protecting the cheese from oxidation or spoilage, but it can result in GUMMY rinds and mushy texture, particularly with blue cheeses.

**Curd:** the solid white mass that coagulates when milk is treated with RENNET or other acid-producing enzymes, leaving the WHEY.

**Curing:** the process of ripening that natural cheeses undergo to achieve peak flavor; often used interchangeably with *aging* or *ripening*.

**Dry matter:** all the components of cheese excluding moisture (water). They include proteins, milk fat, milk sugars, and minerals.

**Earthy:** a term describing hearty, RUSTIC flavors and certain cheeses with ASSERTIVE flavor or aroma, particularly monastery types but also sheep or goat cheeses. It is not negative unless excessive.

**Eyes:** the holes found in some cheeses, especially Swiss or Gruyères. Eyes are formed by gases that are released during the CURING process.

**Fat content:** The fat content of a cheese is measured only in the DRY MATTER, because moisture content varies as the cheese gets older. Fat content for most cheeses is 45% to 50% of the dry matter; a few have only 10% or less, double creams have 60%, triple creams have 75%.

**Ferme,** or **Fermier:** the French term for farm-produced cheeses.

**Fresh:** a classification of cheese. See p. 9.

**Formaggio:** Italian word for cheese.

**Fromage:** French word for cheese.

**Fruity:** a descriptive term for the sweet and appealing fragrance or flavor of certain cheeses, common to some of the monastery types or semi-firm mountain cheeses.

**Gamy:** a descriptive term for STRONG cheeses with penetrating aromas.

**Gassy:** a descriptive term for defective cheeses that have gassy or fermented ordors.

**Goat:** a classification of cheese. See p. 7.

**Grainy:** a term used for describing gritty texture, desirable in certain hard, grating cheeses though not to the point of mealiness. Unless it is typical of the cheese, graininess is an undesirable trait.

**Grana:** Italian term for hard, grating cheeses like Parmigiano-Reggiano, Grana Padano, Sapsago, etc. See p. 3.

**Gummy:** a negative term used to describe an overly plastic texture, as well as overripe rinds that have become sticky or gooey. Gumminess is undesirable in any context.

**Hard:** a classification of cheese. See p. 3.

**High:** a descriptive term sometimes applied to strong-smelling cheeses that have reached full ripeness or are just over the edge.

**Interior:** the part of the cheese inside the rind or crust; also called PASTE.

**Kaas:** the Dutch word for cheese.

**Käse:** the German word for cheese.

**Lactic:** a generally positive description applied to cheeses with a clean, wholesome, milky flavor.

**Lait cru:** French term for raw milk.

**Laiterie or laitier:** French words for dairy or dairyman; appears on French cheeses made in creamery or factory. (See "Ferme.")

**Marc:** white brandy or *eau de vie* made from grape pomace; sometimes used as the solution for curing WASHED-RIND cheeses.

**Matieres grasses:** the French term for DRY MATTER.

**Mild:** a descriptive term for cheeses that have bland or unassuming flavor; also a term for young Cheddars that are aged briefly.

**Mold**: a condition created by the spores of various fungi during ripening that also contributes to individual character. Surface molds ripen from the rind inward; internal molds (such as those used for blue cheeses) ripen from the interior outward. A *moldy* character can be clean and attractive or unpleasantly ammoniated. *Mold* also refers to the fungus itself.

**Monastery**: a classification of cheese. See p. 4.

**Mushroomy**: a descriptive term commonly applied to some soft-ripened cheeses that have developed the pleasant aroma of mushrooms.

**Natural rind**: rinds that develop naturally on the cheese's exterior during ripening, without the aid of ripening agents or washing. Most semi-firm or hard cheeses have natural rinds that may be thin like Cheddar or tough and thick like Parmesan, Pecorino Romano, Swiss Emmentaler and others.

**Nutty**: a term used to describe flavors reminiscent of nuts, often hazelnuts or walnuts.

**Oily**: a term used to describe the texture of some semi-firm or hard cheeses; it can also apply to aroma and flavor.

**Open**: open-textured cheeses are those that have holes. They may be small or large, densely patterned, or randomly scattered and irregular in shape (see "Close").

**Ost**: the Scandinavian term for cheese.

**Paraffin**: the wax coating applied to the rinds of some cheeses, intended to protect them during export and add to their lifespans. The coating may be clear, black, yellow, or red.

**Pasta filata**: Italian term for cheeses whose curds are dipped in hot whey, then kneaded or stretched to an elastic consistency. (See p. 8.)

**Pasteurized**: a term describing milk that has been heat-treated to destroy bacteria. Most factory-made cheeses are made from pasteurized milk to ensure greater control over quality and more uniform consistency. Processed cheeses may also be pasteurized to check further ripening.

**Paste**: a term for the interior of a cheese, most commonly used with soft-ripening varieties that are semi-soft to runny.

**Penicillium**: principal species of fungi used to develop molds on certain cheeses during ripening. *Penicillium candidum* is used to develop many soft-ripened cheeses, such as Brie; *Penicillium glaucum* or *roqueforti* is used for blue cheeses.

**Persillé**: French word meaning "parsleyed;" applied to delicately veined blues where the MOLD resembles sprigs of parsley.

**Pickled**: a term sometimes used for cheeses cured in BRINE, such as Feta.

**Piquant**: a term used to describe an appealing sharpness or exhilarating accent of flavor or aroma.

**Processed**: a classification of cheese. See p. 10.

**Pronounced**: a descriptive term for forceful aroma or flavor.

**Pungent**: strong, sharp, penetrating aroma or flavor.

**Queso**: Spanish word for cheese.

**Rancid**: a term referring to stale, fetid, or otherwise tainted character.

**Rennet**: a substance, found in the mucous membrances of calves' stomachs, that contains rennin, an acid-producing enzyme that aids in coagulating milk, or separating the curds from the whey.

**Rind**: a cheese's outer surface, which varies considerably in texture, thickness, and color. Some cheeses are rindless, some have natural rinds, others possess rinds that are produced by MOLD (BLOOMY RIND).

**Ripe**: a specific term referring to cheeses that have arrived at peak flavor through aging. The optimum period of aging varies widely with the type of cheese.

**Robust**: descriptive term for earthy, full-flavored cheeses.

**Rubbery**: generally a pejorative term for cheeses that are overly chewy or elastic in texture.

**Rustic**: generally ascribed to country or mountain cheeses that have hearty or earthy flavors and assertive or barnyardy aromas.

**Salty**: most cheeses have some degree of saltiness; those lacking in salt are said to be dull or flat. Pronounced saltiness is characteristic of some cheeses, but oversaltiness is a defect.

**Semi-firm**: a classification of cheese. See p. 4.

**Semi-soft**: a classification of cheese. See p. 4.

**Sharp**: a term applied to fully developed flavor in aged cheeses like Cheddar, Provolone, and certain blues. If a cheese is too sharp, however, it has become bitter or biting.

**Sheep**: a classification of cheese. See p. 7.

**Soft-ripened**: a classification of cheese. See p. 5.

**Sour**: a mild, sourish tang can be attractive in young cheeses like Stracchino, but this term usually refers to excessive ACIDITY, which is very unpleasant.

**Spicy**: a descriptive term for cheeses with peppery or herby character. It has a different meaning than *spiced,* which refers to cheeses flavored with herbs or spices like caraway, cumin, pepper, chives, etc.

**Springy**: a descriptive term for resilient texture that "springs back" when you gently press it. Ripe or nearly ripe soft-ripened varieties should be springy.

**Starter**: the culture of milk bacteria used to increase lactic acid and to begin the process of flavor development. Starters are carefully selected or cultured by conscientious cheese producers; they are very important in determining the cheese's ultimate character.

**Strong**: a descriptive term for cheeses with PRONOUNCED or penetrating flavor and aroma. See strong-smelling, p. 9.

**Supple**: a term used to describe the resilient or pliable texture usually characteristic of semi-soft cheeses. It implies just the right degree of elasticity—the cheese is bendable but not rubbery.

**Surface-ripened**: a term referring to cheeses that ripen, from the outside in, as a result of the application of MOLD, yeast, or bacteria to the surface. Bloomy rind and WASHED-RIND cheeses are surface-ripened.

**Tangy**: a generally positive descriptive term that refers to a pleasing acidity or tartness, a thrust of flavor common to CHÈVRES and certain blues.

**Texture**: the "fabric" or "feel" of cheese, which may be smooth, GRAINY, OPEN or CLOSE, CREAMY, flaky, dense, CRUMBLY, etc., according to the specific variety.

**Turophile**: the Greek term for one who loves cheese.

**Washed rind**: a term used to refer to SURFACE-RIPENED cheeses such as Pont l'Eveque, Chaumes, Rollot, whose rinds are washed or BRUSHED with brine, beer, brandy, or other solutions during the curing process. The washing promotes the growth of a reddish-orange bacterial "smear," which contributes to aroma and flavor. See p. 5.

**Weeping**: a term that describes holes or eyes that are shiny with butterfat. Weeping is a sign of maturity in Swiss-type cheeses such as Emmentaler, Gruyere, Jarlsberg, and others.

**Whey**: the watery, yellowish liquid that is separated from the coagulated CURDS as the first step in cheese-making. Some cheeses, such as Ricotta or Gjetost, are made from the whey. See p. 10.

# INDEX OF CHEESES

◆◆◆

◆

# A Directory of
# Fine Cheese Shops

**Avon**
    The Cheese Shop
    802 Fishponds Road
    Bristol

**Berkshire**
    E P Spackman
    25 High Street
    Hungerford

    Wells Stores
    Streatley
    Reading

**Cheshire**
    George Dulton & Son Ltd.
    Godstall Lane
    Saint Werburgh Street
    Chester

**Cornwall**
    The Real Ale
        & Cheese Shop
    9 New Bridge Street
    Truro

**Devon**
    N H Creber Ltd.
    48 Brook Street
    Tavistock

    Dartington Farm
        Food Shop
    Cider Press Centre
    Shinners Bridge
    Totnes

**Hertfordshire**
    Cheese Plus
    116 Darkes Lane
    Potters Bar

**Lancashire**
    Bambers Cheese Shop
    13 Orchard Street
    Preston

**Leicestershire**
    The Cheese Shop
    17 Church Street
    Market Harborough

    Farmhouse Cheese &
        Farmhouse Mill
    55–56 King Street
    Melton Mowbray

    David North Ltd.
    289 Station Road
    Rothley

**Lincolnshire**
    The Cheese Shoppe
    25 Market Place
    Spalding

**London**
    Bartholdi
    4 Charlotte Street, W1

    The Common Wine
    14 Bellevue Road, SW17

    A Cordeau & Son Ltd.
    32 Streatham High Road
    SW16

    Delicatessen Shop
    23 South End Road, NW3

    Fortnum & Mason
    181 Piccadilly, W1

    Harrods
    Brompton Road, SW1

    Mainly English
    14 Buckingham Palace Road
    SW1

    Osio & Gioberti
    62–64 High Road, N2

Paxton & Whitfield
93 Jermyn Street, SW1

Rosslyn Delicatessen
56 Rosslyn Hill, NW3

Selfridges
Oxford Street, W1

## Lothian
Choosa Cheese
178 Bruntsfield Place
Edinburgh

R W Forsyth Ltd.
30 Princes Street
Edinburgh

## Manchester
The Cheesery
1 Regent Road
Altrincham

## Merseyside
Fashoni's Cheese Centre
The Market
Southport

## Somerset
Chewton Cheese Dairy
Priory Farm
Chewton Mendip

## Suffolk
The Cheese Shop
74 Beccles Road
Oulton Broad

## Surrey
Mrs Graham's Delicatessen
14 Red Lion Street
Richmond

## Sussex
The Cheeseboard
58 High Street
Hastings

The Cheese Shop
17 Kensington Gardens
Brighton

## Yorkshire
Farnley Shop
Farnley Lane
Otley

Powells of Ilkley
19 The Grove Promenade
Ilkley

Reginald P Bush
495 Glossop Road
Sheffield

# ACKNOWLEDGMENTS

I wish especially to thank my editor, John Smallwood, and Bill Logan for his help with research and the charts in the book.

Numerous people in the cheese trade were helpful to me in preparing *The Pocket Guide to Cheese.* I wish particularly to express my gratitude to Helen Allen of The Wine and Cheese Center in San Francisco, William Hyde of Balducci's and Giorgio DeLuca of Dean & DeLuca in New York City. Others who provided special help and expertise included the following:

Richard Allen, The Wine & Cheese Center, San Francisco, Ca.
Amazon Coffee & Tea Co., Inc., New York, N.Y.
Austrian Trade Commission, New York, N.Y.
Hans Bogge, Nyborg & Nelson, New York, N.Y.
British Trade Information Office, New York, N.Y.
John Ciano, Crystal Food Import Corp., Boston, Ma.
DiPalo Dairy Foods, New York, N.Y.
Domestic Cheese Corp., San Francisco, Ca.
Don Epstein, Robin Packing Co., New York, N.Y.
Stephen Fass, Macy's, New York, N.Y.
Heinz Höfer, Switzerland Cheese Association
Holland Cheese Exporters Association
Douglas Johnstone, Marin French Cheese Co., Petaluma, Ca.
Murray Klein, Zabar's, New York, N.Y.
George Lang, New York, N.Y.
Mary Lyons, Food and Wines from France, New York, N.Y.
Milk Marketing Board, Surrey, England
Fritz Maytag, Napa Valley, Ca.
Rosemary Miller, New York, N.Y.
Monterey Cheese Company, San Francisco, Ca.
Yvon Moller, Denmark Cheese Association, Elmsford, N.Y.
New Zealand Milk Products, Inc., Rosemont, Ill.
Thomas B. Phiebig, Galaxy Trading Company, Englewood Cliffs, N.J.
Otto Roth & Co., Moonachie, N.J.
Sonoma Cheese Factory, Sonoma, Ca.
Stephen Spector, Le Plaisir, New York, N.Y.
Switzerland Cheese Association
The Farmhouse English Cheese Federations, London, England
Janet Trefethen, Napa Valley, Ca.
Oulton Wade, J.P., Chester, England
Wisconsin Cheese Makers Association, Madison, Wisc.
Olga Domingez, Zabar's New York, N.Y.